THE TEXAS SENATE

THE
TEXAS SENATE

VOLUME I

Republic to Civil War, 1836–1861

EDITED BY

Patsy McDonald Spaw

·

FOREWORD BY

William P. Hobby

LIEUTENANT GOVERNOR

·

Texas A&M University Press
College Station

LIBRARY OF CONGRESS CATALOGING-IN-PUBLICATION DATA

The Texas Senate / edited by Patsy McDonald Spaw ; foreword by
William P. Hobby. — 1st ed.
    p.   cm.
    Includes bibliographical references (p.) and index.
    Contents: v. 1. Republic to Civil War, 1836–1861.
    ISBN 0-89096-442-4 (v. 1 : alk. paper)
    1. Texas. Legislature. Senate—History. I. Spaw, Patsy Mc-
Donald, 1945– .
JK4876.T48 1991
328.764′071—dc20   90-10988
                                                    CIP

Contents

CONTENTS

Illustrations

Foreword

For nearly two decades, I have had the rare privilege of presiding over the Texas Senate. It has been an adventure in a fascinating institution, rich in history and tradition, in collegiality and camaraderie, and in quirks and eccentricities.

Like the U.S. Senate, the Texas Senate was conceived as a deliberative body. With only thirty-one members, it retains that characteristic, while the U.S. Senate, with one hundred members, has become more of a town hall meeting.

Like the U.S. Senate, the Texas Senate jealously guards the rights of the minority. It is a time-honored tradition that no bill comes to the floor without a vote of two-thirds of the members present. And even when a two-thirds vote is mustered, there remains the possibility of a filibuster. This is an annoyance at times, and frustrating to some, but those who would try to circumvent this process do so at their well-deserved peril. There are always fashionable proposals afoot that catch the fancy, but that would, for all their appeal, trample roughshod over the interests of some citizens. The Senate exists to temper these projects.

The Senate, to a greater extent than the House of Representatives, can take the long view. Its members are more insulated from the turning electoral tides. They represent a broader-based constituency. It has been said that the Texas Senate has no rules, and sometimes it seems to operate that way. Rules are less important than consensus.

I love the Texas Senate, and I am proud of its accomplishments. These public servants are paid the princely sum of six hundred dollars a month to work long hours, listen endlessly to complaints and problems, master complicated issues, and balance fiercely competing interests. For that service, they usually attract an opponent in the next election.

In recent years, the Senate has taken great steps to provide a reliable supply of water to the state, to upgrade public schools and equalize state aid to public education, and to preserve our investment in our universities through economic hard times. There were momentous issues and trivial ones. There were moments of high drama and low comedy.

Not long ago, Sen. Chet Edwards asked me where he could find a history of the Texas Senate. It quickly became apparent that there was no such volume, and we decided to remedy that situation.

This history of the Senate is the history of Texas. It is also the history of one of its most venerable institutions. This is the first attempt to put it all down in writing.

This excellent history could not have been written without the leadership and guidance of the indefatigable secretary of the Senate, Betty King. Patsy Spaw, director of engrossing and enrolling, took on the formidable task. Working from archives, newspaper clippings, and interviews with former members of the Senate, Ms. Spaw and her staff compiled this history during the period between legislative sessions. Considering the demands on their time, it is totally remarkable that they have produced such a fine product as this.

WILLIAM P. HOBBY
Lieutenant Governor of Texas

Preface

This project was begun in the fall of 1982 after a newly elected state senator attempted to obtain a history of the Texas Senate, only to discover that it did not exist.

Initially, the history was envisioned as a small pamphlet with a brief narrative and a few pictures. As work progressed, it became apparent that the story was too big and too important to be condensed into a five-paragraph glossy fold-out. The project has grown to what will be a set of five volumes that will provide a glimpse of each session of the Senate since that first Senate convened on October 3, 1836, in Columbia, Texas.

The book is not a spellbinding novel, but rather an informal reference work, giving information on who the members of the Senate were, providing vignettes of the more colorful members, detailing issues of the time and their resolution, and describing interesting Senate proceedings and controversies.

As amateur researchers and historians, but lovers of Texas, we found that the perception of our forebears as rowdy drunkards, criminals, and ne'er-do-wells is skewed. While some of these descriptions fit some, we found men and women of unparalleled courage and determination — educated, intelligent, self-sacrificing. We have not attempted to cover up any of the less than favorable actions of members, but rather to tell what our research revealed.

Using primary sources as our starting point, we reviewed the *Senate Journal*, newspapers of the era, committee reports, legislation, and the personal papers of some of the former members. Quickly recognizing the need for information relating to the state and the times, we expanded our search to include general histories, historical quarterlies, biographies, and histories of counties, religious groups, the railroads, education, newspapers, political parties, early settlers, and the penal system, among others.

Our work would have been impossible had it not been for the invaluable assistance of the staff members of the Eugene C. Barker Texas History Center at the University of Texas at Austin, the Texas State Library and Archives Commission in Austin, the Texas Legislative Reference Library, and the Austin History Center in the Austin Public Library.

I am personally grateful to the staff of the Engrossing and Enrolling Department, who never wavered in their assignments, never questioned whether we amateurs could do what we had set out to do, never lost their zeal for the project, and never compromised the need for attention to details. Principal writers for the project were Robert Henderson, B.A., University of Texas; Mary Hobart Key, LL.B., University of Texas School of Law; and Richard B. McCaslin, Ph.D., University of Texas. Essential information was gathered by Nancy Alliegro, Kelley Burcham, Leigh Anne Rives Crowell, Stephanie Fariss, Myrtle Guinn, Patty Michels, Todd Moore, Guadalupe Maria Shaikh, Ione Stumberg, Virginia Townsend, Heather White, and Kathryn Williams. Typing, copying, and proofreading chores were ably handled by Mary Arnold, Victoria Barnaart, Kristy Baston, Charles Crawford, Debbie Dodds, Bob Edwards, Tommy Gandy, Patsy Harelik, Shirley Hearn, Greg Johnson, Sam Menon, Doris Parker, Howie Richey, Lisa Simpson, Stephen Stanton, and Frances Tate.

Appendixes A–J, listing members of the Congresses of the Republic of Texas, were compiled by Thomas Phillips, chief justice of the Texas Supreme Court. Fascinated by this period of Texas history, Judge Phillips had begun collecting this information years ago. When he heard of our project, he offered to let us use it. I am truly grateful.

Finally, I wish to thank Betty King, secretary of the Senate, who had enough confidence and faith in me and my staff to give us the job and who has encouraged us in every possible way.

The real inspiration for the work has been Lt. Gov. Bill Hobby, whose family history can be traced side by side with the history of Texas and the Texas Senate. Although his place in Texas history has been assured by virtue of his able leadership during economic distress, his commitment to education, and his concern for the underprivileged and the handicapped (as well as by his tenure as lieutenant governor, which has been longer than that of any prior lieutenant governor), his place in our hearts is assured because of his great love for our state and its rich history and his great love and reverence for the Texas Senate—the institution, the tradition, the people.

PATSY McDONALD SPAW
Austin, Texas

PART I
Senates of the Republic

CHAPTER 1

The Senate of the First Congress, 1836–37

The First Congress of the Republic of Texas met on October 3, 1836, in Columbia in a large dogtrot house "meager in every respect." The fourteen senators who convened there must have been amazed at the circumstances that brought them together and fearful of the impermanence of their offices. Only a year earlier the representative body of their territory had been a provincial government of the Republic of Mexico, and not too long before that citizens of the country had sworn fealty to a Spanish king. On this October day, however, the inhabitants of the lands north of the Rio Grande were calling themselves Texans, creators and subjects of a country recognized only by themselves as the Republic of Texas.

Sen. Francisco Ruiz, from the district of Bexar, was the only native Texan in the Senate; the rest of the senators and most of the voters were recent immigrants from the United States. Of the fourteen senators, four had fought at the Battle of San Jacinto, which won the new country's precarious independence, and six had signed the Declaration of Independence on March 2, 1836. The same voters who elected the first Senate of the Republic unanimously ratified the constitution that had been drafted by the convention in March.

The Constitution of 1836 forms the basis of the law that governs Texas today. The framers of the document worked in an unfinished building in an unfinished town only a few hours from invading Mexican armies; they worked in haste and fear and produced a constitution as protective of rights as if it had been drafted in the relative security of a hall in Philadelphia. The common law with which most of the signers were familiar was adopted "with such modifications as our circumstances may

The first capitol of Texas was a large dogtrot house in Columbia on the Brazos, 1836.
Courtesy Texas State Archives.

require"; this proviso protected land titles that had been acquired under Spanish and Mexican law. The common-law distinction between courts of law and courts of equity was eliminated and direct procedures were instituted, so that rights could be remedied in a single court and proceeding. Married women were granted separate rights of property and shared equally in marital property, and debtors were accorded a system of exemption from execution that protected their homes and means of support.

In addition to these provisions, which later influenced reform legislation in older states, the Texas Constitution provided for popular election of the president and members of the legislature. Residency restrictions were loose and there were no property or militia requirements for voting or officeholding. Members of the House of Representatives were apportioned on the basis of white population and senators on the number of qualified electors; this was to appease the frontier regions of the state where there were not many women and children. These provisions for

4

apportionment and for qualifications of the electorate were very progressive, as was the direct popular election of officials, which was an untried idea in most of the United States.

The constitutional organization of the new government required a bicameral Congress, with a lower house of no less than twenty-four and no more than forty members until the population should be greater than one hundred thousand, at which time the number of representatives would increase to not less than forty members or more than one hundred. The representatives served one-year terms. The Senate of the Congress was to be composed of not less than one-third nor more than one-half of the membership of the House of Representatives. Senators served terms of three years, one-third of the members to be elected each year so that the terms would overlap. The length of senatorial terms in the First Congress was decided by lot. Two-thirds of the membership of the Senate constituted a quorum, and the vice-president of the Republic was the presiding officer of the Senate. Since the members of the House of Representatives held one-year terms of office, each Congress necessarily lasted only one year, so that during the ten-year life of the Republic there were nine congressional sessions.

Both houses of the new Congress organized on October 3, the day of assembly. The Senate adopted the rules of the Constitutional Convention as the rules for the "government of this house" and elected Sen. Richard Ellis of Red River County president pro tempore, to replace Vice-President Zavala, who was ill. Richardson A. Scurry was elected clerk and secretary. Robert A. Irion, from Nacogdoches, was permitted to take his seat for the time being until the contested election for his district was resolved. The next day Pres. David G. Burnet sent in his message to the two houses of Congress. In it, he outlined the major problems the new government would confront: finances, tariffs, land speculation, and "a multitude of other subjects that would naturally present themselves to the legislators of Texas. But they belong to your successors, while to us pertains the arduous task of adjusting the controversy with Mexico . . . the defense of our country and the achievement of our independence, are absorbing and permanent subjects to which all the functionary [*sic*] of government, and all patriotic citizens should devote their most strenuous and indefatigable exertions." In spite of this exhortation, the earliest exertions of the new Congress were directed toward organizational wranglings, chiefly involving senatorial seatings from the contested districts:

David G. Burnet, first president of the Republic, March–October, 1836.
Courtesy Texas State Archives.

From the district composed of Matagorda, Victoria, and Jackson counties the contested election between Albert C. Horton and George Sutherland was resolved in favor of Horton on October 6.

From the district of Brazoria the contested election between William H. Wharton and Walter C. White could not be resolved and another election had to be held, which resulted in a vote of 189 for Wharton and 181 for White, so that Wharton took his seat on October 17.

From the district comprising Shelby and Sabine counties the contested election between Willis H. Landrum and (Robert O. [?]) Lusk was resolved in favor of Landrum on October 11.

From the district of Nacogdoches the contested election between Robert A. Irion and Isaac W. Burton was resolved in favor of Irion on October 14.

From the district composed of San Patricio, Refugio, and Goliad counties the contested election between Edwin Morehouse and James Power was resolved in favor of Morehouse on October 15.

Meanwhile, the process of organizing these senators to establish and govern a country proceeded. On October 7 the standing Senate committees were appointed. There were eleven of them:

> The Committee on Ways and Means
> The Committee on Judiciary
> The Committee on Post Offices and Post Roads
> The Committee on the State of the Republic
> The Committee on Military Affairs
> The Committee on Roads, Bridges, and Ferries
> The Committee on Claims and Accounts
> The Committee on Public Lands
> The Committee on Indian Affairs
> The Committee on County Boundaries
> The Committee on Naval Affairs

The joint rules for the regulation of both houses were adopted on October 11, and on October 21 the first bill to enact legislation was introduced; this was "a bill for the further protection of the Indian frontier," drafted by Sterling C. Robertson. Later, on November 7, Senator Wharton's resolution for adopting *Jefferson's Manual* as the common law of the Senate was passed.

The lottery for length of senatorial terms was held on November 11, with Senators Shelby Corzine, Stephen H. Everitt, Francisco Ruiz, and Robert Wilson winning three-year terms. Albert C. Horton, James S. Lester, Sterling C. Robertson, Alexander Somervell, and William H. Wharton drew two-year terms; and Richard Ellis, Jesse Grimes, Robert A. Irion, Willis H. Landrum, and Edwin Morehouse held one-year terms. With the completion of these arrangements the Senate was finally organized.

Report of Committee on Claims and Accounts, First Congress. Courtesy Texas State Archives.

The constitution provided for the inauguration of the president and vice-president on the second Monday in December. However, President Burnet and Vice-President Zavala of the Provisional Government resigned on October 22, so Sam Houston and Mirabeau Buonaparte Lamar were invested as executives of the new government on that day. On Oc-

Sam Houston, circa 1837. Courtesy Texas State Archives.

Stephen F. Austin. Courtesy Texas State Archives.

tober 26 the Senate received and quickly confirmed Houston's cabinet nominations. The country's officers now included: Stephen Fuller Austin, secretary of state; Henry Smith, secretary of the treasury; Thomas J. Rusk, secretary of war; Samuel Rhoads Fisher, secretary of the navy; J. Pinckney Henderson, attorney general; Robert Barr, postmaster general. General Rusk soon resigned and was replaced by William S. Fisher.

The multitude of subjects that President Burnet had outlined and the overriding problem of relations with Mexico were not seriously addressed until after the installation of Houston and his cabinet.

The Mexican problem centered around the person of Mexico's president Santa Anna, a prisoner of the Texans since the Battle of San Jacinto. The issue of whether or not to execute him for his massacre of the Texans at the Alamo was fiercely debated, with first Burnet and then Houston insisting that he be left alive on political grounds. So long as Santa Anna was imprisoned in Texas no unprovoked Mexican army would invade.

The problem of how to dispose of Santa Anna also vexed U.S. president Andrew Jackson, who took time to write Houston in a letter that was read to the Texas Senate on October 25: "I have seen a report that General Santa Anna was to be . . . tried and shot. Nothing *now* could tarnish the character of Texas more than such an act. . . . It was good policy as well as humanity that spared him."

Provisional president Burnet had temporized on the question of a speedy execution, claiming that only a duly elected Congress under a ratified constitution could legally deal with the prisoner; now that these conditions were met, action must be taken. Houston requested permission from Congress to send Santa Anna to Washington to make a treaty with Jackson. In response, Congress passed a resolution ordering that Santa Anna be kept in Texas until the Senate consented to his removal, which resolution Houston vetoed. In the debate that followed, Senator Everitt led the opposition in the upper house, alleging a usurpation of the powers of that body. In spite of the rebellious and vengeful mood in Congress, the resolution was reconsidered and withdrawn; Santa Anna was made the president's sole responsibility and Houston released him, saying that "restored to his own country" Santa Anna "would keep Mexico in commotion for years, and Texas will be safe."

Another question that disturbed the government for several years was the location of the capital of the Republic. Columbia, a struggling settlement in Brazoria County, where the House and Senate met in separate frame buildings, was inadequate as a permanent seat of government. Committees were formed to make recommendations but they disagreed, the Senate favoring a site at San Jacinto and the House one at Nacogdoches. Petitions proposing location at Matagorda, Fort Bend, Washington, Columbia, and Houston circulated in the Senate, but no accord was reached. It was decided to put the question to a joint vote of both houses of Congress on November 30. At this assemblage the Allen brothers, developers of Houston, offered a "handsome and beautifully elevated, salubrious" city as well as government buildings and lodgings. After four

Proposal for a seal and flag design for the Republic, submitted by Pres. David G. Burnet. Courtesy Texas State Archives.

<u>A large golden Star central</u>

A flag for Ordinary uses has already been adopted by the Government for use in the Navy and is now in use. I would receive much approbation, recommend to Congress their Sanction being given to it— Flags Constitute the primary evidences of Nationality to vessels on the high Seas, and it is needful they Should be formally adopted and made known.

The flag in use by the navy is constructed as follows:

Union; blue— Star Central

Thirteen Stripes prolonged, alternate red and White.

The allusion of the 13 Stripes is emphatic, and will Constitute an agreeable Memorial of our Common descent.

signed David G. Burnet.

ballots, Congress accepted and passed an act on December 15, 1836, which situated the capital at Houston until after the 1840 legislative session.

After grappling with the international problem of Santa Anna and the domestic question of the capital, the Congress turned to the universal dilemma of finances. Texas faced a debt of almost $1.25 million from the recent and as yet unresolved war and had no money. Her only asset was her land: Texas comprised more than 200 million acres, only 26 million of which had been granted to individuals by Spain and Mexico. The rest was public domain, the lure to attract settlers, the raw material from which commerce and civilization could be formed.

The Texas Congress had already authorized grants of land to veterans and volunteers in the army to pay them for their services and had granted headrights to residents. The government's shaky financial position and its reliance on land as collateral for credit are apparent in an amendment to the bill for the better protection of the Indian frontier:

> That all the troops who may be enlisted . . . shall be entitled to pay at the following rates, viz: three hundred and sixty-five dollars per annum, in money to be paid quarterly; *provided*, the government be in such a situation as to make said quarterly payments; and a bounty of three hundred and twenty acres of land per annum. . . .

The legislators also hoped to use land as collateral for a highly touted scheme known as the Five Million Dollar Loan. An act providing for the issuance of bonds in that amount was passed on November 4, pledging the public domain and real property taxes. Prospective buyers were to be U.S. banks, but by the time the issue was ready the Panic of 1837 had paralyzed these institutions and no market for the bonds could be found. Other attempts to sell Texas land directly through the issuance of scrip, or drafts against unclaimed Texas land, met the same fate.

One of the problems associated with the use of the public domain for capital was that all of the real property rights in the new Republic, including the boundaries of the country itself, were unsettled. The lands given to soldiers and citizens had to be surveyed and good title given to their proper owners. To further this objective, the constitution provided for the establishment of a General Land Office to recognize valid claims. President Houston was opposed to speedy compliance with this provision because he felt that speculators would take advantage of the confused condition of the country to validate worthless titles. Congress thought differently and, in one of the most bitter contests of the session,

[Nov 8, 1836]

Report of Committee on Finance, First Congress. Courtesy Texas State Archives.

passed the land bill over the president's veto. The bill had a troubled
history even before the veto, passing through two conference committees before final passage. During the December 16 debate on the question of accepting the House's reasons for rejecting the conference report, Senator Everitt moved for the first call on the Senate, and the
doorkeeper was sent to corral absentees. The land office bill eventually
passed the Senate by unanimous vote on the last night of the session,
the rare unanimity apparently being achieved because of collective outrage at President Houston's veto.

The traditional avenue of raising governmental revenues was and is
to raise taxes, but this approach was unproductive for Texas, for embarrassing reasons. Citizens who paid taxes tended to pay in drafts and warrants of the provisional government, which were worthless as currency
but which the government was forced to honor at face value. Although

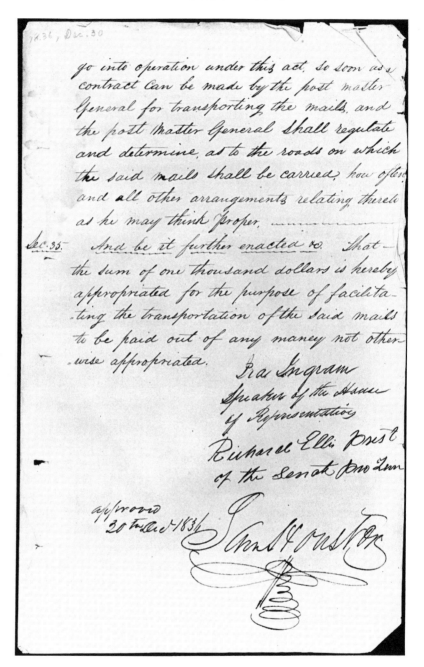

go into operation under this act, so soon as a contract can be made by the post master General for transporting the mails, and the post Master General shall regulate and determine, as to the roads on which the said mails shall be carried, how often and all other arrangements relating thereto as he may think proper.

Sec. 35. And be it further enacted &c. That the sum of one thousand dollars is hereby appropriated for the purpose of facilitating the transportation of the said mails to be paid out of any money not otherwise appropriated.

Ira Ingram
Speaker of the House
of Representatives

Richard Ellis Prest
of the Senate Pro Tem

approved
30th Dec 1836
Sam Houston

Act creating a post office, First Congress, December 30, 1836. Courtesy Texas State Archives.

these payments did reduce the country's debt, they did not bring in hard cash. The First Congress enacted taxes, and the secretary of the treasury collected them, but the coffers of the state remained empty.

On December 20, 1836, the Congress passed the Customs Act, which required payment of import duties in specie and which did earn some real money. More than half of the government's revenues from 1836 to 1840 came from customs duties; from 1840 to 1845 this share was 80 percent.

The money-making scheme that generated the most controversy and that became one of the first real political issues in Texas was the chartering of the private bank known as the Texas Rail Road, Navigation and Banking Company. The charter members were all eminent Texas politicians, including two senators, and the company had the support of President Houston. It was doomed to failure, however, due to political opposition and the endemic shortage of cash to pay for its charter and stock.

As each of these expedients to increase revenues—donations of land, attempted sales of bonds and scrip, the enactment of taxes and tariffs, the chartering of ephemeral banks—proved inadequate, Texas, like other distressed countries, was forced to print paper money in an effort to survive until credit could be established.

Credit depended largely on Texas' credibility as a nation, and this credibility depended on recognition by the United States. Until such recognition was earned, Texas was only a rebellious province of disorganized Mexico with no legitimate power to issue bonds, money, or land grants. Recognition was also a prerequisite for annexation, because the United States could not expect Mexico to give up half of the national territory without a war if that territory was in fact part of Mexico.

On November 12 Senator Ellis introduced an effusive resolution whose enthusiasm later proved to be misplaced:

A joint resolution for sending a Minister to the United States of America

Whereas, the good people of Texas, in accordance with a proclamation of his Excellency D. A. Burnet, president ad interim of the republic, did on the first Monday of September last past, at an election held for president, vice president, senators, and representatives of congress, vote to be annexed to the United States of America, with an unanimity unparalleled in the annals of the elective franchise, only ninety-three of the whole population voting against it. . . .

The man nominated by Houston in response to this request to fill the position of "minister plenipotentiary to the court of the United States of America at Washington City" was Senator Wharton, who was immediately confirmed by his colleagues, and on November 30 James W. Collinsworth took the seat that he had vacated.

Although the annexation of Texas by the United States had been a long-term ambition of President Jackson, and most of the Americans in Texas had supposed that it would be automatic, there were serious obstacles even to recognition. The first was President Jackson's reluctance to antagonize Mexico while the question of unpaid American claims was unsettled. The other and more serious objection was raised by the antislavery forces in the United States. Abolitionists correctly foresaw that recognition would lead to annexation and that Texas would enter the union as a slave state, upsetting the balance of slave against free states in the Senate. No American politician wanted to deal with this incendiary problem until after the November elections, so the recognition of Texas as an independent nation was delayed until March 3, 1837. The intervening months were filled with the frantic efforts of the various Texan ministers to the United States to wring the all-important recognition from a reluctant and divided U.S. Congress.

The Texas Congress meanwhile turned to the task of creating a functioning machinery of civil and military government. Under the constitution, counties and county governments were to be organized by the Congress, and county judges, surveyors, and land commissioners were to be elected by its members. This unusual concentration of power was justified by the chaotic condition of the country. On December 16, 1836, the two houses met in joint session to elect officers of the Republic, and in this election the Senate lost James Collinsworth, senator from Brazoria, to the position of chief justice of the Supreme Court and Senator Shelby Corzine of San Augustine to that of judge of the First District and associate justice of the Supreme Court.

One of the earliest organizational measures of the First Congress replaced the large Mexican municipalities, which were without boundaries, with smaller surveyed counties. An act requiring each county judge to send an accurate description of his county to the secretary of state was passed; when these descriptions were filed, Congress made them legal by statute and gave Texas for the first time a well-defined system of governmental districts.

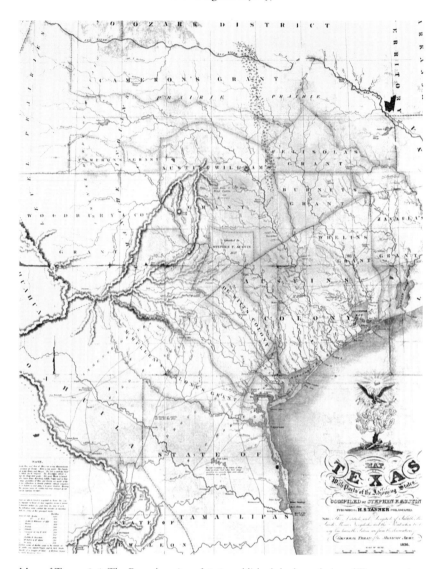

Map of Texas, 1836. The Boundary Act of 1836 established the boundaries of Texas, creating controversy that still exists today. Courtesy Texas State Archives.

Definition of the limits of counties led to a definition of the limits of the country itself, and on December 19 the Boundary Act was passed. This act claimed as territory of the Republic all lands to the north and east of the Rio Grande from its mouth to its source and the waters of the Gulf to a line three leagues from shore. The northern and eastern boundaries were acknowledged to be those established by the Adams-Onís Treaty of 1819 between the United States and Spain. The Boundary Act has contributed to a great deal of controversy, including the Mexican War of 1845. The claim to what is now eastern New Mexico provoked conflicts that continue today, and the Gulf claims led to extended legal battles over title to the offshore oil fields.

The organization of military authority proceeded less smoothly than that of the civil government. A state of war against Mexico still existed so that maintenance of an army was imperative, but the Republic had no money with which to pay its soldiers, and the morale and the caliber of these men were deteriorating. Hordes of adventurers had come from the United States after the Battle of San Jacinto to seek their fortunes as soldiers on the frontier; however rough things might be in Texas, they seemed better than the perilous state of affairs in the United States. But after several months of no pay and no action, the army began to seek excitement and booty on its own initiative.

When General Rusk accepted his appointment as secretary of war he resigned as commander in chief of the army. The Senate refused to consent to Houston's nomination of Thomas J. Green for senior brigadier general, so when the nomination of Felix Huston as junior brigadier general was confirmed on December 21 he succeeded to the command of the army. Huston was a popular officer who had brought a troop of volunteers to the Republic after the Battle of San Jacinto and who was eager to win military glory on another field. He loudly advocated an invasion of Matamoros, an idea that haunted the Republic for years and that the country could not afford.

When the Army Reorganization Act was passed, President Houston filled the position of major general with the appointment of Albert Sidney Johnston, an outstanding West Point graduate who then became Huston's commanding officer. It was hoped that Johnston would be able to control the troublesome element in the disaffected army; but Huston's pride was so offended that when Johnston took command in February, 1837, he was met by a challenge from his subordinate. Johnston accepted the challenge and was so severely wounded in the duel, in which he refused to aim, that he could not carry out his duties, and the actual command was again resumed by Huston. The problem of an unruly military was not resolved until the First Called Session of the First Congress in May, 1837.

Neither was the problem of unruly Indians resolved during the First Congress. On February 23, 1836, in its distress, the provisional government had made a treaty guaranteeing the Cherokees' land titles in exchange for their neutrality in the war with Mexico. President Houston submitted this treaty to the Senate for ratification on December 21, together with a plea for favorable action. The next day the treaty was laid on the table until the first Monday in May, so that the Congress of the Republic refused to ratify the treaty and the Indians understandably renewed sporadic hostilities. Laws had been enacted earlier in December to provide for a large army and a chain of forts to protect the frontier from their depredations, but President Houston refused to execute these provisions, not only out of sympathy for the Indians but on the sensible ground that there was no money to pay for them.

The countless questions facing the organizers and legislators of the new country, as well as its voters, did not become political issues. Politics in the Republic were not a matter of organized parties; most issues were readily agreed on, but personalities were not. In Texas, voters were partisans not of a policy but of a person, and that person was Sam Houston. George Bernard Erath wrote: "We here in Texas had nothing to do with parties in the United States. We were Sam Houston or anti–Sam Houston; Eastern Texas was largely for and Western Texas against him."

The political split of East Texas versus West Texas, which persists today, had roots in the circumstances of the adoption of the constitution. In March, 1836, the drafters of the document had apportioned the membership of Congress before the Mexican invasion and the depopulation of the western part of the state had taken place. Consequently, that area, with one-third of the population of Texas, had more than a two-thirds majority in Congress. No reapportionment could be made until after a census, which West Texas managed to prevent. The easterners naturally resented their heavier burden of taxation, but western citizens claimed that their burden of the brunt of the wars against Mexicans and Indians more than compensated their eastern compatriots.

The effect of the east-west division on Houston's support became more pronounced after his first term, but even in the First Congress the luster of his celebrity as the hero of the Battle of San Jacinto did not dazzle or inhibit bitter opponents. His friendship with the despised Indians, epic drinking bouts, and irregular private life contributed to the growth of anti-Sam movements, and a serious accusation of cowardice on the battlefield threatened to extinguish entirely the glorious light that beat about him. Sam's supporters had to rely on his political and not his personal record; an endorsement by Col. James Morgan when Houston was running for his second term as president expressed the attitude of most Texans: ". . . Old Sam Houston with all his faults appears to be the only man for Texas—He is still unsteady—intemperate but drunk in a ditch is worth a thousand of Lamar and Burnet. . . ." This may seem an unduly harsh picture of a chief of state, especially from a supporter, but descriptions of his fellow countrymen and statesmen were frequently even less flattering. A friend of the Texan character began his defense of the people's honor with a statement of the opposing case: "Did we believe all that we hear, we should be led to regard the people of Texas as a collection of outlaws from the four corners of the earth, driven from other lands for their crimes and having met here as in a common SEWER, have united themselves . . . to plunder Mexico. . . ." This same friend gives his own opinion of the First Congress: "If there was anything like statesmanship or business faculties among the members of Congress . . . it surely escaped the observation of myself. . . ."

Various travelers reported that the occupations of the populace seemed mainly to be drinking and gambling, interspersed with occasional dueling; unruly behavior disgraced even the halls of the Texas Congress. The *Senate Journal* of November 30, 1836, records the appointment of a committee of three "to investigate the affray in the Senate chamber."

But these rowdies, fugitives, and dreamers worked better than they knew, and better than any could have expected. The titles of the bills they introduced and enacted give some idea of the extent of their labors:

> An act to establish and organize the Supreme Court and to define the powers and jurisdiction thereof.
> An act to establish rules and articles for the government of the armies of the republic.
> An act to create civil officers.

Together with the complex personality who was their president, the Republic of Texas' first senators and representatives had created in a few months a new and viable country out of a thinly populated wilderness the size of France. In the words of a contemporary historian:

Nomination of John W. Moody as auditor of public accounts, sent by President Houston to Senate, December, 1836. Courtesy Texas State Archives.

The labors of the first Congress demanded the highest exercise of wisdom and prudence. They were herculean in magnitude, involving the enactment of primary laws embracing within their scope the entire machinery of civil government under a written constitution. Not only were the general principles pertaining to such a form of government to be securely embedded in the laws, but the rights of individual citizenship defined and protected. . . . These grave responsibilities, embarrassed by the confusion incident to the times, were met with a wisdom that challenges the admiration of after times. . . .

On the 22nd of December, after a session of two months and eighteen days and the enactment of many wise, and a few imperfect or unwise laws, and selecting the new town of Houston as a temporary seat of government, the Congress adjourned to meet in that place on Monday the first day of May, 1837.

When the legislators reached their capital on May 1 the six hundred or seven hundred inhabitants, mostly male, of the new town had constructed a block-long, one-story building for their use. At one corner of the block a large room was intended for the Senate, while the House was to meet in a room at the other corner. Administrative offices were located in the space between them. This impressive structure was still unfinished when the congressmen arrived, and lack of a roof prevented timely assembly. When it became apparent that no senatorial quorum could be mustered, Senator Everitt moved that Noah T. Byars be appointed sergeant at arms and sent in search of absent members. This measure proved successful; later that day Senators William G. Hill and Henry W. Augustine took their oaths and were seated. On May 4, Jesse Grimes was elected president pro tempore of the Senate during Vice-President Lamar's absence, and Arthur Robertson was named chief secretary. By May 5 a quorum in both houses of the Congress had assembled, a roof had been rigged, and both houses were organized and prepared to receive the president's message. The presence of Joseph Tucker Crawford, Esq., His Britannic Majesty's consul at Tampico, now commissioned to Texas, at these ceremonies attested the improved prospects of the Republic since its recognition in March by the United States. President Houston was pleased to allude to the country's new status: "We now occupy the proud attitude of a sovereign and independent Republic, which will impose upon us the obligation of convincing the world that we are worthy to be free."

The remainder of the president's message detailed the problems facing this second or adjourned session of the First Congress: the country's perilous financial condition; the unsatisfactory land law; the agreement of the Indians to furnish three thousand warriors, well armed, to the Mexican government as soon as that nation should invade Texas; the state of the army; the attempts to create a navy; and the slave trade.

There were other notables in Houston at the opening of Congress

The first capitol in Houston. Construction was begun on April 16, 1837, and completed about May 4, 1837, in time for the First Called Session (Second Session) to meet in the new, peach-colored building. Courtesy Texas State Archives.

besides Crawford; they included several tribes of Indians preparing for a "big talk" with President Houston; Alcée la Branche, the U.S. chargé d'affaires; Robert J. Walker of Mississippi, Texas' most ardent advocate in the U.S. Senate; and John J. Audubon, the naturalist. Mr. Audubon's diary records one of his walks in the Capitol, "which was yet without a roof, and the floors, benches, and tables of both houses of Congress were as well saturated with water as our clothes had been in the morning. Being invited by one of the great men of the place to enter a booth to take a drink of grog with him, we did so; but I was rather surprised

25

that he offered his name instead of cash to the barkeeper." Every traveler to Houston noticed something about the drinking habits of the populace; one observer reported that "the Texians, being entirely a military people not only fought but drank in platoons. Gambling too was carried to such a disgusting extent at all times that Congress, during the spring session, passed a law making it highly penal to play. But as those who passed the law were the most active in breaking it, the law itself was of little consequence any further than it afforded the gambler the double satisfaction of knowing that he was breaking the laws of God and those of man at the same time." Since, as this same writer commented, half the citizens of Houston were regularly engaged only in drinking and gambling, "riots of all kinds were to be expected." Some of these involved the people's representatives, as well as the citizens themselves, and disturbed the precarious peace of the Senate chamber; a new Texan named Francis R. Lubbock, who later became governor, reported that "while seated in the Senate chamber rapid firing took place in the hall of the building, which caused everyone to leave the chamber. Repairing to the hall to see what was going on, he (Hedenburg [a Jersey visitor]) witnessed the bearing off of Algernon Thompson, badly shot by one Brashear, both clerks in the Senate." The task of "convincing the world that we are worthy to be free" was not to be easy.

The major task of the convened Congress was to resolve the critical financial situation of the Republic. The government was penniless and faced unpaid bills from its army, which threatened mutiny; from its U.S. minister's landlord; from the outfitters of its navy, who refused to release the ships; and from its own governmental officers, who threatened resignation. To raise money to meet these demands, the Congress passed acts levying taxes on real and personal property and increasing the tariff. Both measures met with outraged opposition from the voters, who refused to reelect four of the five senators who had to run in the fall elections. To prevent the escape of any money that might find its way into the treasury, an act was passed to consolidate and fund the national debt, so that interest-bearing stock certificates redeemable at a later date would be issued to holders of valid claims against the Republic. This "later date" was first defined as 1842, but most of the certificates were not redeemed until 1852.

Although the funding of the debt relieved the pressure of payments, the treasury was still empty. Congress, at President Houston's request, authorized the issue of interest-bearing promissory notes. An act was

passed authorizing the printing of $1 million of this paper money; Houston vetoed this bill but approved another for $500,000 worth of the notes to be redeemed in a year, hoping that an issue of this size could be kept at par. This was not to be the case; at the end of the year the notes could be paid only with more promissory notes, which had depreciated almost 90 percent. So low had the country's credit fallen that Senator Everitt, chairman of the committee on printing, reported on May 27 that his committee could make no contract for public printing unless some advances were made by the government.

The destitution of the Republic was reflected even in its most grandiloquent gestures. Houston's nomination of Memucan Hunt to replace Wharton as minister plenipotentiary to the Court of the United States at Washington City was met with antagonism in the Senate, which requested further communication from the president showing cause for the nomination. The president replied that Mr. Hunt was a gentleman of fortune and would cost the Republic no money; the Senate confirmed him.

The Congress and the president agreed fairly well on financial measures, but on the next major issue facing the government they were at odds. The problem of how to survey the country and grant valid titles to its lands had been bitterly debated in the first session of the Congress and had been resolved with the passage, over Houston's veto, of a bill establishing a General Land Office. The bill passed in the final hours of the session, and after adjournment Houston did nothing to effect its measures.

When Congress met again another land office bill was of high priority. A bill passed both houses and was sent to the president, only to be returned with his veto and a message that it would be better that "no land law at all should be passed at the present, than that one should go forth to the world containing imperfections calculated at once to alarm and distress our friends and inflict in the end irretrievable mischiefs and injuries to the community." Congress again disagreed, and in a reprise of the performance at the close of the previous session "an Act Supplementary to an act entitled 'an act to establish a general land office for the Republic of Texas passed December 22, 1836'" was passed over the president's veto by the constitutional majority in both houses on June 12, 1837. This new land act contained an October deadline for presidential action.

The depredations of the Indians during the birth of the Republic had increased, since there was little official resistance during the war with Mexico and the early organizational struggles of the new government. Massacres and livestock raids had depopulated parts of the frontier, and the government was anxious to secure its safety. In May Congress authorized the issuance of $100,000 in the new paper money to a battalion of mounted gunmen, which the president was given a thirty-day leave to organize. These gunmen were the predecessors of the Texas Rangers, and their mobile companies were an effective foil to the marauding Indian warriors.

The Indians posed another threat to the stability of the Republic because they stood ready to join with Mexico in the event of an attempt by that country to regain its lost province. The natural answer to this threat would have been a sizable army, but due to the restless personality of the Texan military forces, the Republic seemed in more danger from its own troops than from Mexicans, Indians, or both. Brigadier General Huston was still in command of the army's nearly twenty-five hundred men, due to Major General Johnston's incapacitation in their duel in February. Huston's prickly pride had not been pacified by his de facto command; he still wanted the rewards of a victorious battle, and so did his soldiers. The soldiers felt also that the constitution had unfairly neglected them in granting preferential headrights in Texas lands to settlers who had been in Texas before the signing of the Declaration of Independence. These claims were all to be settled when the land office opened. President Houston's reluctance to open such an office is partly explained by the open threat of the soldiery to march on Congress and effect a more favorable distribution of the lands by military methods.

While the unpaid army grumbled, General Huston went to the capital to lobby members of Congress to authorize an invasion of Mexico. During his absence from his command, President Houston with Secretary of War Fisher appeared in the army's camp on May 18 and furloughed three-quarters of the men. Without his army, the bellicose general presented much less of a threat, although the Congress, in partial response to his urging, passed a Senate joint resolution on May 26 to appoint a committee "to act in conjunction with a like committee from the house of representatives to inquire into the propriety of carrying on an offensive war. . . ." Later in the session, on June 8, a House joint resolution authorizing the president to empower Brigadier General Huston to raise one thousand men for the purpose of carrying on an offensive

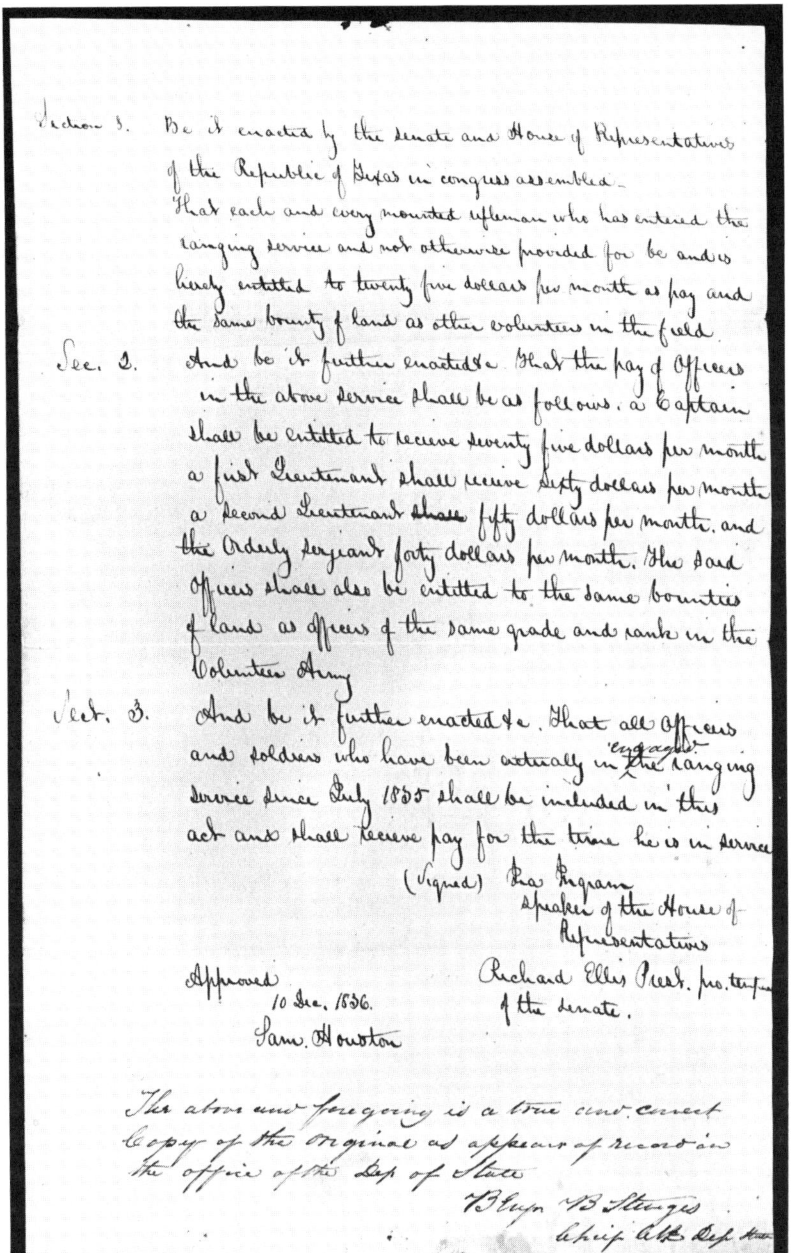

Section 3. Be it enacted by the senate and House of Representatives
of the Republic of Texas in congress assembled—
That each and every mounted rifleman who has entered the
ranging service and not otherwise provided for be and is
hereby entitled to twenty five dollars per month as pay and
the same bounty of land as other volunteers in the field

Sec. 2. And be it further enacted &c. That the pay of Officers
in the above service shall be as follows. a Captain
shall be entitled to receive seventy five dollars per month
a first Lieutenant shall receive sixty dollars per month
a second Lieutenant shall fifty dollars per month. and
the Orderly serjeant forty dollars per month. The said
Officers shall also be entitled to the same bounties
of land as officers of the same grade and rank in the
Volunteer Army

Sect. 3. And be it further enacted &c. That all Officers
and soldiers who have been actually in the ranging
service since July 1835 shall be included in this
act and shall receive pay for the time he is in service

(Signed) Ira Ingram
Speaker of the House of
Representatives

Approved   Richard Ellis Prest. pro. tem
    10 Dec. 1836.   of the Senate.
    Sam. Houston

The above and foregoing is a true and correct
copy of the original as appears of record in
the office of the Dep of State
                        Blyn B Sturges
                        Chief Clk Dep State

An act providing pay for mounted riflemen (forerunners of the Texas Rangers), First Congress. Courtesy Texas State Archives.

29

Mexico's capture of Texas Navy's *Independence*. Painting in collection of San Jacinto Museum, reproduced from the holdings of the Texas State Archives.

war against Mexico was read to a secret, or executive, session of the Senate, but seems to have gone no further.

The Republic's navy was almost as much of a liability as the army. The bills for repairs of the *Independence* had finally been paid and the ship was returning to Texas in April of 1837 when it was captured by Mexico and its crew and passengers taken prisoner. This reduced the Texas Navy to two ships, the *Invincible* and the *Brutus*, and reduced the international status of the country considerably, since one of the prisoners was William H. Wharton, the former minister plenipotentiary to the United States. Enraged instead of chastened by these events, Congress and the secretary of the navy were eager to punish Mexico with an invasion. On May 29 the Congress submitted to the president a Senate joint resolution instructing him to "send the vessels of war, Brutus and Invincible to Matamoros, for the Texian prisoners." Houston's veto message was a masterpiece of constitutional as well as military logic, and persuaded even the belligerent Senate to answer in the affirmative, with one dissent, the question "Are the reasons of the President (for the veto) satisfactory?" Congress then adjourned *sine die*, after little more than a month in session. Even that short period had been too much for the senators, who as early as mid-May had been moving for adjournment on June 1. The editor of the Houston *Telegraph and Texas Register*, Francis Moore, Jr., later a senator himself, resented this attitude: "In our humble opinion some mechanical means ought to be devised to induce our members of congress to hold longer sessions . . . they ought to be supplied by their constituents with seats of tough sticking plaster."

Although there is little reflection of its importance in the records of Congress, the issue of overriding significance during the entire life of the Republic was that of annexation by the United States. The annexation proposal so hopefully submitted to the U.S. Congress by Minister Hunt had been emphatically rejected; by the time the First Called Session of the First Congress convened it was apparent that Texas had been left to her own resources. It was in response to this realization that James Pinckney Henderson had been nominated and confirmed as agent and commissioner to the government of His Britannic Majesty, near the Court of St. James. Texas must seek friends elsewhere than in the United States and must become an independent nation in fact as well as in hope, because no welcome was held out by her northern neighbor. The antislavery forces in the United States magnified the numerous deficiencies of the young country and even went so far as to ennoble Santa Anna as a great humanitarian. The probability of Texas' surviving the depredations of Indians, invasions by Mexico, the collapse of the military, bankruptcy of the treasury, and chaos in civil government long enough to be anything but an embarrassment seemed slim. Besides, the Texas citizenry were seen as a violent rabble composed of fugitives from every corner of more respectable states, a collection of scoundrels whose least crime was slavery. It was the task of the citizens and delegates of the new nation to prove this assessment wrong.

CHAPTER 2

The Senate of the Second Congress, 1837–38

The Senate of the Second Congress did not find itself addressing issues of monumental importance as it had during the previous year. Despite continuing rumors of Mexican invasions and Indian depredations, the Republic enjoyed a peaceful breathing spell of almost a year, and the financial pressure of the Panic of 1837 in the United States did not reach Texas until after the senators had adjourned and returned home in the summer of 1838. The immediate result of the depression in the neighbor to the north was a failure by the Republic to secure loans and a promise of annexation, but that was also the fault of abolitionist sentiment in the United States. Newly independent Texas, secure in a period of relative financial stability and declining militarism, could well afford to wait for annexation and even took the luxury of withdrawing its standing petition in 1838.

The Second Congress met in three sessions: the called session, from September 25 to November 4, 1837; the regular session, from November 6 to December 19, 1837; and the adjourned session, from April 9 to May 24, 1838. Of the fourteen senators present for the called session, eight—Augustine, Ellis, Everitt, Horton, Lester, Robertson, Somervell, and Wilson—had served in the Senate during the First Congress. Six were newly elected: George W. Barnett, Isaac W. Burton, John Dunn, Thomas J. Green, Emory Rains, and William H. Wharton. Juan N. Seguin succeeded Green, who lost his seat, on December 5, 1837, and William J. Russell and John A. Greer joined the Senate for the adjourned session in place of Wharton and Augustine, respectively, both of whom resigned from the Senate near the close of the regular session.

Like their predecessors, the senators of the Second Congress were mostly southern by birth (the sole exception being Everitt, who was from New York) and veterans of the independence movement in Texas. Russell had fought at Anahuac in 1832, and Augustine and Burton at Nacogdoches; the latter had won immortal fame as commander of the "Horse Marines," which captured three Mexican warships off the Texas coast in 1836. Five senators had signed the Declaration of Independence, and John Dunn's signature was proudly affixed to the declaration penned at Goliad, which he carried to the later convention at San Felipe. The senators were quite prosperous, with active business and political interests; they were devoted to Texas and experienced in the infighting of the military and political arena.

The called session convened at Houston on September 25, 1837, but the Senate did not muster a quorum until two days later. On the twenty-seventh, the senators assembled to choose their officers and organize the staff. They elected Stephen H. Everitt president pro tempore and appointed James G. Wilkinson as doorkeeper and Manasseh Sevey as assistant secretary. The other positions remained unchanged from the First Congress: Noah T. Byars, sergeant at arms; Arthur Robertson, chief secretary; Oscar Farrish, engrossing clerk; E. L. Stickney, enrolling clerk; and A. H. Tompkins, reporter. The officers changed following the close of the regular session in December. William F. Gray replaced Robertson as chief secretary for the adjourned session in early 1838, while Edward H. Winfield became assistant secretary after Sevey, who moved over to take Stickney's place as enrolling clerk. William P. Brashear succeeded Farrish as engrossing clerk, completing an almost total change of the old guard. The Senate on September 30 adopted revised rules of order, establishing *Jefferson's Manual* as their reference, and later provided funds to purchase a small law library in an attempt to complete a more professional appearance.

The work completed by the Second Congress was less vital than its predecessor's. Most of the called and regular sessions were taken up with "private" bills for the relief of individual citizens, the incorporation of cities, the chartering of companies, and the creation of counties. Among the new or relatively new towns incorporated by the Second Congress were Houston, Shelbyville, La Grange, Richmond, Matagorda, Lexington, Milam, Bevilport, Texana, Columbus, Independence, and Clarksville. Older settlements that received corporate charters were San Antonio, Gonzales, Victoria, San Felipe, Brazoria, Columbia, Bastrop (or Mina), San Augustine, Velasco, Liberty, Nacogdoches, Goliad, Wash-

President Houston's first Official Residence at Houston 1837

President Houston's official residence in Houston, 1837. Courtesy Texas State Archives.

ington, Refugio, and Jonesborough. The Senate Committee on County Boundaries, comprising Barnett, Augustine, and Lester, found its calendar filled as an increase in population occasioned the creation of the counties of Fannin, Montgomery, Fayette, Robertson, Fort Bend, and Houston. At least a dozen businesses were chartered as commerce prospered briefly before the onset of the Panic of 1837. New companies included the Colorado Navigation Company, which proposed to remove the raft that obstructed navigation along the lower Colorado River. The act of incorporation was signed by Houston on December 27, but it did not extend the broad banking privileges given to the earlier Texas Rail Road, Navigation and Banking Company. The second company made little headway before folding, like its predecessor, for lack of funds.

The ostensible reason given by Houston for convening the Called Session was the execution of the land law. The immediate problem centered on the indefinite location of the line that was agreed upon by the United States and Spain in the Adams-Onís Treaty of 1819 but was never surveyed. After the United States had recognized Texas, Secretary of State John Forsyth approached Memucan Hunt on the matter. Texas professed, by its boundary statute of December 19, 1836, to accept the treaty of

1819, and Forsyth proposed the formation of a joint surveying commission to accurately survey the international boundary. To Texas, an important ramification was the location of a number of headright and bounty lands in the disputed area. If an investigation revealed them actually to be on the Arkansas side of the line running from the intersection of the Sabine River and the thirty-second parallel north to the Red River, a significant number of settlers, along with future tax revenues, might be lost, as well as a portion of the public domain.

Houston was determined to circumvent the faulty land law that Congress had twice passed over his veto, and he hoped to find the Second Congress more malleable than the First Congress. His proclamation calling for the session declared that the unsettled boundary prevented his execution of the land law, for which he had been given an October deadline, and thus merited the special attention of the legislators. His opening message to Congress began with the boundary problem, but in reality asked for a revision of the land law. The first official act of the Second Congress was to suspend the controversial measure through a resolution introduced by Senator Wharton on September 29, and to adopt a substitute measure, which allowed for the issuance of military scrip with the land grants pledged as collateral, thus converting the bounties into cash. Houston vetoed this legislation on October 24, stating that such action was in conflict with Congress's own suspension of the land law and would further depreciate the promissory notes already in circulation. Angrily, both houses promptly adopted the resolution over his veto and proceeded to revise the general land law.

The difficulty with enacting a land law lay in finding a method of apportionment that would satisfy both the veterans and the old settlers, while at the same time excluding land speculators. The soldiers believed that they had as much right to the public domain as those who had settled in Texas before the revolution but did not serve in any of the campaigns. Joint resolutions passed by the Senate on December 4 and 14, 1837, provided that veterans who served for three months would receive 320 acres; for six months, 640 acres; for nine months, 960 acres; and for twelve months or more, 1,280 acres. Additional grants were made to those who had participated in the war against Mexico and for those who had become incapacitated in the service of the Republic. The Senate did not require the land to be surveyed into sections one mile square, as the constitution mandated, believing that such action would be prohibitively expensive and would encourage land speculation. Houston, "with great reluctance," vetoed the bill on that ground, insisting that the task could be done in less than six months. The Congress bristled and overrode his veto once more. Houston again did not open the land office, and Congress ignored the advice of John P. Borden, the harried commissioner of the General Land Office, to reconsider the bill when it reconvened in April, 1838. The controversy remained unsettled in the Senate and contributed to a rising tide of antagonism against the chief executive.

The indefinite boundary between the Sabine River and the Red River caused no small discomfort for Senator Ellis. He arrived late in the called session, on October 30, and presented his papers. The following day, when the Committee on Privileges and Elections reported favorably on seating him, a heated debate ensued on the floor of the Senate. Ellis lived at Pecan Point, well within the area claimed by Arkansas as Miller County and by Texas as part of Red River County. While he had served as president of the Convention of 1836 and as a senator in the First Congress, his son, who lived with him, sat in the Arkansas legislature. Arkansas in 1837 made it illegal for any of her citizens to hold an office in the Republic of Texas, but this was an empty threat because its claims to the region were still in conflict. During the debate in the Senate, Wilson spoke at length, insisting, "I am shewn conclusively that in point of jurisdiction in law the gentleman represents a part of Arkansas." Ellis took his seat on a vote of eleven to four; petulantly, the dissenting senators, Everitt, Burton, Dunn, and Wharton, entered a protest into the *Senate Journal*, stating that if and when the boundary was surveyed northward, it might well show all or part of Ellis's jurisdiction, "and probably the honorable senator's own residence," to be in Arkansas. As a final gesture, on November 4 a resolution to investigate the political condition of Red River County was adopted by the Senate.

Today, most of the disputed area embraces Bowie County, Texas. The Second Congress of the Republic adopted a resolution requiring Houston to appoint a commissioner to work with agents of the United States to survey a boundary as soon as possible, but the effort failed. Memucan Hunt negotiated a second convention between the Republic of Texas and the United States relative to the surveying of the northeastern boundary in April, 1838, and the Senate ratified it in May. A more refined agreement, it provided for the recognition of each nation's land grants in the disputed territory and for the establishment of a joint surveying commission to locate the line. Houston proclaimed the agreement on November 6, 1838, and the boundary was surveyed the following year.

Ellis was not the only senator to have to fight for his seat. The rhetoric that flowed regarding his credentials barely mirrored the acrimonious debate of the preceding month over the seating of Thomas J. Green from Bexar. Green apparently incurred the rancor of the Senate at an early date; his appointment as commander of the army by Houston had been refused, and his endorsement of the Texas Rail Road, Navigation and Banking Company had drawn the opposition of both Congress and the public. Two senators in the First Congress, James Collinsworth and Albert C. Horton, became early subscribers to the scheme, then adamantly disavowed their connections when sentiment turned against the company.

The arguments over Green's seat centered on whether he had truly established residence in Bexar. He represented its citizens in the House of Representatives of the First Congress, but clearly did not occupy a permanent domicile in the district. The people did elect him senator, however, and the constitution did appear to provide a waiver from the residency requirements for those serving in the legislature. Green claimed illness during the first few weeks of the session, often preventing the muster of a quorum to consider his credentials, but a frustrated Senate finally began meeting at his home, flushing out the recalcitrant and, possibly, very ill legislator. The discussion continued, notably without rancor, in the Senate chamber for another ten days.

The debate took a nasty turn with the arrival of Horton to take his seat on October 12. Wharton, who had introduced the motion to meet at Green's home, proposed that he be allowed counsel in his defense of his seat, but was twice ruled out of order by the chair, Vice-President Mirabeau B. Lamar. Wharton appealed the decision each time and won the right for Green to appoint counsel on October 19. Thomas J. Rusk was appointed over the bitter and loud protests of Horton and Everitt. Barnett introduced a motion to declare the seat vacant, which would force another election. Rusk spoke at length against that resolution, alluding to Green's service in the House during the previous year, which brought the stinging retort from Horton that he "did not believe then that Mr. Green was entitled to a seat in that house; nor does he believe him to be competently qualified as a senator now." Rusk also invoked the principle of popular sovereignty, pointing out that Green had been legally elected. Horton declared that he had as much respect for the choice of the people as anyone, "yet they sometimes are liable to be mistaken, and particularly so in the especial instance, as the majority of voters in *Bexar* did not speak our language, or were they acquainted with the laws." Exhausted, Horton then insisted that he could not constitutionally vote for the gentleman's taking his seat. On Wharton's motion, the Senate adjourned.

It reconvened that afternoon, on October 19, to continue a heated debate over Green, and Horton was not the only senator to engage in polemics against his fellow legislators. Wilson confessed that he would vote against Green because:

> the eloquence of the gentleman's counsel, and his own personal and warm friendship which he had for General Green, had almost caused him to lose sight of that pole star of rectitude, truth, and honesty, which he had endeavoured should be his guide, during his course in the senate; yet a ray from that star had flashed across his breast and warned him that his responsibility to his constituents; his oath to the constitution and his duty to his country, together with the received opinions of learned men and the established usages of the republic all prompted to take truth instead of prepossession — duty instead of prejudice — and justice before personal gratification.

The next day, before the final vote was taken, Wharton rose from his chair to "protest, most seriously protest, against members holding up the constitution and their oath, as if to threaten, and indirectly insinuate and allude to senators who differed with them." Green had obviously not met the residency requirement of the constitution, however, and only Burton voted against his removal from the Senate. On October 21, Burton entered a prepared statement into the *Senate Journal,* which concluded: "I here enter my solemn protest against the decision of the senate on this question, and confidently appeal to my God, my country, and posterity for the correctness of my decision." Green moved on, later serving in the legislature of California and commanding its state militia in a triumphant campaign against the Indians along the frontier.

With the business of organization finally settled, the Senate set to work on five important topics. The first involved the creation of a commission to locate a permanent capital for the Republic. Moving chronologically, the Senate next became deeply mired in the squabble between Houston and his secretary of the navy, Samuel R. Fisher, which nearly dissolved the cabinet. Perhaps most importantly, it took up the issue of finance, although it failed to effect a permanent remedy for the monetary ills of the Republic. Optimism over finances led to the organization of a consular system in the fall of 1837, but changing fortunes led to acts that laid the groundwork for annexation by the United States. The debate over Indian policy stagnated in rhetoric, tragically leading to efforts to bolster the militarist faction in Texas and to warfare before the Third Congress convened.

The City of Houston remained a muddy village on Buffalo Bayou, an eyesore and a constant source of argument among the senators. The most lasting measure of the Second Congress was the creation of a five-man commission to find a suitable location for a permanent capital. The Senate concurred in the joint resolution creating the committee on September 29, and Senators Wharton, Lester, and Rains served on the board. Over the course of the next two years they examined a number of sites and reviewed numerous petitions from aspiring towns. The commission's report to the assembled Congress in April, 1838, recommended a site near La Grange along the Colorado River, but Houston vetoed the resulting measure on the grounds that the selection was premature. The president did sign the commission's second bill, which stipulated that when located the name of the new capital was to be Austin and that a portion of the land set aside would be reserved for a state university. The ultimate decision of the group was in favor of a city on the western frontier, a decision strongly influenced by Houston's successor, Lamar.

The navy in the fall of 1837 had foundered completely. Houston had not executed an act of the First Congress calling for the purchase of four new ships. His primary reason was a lack of funds, but the president also wanted to avoid increasing his problems with military opportunists. Moore, the editor of the Houston *Telegraph and Texas Register*, chided on October 28, 1837:

> Most of the members of congress appear to be so fascinated by the new land bill that they have entirely forgotten the navy. Land, land, land, seems to engross their whole attention; if their disgraceful apathy should continue much longer, the thunders of the Mexican cannon pealing along our coast may announce to them the startling fact that the *title to the lands of Texas, is not yet secured.*

The president's refusal to sanction an official rescue attempt after the capture of the Texas warship *Independence* brought about a conflict that did precipitate some interest. Secretary of the Navy Fisher ordered a cruise on his own responsibility, prompting his dismissal from the cabinet. Fisher was very popular among the legislators. His removal led to even more disharmony and loss of backing for Houston, although the chief executive's argument that the navy had only three ships and no funds for new construction held great merit.

The senators shared the general dismay at Fisher's removal. They sent a delegation to meet with Houston and demand an explanation for the secretary's absence from office. The president insisted that it was for the sake of unity within the cabinet, and after heated debate over the course of a few months the Senate concurred in his judgment. Burton and Wharton tried to insert an official protest against the decision in the *Senate Journal*, but in a rare show of unity with the executive branch the other senators voted them down. Many vicious rumors circulated about the true nature of the secretary's dismissal, but the Senate was careful to publicly announce that its sole motive was to "harmonize and reduce to a calm, the ruffled and agitated spirits of the cabinet." Editors of several newspapers, particularly the *Matagorda Bulletin*, still condemned the Senate for its vacillation, insisting that the matter should have been resolved in a few days, not months. The Second Congress later appropriated $280,000 to acquire six new ships and provided for the appointment of a commissioner whose function would be to acquire and equip what would in a few years become the second Texas Navy.

Cantankerous Horton nearly lost his life in the course of his actions involving this dispute. He had long-standing feuds with many men, including both Fisher and Houston. When the Senate at last adopted a resolution on November 28, 1837, requesting the resignation of the secretary of the navy because he was unable to work effectively with the president, Horton quickly requested and received the malicious honor of delivering the message to Fisher. Although Horton, by supporting the resolution, landed squarely in Houston's camp in that controversy, a public note endorsing Lamar for the presidency appeared on December 1, 1837, bearing the signatures of Horton and eleven other senators. Horton further alienated himself from the Houston faction when he declared in the Senate on December 14, 1837, that he "would thank God if the President were dead." Wharton took exception to his remark and stated that he would challenge Horton to a duel after the claims of Horton's earlier adversary, Fisher, had been satisfied. Horton responded that Wharton should have the previous claim, and the duel was avoided by disagreement over who would get to shoot the argumentative senator from Matagorda first.

The financial situation of the young Republic looked good in late 1837. New businesses were springing up everywhere, and the value of imports, especially at M. B. Menard's new city of Galveston, rose to unexpected highs. Crops were bountiful, and the value of the cotton harvest alone was estimated at two million dollars. Good times, however, would not last. A money panic which had begun in Europe spread to the United States by May, 1837, causing the most serious economic setback that country had yet seen. The resulting depression lasted almost eight years and by the close of 1838 had reached Texas.

Secretary of the Treasury Henry Smith informed the Congress of the precarious financial situation of the Republic on October 13, 1837. He characterized the act for the issue of promissory notes "as a hasty and unfortunate measure," which "if carried into execution will prove extremely injurious to the Government in various ways." Smith recommended the recall of all paper currency, "which now hovers over and paralyzes her [Texas'] energies like a floating incubus," as revenues would not prove sufficient to pay more than a third of the promissory note when it came due for $550,000 at the end of the year. Secretary Smith urged Congress to authorize the issue of one million dollars in treasury notes, to bear an interest of 5 percent per annum, redeemable in five years with the public faith pledged as credit rather than proceeds from the sale of specific portions of the public domain. Revenues of the Republic would be payable in gold, silver, or these treasury notes. By keeping up duties and direct taxation on a moderate scale, demand would be equal to the quantity that might be out, and thus the notes would remain at par and become a "sound circulating medium." Few, if any, would be out at the time of maturity, unlike the promissory notes, and bearers would be more likely to refinance because of the low interest rate, 5 instead of 10 percent.

Houston, sick in bed for several weeks, rallied to present his opening address to Congress on November 21, 1837. In his address he endorsed the financial plan proposed by Smith. Congress did not heed their advice, and half a million dollars in promissory notes issued on November 1, at 10 percent annual interest to be redeemed in one year, remained in circulation and were further supplemented on December 14 by the authorization of the issuance of treasury notes in small denominations, in an amount not to exceed $10,000, with an additional issue of $150,000 if necessary. Customs duties were made payable only in specie or treasury notes. By January, 1838, $514,500 in notes had been issued.

Congress convened in a rebellious mood on April 9, 1838, for the Adjourned Session. Financial matters called for immediate resolution and

Henry Smith, first secretary of the treasury. Portrait by William H. Huddle, courtesy Texas State Archives.

were considered first. The issue of interest-bearing promissory notes continued until, by September 30, 1838, the amount in circulation totaled $684,069.59, or $34,069.59 above the amount contemplated by the government. A bill to increase the amount to $1 million was vetoed by Houston on May 12, 1838, on the theory that such a large amount would lead to a serious decline in the value of the currency. Six days later conditions were so bad that Houston did sign a bill authorizing continued issues until an appropriation of $450,000 should be met. The result was widespread depreciation of Republic currency. In April, 1838, the notes were worth fifty cents on the dollar in New Orleans and little more in Texas. The situation facing Lamar and the Third Congress would be even more serious. In less than two years the Republic had amassed a public debt of nearly $2 million.

The optimism of 1837 led in December to the establishment by Congress of a consular service for the Republic. The Consular Act of 1837 was not detailed, but it did place supervision of the service in the state department. Upon application, appointments were made of men who already lived in major cities in the United States. They received no salary, but did derive some income from fees and commissions. Consulates were soon established in Boston, Baltimore, Philadelphia, Charleston, Vicksburg, Natchitoches, St. Louis, Cincinnati, and Richmond, as well as in such unlikely places as Key West, Bangor, and Detroit. Early consuls in New Orleans, Mobile, and New York worked to dispose of the promissory notes and bonds to interested investors, to buy necessary supplies for the government, and to make the necessary exchanges of those bank notes drawn on U.S. banks that had been received in Texas. During the last half of the Republic's existence, offices also opened in Europe: in England in London, Liverpool, Plymouth, and a half-dozen smaller towns; in France in Paris, Bordeaux, Cette, Rouen, and Bayonne; in the Netherlands in Amsterdam and Rotterdam; and in Glasgow, Dublin, Antwerp, and Bremen. These agents in the United States and Europe, along with conducting their business affairs, served as valuable sources of information for would-be immigrants, dispensing a modicum of advice and a great deal of encouragement to those contemplating a move to Texas.

U.S. Secretary of State Forsyth consistently refused to discuss the question of annexation with Hunt. In January of 1838, Hunt, hopelessly discouraged, asked to be recalled, but Irion, now secretary of state for the Republic, persuaded him to remain in Washington. Hunt then suggested that the Republic "appear indifferent" to the annexation question, with the hope that the United States would make the next advance. The Texas Senate in April discussed at length the advisability of withdrawing the petition for annexation. On April 17 the Committee on Foreign Relations recommended that the annexation request be "unconditionally withdrawn," but, by a slim margin, the House twice defeated a joint resolution to that effect introduced by Anson Jones. The Senate did not press, preferring not to disturb the status quo. The defeat of a resolution to annex Texas, which was introduced in the U.S. Congress in June, infuriated Houston, who moved to save the dignity of the Republic by the "formal and absolute withdrawal" of the annexation petition. He appointed Jones as Hunt's successor in Washington, with specific instructions for the formal withdrawal of the proposal for annexation. Jones did this on October 12, 1838, after the Houston faction had lost the election, leaving the matter for Lamar to resolve when he came into office.

Although there was still much talk of an invasion by Mexico, the most immediate danger in the Republic was from Indians. Scarcely any place in Texas was safe from possible attack. Many of the Indians along the frontier were hard pressed from the north by the tribes that the United States had crowded into the Indian Territory in its removal program and, like white settlers, were harassed by the fierce Comanche and Kiowa bands from the west. The encroachment of immigrants from the east into their traditional hunting grounds heightened already existing tensions. Of special interest to the investigating committee convened by Congress in the fall of 1837 were the Caddoan tribes around Nacogdoches, said to be the "greatest rogues" on the frontier; the Keechi, Pawnee, Waco, and Tawakoni, who considered themselves at war with the Republic; and the Cherokee, a complete enigma to the committee. Houston, an adopted Cherokee, signed a treaty that guaranteed Indian land claims in 1836, but, despite his best effort, the Senate refused to ratify it on October 24, 1837. It based its final refusal on both the fact that the provisional government that Houston represented when he negotiated the treaty was virtually defunct, with no right to speak for either Texas or Mexico, and the fact that the twelve Cherokee chiefs who signed also did not truly represent the bands listed in the agreement. The decision, although entirely legal, would lead to tragic and bloody warfare within a year. The Senate demonstrated a similarly narrow attitude in its consideration of matters involving other tribes, characteristically refusing to act until all procedural requirements had been satisfied and the evidence had been carefully weighed, sowing seeds of disharmony on both sides by not acting swiftly to resolve conflicts.

The failure of negotiation led to renewed efforts to provide for frontier defense. In his opening address Houston included a request for reorganization of the militia, along with recommendations for finances and a consular service, but unlike those issues the attempt to provide for defense resulted in a direct reduction of his authority as chief executive, a wholly unanticipated result. Since May, 1837, Secretary of War William S. Fisher had steadily furloughed the soldiers of the army in accordance with Houston's orders. For defense against the Mexicans and the Indians and for the maintenance of order on the frontier, the government depended upon the militia, upon ranger companies, and upon regular troops enlisted as the need arose. Periodically, a raiding party from Mexico would raise a furor as rumors flew of renewed invasions across the Rio Grande into San Antonio and other towns. Fisher was forced to resign, and Barnard E. Bee was confirmed in his stead on November 11, 1837, signaling the opening of an extended struggle between Congress, particularly the Senate, on one side, and Houston on the other, unhappily allied with the militarists.

A few months after completing the furlough of the army, a supplement to the Militia Act of 1836 was passed over Houston's veto on December 18, 1837. Henceforth, until the passing of the supplementary Militia Act of January 24, 1839, the major general in command of the militia would be appointed by both houses of Congress, not elected by his field officers. The militia was divided into four brigades, each commanded by a brigadier general elected, before December, 1837, by the commissioned officers of that brigade. By the new law the initial election of a brigadier general was to be by Congress. Thereafter, whenever a vacancy occurred, it would be filled by the officers of that brigade. Lesser field grades would be elected by the members of each regiment. Each of the four military districts to which the brigades were assigned were now subdivided into precincts, with one militia company of not less than fifty-six men to be raised in each precinct. Houston had no quarrel with such measures; they very effectively carried out his plan to streamline and control the militia organization. He did strenuously object when Congress stripped the executive of all power over the mustering of the militia and conferred that right on the major general in command, whom they had selected, but both houses overrode his veto.

The same law required the president to order a sufficient number of mounted gunmen from each brigade to commence active operations against the hostile Indians on the frontier and to place at the disposal of a quartermaster, appointed by the major general of the militia, twenty thousand dollars to take care of expenses. Organization of the militia proceeded slowly, delay being Houston's favorite tactic, and the problems lingered along with a growing rift between Congress and the president. Also in May, Congress determined to create a "Corps of Regular Cavalry" of not more than 280 men enlisted for a term of not less than one nor more than three years, as the president would deem suitable, for protection of the frontier. Recruiting offices opened in Houston, Galveston, and Matagorda. Enlistments in this regular military establishment also proceeded slowly; mustered at Houston in October, 1838, they were stationed on the western frontier for only seven months before being reassigned to the Indian campaign along the Brazos and Trinity rivers. Although these efforts to create a military organization under the nominal control of the Congress rather than the chief executive did not result in the disaster Houston had predicted, they did interfere in the sincere attempts of others to resolve frontier conflict by negotiation and weakened the Republic's ability to respond to threats when they did occur.

A threat from within that preoccupied the mostly southern and property-holding senators was that of slave revolt. Although the slave population of Texas was not yet large, the status of this group was a major determinant of the future of the Republic and received more legislative attention than the numbers might have suggested and certainly more than many people desired. A joint resolution signed by Houston on December 14, 1837, entitled "An Act to Provide for the Punishment of Crimes and Misdemeanors by Slaves," contained a detailed list of offenses to be considered capital when committed by a slave or free person of color in an effort to impose a greater measure of control over the growing black population.

The association of the senators and their influence on politics in the Republic did not end with their role in Congress. Eight of the seventeen members who served in the Senate of the Second Congress were Masons: Augustine, Burton, Everitt, Green, Greer, Horton, Russell, and Seguin, as well as vice-presidents Lorenzo de Zavala and Lamar. The Holland Lodge met regularly in the Senate chamber and was particularly active in the creation of early educational institutions. The Philosophical Society of Texas met for the first time in Houston on December 5, 1837. Eighteen of its twenty-six founders were Masons, including Rusk, Horton, Lamar, Collinsworth, Houston, Henry and Ashbel Smith, and Anson Jones. Former senators Irion and Wharton were also charter members, although they apparently were not Masons. This group initiated a petition presented by Rusk to the adjourned session in April, 1838, encouraging the rapid establishment of a state-supported public education system. The Holland Lodge became the catalyst, too, for the establishment of the Grand Lodge of Texas, created on December 20, 1837,

Lorenzo de Zavala, Texas' provisional vice-president, 1836. Courtesy Texas State Archives.

Francis R. Lubbock, appointed comptroller of the Republic in 1837.
Courtesy Texas State Archives.

at a meeting in the Senate chamber, with Jones as the first Grand Master.

Masonic ties can be discerned in at least one of the decisions made by the Senate on censuring members of Congress. Following Houston's speech to a joint session of Congress on April 14, 1838, a scuffle had ensued between Francis R. Lubbock and Thomas W. Ward in the gallery of the Capitol. Ward struck Lubbock with a stick; Lubbock drew a derringer and fired, with only the timely intervention of a bystander preventing bloodshed at that range and allowing Ward time to flee. On April 16 the Senate adopted a resolution for Sergeant at Arms Byars to arrest Ward and Lubbock and bring them before the Senate for trial on "an act of contempt committed on Saturday last." Lubbock was brought in, but on a motion from Russell, a fellow member of Holland Lodge, the Senate honorably discharged Lubbock from his arrest. Ward locked himself in his house and refused to be arrested or even seen. He was brought in later that same day and was officially reprimanded by the Senate for his assault on Lubbock in the gallery, although he was apparently unarmed and was the only combatant in danger of losing his life. It is interesting to note that Lubbock earlier had sold his warehouse to be converted into an official residence for President Houston, also a Mason.

The Senate often worked, despite the inflammatory character of members such as Horton, like a private club, with the senators closing ranks against external threats. They legislated surprisingly well, but their clannishness constantly received reinforcement from the headstrong actions of Houston as president. The senators formed a strong cadre for the election of Lamar, even against the candidate who appeared to be one of their own, Robert Wilson. It may be recalled that he did not "fit in" with the usual professional and social circles of the more eminent members of that body. As the Republic developed, the Senate remained a bastion of personal politics, a colorful maelstrom of personality and even violence whose support was necessary for success.

CHAPTER 3

The Senate of the Third Congress, 1838–39

The Senate of the Third Congress convened on November 6, 1838, in an atmosphere of great public anticipation. Francis Moore, editor of the Houston *Telegraph and Texas Register,* declared, "we look forward to this session with more confidence than we have experienced at any previous period." The general mood of optimism could be traced directly to a change in the office of president: Vice-President Lamar had defeated Senator Wilson, candidate of the political faction led by Houston, quite easily. His impending inauguration was welcomed as a turning point in the fortunes of the Republic by those who opposed the Houston administration. The source of renewed progress would be Congress. Although men such as Moore believed that the legislators had "hitherto made but a few desultory attempts at general legislation, and [had] left too many monuments of their folly and selfishness," the coming change in leadership would force them to act responsibly in the future.

The Third Congress met for only one session, from November 6, 1838, to January 24, 1839. The senators who returned included Barnett, Burton, Dunn, Ellis, Everitt, Greer, Rains, Seguin, Wharton, and Wilson, who had lost the presidential campaign. Only four of the total of fourteen were new in the Senate chamber. Edward Burleson, formerly of North Carolina, had won great distinction for his military leadership in the Texas Revolution and for the Republic and had previously served as a representative in the Second Congress. Oliver Jones, also a member of the House in the Second Congress, was a veteran of the War of 1812 from New York and had emigrated to the Austin Colony in 1830. When the Senate revised the flag and seal of the Republic in an act approved in January, 1839, Jones submitted the design that still serves as the state flag of Texas. Harvey W. Kendrick and Beden Stroud, both Georgia natives, were newcomers to Texas and neophytes in the government of the Republic.

The Senate mustered a quorum on the first day and quickly elected the officers for the session. E. Lawrence Stickney became the new reporter, and Jonathan D. McLeod served as chief secretary. The assistant secretary was Algernon P. Thompson, personal attaché to president-elect Lamar. Other appointments included William T. Brannum, enrolling clerk; William P. Brashear, engrossing clerk; William L. Foster, sergeant at arms; and James G. Wilkinson, doorkeeper. Lamar withdrew as president of the Senate due to the pressing duties commensurate with assuming office in December, so Everitt's reelection as president pro tempore placed him in a very active role for the coming month. Before taking the chair, Everitt proposed the appointment of a chaplain for the Senate. Dunn, a Catholic, opposed the idea, insisting that it was an unnecessary expense, as the applicants listed for the position were all missionaries from the United States, each well paid by their respective organizations. After a short debate, the Senate approved the motion; only Dunn and Seguin, both Catholics, voted in opposition.

The most pressing issue facing the Senate was the defense of the frontier from hostile Indians. Its failure in 1837 to ratify the treaty negotiated by Houston with the Cherokees antagonized that tribe and its allies. President Houston attended several conferences with Chief Bowles of the Cherokees in an attempt to placate him, but the Indians grew impatient for confirmation of title to their lands. Distrust of the white men spread, and by early 1838 virtually all of the bands in East Texas were ready to fight.

The catalyst came from the smoldering conflict between Mexico and Texas. Throughout 1837 rumors of Mexican attempts to ally with frontier tribes against Texas had been common. As the bitterness of the Cherokees and their friends mounted, the task of fomenting warfare on the frontier undoubtedly became easier. In the summer of 1838, Vicente Cordova, a former *alcalde* and member of the *ayuntamiento* at Nacogdoches, initiated rebellion against the Republic. Cordova had been planning an assault since the outbreak of the revolution. He had first allied with Chief Bowles and the Cherokees in December, 1835, but action was delayed by the defeat of Generals Cos and Santa Anna by the Texas troops. In the spring of 1838, Cordova received a new commission from General Vicente Filisola to enlist the East Texas Indians as auxiliaries in the Mexican army.

Cordova renewed his alliance with Chief Bowles and the Cherokees and laid plans for rebellion. An uncontrolled outbreak of thefts and murders attributed to his allies in August, 1838, forced him to instigate his plans prematurely. With a combined force of nearly six hundred Indians and Mexicans he established his headquarters on an island in the Angelina River. Texans were aghast to learn of the perfidy of Chief Bowles, who appeared to have been a party to the rebellion the entire time he was pledged to a treaty of alliance with the Republic. The militia was called out, and the insurgents dissipated almost immediately. Cordova fled at the head of about one hundred men. Major Henry W. Augustine, a senator during the Second Congress, pursued Cordova at the head of a detachment of about one hundred and fifty volunteers, but failed to snare him.

General Thomas J. Rusk, with the remainder of the Texas troops, moved against the Cherokee village. Most of the warriors had fled, but Chief Bowles stood his ground. The chief denied aiding Cordova, insisting only a few "bad" Indians had joined. Cordova meanwhile enlisted the Kickapoo to supplement his small force of Mexicans. A gruesome attack on the Killough family by a motley group of Mexicans and Kickapoos led by Manuel Flores, Cordova's lieutenant, precipitated a battle on October 16, 1838, between General Rusk and a band of some nine hundred Mexicans and Indians believed to be commanded by Cordova himself. Following a furious exchange of about an hour's duration the rebels retired. Early in 1839, Senator Burleson, commanding a second detachment of volunteers, decimated Cordova's remaining followers in a skirmish near the town now known as Seguin, and the remainder withdrew to Mexico. The peace with the Indians, however, was temporary, and the victory a hollow one. The Cordova Rebellion of 1838 was just the prelude to bloodier conflict the next year.

Meanwhile, in the fall of 1838 the tempo of Indian attacks in East Texas continued to quicken. Houston, desperately hoping to avert open warfare against his friends the Cherokees, tried to contain the Indians on the one hand and restrain the settlers on the other by using the Texas Rangers. He sought to minimize the growing conflict and delayed taking action in the vain hope that time would ease the situation. New treaties were made and ratified by the Senate with the Tonkawa, Lipan, Coman-

Chief Bowles of the Cherokee Indians. Sketch by William A. Berry. Courtesy Jenkins Co.,
reproduced from holdings of Texas State Archives.

che, Keechi, Tawakoni, Waco, and Tawekash Indians before President Houston left office.

Within the Senate, Houston's attempts to downplay the Indian problem added to the members' exasperation with him. Pursuant to a resolution by Wharton, a joint committee formulated an emotional address to the people of Texas "urging them to rush to the rescue of the inhabitants of our frontier, who are now experiencing all the horrors of a savage war." Five hundred copies of the appeal, one hundred in Spanish, were ordered to be posted throughout the Republic, and the Senate concurred in a House resolution which required Houston to appropriate arms and money for defense of the frontier. The president signed this measure on November 7, 1838, along with another that authorized him to draw on the treasury for the transport of these arms. Houston proved dilatory, however, on the issue of commissions for the militia that had been mustered for the conflict, insisting that the laws passed in May by the Second Congress had usurped his authority to do so. The president did not want to increase support for Rusk, who had been operating almost at will in East Texas with the endorsement of Congress. Total chaos was averted by Houston's recognition of the growing hysteria in Texas, which led him to act by the end of November.

Debate over military finances became heated in the second week of the session. The Senate had concurred in a bill to appropriate twenty thousand dollars to fund an expedition of two hundred and fifty men to join General Rusk in the field. A pointed question, however, revealed that the treasury apparently did not have the money. Burton called up a House bill that authorized the president to issue the amount in more promissory notes. Wharton objected to the introduction of more potentially worthless scrip and called for an investigation by committee to ascertain if all previously provided funds had indeed been paid out. Burton, perhaps put out by the turmoil in his home district surrounding Nacogdoches, pressed on, insisting that an inquiry would take too much time. When Wharton said that he could return with an answer in five or six hours, Burton retorted that the volunteers would disband if not paid immediately. Furious, Wharton exploded, "then let them disband—let them even go to the enemy—Texas wants not such men—a fig for their patriotism! a curse on the motives which brought them together!" Fortunately, a representative of the treasury had entered the chamber as they argued, and a relieved Senate learned that funds for the troops already existed. They amended the bill accordingly, and Houston signed it on November 16, but the Houston *Banner* publicized Wharton's words as evidence of his indifference to the topic at hand.

Petitions from frontier counties flooded into the Senate during November. One particularly dramatic appeal from Gonzales ended with the prediction, "If you do nothing for us at this session, I can foresee but one consequence of our difficulties here, to wit: *the bloody extermination of every man, woman, and child on our western frontier.*" The poignancy of such missives did not fail to capture the attention of the executive branch. In his address to the joint assembly of Congress on November 19, 1838, Houston sounded a similar note, declaring, "It requires little foresight to predict, if some prompt and decisive measures are not adopted by the Honorable Congress, that sixty days from the present, there will not be a family residing between the Neches and the Attoyac." The president repeated his complaint that the removal of his power to direct the military had brought the Republic to the edge of disaster. He did, however, act to ameliorate fears on both sides, most notably by sending former senator Albert C. Horton to delineate Cherokee land claims in East Texas, which temporarily forestalled the encroachment of land speculators and removed a major source of Indian discontent. Final settlement of the matter lay with his successor.

The Senate had become a strong base of support for Lamar early in the presidential campaign. In May, 1837, while then vice-president Lamar was on a trip to his native Georgia, he received a letter from Senator Everitt which implored him to return to Texas "ere this Scrawl can Reach You" because "Houston worn-down by one continuous course of Debauchery, is fast sinking under its effects and is at times Entirely unfit for business of Every Kind." Six of nine senators in the Second Congress who signed a petition urging Lamar to declare his candidacy for president in December, 1837, also served in the Third Congress: Everitt, Burton, Wharton, Rains, Dunn, and Barnett. Lamar was popular with a majority of the congressmen throughout the campaign; when Rusk declared that he would not be a candidate, the outcome almost appeared preordained. Rusk, according to Representative John S. Ford, was "the only man in Texas who could show the shadow of a claim as the peer of Gen. Houston in the esteem, love, and admiration of the people." The Houston faction knew this and tried to persuade Rusk to change his mind, but the general was adamant. Burleson was one of those in the delegation sent by Houston to meet with Rusk; he and Wilson became the center of opposition to Lamar in the Senate of the Third Congress.

The constitution prevented Houston from succeeding himself as president. The election of 1838 promised to be hotly contested, but ended in a macabre runaway. There were no real issues, and in the end only a few candidates. It was a personality contest, the public and the candidates soon dividing into pro-Houston and pro-Lamar factions. Lamar threw his hat in the ring first, after he had ascertained in December, 1837, that Rusk would not run. The Houstonites chose Peter W. Grayson, who had immigrated to Austin Colony in 1830 and served as Austin's aide during the revolution and as attorney general for the Republic. Lamar attacked him as being involved in the speculation of confiscated Mexican lands, and it was reported that Grayson had opposed the land law of December, 1837, stirring up the forces of sectionalism by playing to the resentment of settlers in western Texas to counteract Houston's popularity in eastern Texas. Houston's actions as president had usually favored East and given offense to West Texas; Lamar's managers understood and used this important fact. Candidate Lamar also correctly pointed out that Grayson had not actually fought in the revolution, reducing his base of support among veterans.

The campaign began in earnest in the summer of 1838. Barnard E. Bee, secretary of war under Houston but a turncoat at election time, wrote to David G. Burnet, a candidate for vice-president, that "where general suffrage prevails no stone ought to be left unturned to enlighten the people." The friends of Lamar actively worked at the process of enlightenment. Tales of the escapades of a black-sheep cousin in Kentucky who bore the same name as Grayson were circulated as if he were the man involved. Grayson was serving as an agent for the Navy of the Republic of Texas in the United States, so he may not have known of all the rumors, but he did commit suicide in Tennessee on July 9, 1838. He had suffered from fits of melancholia as a young man, from which he tried to escape by migrating to Texas from Kentucky. The evidence would seem to point to a return of the mental illness from which he suffered; no other satisfactory motive has been uncovered.

The Houston faction hastily chose another candidate, former senator James W. Collinsworth, then chief justice of the Supreme Court. Collinsworth was a poor choice because he was only thirty-two years of age, three years younger than the required age of a president, and a known alcoholic. His selection indicated the chaos that existed within the Houston camp. A few weeks after his nomination, Collinsworth committed suicide by jumping from a steamboat into Galveston Bay. According to his friends, he had been under the influence of alcohol for nearly a week prior to his death. With little hope of success, the Houston men frantically chose Wilson, a colorful and controversial member of the Senate. It was far too late for an effective campaign, however, and he was an unpopular candidate.

Lamar based his campaign platform on several points: protection of the frontier and a firm policy toward the Indians; attainment of a lasting peace with Mexico, based upon recognition of Texas independence; adherence to the land law of 1837, including the opening of the land office and the awarding of patents; renewed attempts to secure English and French recognition and a foreign loan; and a free-trade policy coupled with a disavowal of the existing tariff. This platform consisted wholly of remedies for mistakes that Houston had made. Lamar conducted his campaign on that basis and defeated Wilson easily, 6,995 to 252. Lamar's running mate, David G. Burnet, narrowly defeated two opposing candidates for the vice-presidency: Senator Albert C. Horton and Representative Joseph Rowe.

Lamar, despite the circumstances of the election, interpreted his landslide as a repudiation of Houston's policies. His aggressive leadership in the next three years frequently left Congress and the people trailing far behind. At the next election the voters turned their backs on his administration, but the few years from December, 1838, to December, 1841, were certainly eventful, exciting, and perhaps the most important ones in the Republic's history. Initially, Lamar's election was hailed as a welcome reprieve from the domination of Houston and his minions. In the Senate, the increasing anger at Houston's obstructionism had already led to angry outbursts against his administration during the Third Congress. Even Senator Wilson, who had been Houston's candidate for a successor, chafed at the introduction of yet another resolution requesting action from Secretary of the Treasury Henry Smith. Wilson thundered that "if the Secretary did not behave himself better, he would vote to jerk him up forthwith and bring him to taw."

President Lamar's inauguration in Houston on December 1, 1838, highlighted a day of drinking and gambling marred by a shooting affray and uncounted street brawls. A grand dress ball through much of the night capped the festivities. The inaugural ceremony itself was turned into one of the greatest practical jokes of the time. Outgoing President Houston knew that Lamar had labored to make his inaugural address a literary masterpiece, and determined to steal the show from him. Dressed in knee breeches and a powdered wig, the very picture of George Washington and the only person at the ceremony in a costume, Houston interrupted the proceedings to make a "few" farewell remarks before introducing his successor. Houston spoke for three hours in an elaborate parody of the famous "Farewell Address," mixing tall stories, bucolic jokes, and gross innuendoes with an exaggerated defense of his own administration, which he characterized as a "pillow of thorns." The delighted audience roared with laughter. Lamar, literally too sick with frustration and nervousness to deliver his speech, had to ask his private secretary, Algernon P. Thompson, to read the prepared address. Not familiar with the text, Thompson read it in a dull monotone. Houston and half the audience left before he finished.

Lamar's message to a joint session of the Congress on December 21, 1838, set the tone for the next three years. He challenged the legislators to be vigorous, the key word of his administration despite his own lingering illnesses. His health was failing when he came to Texas, and he was sick on several occasions during his presidency, once being incapacitated for nearly three months. The initial message was lengthy, touching on frontier defense and the Indians, the army and navy, and the eternal problem of finance. He endorsed the creation of a National Bank of Texas, to be modeled somewhat after the old Bank of the United States. The president also urged creation of a system of public education, crowned with a university.

In the area of domestic accomplishments, Lamar's Indian policy was the most notable feature of his term in office. He insisted that the Cherokees and their allies had never received the patents to their lands from the Mexican government; that they had no rights under the treaties negotiated by the provisional government since these had never been approved by the Congress of the Republic; and that they could expect no financial redress from his administration. Lamar admitted that the speculation of certain land agents had perhaps goaded the Indians into rebellion, but although this was to be regretted, the Republic must maintain its Indian defenses. The harshness of his proposed remedy for the Indian problem was obvious when he wrote:

Mirabeau B. Lamar, secretary of war in Burnet's cabinet and vice-president in 1836. Oil portrait by William Henry Huddle, hanging in Capitol, reproduced from holdings of Texas State Archives.

> If the wild cannibals of the woods will not desist from their massacres;
> if they will continue to war upon us with the ferocity of Tigers and Hyenas,
> it is time we should retaliate their warfare, not in the massacre of their
> wives and children, but in the prosecution of an exterminating war upon
> their warriors which will admit of no compromise, and have no termi-
> nation except in their total extinction, or total expulsion.

His terms were ameliorated only by his request that peaceful Indian families be allowed to keep their land, if they would continue to actively
cultivate it. His concern for defense overruled his repugnance for standing armies, and he asked for authorization for a sweeping increase in
the military.

Unfriendly Indians were the primary reason for the Third Congress's
concern with frontier defense. A line of military forts had been contemplated for some time and had the support and recommendation of
Secretary of War Albert Sidney Johnston. On December 16, 1838, Congress ordered the discharge of all persons in the First and Second Regiments of Permanent Volunteers, those mustered to aid General Rusk,
and then enacted a measure, signed by Lamar on December 21, to establish a line of military posts six hundred miles in length along the western frontier, from the Red River to the Nueces River, which would provide better protection and serve as bases for more vigorous prosecution
of a war against the Indians. Fifteen companies, 840 men in all, would
be posted at eight specified locations. Three leagues of land would be
laid off at each site and surveyed into lots of 160 acres each. Two lots
would be reserved for the government to build fortifications, one lot
would be given to the soldiers who adhered to the term of enlistment—a
long three years—and the remainder was to be given in quarter-section
homesteads to settlers. The law optimistically authorized the erection
of sixteen trading posts for the Indians and the construction of a military road to run the entire distance between the forts.

Anticipating that the line of posts would take some time to be fully
implemented, Congress, in a measure approved on December 29, 1838,
authorized the president to raise eight companies of mounted volunteers
for the protection of the frontier against Comanches and other Indians
for a term of six months. These troopers would constitute a regiment
with officers appointed by the president, to be used as he saw fit. Less
than a month later, Congress also authorized the enlistment of a company of mounted rangers, led by officers appointed by the president, for
a term of three months to patrol the frontier of Gonzales County. Eight

Albert Sidney Johnston, secretary of war, 1838. Courtesy Texas State Archives.

days later three companies of mounted volunteers for a term of six months were authorized for immediate service against the hostile Indians on the frontier of Bastrop, Robertson, and Milam counties. Unlike the previous measures, which repudiated part of the acts of May, 1837, by allowing the president to select the officers with the advice and consent of the Senate, this act permitted these units to elect their own officers, who in turn would select a major to command them.

By an act approved on January 24, 1839, President Lamar was required to discharge all officers and soldiers in service except those belonging to the regiment for the protection of the northern and western frontier. One million dollars was appropriated for their support and for such additional forces as the president might deem necessary for the defense of the Republic. Senator Burleson was placed in command of the First Regiment of Regular Infantry after Congress adjourned, but recruiting proceeded slowly. Only one of the eight volunteer companies completed muster, and Burleson was able to enlist only a slim cadre of officers. The provisions of the law of December 21, 1838, authorizing the posts were never completely fulfilled. A portion of the military road, from Austin to San Antonio, was finished, and a post, named Fort Johnson, was established on the Red River in what is now Grayson County, but the rest of the scheme was never accomplished. The plans were too grandiose and expensive for the limited resources of the struggling Republic. On January 26, 1839, an act was approved creating a ranger corps, consisting of two companies of fifty-six men, for the protection of the counties of San Patricio, Goliad, and Refugio. The rangers would serve six months under officers appointed by the president. These men, along with the earlier ranger contingents, bore the brunt of frontier defense during the Third Congress.

Lamar had urged a timely settlement of the outstanding conflict with Mexico in his address to Congress. At his suggestion, the legislators in a joint resolution on January 14, 1839, authorized the opening of frontier trade, heretofore legally conducted only under executive proclamation. This action, they believed, would help to ease tensions, raise the possibility of a cessation of hostilities and even recognition, and facilitate exploration and settlement of the region between the Nueces River and the Rio Grande. The act did result in a gradual resumption of trade within the region and an influx of settlers into the region, commensurate with a swelling tide of immigration into Texas. The government of Mexico neither relaxed its belligerent attitude nor relinquished its claim to the territory; strong public opinion would not allow any administration to appear "soft" on the Texas question by trying to negotiate a settlement. Renewed trade did bolster the sagging economy of the area, indirectly leading to later conflict.

In order to expedite commerce, Secretary of the Navy William M. Shepherd requested authorization on November 21, 1838, to have surveys made of the Texas coastline and to mark its harbors and passes with permanent buoys to facilitate waterborne traffic. His successors under Lamar, Memucan Hunt and Louis P. Cooke, did receive funds for the project, beginning with the Third Congress. By October, 1841, the bar and pass of Sabine had been surveyed, the surveying of the bar and anchorage at Galveston was nearly complete, and the coastline had been mapped as far west as Paso Cavallo, with the depth of the water upon the bars recorded along with the sailing directions for entering each harbor. Despite Lamar's request for appropriations to bolster a navy that could protect shipping, the Third Congress did not act to rebuild that arm of the military.

Domestic affairs absorbed almost all of the energy of the Lamar administration during the Third Congress. One of the stellar achievements was the creation of a system of public education in Texas. Lamar was a Mason, as were seven of the senators (Stroud, Burleson, Burton, Everitt, Greer, Kendrick, and Seguin), with the active involvement in education that membership in that society entailed. Before Lamar took office as president, the Congress under Houston, also a Mason, incorporated DeKalb College in Red River County on November 21, 1838, and endowed it with four leagues of land for support. Lamar's opening address contained many Masonic allusions in the passages on education. One has become immortal: "It is admitted by all, that a cultivated mind is the guardian genius of Democracy, and while guided and controlled by virtue, the noblest attribute of man. It is the only dictator that freemen acknowledge, and the only security which freemen desire." On January 26, 1839, President Lamar signed a joint resolution setting aside three leagues of land for each county, to be surveyed in any empty section of the public domain, to support the establishment of public schools. Another fifty leagues were to be surveyed and set aside for the endowment of two major universities.

Because it did not provide for the immediate organization of the resources appropriated for public schools, the law fell short of the expectations of more ardent supporters of public education. Despite their dour protest, the act has served as the foundation of all state-supported education in Texas, its effectiveness having been multiplied and implemented by additional legislation in the years that followed. The university land was originally located in Central Texas, but the pressure of settlement later caused the legislature to substitute acreage in West Texas, where the discovery of oil reserves in the twentieth century resulted in the enrichment of the Permanent University Fund. The provision for two universities was also later abandoned and the endowment given to the school established in Austin.

Of almost equal social significance was the Homestead Act, signed into law that same day. It provided that every head of a family could hold, free from any financial judgment or execution, his homestead of fifty acres or a town lot with certain improvements, his beasts of burden, his basic household goods, and the tools of his profession. This meant of course that no matter how indebted a man might become, no court could enforce the foreclosure of his minimum property. Designed particularly to protect those who had suffered in the Panic of 1837, this legislation was largely the creation of the Third Congress, although it had some roots in an earlier decree of the Mexican state of Coahuila-Texas and in a suggestion made by Stephen F. Austin before his death in 1836. The law, through extensions and modifications, continues in force to the present time.

The Third Congress under Lamar also provided a permanent capital for Texas. A commission was created to locate a site for the capital on January 14, 1839. Its five members included Senator Burton and former senator Horton. The measure limited their selection of possible locations to a site "at some point between the rivers Trinity and Colorado, and above the old San Antonio road," and stipulated that it be named Austin. A supplementary act, approved ten days later, superseded the earlier requirement that the capital could not move from Houston until 1840, removing the obstacle placed in the way of relocating the seat of government by President Houston. Unlike the commission appointed by the previous administration, the men appointed by Lamar received full support for their recommendations.

The purpose of the new bill was to move the capital from Houston at all costs and placate the western factions by placing it in their section. Although the senators quibbled over details such as the cost of moving and the time required to build a new legislative hall, they were frightened by the nastiness of Houston, where—despite the seductive promise of the Allen brothers—disease and violent crime were the most conspicuous local products, and the senators were eager to leave. The final report, drafted on April 13, 1839, recommended the small town of Waterloo. It lay on the east bank of the Colorado River about thirty-five miles north of Bastrop, the only town in the area that could boast of more than one hundred inhabitants. Despite protests from the press, who themselves dreaded the expense of relocation or the consequence of remaining far from the scene of governmental activity, rapid preparations were underway almost immediately. Edwin Waller was appointed the Republic's agent to oversee the sale of town lots beginning on August 1, 1839, and removal of the government archives was completed in late October of that same year.

Other domestic legislation included the establishment of the State Library and the creation of a patent office. The Third Congress also incorporated a number of new and old towns, including Beaumont, Jasper, Milam, Lavaca, Galveston, Matagorda, San Augustine, La Grange, Rutersville, Fort Preston, Nacogdoches, San Patricio, Refugio, Goliad, Aransas, Comanche, Zavala, and Waterloo, later renamed Austin. Houston achieved a measure of respectability by its incorporation and the establishment of a chamber of commerce by the Third Congress. Several businesses received charters, most notably steam mill enterprises in Matagorda and Bastrop and along the Neches River. The postal service was reorganized, and two gentlemen were engaged to print a code of laws for the Republic. The land act was extended to provide for later immigrants and all soldiers of the Republic. After lengthy debate, the Senate did approve the selection of Rusk as the new chief justice of the Supreme Court, replacing the unfortunate Collinsworth.

The Senate also acted in concert with the House to legislate the development of a more secure Republic. Not passed was a resolution, introduced by Everitt, that ordered all free Negroes who had arrived in Texas since the signing of the Declaration of Independence to leave the country; but an amended bill prohibiting the further entrance of free Negroes was approved on December 21, 1838. More stringent laws against aiding escaped slaves were signed by Lamar on January 15, 1839, mandating strict penalties of five hundred to one thousand dollars and six months to a year in jail for harboring runaways. Although the punishment of branding for manslaughter was repealed on January 23, 1839, new laws against vagrancy approved on January 10 listed penalties of up to one year's imprisonment or thirty-nine lashes for a third offense. The last act of the session mandated the death sentence for horse thieves and their accomplices.

Domestic improvements on the scale envisioned by President Lamar were expensive. In the area of finances, Lamar proved to be an extravagant spender. One of the most far-reaching acts of the Third Congress, unbeknownst to its framers at the time, pledged the revenue of the customs houses to support the payment of the bond issue, little of which had yet been sold. The act provided the basis for the future claim of the State of Texas that since the United States took over the collection of customs after the act of annexation, it also must assume the bonded obligation. During the Third Congress, however, the primary concern was locating the money to conduct the daily business of the Republic, money that was not forthcoming from customs revenues.

The Houston administration had failed in the area of finance and had left Texas almost two million dollars in debt. As an expedient to meet the emergency, President Lamar hoped to secure a loan of five million dollars in either Europe or the United States. He was particularly eager to avoid the pitfall into which Houston had stumbled: the continuing issue of paper money. James Hamilton, former governor of South Carolina and a member of the U.S. House of Representatives from 1822 to 1829, was appointed the Republic's agent to negotiate for the loan. Previous Texan agents had failed because of the hard times in the United States, but Hamilton called on Nicholas Biddle in Philadelphia. He failed to secure five million dollars, but did receive a small advance of four hundred thousand dollars in discounted U.S. post notes from Biddle, who promised to help Hamilton secure a more substantial loan in Europe.

With prospects of a quick loan dimming, the Lamar administration, forced to find another solution for its fiscal woes, reluctantly turned to promissory notes. Lamar allowed the expenditures of the government to soar far beyond those of Houston, from $192,000 under Houston's Second Congress to $555,000 under Lamar's Third Congress. The problem was Lamar's lack of financial perspective, which led him to advocate extensive increases in the funding for the postal service, for bureaucratic staff in the executive branch, and for the removal of the capital from Houston to Austin. In addition, expenditures for the military grew from $881,000 under the Second Congress to over $1.5 million under the Third Congress. The outstanding circulation in paper money when Houston left office in December, 1838, was $800,000. From January to September,

1839, another $1,569,010 was issued, and by September, 1840, an additional $1,983,790 had been released—a total, not including reissues, of $3,552,800. The first issue of paper money, or "redbacks" as the bills were called, was valued at only about 37.5 cents on the dollar and by November, 1840, had fallen to 16.66 cents on the dollar.

The poor sale of bonds, the rapid decrease in acceptance of the promissory notes, and the almost complete lack of a circulating medium of any kind all persuaded Congress to follow Lamar into the quagmire of paper money. By acts of November 16, 1838, and January 19, 1839, the president was authorized to issue the new form of non–interest-bearing promissory notes; the issue was at first limited to a total figure of $100,000 but was later extended whenever specific appropriations were made. Within a few months of issue, the notes circulated for as little as fifteen or twenty cents on the dollar and by the end of 1840 their value utterly collapsed. The issue of $10,000 in small "change" notes by Houston was supplemented by an additional printing of $150,000 by Lamar. Tragically, Lamar's pledge to secure a loan of five million dollars either in the United States or Europe to capitalize a national bank in Texas never materialized. He believed that Texas would prosper if the issue of annexation was allowed to die and the Republic were left to its own devices, but the legislation enacted by the Third Congress proved a disastrous first step.

Major factors in the weak finances of the Republic were a lack of specie and insecure tax revenues. On December 21, 1839, Lamar had to sign legislation that exempted six counties—Gonzales, Bexar, Goliad, Victoria, Refugio, and San Patricio—from taxation for an extended period of time due to Indian depredations. Constant warfare was eroding the Republic's tax base. At the same time, the Senate debated a futile measure to establish a specie standard for Texas currency. At the third reading of the bill, Dunn stood and spoke against further discussion of the issue, as it was obvious that the Republic had no precious metal. Wilson, holding aloft a silver dollar, interrupted him, and Dunn sat down. On January 15, 1839, President Lamar approved a law that set the gold and silver standard in the Republic at the levels used in the United States.

Frustration in the Senate chamber over matters of finance led to a bizarre climax. During a debate in executive session over the proposition of several Mississippi banks that they loan Texas their issue, Senator Wilson became quite excited. He denounced the banks as being truthfully in a failing condition, but went well beyond the bounds of decorum when he "invoked the vengeance of *Almighty God to strike dead* any member who voted for that bill, or any measure calculated to injure the country." Vice-President Burnet directed Wilson to compose himself, but the senator replied that he would be "damned if he would come to order." Burnet ordered Sergeant at Arms Foster to seat Wilson, but the excited senator ordered him to stand back and not touch him, "swearing that no power but God could seat him." The other senators, led by Seguin, ordered Wilson arrested and agreed to delay action for two days to allow time for tempers to cool.

Wilson struck a pose of defiance when the issue was raised two days later on December 26, 1838. He demanded counsel and, when questioned, repeated his inflammatory statements of the previous Monday. Denied an attorney, Wilson declared, "I am determined to rise or fall with Texas, and rise or fall upon my own merits." When the intention of the Senate to expel him became clear, he stood again to proclaim belligerently, "although you may expel me, I stand upon a rock of freedom, which I helped to build, and liberty is my motto." He scorned the proceedings, insisting, "you may impeach me, but you cannot ruin me." He was again placed under arrest when he threatened to leave the room. In a last outburst he exclaimed, "Now condemn me, I defy you. . . . This senate shall not put me down, you may turn me out but you shall not cow me." Left with no other choice, the Senate declared his seat vacant on December 26, 1838.

On January 11, 1839, the Senate proceedings were interrupted by a mob rushing into the Capitol, bearing a triumphant Wilson lustily blowing a bugle to announce his arrival. The election being held within ten days of his expulsion, the counties of Harrisburg and Liberty had returned "Honest Bob" to his seat. On the day when he was to take his place again, some of his constituents secured a large carriage and pulled him amid loud celebration through the streets of Houston to the Capitol. There he thanked them, saying, "my friends, you make me a great man in spite of myself." He was then borne upon their shoulders into the legislative hall. The hapless sergeant at arms was prevented by the drunken crowd from snaring Wilson, although an outraged Wharton had instructed him to bring the rebel before the Senate "dead or alive." The Senate had to ask the sheriff to arrest Wilson and the ringleaders of the mob. Despite Wharton's resolution that Wilson be imprisoned for the balance of the session, the other senators realized the wisdom of Wilson's declaration: "I have gained a proud laurel, you cannot rob me of that sweet reflection." Refusing to become a lens for the further magnification of Wilson's glory, they sentenced the crowd leaders to only one day in jail and let the senator retake his seat with only a reprimand.

The Senate chamber was also the scene of a more violent exchange involving one of its members. Early in January, Everitt had called into question Ashbel Smith's execution of his duties as surgeon general of the Republic, and the matter had been referred to a Senate committee of inquiry. Before they could convene, Smith confronted Everitt in the Senate hall. Not satisfied with Everitt's reply that the verdict was in the hands of others, Smith pressed on to ask if it was true that Everitt had called him an enemy of the president. When Everitt refused to answer, Smith said that he told a "damned lie" and began to beat the senator about the head with a loaded horse whip. Witnesses were helpless to aid Everitt, as Smith's younger brother brandished a knife and pistol. The next day, January 7, 1839, Smith informed the Senate that he intended to have Everitt arrested for "subordination of a witness." The senators refused to deliver their fellow member and instead passed a resolution demanding the recall of Smith from his office. In a puzzling reversal, on January 8 the Senate reconsidered the motion for a recall and defeated the measure, ending the matter without any further debate. They refused to allow their responsibilities as senators to be sullied by public discussion of violence within the legislative arena.

President Lamar had taken office amid great anticipation of the improvements to come. The Senate, frustrated with the dilatory tactics of Houston, had willingly followed him into a labyrinth of increasing militarism and debt. Their continued frustration found defiant and sometimes violent expression in the legislative halls, endangering the image of public peace and prosperity that they wished to promote both within the Republic and abroad. Nevertheless the achievements of the Third Congress were notable, particularly in education and personal credit. Texas could still depend on an influx of immigrants, especially into the region along the Nueces River, which had opened up with the renewal of frontier trade. Unfortunately, when the Senate convened again, it would have to face ever more perilous questions of war and finance as it relinquished the active quest for annexation and worked to establish a stable republic. The debates hardened the lines of sectionalism and aided the cause of personal politics, detracting from the support for the new president who had been anticipated so eagerly.

CHAPTER 4

The Senate of the Fourth Congress, 1839–40

The Fourth Congress met in the new capital of Austin, described by Vice-President David G. Burnet as a "beautiful and picturesque spot, fit residence of the fabled Hygeia." The finances of the Republic, however, presented a much less pleasing picture. Francis Moore, the editor of the Houston *Telegraph and Texas Register,* declared that a "retrenchment of the government expenses even to the borders of parsimony is imperatively necessary." Many of the senators clearly realized the situation, but their actions increasingly took on a partisan aspect. Houston had been elected once more to the House of Representatives, where he began to rally his supporters into a strong opposition to the administration of President Lamar. This factionalism spilled over into the Senate. Houston followers took every opportunity to discredit Lamar and his loyal coterie. George W. Bonnell, editor of the *Texas Sentinel,* established in Austin, wrote in January, 1840: "We think this country too young to become the prey of party politics, and we hope the day is far distant, when parties shall be organized, for the purpose of elevating individuals." Reality, however, had already rendered such sentiment anachronistic.

The membership of the Senate initially appeared to be perfect for promoting the "wisdom, harmony, and singleness of purpose" urged by Burnet. The senators totaled fourteen in number, including four new members elected in September, 1839, but the resignation of Ellis in November due to illness and the late arrivals of several senators prevented the full complement from sitting together. The volatile Robert Wilson had been replaced by Francis Moore, Jr., a veteran of the Texas Revolution who, as the editor of the Houston *Telegraph and Texas Register,* had

Sketch of Austin, 1839, attributed to a Mr. Sandusky. Capitol on the right.
Courtesy Texas State Archives.

urged unity and responsibility in the Congress. James T. Gaines, who supplanted Emory Rains, was one of the oldest members of Congress and had the longest residency in Texas. Born in 1776, he had first come into the area in 1812 with the Gutierrez-Magee expedition and by 1819 operated a ferry across the Sabine River where it intersected the Old San Antonio Road. Gaines had joined the Fredonians in their rebellion and later signed the Declaration of Independence. To many Texans his career reflected a staunch loyalty to independence and to the growth of the Republic, regardless of partisan affiliations. James S. Lester returned to the Senate after a term in the House, bringing an established record of moderation in voting.

The seeds of discontent were sown in the election of Dr. Anson Jones, the fourth new senator. He replaced Wharton, killed by an accidental discharge of his own pistol while dismounting from his horse. During the session the senators wore an "emblem of mourning" on their left sleeve in memory of Wharton. Anson Jones boasted a distinguished list of accomplishments in the service of Texas, but was also a devoted Houston man. Much of his partisanship can be traced to his displacement as minister in Washington by Lamar's appointment of Richard Dunlap. All four of the new senators, led by Anson Jones, would form a solid core of pro-Houston sentiment in the Senate, opposed by a nebulous group who supported Lamar; the latter group always included Everitt, Burton, and Burnet, who in 1841 would campaign unsuccessfully for the office of president as Lamar's candidate.

The senators elected a full slate of officers: McLeod as secretary, Thompson as assistant secretary, and Byars as sergeant at arms; the newcomers were William Grimes as engrossing and enrolling clerk, Robert D. Mc-Anelly as doorkeeper, and Amos Roark as chaplain. Everitt apparently resumed the office of president pro tempore, although there is no name recorded for that position. Unfortunately, factional squabbling prevented an appropriation for publishing the laws and journal of the Fourth Congress, an inexcusable oversight which could be only partially justified by a desire for economy.

The Fourth Congress was the first to convene in the new Capitol in Austin, where it met from November 11, 1839, to February 5, 1840. Surveyors directed by Edwin Waller had laid out the town between Shoal and Waller creeks on the north bank of the Colorado River. Most of the buildings that were clustered along Congress Avenue were of hewn post oak logs. Double log cabins provided office space for the president, the adjutant general, and the departments of war, state, justice, and the navy. The temporary Capitol, however, was a frame building, as was the structure that housed the Treasury Department. The president's house would not have attracted notice in a more settled town, but its two-storied plank facade with porticoes front and rear set it apart from the rough shanties that sheltered a majority of the settlers now flocking to Austin. North of the center of activity lay College Hill, still a knob covered with live oaks whose only value was the view it afforded of the surrounding countryside.

The capital center proved an easy target for the Houston faction. The town, situated on the frontier, was exposed to Indian raids, and Houston men facetiously stood guard at the windows whenever Congress met. Unpleasant living conditions coupled with a high cost of living provided another focus for dissent. Despite the rhetoric, people continued to flood into the area, swelling the settlement's population from less than four hundred in November, 1839, to well over eight hundred after the

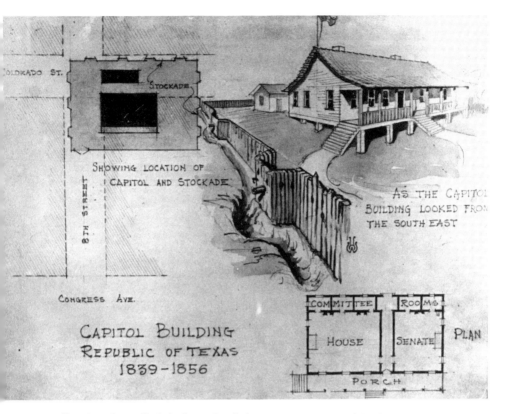

Drawing of 1839 Capitol, shown in relation to present streets of Austin.
Courtesy Texas State Archives.

turn of the year. A great number of these new faces were present for the session only, straining the town's limited capacity for travelers. Many legislators stayed at Bullock's, the first hotel in Austin, which had been built on Congress Avenue soon after lots went on sale in August, 1839. Its ground floor was constructed of logs, and the second of cottonwood planks; patrons often slept on the floor. The inevitable wave of shady tavern keepers and gamblers accompanied the tide of immigration into the capital, but the sessions of the Fourth Congress were remarkable for their lack of violence both in chambers and on the street.

Finances remained the most immediate concern of the senators. The Republic still hoped to ease its desperate financial straits by attracting foreign capital. James Hamilton, who as president of the Bank of South

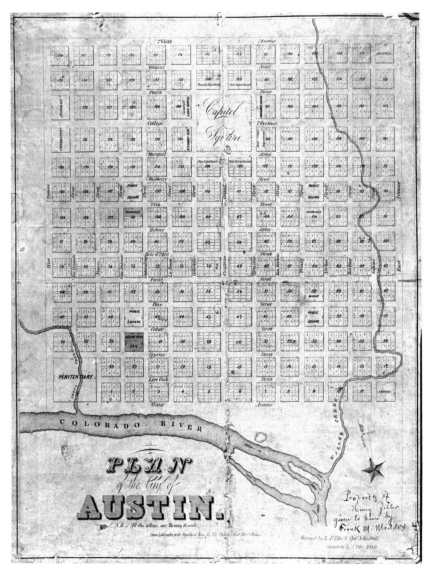

Plan of the City of Austin, 1839. Courtesy Texas State Archives.

Carolina had obtained a loan from abroad for his native state, was commissioned to locate funds for Texas in Europe. He stopped initially in England, but English investors expressed little interest. Their country had suffered a poor harvest in 1838, and the resulting unfavorable balance of trade had forced the export of almost seven million pounds of bullion. The Bank of England had been forced to borrow two million pounds sterling from the Bank of France. Not even a recommendation from Nicholas Biddle, the scion of the once powerful Bank of the United States, could wring a concession from the hard-pressed capitalists in England.

Hamilton traveled next to France, hoping to secure recognition for the Republic. Such a diplomatic achievement could bring a French loan, which in turn might spur the English to invest. J. Pinckney Henderson, at Paris in his capacity as minister of the Republic of Texas to England and France, worked with Hamilton. The latter, whose primary interest lay in obtaining capital, believed that the success of his mission depended on recognition. He sacrificed commercial goals to get it, alienating Henderson. A treaty was signed on September 25, 1839, but, ironically, Hamilton never received his loan, so returned to Texas empty-handed. The depressed money market and difficult French demands for aid in establishing trade with Mexico for them through Texas combined to thwart his efforts. An additional frustration for Hamilton was the fact that England stalled for another year, not recognizing the Republic of Texas until the fall of 1840.

The Lamar administration, having watched its hopes for a loan be dashed on the shoals of European diplomatic intrigue, again cast about for an expedient solution to its fiscal problems. Despite loud opposition, the Senate concurred in the House's decision to issue more scrip, which after the turn of the year sold for less than seventeen cents on the dollar in the wake of a brief recovery due to the mood of optimism surrounding the prospects for a loan. Secretary of the Treasury James H. Starr in November advised the Congress to enact laws for a substantial direct tax on real as well as personal property, and urged the revision of the existing tariff statutes. Everitt, as chairman of the Senate Finance Committee, futilely reported against the issue of more promissory notes, but his recommendation that an impost of 15 percent be levied on all imports except alcohol, which paid a generally higher duty, became law on January 14, 1840. Similarly, an act for direct taxes on real, personal, and mixed property was signed by Lamar, despite strong public opinion against the measure.

Finances made another fine target for the Houston faction. Lamar compounded his mistakes by increasing the civil list when the government should have been practicing the strictest economy. The Senate responded with hostile inquiries about the actual number of clerks and officials necessary to conduct the affairs of the Republic. The senators did, however, initiate a measure to raise government salaries to a living wage, recognizing that the levels had been established in anticipation of payment in specie, not the depreciated scrip of the Republic. As president, Lamar consistently displayed a tragic inability to understand the financial problems besetting the nation. Times were indeed hard; James Morgan, writing to his friend Samuel Swartout about a business deal, noted that property selling for fifty-five thousand dollars in Houston in 1838 sold at sheriff's sale for eight hundred dollars two years later due to the lack of capital. A significant fiscal retrenchment had to wait for the Fifth Congress, however, because Houston's followers could not quite muster enough power to force passage of measures for economy. They did relish their role as spoilers, reducing a tough scenario to an almost impossible situation. In their zeal to disgrace the president, Houston's faction uncovered scandal in the administration of the customshouse at Galveston, adding to Lamar's difficulties by forcing him to request and accept the resignation of Treasury Secretary Asa Brigham and appoint the supposedly nonpartisan Starr, who was unanimously approved by the Senate.

Lamar also continued to push for an increase in appropriations for the military, aggravating the friction between himself and the Senate. The departments of war and the navy received $1.6 million from the Fourth Congress, but the senators rebelled when the fund appeared to be spent for naught. The delivery of six new sailing ships for the second Texas Navy, to complement its one steamship and a "wharf-bound schooner," was completed by April, 1840. The Senate approved the appointment of Edwin W. Moore as "post captain" of the navy in November, 1839, but exploded when Lamar flippantly replied to their request for an explanation of the appointment of ninety naval officers of all ranks while Congress had been adjourned. Lamar asked if they were concerned more for the number or the authority he had assumed, explaining both as being necessary because the Republic existed in a "State of War." Many members of the Senate Committee on Naval Affairs agreed that their protest had been ambiguous, but Oliver Jones dissented, retorting that a "school-boy of ordinary capacity, over the age of ten years, ought to have understood" the question.

Lamar signed a bill on February 5, 1840, directing that the entire fleet, with the exception of two schooners employed in the coastal survey, be laid up in ordinary, but delayed its implementation. In 1841 the *San Antonio* sank, and after their first engagement all but two of Moore's remaining ships were decommissioned. The Senate on January 7, 1840, approved a measure for the merger of the departments of war and the navy and concurred in a House bill forbidding the secretary of the navy on the same date to remove the Navy Yard. Willing to fund an army and navy large enough only to defend the Indian frontier and collect the revenues of the Republic, they gladly incorporated paramilitary units such as the Milam Guards in Houston and the Fannin Guards to bolster local defense.

The financial plight forced Lamar to grasp at straws. One scheme was to win the trade of the Santa Fe region of New Mexico, worth an average of five million dollars each year to merchants in the United States. The Santa Fe trade became a panacea for solving all the fiscal woes of the Republic: that commerce, diverted into Texas ports, could generate enough revenue through the revised tariff laws to ensure solvency. Lamar, informed that the time was ripe because Santa Fe's ties with Mexico were unraveling as revolutionary spirit built, urged Congress to fund his scheme to send a regiment to encourage the region to rebel. In his address to the joint session on November 12, 1839, Lamar pointed out that those people were, after all, "a part of our citizens" who, "if not already prepared to identify their fortunes with ours," would "readily become so if correct information in respect to ourselves were disseminated among them." Congress refused to sanction his plan because of the expenses involved and because there was genuine doubt that the residents of Santa Fe were ready for revolt. Lamar on his own made contact with agents in Santa Fe, but failed to win support from the Fifth Congress. In the summer of 1841, after they adjourned, Lamar took executive action. General Hugh McLeod led five companies, a total of 265 men, into disaster. Their abject surrender on the outskirts of Santa Fe prompted an international protest and a later investigation by Congress.

Even as he worked to foment revolt in Santa Fe, President Lamar in a message delivered on December 10 assured the Fourth Congress that his efforts to make peace with Mexico would soon bear fruit. His plan involved two coordinated actions: an envoy had been sent to Mexico while a minister had been dispatched to Washington to ask for the mediation of the United States. Accordingly, in March, 1839, Richard Dunlap approached U.S. Secretary of State John Forsyth, who assured him that the United States would be willing to help if invited by Mexico. Barnard E. Bee landed at Vera Cruz two months later, but the Mexican government, faced with severe domestic turmoil in the wake of the disastrous "Pastry War" with France and a rebellion in its northern provinces, understandably refused to receive Bee when it learned of his instructions to insist on Mexico's recognition of Texan independence. Lamar's optimism in December stemmed from his commission of James Treat to negotiate secretly with Santa Anna, who was nominally in retirement but was actually conducting many of the affairs of Mexico from his ranch. The Senate agreed with this plan, and Treat reached Mexico in December, 1839, but the involvement of Texans in the short-lived Republic of the Rio Grande and the demonstration by the Texas Navy in support of the Yucatan insurgents in the summer of 1840 ruined what small chance he had for success. Treat, like Bee and Dunlap, returned to Texas empty-handed.

The Houston faction applauded the unsuccessful outcome of Lamar's diplomacy and even contributed to its failure by a meanspirited but clever stratagem on the floor of the Senate. Led by Anson Jones, the followers of Houston prevented the ratification of Dunlap as minister to the United States and forced his return from that country. Playing on the pride of the congressmen, they pointed out that only a chargé d'affaires had been sent to the Republic by that country, and they should not embarrass themselves by committing the faux pas of sending a minister in return. A bill to create the position of chargé d'affaires easily passed both houses and was signed by Lamar on January 25, 1840, as a matter of course. Dunlap, possessing only a useless commission as minister, had no choice but to resign.

President Lamar enjoyed a few victories over his opponents, but in the end they proved to be only a source of even more friction. He was elated at the expulsion of the Cherokees following a clash in the summer of 1839, which ended in disaster for the Indians and death for Chief Bowles. The last remnant of the Cherokees in the field, a small band attempting to reach Mexico led by the chief's son, John Bowles, was intercepted by Edward Burleson on Christmas Day, 1839, and dispersed. The rest fled north across the Red River in the wake of Lamar's expulsion order.

Houston's legislative counterattack was as brilliant as it was emotional. He introduced a bill in the House to section and sell the lands formerly occupied by the Cherokees, an action that would acknowledge that the tribe had indeed owned the land, that it had not belonged to the Republic of Texas while the Cherokees were in possession of it, and that now it must be divided and sold regardless of previous claims by private interests. The Senate Committee on Indian Affairs reported in favor of the Cherokee land bill, declaring that "no Indians under the sun ever had rights better established than the Cherokee" and adding that "none but those who regarded filthy lucre more than their country's peace and quiet, or the blood of their citizens, have called that matter into question." In sum, they were "unwilling to see those evil disposed persons profit by their own wrong." Burton dissented, protesting "the *rumor* of title in favor of the Cherokees." The intent of the Houston followers to discredit the administration was obvious; in the course of debate on the floor, Moore was chastised for declaring, "I do not wish Senators to bow down like grovelling curs to party spirit."

Although the wording was changed slightly, in large part due to the determined stance of Burton, the Cherokee land bill passed the Senate on January 25, 1840, with only Burton, Kendrick, and Moore opposed. Lamar signed it into law on February 5, codifying the Cherokees' rightful ownership of the land before their expulsion. The House later approved an appropriation of forty-five thousand dollars to implement the survey of the Cherokee lands, but the senators, having made their statement in favor of principle and of Houston, balked at the expense. Burton registered another strong protest, but his effort was wasted. The measure was referred to a series of committees, where it died without a vote at the close of the session. The law to section the lands was revoked within a few years, and the rights of the early claimants were reestablished in a statute that was more consistent with the public land policy of the Republic.

The Indian policy of the Republic under Lamar was more indulgent toward peaceful tribes. On January 31, 1840, Anson Jones introduced a bill for the support of the Caddo Indians, a small tribe impoverished by the incessant warfare in its region. The rules were suspended and the measure passed immediately, with the House concurring that afternoon. Lamar signed the bill on February 5, 1840. Some indication of the motives behind the support for this act can be gleaned from the debate over the establishment of a reservation for the Alabama-Coushatta Indians, which became law on January 14, 1840. George W. Barnett, chairman of the Senate Committee on Indian Affairs, reported in favor of its passage, saying that "they are only the remnant of a people, and unable to sustain themselves against the Cumanchees [*sic*], if driven to the frontier [they] must from necessity [and] from principles of self-preservation unite with our enemies." Occasionally the goal of frontier defense could bring about humanitarian action instead of military reaction. President Lamar, quite possibly with a sigh of relief, signed a bill authorizing him to spend twenty thousand dollars to ransom prisoners held by the Indians, giving him a more peaceful alternative to punitive expeditions.

Domestic affairs became an increasing burden on the Department of State as the Republic developed. Lamar asked Congress to create a Department of Government, with separate bureaus for education and internal improvements, but it refused on the grounds of economy. Congress did act, however, to better conditions in those areas. Two bills, signed by Lamar on January 14 and February 6, 1840, provided for a sweeping reorganization of the postal system and the construction of additional post roads. Private industry was encouraged as a solution to the Republic's lack of internal improvements. The charter of the Brazos and Galveston Railroad Company was amended to give it the responsibility for building canals, and enterprises such as the Sabine Steam Mill and Water Works Company and the Trinity Coal and Mining Company were expected to aid in the development of natural resources within Texas. Laws to detect fraudulent land certificates and provide strict penalties for land fraud and swindling passed, the former over Lamar's veto. The president had requested a bill that would punish both those who sold false land certificates and those who bought them, and initially rejected the more lenient measure of Congress, which did not penalize the perhaps unwary purchaser. Houston, who had consistently refused to carry out legislation ordering him to open the General Land Office because he believed that widespread speculation and fraud would result, must have relished his opponent's predicament. Congress also ordered the surveyors of each county to send in maps of their region to aid in settling disputes and reducing the possibility of swindles.

The senators of the Fourth Congress, eight of whom were Masons, worked to prevent partisan demands for government economy from impeding the development of a system for public education in Texas. A bill introduced in the House to create a Board of School Commissioners for "Common Schools and Academies" received the immediate approval of the Senate Committee on Education, and was signed by President Lamar on February 5, 1840. It assigned the chief justice and two associate justices of each county to sit as a panel to review decisions for employment as teachers and to regulate the lands set aside for the support of schools. The Senate also provided for higher education: a bill to charter Rutersville College became law on February 5, and another signed on the previous day incorporated the trustees of Union Academy. Unfortunately, the acts of Congress in favor of education were ahead of their time and received little support for implementation. In 1840, no country had a fully developed free public school system such as the legislators of Texas were trying to establish. Land endowments by themselves were not enough to fund continued growth and did not attract other sources of support. The people of Texas were also scattered and more concerned with the obstacles of settling an almost virgin territory. Effective organization of schools for primary public education came only after statehood.

Under the aegis of the Fourth Congress, the Republic began to adopt more of the trappings of a civilized nation. The capital town of Austin was incorporated on December 27, 1839, followed by new charters for Beaumont, Goliad, Victoria, Galveston, Gonzales, Matagorda, and Texana. A bill creating Travis County was signed on January 25, 1840. Congress authorized a chamber of commerce for both Houston and Matagorda. Lighthouses were ordered to be erected at important ports in a law of January 7, 1840, despite bitter protests from some senators who insisted that the money could be better spent for frontier defense. An act for the construction of a penitentiary using the Auburn model of penal labor was introduced by Senator Moore and adopted by the Senate, but the House refused to sanction the expense. Senator Lester introduced a joint resolution for a hospital on January 29, 1840, which became law on February 5.

The rush to become a civilized nation also involved a revision of the basic laws of the Republic. Lamar signed an act establishing English common law as the legal foundation of the Texas legal code on January 20, 1840. One salient point of Spanish law was retained in an act approved on the same day which stipulated that the land and slaves owned by a woman before marriage remained her separate property after marriage, although her husband would exercise sole management over them. All other possessions, unless otherwise stipulated in a prenuptial agreement, would be common property. The Senate also gave its approval to a broad reorganization of the judicial system, creating two new districts to complement the five already extant. New laws defined the status of wills and

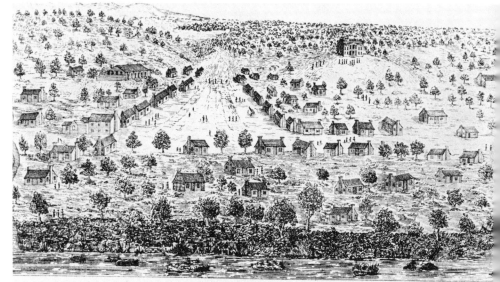

CITY OF AUSTIN THE NEW CAPITAL OF TEXAS IN 1844.

Austin, 1840, showing President Lamar's home on hill at right.
Courtesy Texas State Archives.

provided for the settlement of succession and intestate estates, to be administered by revitalized probate courts.

Morality was a key element in the quest for a civilized Republic. A law of February 5, 1840, required tavern keepers to post a bond of twenty-five hundred dollars, paying 10 percent to the county clerk to obtain the mandatory license. Gaming with cards and dice was forbidden by an act of the same date, although billiard table operators were amended out of the bill requiring that public houses be licensed. A vote in the Senate on an act to legalize horse racing ended in a tie on January 10, 1840, before Burnet cast a deciding vote in the negative. Oliver Jones, chairman of the special committee on the matter, reported in favor of the bill, saying that "a law authorizing turf racing cannot have any unfavourable effect on sosiety [sic], but would have the tendency to Encourage the raising [of] fine blooded Horses, a discription [sic] of animals much required in this Republic." This report was read again and adopted by the Senate on January 22, but the bill, which was put to another vote, again failed to be passed. Such actions contributed in no small measure to the overall peaceful conduct of the Fourth Congress as they placed beyond the pale of the law many activities that generated violence.

A heated exchange ensued when the House requested the concurrence of the Senate in its bill for the suppression of dueling. Anson Jones, chairman of the Committee on the Judiciary, reported in favor of the measure. Oliver Jones, in the course of debate on the floor, moved that its title be changed to "An Act for the Protection of Cowards," but the other senators refused to allow such mockery. Only Kendrick supported Oliver Jones on his second proposed amendment, which would have stricken the section that prevented those who had taken part in a duel from holding public office. The day after it was introduced, the measure passed the Senate, with only Oliver Jones, Kendrick, and Burton voting in opposition. Lamar signed the bill on January 28, 1840, to the general approbation of the Texas press.

The Fourth Congress of the Republic enacted a particularly harsh law to drive "free persons of colour" from Texas. It forbade them to immigrate to the Republic and commanded all those residing in Texas to leave within two years. If found in violation of the law, the offenders would be required to pay a bond of one thousand dollars or would be sold into bondage for one year. At the end of twelve months of bondage, if the Negro had not yet paid the fine, he or she would be sold at auction into slavery for life. A similar bill had failed to muster enough support during the previous session, but this one passed and was signed into law on February 5. Despite their support for this harsh statute, members of the Senate did approve most of the petitions submitted during the Fourth Congress by free Negroes requesting permission to stay in Texas, and did not strictly enforce the provision requiring expulsion in the case of manumission. Anson Jones, as chairman of the Committee on the Judiciary, often led the fight in favor of the humanitarian alternative of letting free Negroes remain in Texas. Those who opposed letting them remain expressed a strong fear that they would become a source of dissatisfaction among the slaves which, ultimately, would lead to insurrection. Houston in 1842 would lead the effort to make this law inoperative, and there is no real evidence that it was ever really enforced. Another law forbade anyone to trade with slaves, but more importantly it defined the killing of a slave through cruelty or carelessness as murder, to be tried as a felony. Significantly, the law's final provision denied slaves the right to bear arms without express permission from their masters.

It was the financial plight and the failure to reach a peace with Mexico that discredited the Lamar administration. The public did generally approve both the expulsion of the Cherokees and the removal of the seat of government to Austin, but both actions also made some influential enemies for Lamar and increased support for Houston. Lamar's position was made even more untenable by his increasingly hostile relationship with Congress. Congress had given him wide latitude and great financial support, and he had failed to bring about the major changes envisioned in the optimism that surrounded his inauguration in 1838. The Fourth Congress became the last to endorse a majority of the expensive measures for civil reform championed by Lamar, although even they set a precedent for the future by rejecting many of his proposals. Subsequent sessions would curtail the budget of the Republic drastically, especially in the areas of defense and public services. The dream of a civilized Republic would endure, but it would be tempered by a more realistic appraisal of the available financial resources.

CHAPTER 5

The Senate of the Fifth Congress, 1840–41

Financial retrenchment dominated the debates within the Senate of the Fifth Congress. Personal politics became increasingly complex as the supporters of the Lamar administration introduced measures for economy in government that the Houston faction opposed. The majority on both sides, however, realized the need for responsible fiscal policies, and the session that met from November 2, 1840, to February 5, 1841, was remarkable for its harmony when faced with dangerously divisive issues. Led by Lamar and Houston, the Republic of Texas in this period teetered on the brink of financial disaster and war with Mexico, a combination of events almost certain to bring about the collapse of civil government. The Senate became a forum for the resolution of many of the most heated controversies and provided stable leadership through a continued policy of conservative action under acting president David G. Burnet.

Of the fourteen senators who sat during the Fifth Congress, there were five new faces. William Henry Daingerfield took the seat of Seguin, who resigned shortly before the session to join the Federalist campaign in Mexico. Daingerfield had previously served as mayor of San Antonio in 1838, less than a year after emigrating from his native state of Virginia. Kindred H. Muse replaced the doughty Burton; Muse was a veteran of Texas politics, having served in the House during the Third and Fourth congresses. James W. Byrne, an Irishman, had fought in the Texas Revolution before establishing the town of Lamar, named in honor of the president. James B. Miller brought a lengthy record of public service for Texas to the Senate, including attendance at the conventions of 1833 and 1835. Robert Potter had perhaps the most remarkable political history; he had been elected to three terms in the South Carolina legislature and once to the U.S. House of Representatives before moving to Texas, where he signed the Declaration of Independence in 1836. After serving as secretary of the navy in the *ad interim* government of Burnet, he retired to his headright grant on Caddo Lake in the present county of Marion, where he almost immediately became involved as a Moderator in the Regulator-Moderator War, appropriately called, which arose from the competition of two essentially indistinguishable, self-styled vigilante gangs for control of a lawless area now embraced by Shelby, Panola, and Harrison counties. It raged for some five years, and the murder of Senator Potter on March 2, 1842, just after the first session of the Sixth Congress, perpetrated by a well-known and unpunished band of Regulators, typified the conditions that at last led President Houston in August of 1844 to send in troops and force the ringleaders to sign a treaty of peace. Despite his own role in a conflict that had only bad sides, Potter had been a strong proponent of responsible government as a senator of the Fifth and Sixth congresses.

The Senate mustered a quorum on the first day of the session and quickly elected its officers. McLeod retained his post as secretary, as did Sergeant at Arms Byars. The offices of enrolling clerk and engrossing clerk were again separated and given to John E. Jones and C. W. Peterson, respectively. Solomon L. Johnson became doorkeeper, and M. H. Nicholson replaced Lamar's personal secretary, Algernon P. Thompson, as assistant secretary for the Senate. Anson Jones was elected president pro tempore when Burnet took over the presidency from Lamar on December 12, 1840. Lamar, a consumptive, was exhausted from the cares of his administration and suffered from an intestinal disorder; he asked leave in order to journey to the United States for proper treatment. He was unable to resume his duties before the spring, so Burnet continued as acting president for the balance of the session.

A spirited debate ensued over the election of a chaplain for the Senate. Kendrick staunchly opposed the motion to elect a chaplain, and the subsequent vote ended in a tie. Burnet, the president of the Texas Bible Society, broke the tie by voting in the affirmative, supported by Senators Moore and Barnett, vice-presidents in the same organization. A number of resolutions introduced during the session to reassure the people of Texas of the continued Christian principles of the senators indicated that this attack was simply the opening salvo in the battle over government finance. Moore, six days after the first clash had been resolved with Burnet's tie-breaking vote, offered his own measure to again combine the offices of enrolling clerk and engrossing clerk and to do away with a chaplain in the interest of economy. Ironically, two days later Barnett's successful motion to indefinitely postpone Moore's resolution effectively ended the assault on the office of chaplain.

Burnet took control of the Republic at a very inauspicious time for his own political fortunes, more especially because he was a Lamar supporter and was recognized as the logical successor to continue the president's policies after the election of 1841. The vice-president knew that a good showing was essential for his future. Burnet took financial retrenchment to heart and, in his first official act, sent a jingoistic message to Congress declaring that an invasion of Texas by Mexico was imminent and prompt action was imperative. Houston had found a more clever opponent in Burnet. While he held the reins, the vice-president would continue to undermine Houston's support in Congress by adopting many of his projects as the administration's own and diverting attention from objectionable circumstances by emphasizing the threat from Mexico.

Financial retrenchment in the Fifth Congress included a variety of actions at many levels. The salary of the chief justice was reduced from five thousand to three thousand dollars annually, and the bill to increase Burnet's salary to a level commensurate with his new responsibilities as acting president was squelched. Repeated efforts to provide for a census of the Republic were frustrated. The senators demanded an accounting of the public buildings in Austin and on January 5, 1841, approved a bill that ordered the sale or lease of all unnecessary government-owned structures in the capital city. Burnet signed the measure into law four days later, initiating the abandonment of every public office south of Pecan Street except for the treasury building and the General Land Office. He was spared the ultimate indignity when a joint resolution introduced by Senator Gaines to halt payment of the salary for a private secretary to the president, authorized in January, 1839, was rejected by the Senate on February 1. The appropriations of the Fifth Congress for civil purposes amounted to about $450,000, a significant drop from the $550,000 voted for by the Third Congress, Houston's previous.

Moore, now a confirmed opponent of Houston, initiated a much more substantial movement for retrenchment. Writing in his Houston *Telegraph and Texas Register* before the session began, Moore advocated the prompt elimination of "many of the most useful and necessary offices of government," according to opposing editor Bonnell of the Austin *Texas*

Sentinel. Moore had introduced a similar proposal as a senator in the Fourth Congress, but it had been soundly rejected. His expanded program included the merger of the Department of War and the Department of the Navy; abolition of the offices of quartermaster, commissary, surgeon, adjutant, and inspector general, as well as that of the colonel of ordnance, with their functions to be assumed by clerks in the war department; dismissal of the stock commissioner, to be replaced by a new clerk in the Department of the Treasury; elimination of the second auditor, with all duties to be concentrated in the first auditor; and the deletion of the postmaster general and his staff, their responsibilities to be assumed by clerks in the state department. Bonnell believed that no good could come of the fight brewing for Congress, and warned, "Let every honest member of congress lay aside party feeling and reflect that we are too young a people to be quarrelling about party politics." His words had some effect: the Lamar faction adopted the issue of retrenchment as its own, and through its own necessity the idea would enforce harmony.

Everitt, a staunch Lamar supporter, fired the initial volley. Everitt stated on November 16, 1840, that within the week he would introduce a bill to discharge the regular army, place the navy in ordinary, and abolish every officer except a single lieutenant in each of those departments; to suspend the issue of the promissory notes of the Republic and to allow holders to fund at six percent payable at the pleasure of the government after ten years; to reduce the number of post offices; to reduce direct taxes to one-fourth of one percent; and to require the payment of all revenues to the Republic to be made in specie, with all public salaries to be paid in drafts upon the anticipated reserve of silver and gold. He was as good as his word; on December 2, Everitt introduced legislation that embodied his proposals. Following a motion by Moore, the Senate rejected that which pertained to the suspension of promissory notes, the reduction of direct taxes, and the payment of public revenues in specie, leaving only the core of Moore's original scheme for streamlining the government.

The debate over this legislation in the Senate became tangled. When Potter offered an amendment that would allow the retention of three hundred men in the regular army, the Senate concurred. Everitt, who had not voted on the change, resigned immediately. He should have remained, because Moore's counterproposal that all officer ranks be reduced and recruiting be suspended was accepted by the Senate as an amendment on December 16, 1840. The final bill signed into law by Burnet on January 18, 1841, required the elimination of the offices named by Moore in his editorial, with a concurrent reduction of the army officer corps and placement of the navy in ordinary, so that it would consist of only sixty seamen and the necessary officers. More importantly, the Senate appropriated no money for the support of the army, and the president was denied the power to issue additional promissory notes for the navy. The total allotment by the Fifth Congress for the upkeep of both the army and navy amounted to only $211,050, compared to almost $1.6 million from the previous Congress. After adjournment, Burnet chose to disband the regular army rather than keep the troops in the hope of receiving the funds to pay them from future sessions.

The bill that reduced the army and navy also eliminated the position of postmaster general. Moore had introduced a resolution authorizing that office to suspend all of its contracts for the delivery of mail, a drastic measure which was alleviated with the organization of a "General Post Office" within the Department of State in January. To support the new organization, postage rates were doubled. Some post offices were eliminated, as well as post roads, but the senators for the time being could congratulate themselves on effecting substantial economy in the postal service of the Republic.

The act to reduce government officers proved to be little more than a temporary stopgap. President Lamar in his annual message to Congress urged the swift acquisition of a foreign loan as an expedient for the Republic's financial dilemma, and declared that prospects were good for selling Texas bonds. The effort depended on Hamilton, who was still in England. The president's decision to order a demonstration by the Texas Navy in support of the rebels in the Yucatan region of Mexico was used as leverage by Hamilton to secure a treaty. The threat of interrupted commerce between England and Mexico was a powerful incentive in troubled financial times. Recognition of the Republic by the Netherlands in September, 1840, through a treaty of commerce and navigation, also brought pressure to bear on the British government. In November, Hamilton was informed that it was ready to sign a formal agreement.

Hamilton initially endorsed two treaties, the first a treaty of commerce and navigation to enhance trade relations, the second to assure Britain's mediation to establish peace between Texas and Mexico in return for the Republic's assumption of a substantial portion of the latter's foreign debt contracted before January 1, 1835. These treaties were carried to Austin by a special English agent and ratified by the Senate on January 28, 1841. A third treaty, which Hamilton reluctantly signed, required mutual suppression by Texas and Britain of the African slave trade through provisions allowing each nation to search the vessels of the other. Hamilton believed, erroneously, that such an agreement would be strongly opposed in Texas, and so he sent it, along with a lengthy letter of explanation, to Austin with Arthur Burnley, his co-worker. Burnley did not arrive until after Congress had adjourned, and consequently the third treaty was not ratified until the Sixth Congress. Despite Lamar's optimism, recognition did not bring about an English loan; the failure of confidential agent James Treat to negotiate a settlement with Mexico undermined the value of Texas bonds as an investment.

In desperation, the Republic continued to issue promissory notes in lieu of a more substantial circulating medium. Anson Jones's proposed amendment to suspend the issue of all promissory notes, similar to the portion blocked by Moore of Everitt's bill for the abolition of certain offices, was rejected by the Senate in the final version of the measure. In an effort to provide substantial revenues to support the scrip, all specified duties were doubled in an act signed on February 5, 1841. *Ad valorem* taxes on imports of 10 to 15 percent were set at 45 percent by the new measure. Only salt, iron, steel, sugar, and coffee were exempt, the latter two products because they came from Cuba by way of the United States and had already had two duties paid on them by the time they reached consumers in Texas. A law enacted on the same date allowed holders of all promissory notes, bonds, certificates on the funded debt, or any other "liquidated claims" against the Republic to exchange their paper for land at the rate of two dollars per acre.

The Lamar administration, faced with constant attacks, attempted to redeem itself in areas of governmental action other than finance. On November 12, 1840, the president transmitted to the Senate a communication from Barnard E. Bee, who was in charge of the legation in Washington, along with a report from an informant that indicated that Indians migrating southward from Arkansas were being enlisted by Mexico "in prosecuting its national war" against the Republic. Lamar had dismissed the possibility of war as too expensive in his opening address, but when the news of the failure of Treat's negotiations reached Texas early in December, he immediately recommended that the armed forces of the Republic be ordered to compel Mexico to acknowledge the independence of Texas. It was an astute political move as well as a diplomatic move.

Many of the followers of Houston joined the Lamar faction in supporting war. A joint committee of Congress met to consider a declaration of hostilities, uniting the opposing political camps to consider the practicality of a march on their common foe.

Burnet encouraged this spirit. Speaking before a joint session, he thundered, "I doubt not that the congress of Texas will be animated and cheered with the prospect of a speedy determination, by the sword, of our protracted controversy with Mexico." Diplomacy had failed utterly: "we have exhibited to our enemy many instances of magnanimity and forbearance; but they have been as 'pearls cast before swine.'" The acting president presented the threat as an opportunity, saying, "Texas proper is bounded by the Rio Grande; Texas, as defined by the sword, may comprehend the Sierra del Madre." Burnet, after his nationalistic message, submitted a plan of action formulated by Felix Huston that included an invasion of Mexico by way of the lower Rio Grande. A report from former senator Seguin, who returned from a campaign with the Federalists in Mexico during December, 1840, reinforced the general alarm over an impending invasion.

Houston and his few loyal supporters objected to an offensive action as one more needless drain on the treasury. Their own solution called for a strategic defense. Congress wrangled over the two plans for weeks without reaching a decision. The Senate stood fast for Houston, tabling a bill to rescind the joint resolution that had earlier insisted on a spirit of amicability between the two nations. News then came from England that Hamilton had signed the treaty that would bring about a settlement between Mexico and Texas. The merits of this plan were quickly recognized, and Congress postponed action on a definite stand regarding war until Hamilton's achievement could be fully investigated. Britain's interest in continued uninterrupted commerce with Mexico had long restrained the government of the Republic from launching a premature attack, and in this case it became a factor in dragging the most ardent war hawks back from the Rio Grande. The joint committee, which had held the two resolutions that would have declared war with Mexico, tabled them indefinitely on January 12, 1841, and reported in favor of continuing a defensive posture. Their words meant victory for Houston and defeat for Burnet.

Proponents of disbanding the regular army experienced a great scare in the war crisis of December, 1840. They did not swerve from their determination to eliminate a burden on the economy of the Republic,

Juan Seguin. Painting by Jefferson Wright, reproduced from holdings of Texas State Archives.

but they did act to strengthen the militia system. At the height of the emergency, Burnet signed an act authorizing him to enlist three "spy companies" of fifteen men each to patrol the western frontier. On February 4, 1841, he approved a law for the reorganization of the militia, with a company of fifty-six men to be raised in each of the twenty frontier counties. These units were to "hold themselves in readiness as minute men." The volunteers' right to elect their own company officers was upheld by this act, but the privilege of appointing officers of higher rank rested with colonels, brigadiers, and major generals, whose ultimate authority devolved from the president. The Senate approved these measures, but also endorsed the purchase of three hundred and fifty muskets for military use in February, 1841, possibly in anticipation of a need for at least a small regular army.

The Senate did not retreat from the common assertion of the Rio Grande as the border of Texas. A bill belligerently entitled "An Act for the Protection of the Mexican [Trade] and the Suppression of Marauding Parties and Cattle Stealers on the South Western Frontier," introduced by Byrne, met with approval and later became law. The lure of Santa Fe remained great; Daingerfield offered a petition from a number of Austin citizens asking for a charter for fifty men to be known as the Santa Fe and Chihuahua Trading Company. The Senate rejected this measure, as well as another that would have authorized the president to enlist a company of volunteers for an expedition into New Mexico. Reports such as Bonnell's assertion that "two additional rich gold mines have been discovered on the route between [Austin] and Santa Fe" proved to be a great temptation, especially when he reported that the people of the region were rebelling against the ecclesiastical authority over the town. The Senate did pass a bill to establish communication with Santa Fe in January, 1841, but refused to allow the Republic to mount a reconnaissance. The decision by Lamar to mount an expedition in defiance of Congress became the most tragic blunder of his administration. Most of the men involved who survived the tortuous march south to Mexico City after their surrender remained prisoners at Castle Perote until 1842.

The Senate also proved its responsibility in the domestic sphere. The section of the land law passed during the previous session that denied the General Land Office the power to issue patents to the purchasers of property had been labeled "one of the most unjust, unconstitutional, and iniquitous laws ever enacted" by Bonnell, the outspoken editor of the *Texas Sentinel.* Owners, although they could not receive their titles, were still bound to pay "extravagant" taxes. Bonnell pointed out that "acts of Congress never settle land titles. . . . The question must and will eventually come to the judiciary—the only legitimate tribunal for its final settlement." It was a hard lesson to learn, but the Senate took the initiative in providing a solution. Potter called for a joint committee to investigate the instance of land fraud, while the Senate as a whole passed measures for the relief of the settlers along the newly surveyed Red River boundary. Satisfied that a large portion of the public domain did legally remain open, except for those portions legitimately claimed by homesteaders, and perhaps chastised by Kendrick's facetious motion to substitute the word "disturb" for "quiet" in the caption of a bill intended to quiet land titles, the Senate authorized the General Land Office to issue patents for claims and extended the deadline for headrights to January 1, 1842, two years beyond the previous limit.

The senators, like most educated men in the nineteenth century, retained a strong belief in private enterprise as the best method of providing for internal improvements and even colonization. The Fifth Congress chartered the Galveston and Virginia Point Bridge Company to link the island with the mainland; the Houston and Austin Turnpike Company to build a road between the towns; the Harrisburg Railroad and Trading Company and the Texas Trading, Mining, and Emigrating Company to expedite new immigration and construction in the Republic. In a notable diversion from regular policy, which is perhaps indicative of the financial straits of the Republic, the latter company was allowed to muster an army of three hundred soldiers, led by officers who had sworn an oath of allegiance to Texas. Despite previous experiences, the Congress awarded banking privileges, including the right to issue scrip, to McKinney, Williams and Company due to "their having made large advances to this government at an early period of its existence." A bill for the Peters Colony, introduced on January 17, 1841, passed quickly and was signed on February 4, 1841. Six hundred families were to be settled between Trinity River and Red River, each head of household to receive the standard headright of 640 acres. Although the colony, from its inception to its final demise in 1852, was a nightmare of ineptness and controversy, it was responsible for the largest immigration Texas received from any single stimulus. Other incorporations included the Galveston Artillery Company and the Travis Guards, paramilitary units to augment the militia's power to respond to emergencies.

The senators did not blindly endorse every private scheme for the colonization of Texas, especially when the proposal came from the pompous representative of a European monarchy, an anathema to their republican spirit. France had dispatched Alphonse de Saligny, formerly secretary of the legation at Washington, to Texas as her first minister to the Republic. Saligny, through his glowing reports of the Republic, had been instrumental in Hamilton's winning a treaty and was initially received with genuine approval. He unfortunately proved to have an un-

French Legation, built in 1839.
Courtesy Texas State Archives.

canny knack for antagonizing his hosts. The first incident of this occurred when he knowingly passed counterfeit currency to the local teamster who had transported his luggage and household equipment. The Republic was forced to make good when the Frenchman haughtily refused to do so. Later, Saligny met his match in Richard Bullock, owner of the Austin hotel where the minister initially made his headquarters. Their spirited feud over the payment of the Frenchman's bill would peak when Saligny ordered his servant to slaughter Bullock's pigs, which had wandered into his stable. The resulting imbroglio was beyond the power of the Republic to resolve, and Saligny asked for his passports at the end of the summer of 1841.

A matter of greater importance set the administration and many of the senators irrevocably against Saligny. He had arrived with a plan, believed to be the creation of Louis Philippe, for the establishment of colonies of French settlers along the Texas frontier. He persuaded Houston to introduce the scheme into the House of Representatives. The bill requested a grant of three million acres of land upon which a company of French capitalists would locate at least eight thousand French emigrants by January, 1849. As an inducement to emigration, the French would have the right to import whatever they chose free of taxation until 1848. Moreover, the land itself would be tax free for the same period. The company, for its part, would establish a line of at least twenty forts along the frontier between the Red River and the Rio Grande and maintain them for a period of twenty years. As soon as the eight thousand colonists were settled around these posts, the company would receive full title to the three million acres. The proposal included other substantial privileges: the French would enjoy the right to work all mines within the ceded area during the twenty-year grant, giving only 15 percent of the annual proceeds to the Republic; would have exclusive rights of trade with the towns of northern Mexico; and could exclude other settlers or companies from homesteading land within their three-million-acre reserve during the twenty years.

The Franco-Texian Bill, as it soon became known, stirred up a hornet's nest of opposition. Houston's support for the bill exposed the former president to bitter political charges. The congressmen also objected to Saligny's personal interference in a domestic matter. Comparisons with the Citizen Genet affair were common. The new editor of the *Texas Sentinel*, J. W. Cruger, called it a "Bill of Abominations." Saligny, for his part, wined and dined the congressmen assiduously. He achieved his goal in the House, but his proposal went down to ignominious defeat in the Senate in February, 1841. Senator Lester, who spoke against the bill as chairman of the Committee on Military Affairs, to which the bill had been referred, scoffed at the idea of yielding three million acres "for the trifling protection this company would give." Moore in his newspaper went even further: "And in this grand scheme of conquest, where would Texas be found?" Texas needed no such protection because in two years the "handful of naked, half-starved, unarmed savages" would be scattered by "hosts of hardy pioneers" coming into the Republic. The debate continued through the summer, and passage of the bill became a campaign promise of the Houston faction. Saligny wreaked his revenge when he prevented the consummation of the five-million-dollar loan arranged by Hamilton after painstaking negotiation with French bankers. Once returned to office, Houston astutely let the matter drop.

Land was not the only domestic issue of import. The senators passed a number of bills to relieve themselves of the burden of endless petitions for relief. Daingerfield introduced a measure to create a system of bankruptcy and to regulate the collection of foreign debts. The sections of the act on bankruptcy became one of the most hotly contested issues of the session, but the measure was signed into law on January 19, 1841. A similar measure provided for those who had taken refuge in the insolvency laws of other countries. Two weeks earlier, Burnet had endorsed a bill that allowed district courts to adjudicate divorce cases and award alimony, actions previously carried out by petitioning Congress. The Senate also approved a blanket exemption from the mandatory expulsion act of the previous session for Negroes who had resided in Texas before March 2, 1836; the exemption extended to their families. Sadly, a law providing for the auction of runaway slaves provided every opportunity for a slaveowner to protect his property rights, but no chance at all for a free Negro to assert his civil rights if wrongfully apprehended. Finally, the senators endorsed a bill that provided for the "support and education" of indigent orphans through a system of indenture, to be regulated by the courts and not by petition.

The Senate of the Fifth Congress also promoted higher education. Among the trustees of Galveston University, which was actually founded before its charter was granted, were two senators, Moore and Anson Jones, as well as Burnet, Lamar, and Houston, all Masons. Galveston University remained open at least through 1844, but its further history has been shrouded in oblivion. The Senate also endorsed the charters of Guadalupe College, to be established in Gonzales, and Trinity College, to be established in the settlement of Alabama in Houston County, but neither institution ever opened. The Austin Lyceum also received a charter to promote learning, but the Senate, led by Moore, rejected its request to be allowed to use the Senate chamber for meetings. Later in the month, the senators would declare their meeting room in the Capitol off limits for any "feasting" or dancing, especially while they were in session. The Senate approved the charter of the German Union, a fraternal organization similar to the Masons, to which eight of the senators belonged, but refused to consider a petition for a charter of the Lone Star Lodge of the International Order of Odd Fellows. Moore, a Mason, introduced the request; rebuffed, he asked for and was granted permission to withdraw the motion.

A spirit of penury reigned over the Fifth Congress. Houston, drawing closer to the election of 1841, made little headway in the Senate as he found himself outmaneuvered by Burnet. The former president introduced a measure in the House that would appropriate seventy-five thousand dollars for the sectioning of the former Cherokee lands, reviving that issue in yet another litmus test of Senate support. The senators failed utterly to buoy Houston's hopes of victory; they added an amendment legitimizing the claims of those settlers resident on the property and steadfastly refused to recede from their position. A conference committee adjourned after two days, reporting that its membership "agrees to disagree" on the issue. The bill was finally laid on the table indefinitely. In turn, the House refused to pass Moore's measure for building a penitentiary. Both sides claimed economy as their motive, but at stake also were more immediate political gains. When confronted by the major issues, however, both houses pulled together to work for the Republic. In the end, Texas would survive and progress, and Houston would return to office as even his Senate foes bowed to the pressure of circumstance. Much as they might dislike him, Houston represented an administration that increased in luster as his successor struggled to the end of his term.

CHAPTER 6

The Senate of the Sixth Congress, 1841–42

The fortunes of the Republic of Texas in 1842 reached their lowest ebb. The dissatisfaction of many people with President Lamar found expression in a growing obstructionism within Congress to his policies. Lamar, when the Senate of the Sixth Congress met in November, 1841, was a lame-duck incumbent, and his chosen successor, Vice-President Burnet, had been soundly repudiated at the polls. Burnet's victorious foe, Sam Houston, faced the most difficult task yet of any president of Texas. Lamar's actions had not only meant political disaster for himself, but they had also brought the Republic to the brink of collapse.

Houston took command of an impoverished and virtually powerless country. Mexico, goaded by Texan incursions in New Mexico and the Yucatan, threatened war. Many in Congress urged a full-scale invasion, which Houston realized the Republic could not conduct successfully with her army and navy in disarray. The Senate of the Sixth Congress, like the rest of the nation, split asunder as a consequence of Houston's efforts to reconcile ideals with reality. Houston, while trying to bring about greater economy in government and to avoid war, lost the support of many followers in the Sixth Congress, which met from November 1, 1841, to February 5, 1842, and gave new impetus to the protests of such vociferous opponents as Senator Moore.

Houston had begun his campaign as a member of the House, where he worked continually to obstruct the efforts of President Lamar and to undermine his supporters. Fortunately for Houston's political fortunes, Burnet and Lamar had grown apart, in large measure due to the former's actions as acting president. Burnet removed some of Lamar's appointees

in a flurry of economy and brought Texas to the brink of war with bellicose declarations at a time when Lamar still hoped to negotiate peace
with Mexico. Lamar, after trying to recruit several other candidates, reluctantly endorsed Burnet, but the division doomed the latter's candidacy from the start.

The campaign quickly became bitter, with foul accusations flung by
the supporters of both Burnet and Houston. Burnet's followers stressed
their opponent's penchant for alcohol, although Houston had apparently
sworn off liquor. Moore gleefully repeated in his *Telegraph and Texas Register* a report that Houston had been carried inebriated and unconscious
into the city that bore his name and had been turned away by friends
who were ashamed at his condition. A tract entitled "Houston Exposed,"
which accused him of cowardice at San Jacinto while under the influence of opium, reappeared during the campaign. In turn, Burnet was
by association burdened with the failures of Lamar, especially the Santa
Fe expedition, which was attributed to Burnet's own hawkish spirit.
Houston himself, in an editorial published under the pseudonym "Truth,"
joined the fray by labeling Burnet a "hog thief" and a traitor whom "the
waters of Jordan could never cleanse from . . . political and moral leprosy."
Burnet more than once was chastened by newspaper editors who were
astonished at the vindictiveness with which he conducted his campaign
against Houston.

Houston was the better speaker, and the Lamar administration had
earned a sad reputation. When Houston won handily, James Morgan
summed up well the majority sentiment when he wrote to a friend that
Houston "drunk in a ditch" was still "worth a thousand of Lamar and
Burnet." Houston's inauguration took place on December 13, 1841, in
Austin. It was a gala event, accompanied by many lavish banquets and
elegant balls, including several held in the Senate chamber in honor of
both the incoming president and the outgoing incumbent. Houston remained notably sober throughout the events but did devote most of his
inaugural address to a denunciation of his predecessor's actions. Unlike
Lamar, who tried to build a coalition cabinet which became a source
of constant antagonism, Houston appointed only his own followers to
executive positions. These included former senator Anson Jones as secretary of state and incumbent senator William H. Daingerfield as secretary
of the treasury. It was a gratifying return to office, attended by a satisfy-
ing aggrandizement of power.

The membership of the Senate, unlike that of Houston's cabinet, of-

Sam Houston. Painting by Martin Johnson Heade, hanging in Governor's Mansion, reproduced from holdings of Texas State Archives.

fered little promise for his efforts to avoid war. Five of the six new senators could boast of distinguished military records, four of them in the
field against Mexico. Wyly Martin had fought under William H. Harrison in the northwestern United States, and later under Andrew Jackson at the Battle of Horseshoe Bend. After killing an antagonist in a
duel, Martin resigned his captain's commission and emigrated to Texas
in 1823. He won distinction as an *alcalde* in Austin Colony and as a delegate to the conventions of 1832, 1833, and 1835, and then took up arms
again in the Runaway Scrape. James Webb had also been an officer in
the U.S. Army, as well as a distinguished attorney. Webb came to Texas
in 1838 after presiding for ten years over the U.S. Court for the District
of Florida; in the Lamar administration he served, in turn, as secretary
of state, attorney general, and envoy to Mexico. It was he who urged
President Lamar to sign an alliance with the rebellious province of Yucatan, which would later lead to embarrassing consequences for Texas.
Clark L. Owen was definitely a scrapper. He came to Texas in 1836 to
fight in the revolution and later fought in the skirmish at Plum Creek
before commanding a unit near Corpus Christi in 1841. A participant
in the Mier Expedition of 1842, he prudently turned back at the Rio
Grande. He was elected captain of a company in the Second Texas Infantry at the outbreak of the Civil War and was killed at the Battle of Shiloh
in 1862. James Shaw and Thomas S. McFarland, like Owen, were veterans of the Texas Revolution. Among the newcomers, only Timothy
Pilsbury, who had served in the Maine house of representatives and in
the House of Representatives of the Republic of Texas, had no military
record.

The first order of business when the senators initially mustered a
quorum on November 2, 1841, was not, however, Houston's war policy.
His election was already a foregone conclusion, but there was still other
business to attend to. The senators elected a slate of officers with little
debate: Alexander C. MacFarlane, secretary; Elijah S. C. Robertson, assistant secretary; Thomas Green, engrossing clerk; H. W. Raglin, enrolling
clerk; and Thomas W. Ward, sergeant at arms. Solomon L. Johnson,
as doorkeeper, was the sole officer from the Senate of the Fifth Congress
to return to his post. The senators elected no chaplain, an oversight that
must have galled Burnet, whose puritanical defense of that position had
come to be expected. The members of the Senate did unanimously elect
John A. Greer, a staunch supporter of Houston, as president pro tempore on December 4, 1841, to preside until the incoming vice-president,

Edward Burleson, a senator during the Third Congress, took his seat on December 14.

At least some of the members of the Senate had learned important lessons from the endless wrangles of past sessions. The senators unanimously voted their thanks to Burnet for his discharge of his duties, thereby refusing to let political rivalries become petty. Muse took more definite action when he introduced a joint resolution that would limit the length of time any member of Congress, Senate or House, could speak. Webb, chairman of the Committee on the Judiciary, to which the bill was referred, recommended that the measure be indefinitely postponed; this was done on November 11. Ironically, the balloting on postponement had ended in a tie, which was broken in the affirmative by Burnet. In one of his last acts as vice-president, the man who would receive the united congratulations of the senators had provided a forum for later divisiveness.

President Lamar, during his last month in office, preferred to remain distant from the Congress, which had largely turned against him. The chief clerk of the House read the president's message to the joint session on November 3, 1841. That same week, Senator Shaw introduced a resolution calling on the president for information relative to the foreign loan, which had failed to materialize, and asking by what authority Lamar had drawn money from the treasury for the expedition to Santa Fe. Although his belligerent missive was laid on the table, it raised two of the most bitter issues of Lamar's presidency, issues that would be resolved only through lengthy debate and only after Lamar had left office. The members of the House considered articles of impeachment against President Lamar, Vice-President Burnet, and Treasury Secretary J. G. Chalmers, but the resolutions were dropped after Houston took office.

Efforts to obtain a foreign loan of five million dollars were suspended as a step in the movement for retrenchment, which took on greater momentum under Houston. In his address to Congress, the new president declared, "We are not only without money, but without credit, and for want of punctuality, without honor." As a gesture of economy, he refused to live in the executive mansion, boarding instead at Bullock's Hotel and recommending the sale of the furniture from the imposing official residence. Following his mandate, the House took the lead in legislating greater financial responsibility, with the Senate's eager concurrence. On January 12, 1842, Houston signed an act repealing the authorization to negotiate a five-million-dollar loan. Other acts suspended the payment of the public debt until such time as the Republic could meet its obligations. Hamilton, upon his return from Europe in the spring of 1842, was dismayed to find that all bond issues had been canceled. Adding a final flourish to its program of contracting its credit obligations, Congress even refused Houston's request for authorization to negotiate a small loan of three hundred thousand dollars.

Credit contraction also required a sweeping reorganization of the Republic's system of currency. The Congress endorsed the issue of two hundred thousand dollars in exchequer bills, secured by customs revenues. Only after long debate and many amendments did the Senate concur in the House bill to authorize Houston to issue bills of exchequer. By its terms, after February 1, 1842, it would be unlawful for the government of the Republic to receive as payment any medium but specie or exchequer bills, and all gold and silver paid in would be applied to the redemption of the latter. All laws for the issue of promissory notes were repealed, and those bills already in circulation could only be taken by the government as payment on land dues. As Texas promissory notes and bonds had decreased in value to as little as ten cents on the dollar in New Orleans, the Senate had little choice but to endorse drastic restrictions. Provisions were made for burning the old issues. Senators Barnett and James T. Gaines formed a joint committee with five members of the House to count the star notes and promissory notes held by the stock commissioner and the treasury, and then incinerated most of the unused bonds and notes, including those printed for the five-million-dollar loan but never used.

The Senate quickly approved an act introduced in the House that increased impost duties to fund the new issue, but measures for reducing the government payroll sparked heated debate. The first bill for reduction passed while Lamar was still in office, but a committee of Daingerfield, Moore, and Barnett had to be appointed to meet with members from the House to reconcile the differences between two heavily amended versions. Barnett had been active in fighting to reduce salaries for many posts and had acrimoniously defended his position. When he introduced an amendment to reduce the proposed pay for district judges, Muse objected, saying that to attract good men the government must pay well. Barnett, in an obvious appeal to his fellow senators, pointed out that members of Congress were competent men serving for much less pay. Muse retorted that "any common school-master would make a very respectable member of Congress," but that it required a different sort of man for a district judge; this remark stung his compatriots to the quick. Barnett countered that "men always maintained more or less damage by their associations," and he was satisfied that he suffered from his association with Muse. Similarly sharp debates accompanied every proposed amendment, but Lamar, two days before leaving office, signed a compromise bill for reduction of the government, which included a cut in congressional salaries.

The passage of the act for further reducing the number of offices set a precedent for retrenchment that persisted under Houston. According to the Austin *Daily Bulletin*, Senator Potter commented: "there was an idea in vogue that this was a two-horse government, and he thought they would soon have it regulated so as to work with one mule." The expenditures of the Republic under Lamar totaled five million dollars; during Houston's second administration, expenses amounted to slightly more than 10 percent of his predecessor's lavish expenditures, despite many crises. The general public, however, was impatient and by the end of the Sixth Congress began to protest against Houston because he had not effected immediate financial relief. Within the Senate, outspoken members such as Moore and Muse began to fulminate against the administration and their fellows. Samuel Whiting, editor of the Austin *Daily Bulletin* and a supporter of Houston, offered a sarcastic riddle to his readers on November 27, 1841, during the debate on the reduction bill. The question was "Why is Nacogdoches no longer a poetical county?" The proper answer was "Because her *Muse* is *Moored*." The exchanges grew more acerbic as Houston steadfastly maintained a pacific stance with regard to Mexico.

When Shaw introduced a resolution to censure Lamar for the Santa Fe expedition, the people of the Republic still did not know the fate of the adventurers. Not until the first of the year were the rumors of disaster confirmed. The reports of atrocities sparked an outcry for revenge from many people, but recognition that the expedition would be seen by Mexico as an act of renewed aggression prompted more sober thinkers to provide for defense. Senator Owen in November, 1841, had introduced a bill to establish a "Texas Californian Territory," but it had been tabled in the move to condemn Lamar for the Santa Fe expedition. The news of the disastrous result of the march rallied the hawks in Congress, which passed a bill over Houston's veto that extended the boundaries of Texas to include the Californias, New Mexico, Chihuahua, Sonora, and parts of the Mexican provinces of Sinaloa, Durango, Coahuila, and Tamaulipas; this made Texas a territory larger than the United States was at that time. More practically, Houston signed acts that provided for the fortification of the harbors at Matagorda and Galveston, the organization of a company of rangers to patrol the southern frontier, and the activation of the militia in the event of an invasion of Texas by Mexico.

Houston's course of action was complicated by the presence of the Texas Navy in Yucatan. President Lamar, following the advice of Webb, had signed a treaty of alliance with the rebellious state of Yucatan on September 17, 1841. In the treaty, he pledged a union of the Texas fleet with the land forces of Yucatan to prevent an invasion of that state by the Mexican army. The *Yucatecos* would advance the funds necessary to fit out the Texas vessels. Commodore Edwin W. Moore sailed eagerly to join the fray, but Yucatan signed a treaty with Mexico before Moore could take an active part. Moore also ignored orders from Houston to return in December. Houston, when called on to make some sort of a gesture toward Mexico after the turn of the year, declared a blockade to be enforced by Moore. Following a few months of this ineffectual effort, the president ordered the commodore to return home. Moore complied and was ordered to New Orleans for refitting, with the promise that funds would be forthcoming. Although Congress quickly passed the necessary legislation in the regular session and the called session, which convened on June 27, 1842, Houston effectively blocked payment, so the Texas Navy remained at the shipfitters' wharves in Louisiana while Moore fumed. Houston, by betraying Moore, sowed more seeds of discord among the general population and the more influential senators.

While Houston laid plans for luring Moore away from Yucatan, the conflict with Mexico escalated sharply. Mexican general Rafael Vasquez, commanding a raiding party of fourteen hundred troops, forced the surrender of San Antonio on March 5, 1842. At the same time, smaller detachments entered Refugio and Goliad. Santa Anna was serving notice that his government might soon attempt the reconquest of Texas, the source of constant irritation to Mexico in its activity at Yucatan and Santa Fe. Vice-President Burleson took to the field with three companies of cavalry, recognizing a great opportunity for further glory and political aggrandizement, but Houston foiled his attempt at glory by appointing more malleable men to command over Burleson and ordering the impetuous politico back to Austin. Rather than force an open confrontation, Burleson reluctantly complied.

The intensity of the situation with Mexico compelled Houston to request a special session of Congress, which met from June 27, 1842, to July 23, 1842. He asked Congress to assemble in Houston as a step in moving the capital back there from Austin, which he claimed was too exposed to invasion. They met for less than a month in one of the most tempestuous sessions ever. Revolt from within the ranks of his supporters, encouraged by Burleson's political sniping, plagued Houston, who refused to recommend an invasion of Mexico and requested only measures to protect against raids from across the Rio Grande. Greer led the defection in the Senate, spearheading a drive for war measures that would give Houston almost dictatorial powers to govern and to lead the army, which would be supported through the sale of ten million acres of the public domain and the conscription of one-third of the population able to bear arms.

Moore was ecstatic at the dissolution of Houston's faction and loud in his protestations of the necessity of war with Mexico. The president's support in the Senate had been further watered down by the replacement of more moderate senators with new, perhaps more hawkish legislators. Ludovic Colquhoun took Daingerfield's place as senator from Bexar when the latter became secretary of the treasury, removing a key proponent of Houston's policies in the Senate. Pilsbury, the only newcomer at the beginning of the regular session who was without a military record, had been replaced by William H. Jack, author of the Turtle Bayou resolutions and a veteran of the Battle of San Jacinto. Potter, a staunch supporter of Houston on retrenchment, had been killed at his home by a Moderator band on March 2, 1842. His place was taken by James Titus, a political unknown who had just come to Texas in 1839. Another newcomer to the Republic, Leonard Randal, sat in place of Senator Gaines. Oliver Jones, who had supported Lamar as a member of the Senate in both the Third Congress and the Fourth Congress, replaced Wyly Martin, who died in April, 1842.

With the defection of such supporters as Greer, Houston was seemingly faced with a strong mandate against pacifism. Most expected Houston to sign the bill granting him broad war powers, but he did not. The president ended his veto message with the sarcastic observation that the act was like a "resolution to appropriate ten million acres of blue sky and conferring dictatorial powers on the north wind." His most serious objections were that the measure's provisions were unconstitutional and that the Texas economy could not bear the cost of offensive war. A letter from "Fayette" in the *Austin City Gazette* of August 17, 1842, expressed the suspicions of many partisans: "I have not been one of those who believed that President Houston ever seriously entertained the idea of prosecuting a war against Mexico, in any shape or form whatever." The president was just posturing because "there is no insult, aggression, or outrage, however gross and palpable, that is sufficient to force him into any war (except one on paper), either with Mexico or the Indians, if there should exist the slightest chance of his crawling or begging out of it." Samuel Whiting composed another of his barbed riddles for the occasion. The correct response to the question "Why is the valley of the Rio Grande like the City of Houston?" became "Because they are both places to which cowards fly when they fear to meet their enemy in a fair and open field of battle." Houston's failure to carry out the provisions for the support of Moore added insult to injury for the senators.

Partisanship spilled over into every issue taken up by the Senate in both the regular and called sessions. Moore reintroduced his bill for a penitentiary on November 3, 1841, the first full day of business during the regular session. The senators approved it after three weeks of debate and amendment, and then sent it to the House for another long month of argument before final passage. Houston, recognizing the importance of the measure but refusing to lend his approval to a bill championed by a bitter opponent, sent it to the Department of State for implementation without his signature on January 4, 1842. The site for the penitentiary was to be selected by a joint vote of both houses. The facility would occupy ten acres, with one hundred separate cells and workshops for "the employment of the convicts who may be there confined, at any kind of labor which may be deemed most profitable and useful to the Republic." No further action was taken on the proposal during the Sixth Congress.

Some of the most bitterly partisan battles took on the aspect of a poor man's struggle against the encroaching privileges of the affluent. Barnett introduced a bill to repeal an act prohibiting the forced sale of slaves in the event of bankruptcy on November 8, 1841. Webb, chairman of the Committee on the Judiciary, reported in favor of the bill, but it was repeatedly laid on the table. Webb spoke often against the exemption of slaves from the execution of debts, calling it an iniquitous measure championed by the slaveowners simply to protect their profits. Greer derided the slaveholders' argument that their interest lay only in preventing the separation of Negro families or the breaking of the crucial bond between master and servant. If a slave did wrong, and "he was taken to the stump, and a hundred lashes given him, . . . where then was the sympathy?" asked Greer. Muse spoke for those who supported the exemption of slaves from forced sale, calling on Barnett, who had initiated the repeal measure, as a Christian to protect slaves "in accordance with Scripture, as children of that God whom the gentleman worshipped."

Barnett turned the constitutional arguments of the slaveholders against them, maintaining that slaves were property and as such should be held in accordance with both the protection and the responsibilities of the law, with no special exemptions. His argument was constitutionally sound, and Houston signed the bill for repeal on December 30, 1841. A bill introduced in the House that provided for the organization of "slave police" passed the Senate in January, but then expired as the senators refused to act on the amendments offered by the representatives. The need for a constabulary to regulate slaves excited little interest in a Senate resentful of the demands of slaveholders.

Moore reserved some of his most bitter verbal venom for debates on the nature of democracy itself. The Senate approved a bill giving the people the right to choose the chief justices of each county on December 3, 1841; it was signed by Lamar four days later. During the course of debate on the measure, Moore had demanded to know if "mere loafers and hangers-on of grog shops were to be permitted to control the purity of the ermine." He said that such people controlled the elections "upon a rainy day" and sent members to Congress; he stopped short, however, of naming the senators who held their offices through such circumstances. Among others, Potter took the opportunity to lambaste his comrade, who refused to back down from his position. Whiting commented later: "the Senator from Harris has a great contempt for those low, vulgar, dram-drinking creatures, the people. The Doctor feels the independence natural to a man who is about to go out of office, and knows he cannot get in again."

The senators were apparently eager to establish the judicial branch of government on its own and not to interfere greatly with its operation. A committee from the House informed the Senate in January that it had preferred articles of impeachment for "high crimes and misdemeanors" against the Honorable John M. Hansford, judge of the Seventh District. The representatives met as a committee of the whole to consider charges against Hansford on January 6, 1842, and the Senate resolved itself into a high court of impeachment that afternoon. In an executive session one week later, the senators rejected a motion by Potter to allow the House to end the proceedings against Hansford that it had requested. Once Hansford resigned his position on January 19, however, the charges were allowed to lapse without further action being taken. Hansford, like Potter, was involved in the Regulator-Moderator War in East Texas. The accusations against him centered on his failure to bring a Regulator to trial; ironically, Hansford was killed two years later when he refused to comply with the demands of a band of Regulators who had taken possession of his home in his absence.

Houston's return as president signaled the adoption of a more pacific general policy toward Indians. The House rejected a bill introduced by Greer and endorsed by the Senate that provided for the expulsion of certain tribes from Texas. In turn, a House act to prevent persons from selling "ardent spirits" to any Indian passed quickly through the Senate. A joint resolution providing for the ransom of five children and two women from their Indian captors easily passed the Senate, as did a general law that set a standard procedure for the redemption of other prisoners in the future. Such actions heralded a more flexible approach which had as its goal the salvation of prisoners, not just the punishment of their captors, as Lamar had advocated so aggressively. In his opening address Houston called for the construction of a series of military colonies on the northwestern frontier to protect against marauding Indians, and Congress responded favorably to this alternative to punitive expeditions, which were so costly in terms of both money and human life.

Moore's companion in vitriol, Muse, introduced an act to repeal an act to section and sell the lands formerly occupied by the Cherokee Indians. If the earlier measure were rescinded, then the chances for passing a bill that would legitimize the claims of squatters in the area would improve. Houston vigorously opposed repeal because he was unwilling to see those who he believed had cost the Cherokee so much profit by their perfidy. Muse played the political game well as the bill passed from one committee to the other like a hot potato. Aided by Moore, he was successful in repeatedly bringing the bill before a reluctant Senate for its vote. Muse suffered a temporary defeat when the senators adopted a substitute for his measure in January, 1842, and refused to accept his amendments to protect the rights of squatters in the region; they did, however, accept his proposal that those with legitimate petitions could "float" to any other section of the public domain claims that had been duly purchased and registered. During the called session, Houston had to bow to pressure from the hawk faction and sign a bill that exempted the claims of squatters from a general sectioning and sale of the former Cherokee lands to provide funds for defense.

Land became one of the most active issues of the Sixth Congress. Greer introduced an act to quiet the land claims of the Republic of Texas on November 22; it passed the Senate with amendments on December 31, 1841, but was not signed by Houston, who repeated his earlier objections to the rapid patenting of land as conducive to fraud. Houston did sign a bill that authorized him to extend the same rights and privileges enjoyed by the Peters Colony entrepreneurs to any other immigration company on the same terms. Muse proposed an amendment that would prevent Houston from extending such a grant to the Franco-Texian Company, but the Senate refused to revive old feuds, and voted it down. The growing spirit of parsimony in land grants claimed some unfortunate victims: the Senate approved Greer's measure to set aside ninety-six hundred acres in land scrip to reward George S. McIntosh, who served as secretary and chargé d'affaires in the Texas legation in Great Britain and France, but the motion was rejected by the House. McIntosh was never compensated for his services, although in order to avoid discredit to Texas Ashbel Smith assumed his indebtedness when he arrived in France as minister.

Houston allowed his personal prejudice against the Texas Navy to influence his decision on another just measure. Potter introduced a joint resolution to allow the secretary of war and the navy to issue certificates of bounty land to the officers, seamen, and marines of the navy. It had been anticipated that they would receive a bonus for their service from the distribution of prize money, and no provision had been made for them to receive land grants like the army. In its activities, however, the Texas Navy had captured precious few prizes. The resolution passed the Senate immediately, but Houston vetoed it on January 6, 1842. His sarcastic veto message, at the instigation of Pilsbury, was written into the *Senate Journal.* The president declared that "generally, the seaman has no interest (except a transitory one) on shore." That transitory interest was of a very specific nature: "The harpies that are generally found in sea-ports, and to whom seamen usually become indebted, are those only who would profit by the bounty and munificence of the Government." Sailors would not be inclined to come ashore and homestead. A joint resolution to override this derogatory veto was passed by the Senate on February 1, but the session ended before the House could take it up.

The question of land played a prominent role in a diverse array of otherwise unconnected bills. Greer on November 23 introduced an act to repeal an act to translate the laws of the Republic into the "Castilian language." Moore read the majority report of the Committee on the Judiciary, to whom the bill went, endorsing its passage. In a rare dissenting opinion, Daingerfield, senator from Bexar, spoke out against the measure and introduced his own proposed amendment to the constitution to delete those sections that prohibited aliens from holding land in Texas except through titles issued by the government of the Republic. Although he was successful in forcing the passage of measures to protect Spanish land titles and provide for frontier defense, Daingerfield could not fight against the tide of fiscal conservatism that eliminated the office of translator in the General Land Office and suspended the printing of laws in Spanish. Undoubtedly, the rising hysteria regarding Mexico had much to do with the anti-Spanish sentiment in the Sixth Congress, a prejudice that found its easiest expression in measures of economy.

The House passed a bill to incorporate Marshall University on December 3, 1841, and Potter, as chairman of the Committee on Public Lands, reported the measure favorably with no amendments to the Senate at the end of the month. The bill encountered stiff opposition in the Senate due to its unprecedented grant of four leagues of land to the school as an endowment. Only a tie-breaking vote in the affirmative by Vice-President Burleson secured its passage to a third reading. An amendment offered by Greer on January 12 provided that each of the schools previously incorporated by Congress would receive similar land grants; when the amendment came to a vote, again Burleson had to break a tie in the affirmative. In its amended form, the measure passed the Senate and was signed on January 18, 1842. Marshall University was never more than a secondary school, but it did remain open until it merged with the public schools of Marshall, Texas, in 1884. Specific measures to give similar land grants to Trinity College and Galveston College were rejected outright by the senators, who apparently could not break fully from their new conservative mold with regard to land policy.

Through incorporation the Senate of the Sixth Congress continued to provide for the economic development of the Republic. The Brazos Canal Company almost lost the fight in the Senate, but with the strong support of Pilsbury received a charter to dig a canal from the Brazos River to the harbor of San Luis. The company gained the right to petition the chief justice of the county for eminent domain if the owner refused to sell outright. Congress retained the option to purchase at par the whole of the capital stock of the company twenty years after incorporation. If Congress did not exercise that right within a year of the expiration date of the original charter, then it would be automatically renewed for twenty more years, at the end of which the canal would belong to Texas. The San Luis Bridge Company received a charter with similar provisions. Other acts incorporated the Colorado Mining Company and allowed Houston to contract for keeping Buffalo Bayou clear of wrecks and obstructions. To provide civil government for a burgeoning population, the Sixth Congress organized the counties of Goliad, Burnet, Trinity, Burleson, Lavaca, Guadalupe, Neches, Smith, DeWitt, Madison, and Hamilton, and incorporated the towns of San Antonio and Refugio. During the Mexican scare, the Senate quickly approved a measure that originated in the House for the organization of the San Augustine Light Horse Company.

Houston had acted in what he considered to be the best interests of the Republic, but in the process had split his support within several notable organizations, most notably the Senate. Even more discord was sown by his increasingly evident desire to remove the capital from Austin to Houston. His insistence that his intent was solely to provide for the better defense of the government brought little more than skepticism and not a few accusations of cowardice. Greer led the fight for removal in the Senate, where opposition probably stemmed more from resentment over policy in other areas than from concern for the location of the national archives. Houston had backed down when confronted by a direct threat from Mexico, and the Senate was unwilling to accept his correct explanation that the Republic was poorly prepared for war, even when he displayed a letter from "Old Hickory" congratulating him for his prudence. Houston had not brought an immediate solution to the fiscal woes of the Republic, and many people resented the drastic reductions in expenditures carried out by Congress under his leadership. In the Senate, as in the population at large, Houston would have to work long and hard to rebuild his support after a rocky first year back in office.

CHAPTER 7

The Senate of the Seventh Congress, 1842–43

President Houston requested that the Seventh Congress of the Republic of Texas convene at Washington-on-the-Brazos on November 14, 1842. The Mexican general Adrian Woll had led yet another raid on San Antonio, and Houston was at last forced to prepare for war. The president's stubborn insistence on defensive tactics rather than an invasion south across the Rio Grande, however, continued to infuriate his enemies and divide his supporters. During the upheaval, Houston also seized the opportunity to press for the removal of the seat of government from Austin, an effort that sparked even greater resentment within Congress, especially from those legislators who represented western districts. They feared that relocation of the capital might also mean fewer appropriations for defense and internal improvements along the western frontier, a region already resentful of an apparent eastern bias in the Houston administration. The president's explanation that Austin was too exposed, especially in light of General Woll's assault on San Antonio, carried little weight.

The solons straggled into the tiny hamlet on the Brazos River, where they sullenly resisted Houston's initiative on a variety of issues during a called session and a regular session that lasted from November 14, 1842, to January 16, 1843. Washington held less than three hundred people in 1842, along with a transient population of gamblers, horse racers, and saloonkeepers. The legislators met in temporary quarters which offered few of the comforts they had provided for themselves in Austin. To console themselves, it appears that they drank and enjoyed the vices of Washington a bit too much for the strict Calvinist standards of many people in Texas. The inactivity of Congress in December, when it appeared to many that the Republic was in imminent peril, further inflamed public opinion against the legislators. Faced with popular condemnation, the Senate and its compatriots in the House stirred from their lethargy by the turn of the year, providing leadership in a time of crisis. They did not, however, heal the deep schisms within the faction that had formerly supported Houston and left the president virtually alone to face the consequences of their actions.

After the adjournment of the called session of the Sixth Congress, rumors abounded that Santa Anna would soon mount a full-scale invasion of Texas. The worst fears of the citizens of San Antonio were realized on September 11, 1842, when General Woll and an army of 950 men captured the city. The entire personnel of the district court were taken prisoner along with three congressmen, including former Senator Colquhoun. Texas troops were unable to decisively defeat General Woll in battle along Salado Creek. Tragically, a regiment under Captain Nicholas M. Dawson, hurrying to the support of the Texans, was cut off by Mexican cavalry and surrendered after a sharp fight. Many of these prisoners were executed on the spot, and the remainder, along with those from San Antonio, were marched south into Mexico.

Even those who had supported Houston's earlier vetoes of measures for war were galvanized into demands for revenge, forcing him to act. The president activated two regiments of militia and placed them under the command of General Alexander Somervell, who also took charge of a regiment of volunteers upon his arrival in San Antonio. General Somervell marched his unruly band to the Rio Grande, where some three hundred mutinied at his decision to turn back. Under Colonel William S. Fisher the rebels continued into Mexico. They were defeated in a bloody engagement at Mier on Christmas Day and marched south as prisoners. Nearly two hundred escaped; following their recapture, they were forced to draw beans. Those who drew black ones were executed in March, 1843. Senator Owen had turned back at the Rio Grande as ordered, but former Senator Green witnessed the fateful lottery. Green later escaped from Castle Perote in the state of Vera Cruz and made his way back to Texas.

While events in the field were moving toward a violent climax, the Senate grudgingly assembled a quorum in Washington-on-the-Brazos. Only Barnett and Leonard Randal attended on the first day, pursuant to the president's initial proclamation; the Senate did not muster a quorum until November 30, 1842, after Houston issued a second angry de-

Mier Expedition, drawing of the beans.
Courtesy Texas State Archives.

mand. The senators spent the day electing their officers: Stephen Z. Hoyle, secretary; Nimrod I. Chappell, assistant secretary; M. H. Nicholson, engrossing and enrolling clerk; Samuel R. Miller, doorkeeper; and Ward, the only returning officer from the Sixth Congress, as sergeant at arms. Turmoil took its toll on the officers: Hoyle barely avoided a Senate investigation into accusations of having taken part in a duel; Chappell resigned on December 19, 1842, and was replaced by H. H. Collier; and Miller's son took his place for a short time as "doorkeeper pro tempore" due to illness in the family. The senators elected no chaplain, but approved a resolution by Senator Muse on December 1 to invite Reverend William Tryon to open each day's proceedings with a prayer.

Unity on the question of war did not preclude deep division on many other questions, most notably Houston's determination to move the seat of government from Austin. Muse was furious with the president. When a resolution was introduced on December 1 that the Senate repair to the House chamber to hear the president's address, a *pro forma* motion, Muse immediately moved that they instead adjourn until five in the afternoon, by which time Houston would have finished speaking or even canceled his speech. Following adjournment the senators could attend the address as individuals, but not as a body that would allow formal recognition of the president's words. The motion by Muse lost, as well as his substitute resolution that the senators retire not to the House chamber, but only to stand at the door.

Muse was not alone in his opposition to the president. Webb on December 3, 1842, moved that a committee be appointed to wait on the House and inform them that the Senate was ready to adjourn *sine die* immediately. A debate continued into the afternoon, with Webb, Muse, Shaw, and John W. Smith, all representing western districts, supporting the idea of immediate adjournment, but to no avail. Only seven senators attended the next day, a Sunday, and on Monday the Senate again failed to muster a quorum because Webb and Muse were absent. Muse pleaded illness, but Webb received a visit from Ward, the sergeant at arms; that afternoon, Vice-President Edward Burleson announced Webb's resignation. With the continued absence of Muse, quorum had become impossible. Ward was sent after Oliver Jones, who had yet to appear, on Tuesday, December 6; Jones arrived three days later. His arrival in the Senate was attended by Muse, rounding out a Senate composed of only ten members. Greer was elected president pro tempore on December 14, following Burleson's announcement that he would be absent for some time.

Only ten senators attended most of the session. Three of those present on November 30 were newcomers, but had strong political backgrounds. William Lawrence, who had held the rank of major while serving as quartermaster of the post at Galveston from 1836 to 1838, had previously sat in the House of the Third Congress and the Fourth Congress. George A. Pattillo was a veteran of the Texas Revolution, a former associate justice, justice of the peace, and postmaster of Beaumont, and a representative in the Sixth Congress. Smith, a veteran of the battles around San Antonio during the Texas Revolution, had carried Travis's last message from the Alamo, thus escaping the massacre. Smith served as mayor and alderman in San Antonio before being elected to represent the besieged town in the Senate. John Rugeley took his seat in the Senate on January 7, 1843, replacing Owen, who had resigned in order to accompany General Somervell. Before coming to Texas, Rugeley had served in the Alabama legislature and in the spring of 1842 had fought in the expedition against the Mexican general Rafael Vasquez following his raid on San Antonio. The hot-headed Webb returned to the Senate on December 31 after an uncontested reelection. He, along with a majority of the Senate, would form a solid faction in favor of war but opposed to relocating the seat of government.

In his address on December 1, Houston demanded the removal of the archives from Austin, declaring that "as to the propriety and necessity of the act no reasonable doubt could exist." He rightly pointed out that the constitution gave the executive the power to provide for the safety of the government in the face of danger, such as General Woll's attack on San Antonio. Houston termed the activities of the "Archive Committee" in Austin, which sought to prevent the removal of the official records, "seditious" in their effect. He called on the Seventh Congress to support him, as the Sixth Congress had not, in his attempt to overpower them.

The president did receive some support from loyal adherents in the Senate. Greer introduced "a Bill to provide for the safety of the National Archives" on December 9. He tried to suspend the rules of order so that passage of the measure through the Senate would be swift, but was voted down through a tie vote which was decided in the negative by Burleson, now a staunch opponent of Houston. With hopes for the passage of his bill dimming, Greer introduced a bill the next day for the removal of the General Land Office; blank spaces were left for the name of the town and county to be honored by relocation. He moved for suspension of the rules requiring three readings, and again lost by a tie vote.

Greer's second bill initiated a controversy over the town that would serve as a repository for the official records and, by implication, as the seat of government. Muse proposed Crockett, and Jones offered Houston; both lost. Barnett moved for location of the archives in Washington, an amendment that the Senate approved on December 12. Lawrence introduced a bill on December 24 that would specifically declare Washington to be the capital of the Republic. Laying aside Greer's proposal, the senators engaged in debate on this new and more definitive measure. Jones read a petition received from San Felipe which requested that it be designated the capital. Jones, Lawrence, and Jack were appointed to a special committee to consider the entire package. When the bill returned to the floor, debate became lively. Greer moved to adopt the measure with one amendment: change the name of the town of Washington to San Jacinto, in honor of Houston. The Senate adopted the amendment, infuriating Webb, who had returned on December 31. Webb tried to get the site changed to San Felipe, and then to Nacogdoches, but failed. The bill once more returned to committee.

In committee, the bill to establish the capital at the renamed town of San Jacinto was combined with another measure that would locate the Supreme Court of the Republic of Texas at Galveston. The impossibility of either measure passing the Senate had become obvious, and Jack, as chairman of the special committee, reported a substitute. This final version contained no provision for the permanent relocation of the seat of government, but did authorize Houston to remove the archives to any place of safety he chose, and allowed him to designate the site of the next Congress if peace with Mexico had not been achieved. Once more, the senators reached a tie vote, but this time Burleson decided in the affirmative. All came to naught: the House refused to concur.

Houston was still determined that the seat of government be moved from the exposed town of Austin. During the debate in the Senate, the president dispatched an expedition to effect the removal of the official archives. Members of his group quietly entered town on December 30, 1842, and quickly loaded the wagons. Angelina Eberly, manager of Bullock's Hotel, realized what they were about and let fly with a round from a six-pound cannon located on the Capitol grounds for defense in the event of an Indian attack. Her shot was accurate enough to damage the General Land Office building, and the intruders wisely retreated, taking the archives with them. A posse from Austin cornered them on Brushy Creek, where the records were surrendered without a fight, ending the brief "Archive War."

Senator Titus subsequently introduced a final resolution to authorize the president to remove the records of the General Land Office from Austin. The select committee reported through Jones "that the only benefit which could result from the passage of the resolution, would be an expression of opinion, approving that illegal and unauthorized act of the President, in secretly raising an armed force, for the purpose of removing the archives from the seat of Government established by law, at a time when the representatives of the people were in Congress assembled, and deliberating on the propriety of their removal." The members of the committee admitted that they had opposed establishing the capital in Austin, but stated that there appeared to be no immediate danger to the city since the return of General Somervell from the frontier. They declared that the president was "morally and legally bound under his oath of office and the action of the present Congress, to remove (with the heads of Departments) to the seat of Government established by law. . . ." The Senate adopted the report, with most of the members of the eastern districts voting in opposition. Houston realized that another attempt to move the records might result in civil war, and wisely allowed the controversy to fade, but did not return the seat of government to Austin before annexation.

As the Senate concerned itself with the issue of relocating the capital and neglected the matter of war with Mexico, popular dissatisfaction grew. Dissatisfaction turned to anger as weeks passed without apparent legislative action, bringing bitter and sometimes slanderous denunciations of Congress. A correspondent for the Houston *Morning Star* reported from Washington on December 9, 1842: "There is but little liquor in town; but nevertheless, it finds its way to the lips of some of the Honorable members." Five days later he reported: "The Senate seems disposed to wait the movements of the House, and not to originate more than they can help." Another visitor reported on December 22 that he found the members of the House lolling about, and that

> finding nothing there to interest me, I proceeded to the Senate, which is held in Bailey, Gay, and Hoxey's old store, where I found the President looking at the Senators, and the Senators looking at him. The Senate, I learned, was waiting for the House to progress with business, and the House, I suppose, often waits for the Senate, and in the meantime certain members steal away occasionally and *consult the book of prophecies*, alas, a pack of cards. Thus our legislators *labor* for their country.

Official reports do indicate a lull in legislative activity, but such was usual after the first flurry of organization while the committees met and before reports were received on the floor.

With the divisive matter of relocating the capital laid to rest, the Senate turned to the more important question of preparing for war with Mexico. Muse introduced an act requiring the president to hold an election for major general of the militia on December 10, 1842. Barnett introduced a counterresolution authorizing Houston to take command of the army that same day. The latter passed the Senate ten days later, but Houston declined to sign it into law. He did not wish to assume the responsibility of prosecuting a war of which he did not approve.

The senators welcomed a second bill, which originated in the House, for the election of a major general. Houston vetoed this bill as well, but they overrode him on January 16, 1843. Through its provisions, the two chambers proceeded to elect Thomas J. Rusk as major general of the Republic, to serve until the first day of 1844, when he or his successor would have been sanctioned by a popular election. Rusk was empowered to take the field at any time and command any number of troops. Since he would receive compensation only if one thousand or more soldiers were under his command, Congress provided a ready incentive for him to muster a large force. The measure provided for a general mobilization of the militia to expedite recruitment. Spoils would be divided among the captors by the field officers, without regard to rank. Six companies would be mustered quickly for patrol along the southern border, and martial law was declared for the region between the Frio River and Nueces River and the Rio Grande. A second bill for the organization of a company of mounted men to patrol the border with Mexico was rushed through both houses on the last day of the session, January 16, 1843, and was signed by Houston.

The Senate did not provide for the navy, but rather, in secret session, authorized the president to sell the entire Texas fleet. This act brought about a heated conflict between Houston and Commodore Moore. Houston, after recalling the navy, had suspended all intercourse with the government of Yucatan. He did not believe that it had been a wise move in the first place to enter into an agreement with Yucatan, and placed the blame for endangering Texas squarely on Lamar. Trying to rally support among the senators, he pointed out that they had been given no opportunity to approve or disapprove his predecessor's "treaty" with Yucatan. As he did not wish to "soil his skirts with the crime of treason," Houston had broken off the agreement. Greer spearheaded the movement in the Senate to sell the navy, which reached a successful climax with the adoption of a joint resolution through a conference committee in January, 1843. Moore returned his fleet to be sold at Galveston later that year, but not before fighting two sharp engagements for the Yucatan government against the Mexicans during the summer. He also challenged Houston to a duel for having labeled him a pirate, but the president declined as he always did, adding to the frustration of his enemies.

The naval protection of the Republic was not entirely neglected, although the provisions made conformed to Houston's scheme of static defense. The president signed an act for the protection of the seacoast on January 14, 1843, which provided seven thousand dollars for the construction and staffing of fortifications at Galveston. An additional one thousand dollars was appropriated for the defense of the mouth of the

Brazos River and a like sum for the pass into Matagorda Bay. Construction of these defenses progressed slowly, and the resulting works were hardly adequate. Fortunately, the Mexican navy was in no condition to carry out an invasion of the Texas coast, especially after the engagement with Moore during the summer of 1843.

Houston realized that the Mexicans derived great benefit from the continued hostility of Indians in Texas toward the settlers of the Republic. Greer on December 29, 1842, introduced a bill to establish peace and maintain a friendly intercourse with Indians. Signed into law on January 14, the act created a Bureau of Indian Affairs, to be attached to the Department of War. This bureau would administer funds for the employment of interpreters, as well as agents to serve under the direct command of the president. Five trading posts would be built along the western frontier from the south fork of the Trinity River on the north to the junction of Las Moras Creek and the Rio Grande on the south. Traders at these posts would be licensed and closely monitored; without a license, one could not legally engage in Indian trade. Even individual transactions, such as the barter of a horse, required permission from a chief justice or a justice of the peace. No war goods or ardent spirits could be traded, although special dispensation for the sale of the former could be had directly from the president. No one without special permission from the president could pass beyond the line of trading houses, and then only for friendly purposes. At the same time, no Indians could come "below the line of their territory," unless permitted by an Indian agent and accompanied by that agent or his proxy.

Houston hoped by these provisions to protect the Indians from the encroachment of white settlers and unscrupulous traders and lessen the ferocity of Indian raids and reprisals. He and the legislators realized that it was almost impossible to isolate so many diverse peoples, so they also provided stiffer penalties for white transgressions. The act made it clear that "any person or persons, who shall attempt to molest the Indians or their property, while they remain peaceable under the treaties, shall be held guilty of felony and punished accordingly." More to the point, "any killing or outrage whatsoever, committed by a white man upon any Indian, in time of peace, shall be punished in the same manner as though the Indian were a white man," provided that the Indian was not illegally within the area of white settlement. Finally, any person who raised a force to wage war on the Indians while they were at peace, without permission from the president, was guilty of a felony and would be prosecuted. The Senate, by approving these measures, cast its vote for a laudable attempt to settle a dangerous conflict peaceably.

The senators also approved a pioneering effort to negotiate with Indians for the return of prisoners. On December 23, Houston informed the Senate:

> that he has been recently assured, that the different tribes of Indians have in their possession as prisoners, no less than eleven Texians, and that they will be brought to the Waco village at the time set apart for entering into a treaty with them, with the intention on the part of the Indians to exchange them for their own people, held by us as prisoners, as well as others held by the Lipan and Toncuhua [*sic*] tribes. . . .

The president requested and received legislation that authorized him to compel the surrender of Indians held by Texans, but the same act also provided for continued executive negotiation for the release of prisoners held by Indians. Despite the dire financial straits of the Republic, Congress did not hesitate to appropriate funds for the ransom of prisoners. The negotiations were not as successful as had been anticipated, but the concurrence of the Senate in attempts to resolve a difficult situation by providing for diplomacy is noteworthy.

Much of Houston's desire to avoid war stemmed from his recognition that the Republic could not afford protracted operations. Before the session opened, he had suspended the issue of all exchequer bills until those already in circulation reached par. The Houston *Morning Star* reported on October 27, 1842, that the value of such notes was steadily increasing in the New Orleans market, but in a separate article of the same date, the editor also reported that currency of any sort was rare in Austin and that merchants were conducting business through a barter system. Houston in his address on December 1, 1842, said, "we find ourselves in a condition utterly destitute of credit, without a currency, without means and millions in debt." Houston later began issuing drafts on the exchequer bills at par, to be drawn on the customshouses. Less than one thousand dollars was thus paid out as an expedient for certain expenses, but Congress still protested loudly. The Senate had earned the approbation of the public for its frugality in relief cases and public works and wished the president to share any blame attached to expenditures.

On December 20, 1842, Senator Jack, a member of the committee on finance, issued a radical report in favor of further fiscal retrenchment. He recommended the recall of all Texas representatives to foreign courts;

their function could be filled by special agents as the occasion arose. The secretary of war and marine and the secretary of the treasury could be eliminated; after all, it was well known that the chief clerks had been carrying out their duties for several years. Jack declared that "these offices are mere sinecures, without any benefit to the nation, and ought not any longer to exist." The secretary of state would take over the functions of the secretary of war and marine, while the treasurer would assume the responsibilities of the secretary of the treasury. A bill to this effect was introduced by the committee as a whole, which included Jack, Jones, and Randal. It met with general approval and passed the Senate, but did not become law. Jack also proposed a *per diem* of five cents for congressmen, but the proposal met with strong disapproval and did not pass until amended to provide four dollars a day. The Senate did expect to provide for its own expenses.

Houston in his address to Congress recognized the poor state of the postal system in the Republic. Reflecting on the finances of the nation, the president stated that "nothing is better calculated to present the deplorable financial condition of Texas than the situation of our post office and mail establishment." The House originated a bill to reorganize postal routes; it was signed on January 6, 1843, but Senator Muse introduced an extensive bill, signed ten days later, establishing uniform postal rates. This measure required postal clerks to receive exchequer bills at par for the payment of postage, a symbolic gesture which was calculated to restore faith in the currency of the Republic. Houston did sign this bill but refused to sign a similar measure that would have required sheriffs, who served as tax collectors, also to receive exchequer bills at par. The president was clearly unwilling to reduce the intrinsic value of the primary revenue to provide a psychological boost for the national economy.

The Senate, while pursuing a course of public parsimony, relied once more on private enterprise to provide for internal improvements. The Senate concurred in a House bill to charter the Matagorda Caney Navigation Company, which proposed to clear Caney Creek in Matagorda County for navigation to the Gulf of Mexico. The firm was given the right to petition for eminent domain and to charge tolls for thirty years. At the end of that period, the county had the right to buy out the stockholders; if the government did not exercise its option, the corporation could charge tolls for another thirty years. Republic vessels would pass free of charge at all times. The Senate denied banking privileges; in fact, the Seventh Congress witnessed a concerted attempt to withdraw such power from the only extant company to which it had been granted. Shaw introduced a bill to repeal the act that accorded banking privileges to McKinney, Williams and Company. Just four days later, on December 23, the bill was laid on the table by the recommendation of Jack, chairman of the judiciary committee to which it had been referred.

The Senate was somewhat more generous with land. Four leagues of land were granted to DeKalb College, chartered by a previous action of Congress, but a similar bill for the benefit of Trinity College failed to reach the Senate floor on the last day of the session, despite a motion by Lawrence. Titus introduced a bill to incorporate the German Emigrating Company on December 30; the bill passed the Senate a week later, although it did not become law. Jack requested the incorporation of the Texian Emigration, Agricultural and Commercial Company on January 3, 1843. His bill went to the committee on foreign relations, where it lay without further action as the session expired. The Senate was cautious about chartering a foreign company with a half-million dollars in capital at its disposal. The memory of the French imbroglio was still too fresh.

The members of the Senate, in this time of military crisis, produced legislation to mold a more ideal Republic in their own conservative image. The Senate approved a charter for the Galveston Orphan's Friend Society, founded by four women who proposed to build an orphanage in that town. The Senate also concurred in a bill which originated in the House for the legal establishment of a Sabbath or day of rest in Texas, but Houston did not sign the measure. The president moved ahead of the Senate in racial matters: on December 21, 1842, by executive decree, he suspended the expulsion of free Negroes from the Republic for three additional years beyond the deadline set by Congress in 1840. By the time this decree had expired, the law had effectively become a dead letter. The Senate did not protest his presumption of executive power, but the sentiments of several members on the status of free Negroes in the Republic were clear. Lawrence introduced a resolution that required the committee on the judiciary to inquire whether "free persons of color" could own real estate in Texas. The senators approved this measure, thereby indicating that the question was important to them, but no definite action came of it.

The Senate of the Seventh Congress, after a slow start, had in the end acted effectively to sustain the Republic for another year. One of its most significant acts was unanimous approval of a treaty of amity, navigation, and commerce with the United States which had been signed by Daniel Webster and James Reily on July 30, 1842. It was a proud accomplishment for the Houston administration, but it did little to bridge the widening gap between the president and his former legislative supporters. The Senate approved the creation of three counties during the Seventh Congress. Two were named in honor of military heroes of Texas, Bowie and Rusk. The third county bore the name of Houston's most bitter opponent, Lamar, symbolizing the continued refusal of the legislators to follow executive initiative blindly. The Senate acquiesced in measures by which Houston disbanded the navy and manipulated the credit of the Republic, but it also stubbornly clung to its own goals for the continued defense and prosperity of the Republic of Texas.

CHAPTER 8

The Senate of the Eighth Congress, 1843–44

The Senate of the Eighth Congress of the Republic of Texas met in Washington from December 4, 1843, to February 5, 1844. The nation could boast of much progress during the past few years; President Houston's speech to the assembled Congress on December 12 focused on the improvements effected during his administration. Through the strictest economy, the treasury had achieved a precarious balance. Because Houston had authorized an armistice with Mexico during the summer of 1843, the Republic for once was free from the threat of imminent invasion by Mexico. Treaties with several Indian tribes had reduced the danger from that quarter. Foreign relations had improved after recognition from certain European nations, most notably England and France, and trade was booming. Lasting peace and prosperity, however, were still not at hand, a fact for which the president chastised Congress. As annexation by the United States remained only a fond hope of a majority of the people of Texas, the Senate continued to legislate for the formation of an enduring independent Republic.

The Senate of the Eighth Congress convened on December 4, 1843, pursuant to the president's proclamation. Stephen Z. Hoyle, as secretary of the previous Senate, called the roll on that day, but only Isaac Parker and William L. Hunter appeared. Both were newcomers to the Senate. Parker, a veteran of the Texas Revolution, had served in the House of Representatives during the Third, Fourth, Sixth, and Seventh congresses. He would sit in the last two congresses as a senator, attend the Annexation Convention in Austin in 1845, and serve five terms as a state legislator before the Civil War. Hunter was a larger-than-life revolutionary hero, having fought at the siege of Bexar and survived the massacre at

Goliad, where he was "shot, bayonetted, and clubbed with a gun butt" before he made his escape. He brought a record of active service to the Republic with him to the Senate, including terms as chief justice of Refugio County and representative for Goliad County in the Fourth, Sixth, and Seventh congresses.

The senators continued to straggle in during the next week. Vice-President Burleson appeared on the second day of the session, December 5, along with Smith, Rugeley, and Gustavus A. Parker. Smith and Rugeley were veterans of the Senate, but Parker had previously attended Congress only as a representative in the fifth and sixth sessions. Returning Senators Webb and Lawrence made their appearance on December 7, Pattillo two days later, and Greer on the 11th. The Senate finally mustered a quorum on December 12, when Robert M. Williamson arrived. A colorful character, Williamson, known as "Three-Legged Willie" for his wooden leg, was a master of wit and oratory. He was credited as much as any one man for sustaining the revolution and as such shared the dubious honor with William B. Travis of being the object of particular hatred by the Mexicans. From 1836 to 1839, he had served as a member of the Supreme Court of the Republic, and then was elected for two terms in the House of Representatives. After annexation, he would sit in the first two state legislatures as a senator before retiring from public life.

The arrival of David S. Kaufman on December 13 completed a muster of the Senate. Kaufman had served in the House during the Third, Fourth, and Fifth congresses and was elected speaker in the last two. He remained a staunch supporter of Houston in the Senate of the Eighth and Ninth congresses and became Texas' first U.S. representative, attending for five years until his death in Washington, D.C., in 1851. During the Eighth Senate of the Republic of Texas, he and Williamson represented the best hopes of the Houston administration for renewed legislative support in that chamber. During the summer of 1843, President Houston and several members of his cabinet conducted a speaking tour of Texas in an attempt to gain the election of an Eighth Congress favorable to the executive. Staunch opponents such as Jack and Webb did return to the Senate, but their opposition was offset by the election of Kaufman and Williamson, both strong supporters of Houston's policies.

The Senate elected their officers on December 12. Thomas Green replaced Hoyle as secretary; other newcomers included N. C. Raymond as assistant secretary, Samuel W. Pipkin as sergeant at arms, and Lewis

Site of the first court of Third Judicial District of the Republic, held in April, 1837, by Judge Robert M. Williamson. Courtesy Texas State Archives.

Goodwin as doorkeeper. M. H. Nicholson returned as engrossing and enrolling clerk, and William M. Tryon served as chaplain once more. Greer was elected president pro tempore of the Senate on December 26. His election marked an important procedural victory for the supporters of Houston in the Senate; as a die-hard proponent of the president, Greer would work from the chair to provide vital support for executive policies.

The Congress met in Washington, where little provision had been made for the senators. As the question of a permanent seat of government had yet to be settled, the accommodations in Washington remained temporary, even primitive. Buildings had been erected to serve as a capitol, but the Houston *Morning Star* reported that they "were very inconvenient, and will hardly afford shelter from the inclemencies of the weather." During the seventh session, the senators had appropriated funds for a stove to heat the chamber; this time they set aside money for a dozen chairs on which to sit while they deliberated. Washington harbored no library, and therefore more funds were spent for the purchase of six copies of the laws of Texas and a subscription to the *National Vin-*

dicator. Although the capital correspondent to the Houston *Morning Star* noted an obvious increase in sobriety among the legislators and the residents of the little town on the Brazos, absenteeism continued to plague the Senate. Throughout the session, Sergeant at Arms Pipkin would be kept busy corralling senators as, more often than not, each morning began without a quorum.

Bitter debate over the election of several senators consumed a large part of the legislative calendar. Shortly after Congress convened, Jesse Grimes, who had served as a senator in the First Congress and a representative in the Fifth and Sixth congresses, sent a petition to the Committee on Privileges and Elections of the Senate, claiming that he, not Williamson, had won the election for senator in the district composed of Washington, Montgomery, and Brazos counties. The committee members had no precedent to follow in their investigation and, more importantly, no definite rules for elections on which to base their decisions. Lawrence, chairman of the committee, consistently obstructed their efforts in an attempt to retain Williamson, a Houston supporter, in the Senate instead of Grimes, whose politics were more equivocal. The other members of the committee, notably Jack and Webb, pressed the issue as a means of removing an impediment to their attack on the president. They were prominent in a movement to impeach Houston, a campaign that could not succeed with a divided Senate. Their goal was to have the seat declared vacant, as neither Williamson nor Grimes would be sympathetic to their cause, and then campaign for a more amenable confederate.

The committee initially reported from the available returns that Williamson did hold his seat legally. But, they added, "These returns do not present any thing like a true statement of the vote which was given at the late Senatorial election in this district." Votes taken at a number of the precincts in Washington County were rejected on objections which the committee regarded as "merely technical." Grimes had presented election returns from Montgomery County, which showed him to be the winner by a large margin, but these had been sent by mail to Washington County and were not counted by the chief justice, who acted as elector. The chief justice had been informed that the returns were at the post office, but refused to receive them, as they had not been relayed to him by the method prescribed by law.

Although the chief justice had acted in strict accordance with the law by refusing to accept the returns sent through the mail, the committee pointed out that "these votes were cast by the free citizens of the district, legally entitled to vote for the candidate of their choice on this occasion." If these returns were rejected "simply because the officers of the law were more particular and strict in the discharge of their duties, it might result in a defeat of the expressed will of a majority of the people of the district, in a case, in which, according to the genius and spirit of our Government, the will of that majority should govern." Other election returns from Brazos and Milam counties had also been thrown out, and Grimes insisted, although he had no evidence, that even more returns from Montgomery had never reached the election officers. Depending on which combination of possibly legal records the committee chose to accept, the verdict could vindicate either contestant.

The committee members, with the exception of Lawrence, said that they were "somewhat at a loss to know what report to make." In the report, written by Jack and Webb, they declared:

> Of one thing, however, it is certain, that the certificate was given to Mr. Williamson upon scarcely a tithe of the entire vote polled in the district; and if certificates, given under such circumstances, are to control the elections and voice of the country, then the boasted right of suffrage, and the principle that majorities shall govern, are destitute of meaning, and should be discarded from the form and system of our Government.

Although they left the question open to the Senate, Jack and Webb had placed the issue in a context that apparently allowed only one decision if the people of the Republic were to be fairly represented, and the pair immediately introduced a resolution to declare Williamson's seat vacant.

Greer temporarily staved off their assault by a motion to lay the resolution on the table; only Jack, Webb, Hunter, Rugeley, and Smith voted against the measure for postponement. On the afternoon of January 3, 1844, the matter once again came before the Senate. Upon a motion by Kaufman, both Grimes and Williamson, or their counsels, were permitted to speak to the Senate, although a time limit of two hours proposed by Greer did not pass. An attorney, B. Gillispie, spoke for Grimes, Williamson for himself. Afterward, Jack and Webb pressed for adoption of their resolution declaring the seat vacant, a move that was loudly opposed by Kaufman. Isaac Parker the next day offered a resolution declaring the votes from Milam County to be illegal and Grimes to be legally elected. Shaw offered a compromise resolution whereby Williamson would hold his seat for the balance of the session, but immediately afterward the seat would be declared vacant and a special election would be called by the president. Through continued opposition, Jack and Webb succeeded in getting both measures tabled and their original resolution adopted by a weary Senate. Greer won a small measure of vindication when he succeeded in passing a final resolution, over Webb's objection, which declared the Milam votes, on which Grimes's elimination rested, to be illegal.

The Senate dragged its feet on the issue, but Kaufman moved on January 20 that Williamson be notified of the vacation of his seat in the Senate. Williamson replied quickly and gallantly:

> Having uniformly entertained and expressed in public and private life the belief that our country was safe of her common enemy, I deem it of little consequence, at this crisis, whether I am in or out of her councils, and having no political or personal asperations [sic] to gratify, I assure your honorable body that it is with but little concern on my own part that I receive such notice. Had I felt myself at liberty to have pursued my own inclinations on this subject, I might have saved the Senate of some time, and perhaps some trouble.

He had understood that he had won a plurality and felt bound to serve until the question could be settled, "and with it I am content." He concluded, "And now, gentlemen, on retiring from your deliberations, allow an old citizen-soldier to tender to you, as a body, his sincerest and kindest regard, and individually, his right hand." Grimes, as senator-elect, took his seat on January 22.

Scarcely had the Senate settled the first contested election when they took up a petition from James Power, who contested the seat of Hunter, on January 9, 1844. Jack, now chairman of the Committee on Privileges and Elections, offered a resolution to disregard the petition because "no notice, as required by law, [had] been given by James Power." Unlike the contest between Williamson and Grimes, this matter contained no clear-cut political advantage to be won through its outcome. Pattillo countered Jack's proposal with a substitute that declared Power to be duly elected, but the next day on a motion by Greer, Pattillo's resolution was laid on the table, and Jack withdrew his motion by leave of the Senate. In the absence of partisan politics, cooler heads would prevail.

Webb proposed a resolution that would permit each contestant to gather information for four weeks, after which he would present his findings to the Senate. It is interesting to note the division between the confederates on the Williamson affair: Jack angrily countered with yet another resolution declaring Hunter to be duly elected and then, having made his point, withdrew the motion. The Senate accepted an amendment from Kaufman that shortened the period of inquiry to three weeks, and refused to grant Hunter a leave of absence because that could be interpreted as a recognition of his legal election. Apparently, Power attempted to dominate the board of inquiry, an effort that angered the Senate. Webb, for the committee, reported that even if all of the contested votes were disregarded, Hunter still had a majority. On the last day of the session, Isaac Parker introduced a resolution that declared Power to be the winner, counting only the votes that he held to be legal. The Senate refused to pass this measure, and instead adopted a substitute offered by Smith that simply declared the seat vacant and called for another election.

A bungled election for a major general of the militia proved to be the last straw. Several counties failed to make returns, and the Senate had to endorse a joint resolution that authorized the president to declare a winner from the returns at hand. On the same day that he approved this measure, February 5, 1844, Houston also signed an act carefully delineating the methods of election, including the officers responsible, the method of specifying the polling places, the procedure for holding elections and handling returns, and the forms that the secretary of state would provide to every county to record the results. In the case of a tie, the chief justice of the county would immediately void the election and order a new poll. Fines would be levied for late or improper returns.

Apart from the almost farcical matter of disputed elections, much of the senatorial debate concerned foreign relations, especially with Mexico and the United States. Soon after Congress adjourned in January, 1843, James Robinson, who had been captured in Woll's raid on San Antonio and imprisoned at Perote, proposed a plan for peace to Santa Anna. The most important tenets of the agreement were amnesty for all past actions and a separate government for Texas under Mexican sovereignty. Robinson had been released to convey the terms of the settlement to Texas, where he met with Houston in March; it was this release, not any international agreement, that seemed to be Robinson's real interest in the negotiations. Robinson was publicly condemned, as was the president for agreeing to meet with him, but Houston had no intention of accepting any proposal that did not recognize the independence of Texas. The president did see in this document a desire for peace on the part of the Mexican government. He requested the British minister in Mexico City to take the necessary steps toward an armistice negotiation, and on June 15, 1843, declared a truce, pending negotiations for peace, an action copied by Santa Anna.

The Senate welcomed the chance for a peaceful settlement, but remained wary of both the Mexicans and the British, who had taken an increasingly active abolitionist stance. On December 23, 1843, the Senate requested copies of all correspondence between Texas and Britain relative to the armistice with Mexico, as well as all documents sent to and from the latter country and those regarding the Texas commissioners, George W. Hockley and Samuel Williams. Shaw added a more comprehensive resolution that same day, calling for "so much of the correspondence, had with Great Britain and the United States, with this Government, since the adjournment of last Congress, as he, in his judgement, may deem advisable for the future interest and prosperity of this Republic." The Senate was willing to support any initiative for a negotiated peace, but not at the expense of national sovereignty.

The prospect of a settlement did not mean that the Senate neglected defenses along the border with Mexico. An act for the protection of the southwestern frontier, which originated in the Senate, was signed by Houston on January 31, 1844. It authorized the expulsion of all those known to have borne arms against the Republic since the invasion of General Vasquez in the spring of 1842. The offenders were to leave within twenty days or be tried by a court-martial. The commander of Texas troops in the region also received the power to regulate Mexican trade. The senators applauded the combativeness of Captain John C. (Jack) Hays and his company, and repaid his expenses in December. A bill was introduced in the Senate on January 10 to authorize Hays to raise a company of forty mounted gunmen. Passed and signed within two weeks, the act provided for a term of four months along the southwestern frontier, but enlistments could be extended by the president if an emergency arose. Bills drafted by Kaufman and Webb to provide for the organization of the national militia failed to become law, however, indicating the generally relaxed situation in January, 1844.

Partisan politics intruded into preparations for defense. Rugeley offered a resolution on December 29, asking Houston to convey all information relative to the sale of the navy, including proceeds and the amount thought necessary to sustain the remaining ships in port at Galveston. It was adopted by the Senate, along with a motion made by Greer on the following day proposing that the president's secret message relative to the sale of the navy, in which he had explained his reasons to the Seventh Congress, be printed in the public journals and five hundred copies distributed. The president was clearly in a bind; public opinion was outraged at the disbanding of the navy and his treatment of Commodore Edwin W. Moore. Even the Houston *Morning Star,* normally a great supporter of Houston, condemned his stance against the navy as a policy pervaded by "obduracy bordering almost on fatuity." The editor echoed the sentiments of a majority of Texans when he predicted that if negotiations with Santa Anna failed, the lack of ships would place the Republic in great peril.

All communications on the navy from the harried president to the Senate were referred to the Committee on Naval Affairs. Its members, Rugeley, Lawrence, and Hunter, were joined by Jack, on motion of Kaufman, and Webb, on motion of Lawrence. An act to provide for putting the navy in ordinary, which committee members originated, was signed by Houston on February 5, 1844, despite the testimony of Secretary of War and Marine George W. Hill that the remaining ships were too decayed to be salvaged. At the time the bill was signed, only the ship *Austin,* the brigs *Wharton* and *Archer,* and the schooner *San Bernard* remained. President Houston vetoed an earlier bill for providing back pay to the navy officers, declaring that the finances of the Republic could not support it. As it provided only for officers, the Senate refused to override it, but did pass a successful act to disburse partial back pay to all seamen as well as officers. Despite loud protests from Houston, the Congress on February 1, 1844, endorsed a joint resolution by a constitutional majority to settle the accounts of Moore, including the expenses incurred while fighting in Yucatan.

The Senate did not forget the prisoners being held in Mexico. The Houston *Morning Star,* like many publications, castigated the president on the issue of the Texan prisoners, demanding that he abandon his policy of inaction and initiate negotiations that would bring them home. An act that originated in the House was signed on February 2, 1844, forbidding the forced sale of any property belonging to a Texan held as a prisoner of war. A second measure signed on February 5, 1844, declared Houston to be "authorized and required, forthwith, to employ any means in the reach of the Government, to feed and clothe our unfortunate countrymen, prisoners of war, who are, at present, starving in the prisons of Mexico. . . ." To facilitate matters, Congress set aside fifteen thousand dollars for that purpose.

The Senate, in the interest of defense, also endorsed the Treaty of Bird's Fort, signed on September 29, 1843, between commissioners George W. Terrell and E. H. Tarrant, of the Republic, and delegates from ten Indian tribes. The conference had been attended by chiefs of the Delaware, Biloxi, Waco, Chickasaw, Tawakoni, Keechi, Caddo, Anadarko, Ioni, and Cherokee peoples who were still within Texas. By the terms of the peace settlement, the Indians agreed to abide by legislation passed during the Seventh Congress: trade to be restricted to nonmilitary items and to be conducted only by designated agents; the boundary between the territories held by the whites and Indians to be defined by a line of trading houses; and travel forbidden by unescorted Indians or whites outside of designated areas. Little public notice was taken of the fact that the most hostile tribes, the Comanche, Kiowa, and Apache, had not attended the convention.

Relations with the United States took a turn for the worse in the spring of 1843. Because the treaty negotiated by James Reily at Washington, D.C., was not ratified by the U.S. Senate, Texas still claimed the territory that lay west of the hundredth meridian between the Arkansas River and the Rio Grande. Because of this claim, the government of the Republic regarded the trade between Missouri and Santa Fe as contraband and the operations of the Santa Fe commerce as an infringement upon the sovereignty of Texas. Houston, accordingly, authorized an expedition by Colonel Jacob Snively which set out in April to capture a wagon train of Mexican traders on the way from Missouri to Santa Fe. Under the terms of Snively's commission, half the spoils would belong to the Republic and half to him and his men. Unfortunately, the Mexican caravan escaped attack when Snively and his command were arrested by the U.S. cavalry on the charge that the Texans were on U.S. soil with intent to do harm. They were eventually released, but it was a diplomatic setback for the Houston administration nearly equivalent to that suffered by Lamar in the wake of the previous Santa Fe expedition.

Houston's opponents in the Senate eagerly took up the issue. Jack introduced a resolution on December 29, 1843, demanding that Houston communicate to the Senate all information relative to the Snively expedition, including the circumstances of the surrender of its members and the treatment of them as prisoners. Jack demanded to know their objective and whether they had been within the territorial limits of the Republic when they were seized. Williamson, always a supporter of the president, moved that the punitive motion be laid on the table, but the motion lost and the resolution was adopted. As the prisoners were eventually released unharmed, however, little political capital could be made of the event within Texas.

The senators, despite the clash with the United States in the spring, seemed confident that annexation was at hand when they convened in the fall. U.S. Secretary of State Abel Upshur, concerned with rumors that Britain had offered Texas a substantial loan in return for the abolition of slavery within its borders, had prevailed upon President John Tyler to reopen negotiations for annexation in October, 1843. Public opinion in Texas eagerly supported the idea, but Houston moved cautiously, having already been rebuffed on more than one occasion. His hope of maintaining a distant stance toward the United States, while making the most of England's friendship, was dashed when virtually nine-tenths of Congress signed a round robin circular endorsing a speedy union.

The Senate's primary concern was that it be consulted at every step. Rugeley offered a lengthy resolution in December that demanded that an agent dispatched by Houston to the United States be recalled because the Senate had not yet been consulted on the matter. Upon a motion by Jack, the senators voted on the measure. The vote resulted in a tie, with Houston supporters Greer, Kaufman, Isaac Parker, Gustavus A. Parker, Lawrence, and Pattillo opposed; Burleson broke the tie in the affirmative, and the message was sent. President Houston addressed Congress on January 20 and pointed out that as the annexation issue would soon be debated in Washington, D.C., it would be well for the Republic to have a special representative on the scene. In executive session four days later, the Senate finally endorsed the dispatch of an agent and appropriated five thousand dollars for that purpose. Kaufman gently chided Houston: "It is an old adage that in a multitude of counsellors there is safety; and if that remark is true in ordinary cases, it cannot be less so where the consequences flowing from such treaty, whether for good or evil, must necessarily be so lasting in their character."

The Senate maintained its position that annexation should be achieved through a treaty against the House's insistence that Texas would and must be annexed by an act of the U.S. Congress. The House declared that to initiate negotiations would only embarrass the Republic; only when the U.S. Congress finally did act, should the Congress of the Republic consider the matter. After heated exchanges through a conference committee, the two chambers agreed on a joint resolution that authorized negotiation, and the Senate approved the appointment of J. Pinckney

Henderson as the commissioner. As the House predicted, and Houston might have expected, the resulting treaty was defeated through a primarily sectional vote when it came before the U.S. Senate on June 8, 1844. The reaction in Texas was predictably vengeful, and the demands for established independence, with the aid of Britain and France, increased. Annexation would be a central issue in the 1844 presidential elections in both the Republic of Texas and the United States.

Debate on defense and foreign relations did not preclude lengthy exchanges on a variety of domestic issues. Greer introduced a motion on December 14 for an amendment to the constitution that would allow for the independent establishment of the Supreme Court. The motion was referred to the Committee on the State of the Republic, which was created by the Senate of the Eighth Congress in addition to the standing committees. Although no roster of members survives, it is known that Kaufman was active on that committee, and Rugeley served as chairman. The committee served as a catchall, charged with numerous bills on domestic administration, often bypassing the standing committees. It approved Greer's motion within the week, and the joint resolution was accepted without protest by Houston on February 1, 1844. Henceforth, the Supreme Court would consist of a chief justice and two associate justices who would be elected by the Congress and hold their office for six years. Houston did veto a bill establishing a site for the Supreme Court at Galveston, labeling the argument that more libraries were available in that city than elsewhere as a facetious attempt to create a local power center.

Jack, on the same day that Greer introduced his resolution for a separate supreme court, proposed a bill to require the executive and the heads of departments to retire to the seat of government at Austin. This measure was also referred to the Committee on the State of the Republic, where it stalled. Williamson, on December 28, introduced a bill for the permanent establishment of the seat of government at Washington, and Greer successfully moved for the rejection of Jack's bill, initiating a heated debate. Numerous motions for reconsideration were voted down as debate persisted for several weeks. Greer's motion to reconsider Jack's bill was finally successful on January 9, 1844, narrowly averting an attempt by Isaac Parker to table it once more. Greer moved for an amendment to the Senate rules that "no motion to lay a motion to reconsider on the table shall be in order," but lost, and to his certain frustration the next motion, made by Kaufman, to table the motion for reconsideration of Jack's bill was adopted by the Senate. Greer's campaign to have Jack's measure called up and soundly defeated had run aground on the shoals of parliamentary procedure.

On December 29, after the second reading of his bill, Williamson moved for its engrossment, but lost. Frustrated, Williamson introduced a bill on New Year's Day, 1844, which authorized the president to immediately transport all of the public archives in Austin to Washington. On a motion by Hunter, Williamson's substitute was sent to the Committee on the State of the Republic, which reported against its adoption. The Senate vote on the report ended in a tie, which Burleson resolved by voting in favor of the report and against adoption of Williamson's second measure. The vote was partisan, as Greer, Williamson, Pattillo, Kaufman, and Gustavus A. and Isaac Parker found themselves on the losing side, opposed by Jack, Webb, Hunter, Shaw, Smith, and Rugeley. The bill requiring the heads of departments and the executive to return to Austin was once more resurrected, hotly debated, and finally adopted by the Senate on January 14. The next day the senators met at ten o'clock and upon a motion by Webb adjourned. Greer had given notice that he would move to reconsider the seat of government bill on the 15th, and now felt cheated. On the 16th he introduced his motion to reconsider the bill, and it was seconded. Webb protested, asking whether Greer was out of order since it was now the 16th, not the 15th. The Senate was evenly divided when asked to vote on the question, after Lawrence failed to move for adjournment, and Burleson decided the matter by ruling that Greer was indeed out of order. Livid, Greer and Isaac Parker said that they would lodge formal protests.

The disgruntled Houston faction did lodge a formal protest on January 18. Greer, Lawrence, Pattillo, and Gustavus A. and Isaac Parker signed, but notably the outgoing Williamson did not. The missive declared that the rights guaranteed to them by the Texas Constitution were usurped by the application of an "extraordinary rule, adopted solely for the purpose of preventing the abuse of the Republican privilege of debate." As a debate had not been allowed to take place on January 16, no privilege had been abused and therefore no "urgent necessity" made it imperative to suspend discussion. Greer and Lawrence insisted that the only reason they had voted for the bill had been to move for a reconsideration of the vote being taken. Greer recalled that he had given notice that he would move for reconsideration, but on the morning in question he was prevented by a motion by Webb for adjournment which succeeded, evidence of the "injustice and procedure of the majority." The protest ended with a vituperative condemnation of Burleson's obvious partisanship and the "tyranny of majorities." Ironically, Houston did not sign the bill that required him to remove the seat of government to Austin, and a Senate bill to establish the capital at Washington, which passed on January 31, was rejected by the House.

Houston's administration of the colonization laws of the Republic also came under attack. The opening salvo came with a resolution offered by Kaufman that Houston be ordered to provide the Senate with all information relative to colonization efforts in Texas. On the next day, December 19, Kaufman introduced a bill to repeal all colonization laws then in force, including all those that allowed the president to negotiate colonization agreements, and to declare forfeit all contracts in which the terms had not been strictly followed. Jack, chair of the Committee on the Judiciary, to which the bill was sent, reported in its favor on December 21, and the bill passed the Senate one week later. The House concurred, but Houston vetoed the measure, declaring: "The dignity, as well as interests of the nation, requires, as the Executive believes, a strict fulfillment of all its pledges." Despite the president's insistence that many European immigrants were on their way to Texas, Congress overrode him by a constitutional majority, with Senators Greer, Pattillo, and Gustavus A. Parker voting in opposition. A separate act repealing all laws that authorized the president to negotiate a loan upon the public faith or the hypothecation of the public lands was signed on January 27, 1844. On January 19, the Senate had rejected a bill to incorporate the Texas Land and Emigration Company.

Houston suffered a final defeat on the issue of public lands. Isaac Parker introduced a measure to repeal the act to section the former Cherokee lands. The measure passed the Senate and became law within a week, annulling both of the earlier measures, signed on February 1, 1842, and July 23, 1842, regarding the Cherokee tracts. All legal and valid land surveys, scrip, bounty warrants, or certificates would no longer be considered binding within the territory itself, and the remaining lands were declared open for settlement without regard to any previous legislation or Indian treaties. Houston had fought to undermine the claims of squatters and land speculators because he believed that they had contributed to the fate of the Cherokee, but the pressure of immigration had proven too much to resist.

The Senate bombarded Houston with requests for strict financial accounting, including audits of the annual expenditures of every department and the disposition of the funds, appropriated in January, 1843, for the ransom of Indian prisoners. On a resolution by Jack, a bipartisan committee of Jack, Greer, and Smith was appointed to determine which public offices could yet be dispensed "without prejudice to the public service," and how much money could be saved. Houston complied with each request with little protest, realizing that a policy of continued fiscal retrenchment would be fortuitous to the Republic.

Partisan politics occasionally became ludicrous. Jack introduced a bill to prevent the sale in the Republic of "spirituous liquors" in quantities of less than a quart. Webb proposed immediate passage, but was voted down eight to four. Williamson moved that the bill be sent to the Committee on the State of the Republic, but also lost. The measure passed the Senate on January 2, with four senators, all Houston supporters, voting in opposition: Pattillo, Isaac Parker, Williamson, and Lawrence. The House refused to approve the bill, and so Houston was never forced to confront such an issue. A bill to exempt distilleries from taxation, which was received by the Senate from the House later in January, was passed from committee to committee, and never reached the floor.

The senators did set aside their differences to legislate for the public good. Rugeley introduced a bill to amend the charter of the Colorado Navigation Company on January 1, 1844, and Jack proposed a similar measure for the Brazos Canal Company on the same day. Both bills were sent to select committees, after Isaac Parker failed to have them submitted to the Committee on the State of the Republic. The Colorado Navigation Company bill was signed on January 18, 1844, granting that corporation greater powers, such as the right to petition for eminent domain, which would aid in the effort to clear the Colorado River and improve navigation by dams, locks, and otherwise, from its mouth on Matagorda Bay as far upriver as practicable. The company was authorized to collect tolls for thirty years, after which the Republic had the option of buying it out.

The Brazos Canal Company failed in its bid for a new charter, but a host of other measures for internal improvements became law. A bill to authorize Sylvanus Dunham to establish a ferry across Matagorda Bay was signed on February 1, 1844. Two days later, Houston approved an act that made it a high misdemeanor to obstruct the navigation of a stream by building dams or by any other means. On the last day of the session, he endorsed an act for the construction of a national road, from within fifteen miles of the mouth of the Elm Fork of the Trinity River to the bank of the Red River, opposite the mouth of the Kiomatia. The threat to the national currency posed by corporations who assumed banking privileges was eliminated by the signing, on February 5, 1844, of an act to suppress private banks.

Nine of the fourteen members of the Eighth Senate were Masons: Rugeley, Greer, Kaufman, Lawrence, Isaac Parker, Pattillo, Shaw, Titus, and Webb. In their efforts to promote education within the Republic, they found themselves confronted by an unforeseen situation. San Augustine University, incorporated by the First Congress on June 5, 1837, had been taken over by Presbyterians, an impractical development in a region dominated by Methodists. Enrollments declined almost from the very first day it opened its doors in the spring of 1843, and the school closed four years later when its president was shot and killed. A bill was received from the House in January, 1844, for the incorporation of the Wesleyan Male and Female College of San Augustine, a Methodist school, and was referred to a select committee of Greer, Kaufman, and Webb. Among the trustees asking for a charter were J. Pinckney Henderson and Henry W. Augustine, a former senator and one of the original trustees of San Augustine University. Because this bill provided for a land grant of four leagues, several senators subsequently tried to attach riders to provide similar grants for Trinity College and Washington College. The measure as passed provided no land for any school, but exempted the Wesleyan Male and Female College from paying any taxes. Kaufman was among the speakers at the laying of the cornerstone. The institution remained open only three years.

A more unusual bill came from the House on January 16. Passed by the Senate and signed on January 27, the measure incorporated Herman's University, which was to be funded by subscriptions of either land or currency. After five years, the trustees were to be authorized to sell no more than one-tenth of the land every year for revenue. The proposed curricula included four faculties: theological, judicial, medical, and philosophical, each modeled after those of German universities. No one was to be considered for a professorship unless he understood both English and German, the only exceptions being those elected unanimously by the trustees. The theological faculty was to have been nondenominational, but Protestant. The president and trustees of the university were to have corporate jurisdiction within a half-mile from campus to "suppress and abate nuisances," including the power to fine sellers of "spirituous liquor" within that region. Like the university at San Augustine, this one was tax exempt but lost its land grant during the Senate debates. The university was to be located on Mill Creek or Cummins Creek, but there is no record of its ever having opened.

The senators also endorsed a charter for an unusual paramilitary organization in Houston. The members were to be exempt from militia duty, payment of the road tax, and the service of overseers of the road. They were authorized to hold their own courts-martial on their members, with penalties limited to expulsion or fines of up to one hundred dollars. In militia reviews, members of the organization were to take the place of honor at the extreme right of the line. Members were to be exempt from individual conscription, but were to take to the field as a body if the need arose. The Congress agreed to supply them with two brass six-pounders, small arms and sidearms, and all necessary ordnance and accoutrements. Grimes objected to this last section of the charter, but the Senate did not adopt his amendment to strike it. The act of incorporation was to remain valid for ten years. A similar bill to incorporate the Galveston Guards passed the Senate February 5, 1844, but did not become law.

The Senate continued to foster the institution of slavery in the Republic. An amendment to the act for the apprehension and return of runaway slaves, which increased the bounties to be paid to slave catchers, was signed on January 27, 1844. Another bill received from the House would have prevented slaves from carrying firearms. It was amended by Pattillo, chairman of the select committee to which the bill was referred, to also include a prohibition on slave ownership of dogs, horses, and hogs. The amended measure passed the Senate on January 26, but the House refused to concur with the amendments to the bill. A conference committee that included Kaufman, Pattillo, and Isaac Parker failed to reach a settlement with the House, as the Senate remained insistent on its changes, and the session expired without a resolution.

Partisan politics dominated the actions of the Eighth Senate. Isaac Parker's proposal for a census of the Republic was blocked by the western members of the Senate, who realized that a new apportionment would probably reduce their proportion of the Congress in favor of more populous East Texas. Isaac Parker's later attempt to increase the terms of the president and Congress, and to require that the latter meet only every two years, was also killed by the opposition of Jack, chairman of the Committee on the Judiciary, who did not wish to provide for an increase in the power of the executive. The movement to impeach Houston, however, failed miserably. Greer, on the last day of the session, offered a resolution commending Houston, stating that although "many grave charges have been made by the enemies of Sam Houston and of Texas . . . against the President, which if true, would deservedly consign his name to infamy and to the loathing of all good men," including charges of "bribery, corruption, treason, and abolitionism," Congress had found "much to admire and approve, and but little to condemn," and therefore "Sam Houston, President, &c., for his able, faithful, honest and economical administration of the Government, is justly entitled to the admiration and gratitude of the nation, and the support of the Senate." Only Rugeley, Shaw, Hunter, and Webb voted against the resolution, indicating that Houston's popularity in Congress was again in the ascendant.

CHAPTER 9

The Senate of the Ninth Congress, 1844–45

The Ninth Senate of the Republic of Texas met in Washington-on-the-Brazos from December 2, 1844, to February 3, 1845, and again from June 16 to June 28, 1845, in a special session called by Anson Jones, who served as the last president of the Republic. Although annexation by the United States became the paramount issue of the period for Texas, most of the business conducted by the Senate during the regular session concerned domestic affairs. That Texas would become part of the United States was by no means a foregone conclusion, so the senators, rebuffed earlier by their neighbor to the north, continued to legislate for an independent Republic. Once summoned to the capital in the summer of 1845 to consider a definite proposal for annexation from President James K. Polk, however, the Senate, along with the House of Representatives of the Republic of Texas, moved quickly to cement the union that would precipitate a final showdown with Mexico.

The senators who had persistently opposed the policies of the Houston administration during the Eighth Congress did not fare well in the elections of 1844. Webb was replaced by John Caldwell, who had served as a representative in the Third, Fifth, Sixth, Seventh, and Eighth congresses. Caldwell was not truly a supporter of Houston, as he had consistently demanded the return of the seat of government to Austin and resigned in protest of the matter during the Seventh Congress, but he did not have the influence Webb enjoyed. Pilsbury reclaimed the seat he had surrendered to Jack in 1842. Pilsbury, during the interregnum, had served as chief justice and judge of probate for Brazoria. Like Caldwell, he would serve several terms in the state legislature after annexation. Richard Roman, a veteran of the Battle of San Jacinto and a representative in the First and Third congresses, replaced Rugeley. Roman would become one of the few senators to fight in the war between the United States and Mexico, joining Captain Hays's company as a private and fighting at Buena Vista and Monterrey. Hunter was supplanted by Henry L. Kinney, founder of Corpus Christi. Kinney would serve in the Annexation Convention, along with Caldwell, and in the first four state legislatures. Finally, Shaw's seat was taken by Henry J. Munson, of whom little is known.

Smith, another foe of Houston, returned to the Senate, but died of influenza and was hurriedly buried on January 13, 1845, a victim of an epidemic that swept the temporary capital of Washington. He was replaced by Samuel H. Luckie, who had served the Republic as a representative in the Sixth Congress and as a soldier in the Woll expedition of 1842, during which he was severely wounded. Luckie took his seat on February 1, two days before the session ended. Influenza also claimed Gustavus A. Parker, the only Houston supporter to lose his seat. Parker was elected instead to the House, which informed the Senate of his death on January 23. James K. McCrearey, who resigned the position of chief justice of Austin, took his place in the Senate. The attendance of George W. Wright, representing Red River, Fannin, Bowie, and Lamar counties, which had elected no senator to the Eighth Congress, completed a muster of fourteen members for the Ninth Senate. Wright was a veteran of the Texas Revolution, a representative in the First and Third congresses, and the founder of Paris, Texas. Following the close of the called session, he also attended the Annexation Convention.

The Senate mustered a quorum on the first day of the session, December 2, and elected its officers on the following day. Greer remained as president pro tempore, and Pipkin returned as sergeant at arms, but the rest were newcomers: Henry J. Jewett, secretary; Alfred W. Luckett, assistant secretary; H. W. Raglin, engrossing and enrolling clerk; and James Neely, doorkeeper. The senators chose Orcenith Fisher as their chaplain after two days of balloting. Fisher was nominated by Jesse Grimes; his rival, William M. Tryon, who had served as chaplain for the Eighth Senate, was introduced by Pilsbury, who thus lost his first motion before the Senate after a two-year absence.

The presidential election of 1844, remarkable for its lack of concrete issues, set the stage for the Ninth Senate. Burleson, with the aid of former Senator Webb and others, had secured the nomination of the fac-

tion led by former president Lamar. The vice-president was eager to secure the sanction of the public for his actions in defiance of President
Houston, especially the skirmishing before San Antonio, when he had
ignored orders to return and had continued to pursue General Woll's
raiding party. Houston officially damned his partner's candidacy in an
open letter, declaring: "On almost every question affecting the policy
of the present administration, which required the casting vote of the vice
President [*sic*], he gave it *against* the Executive." Instead, President Houston gave his endorsement to Anson Jones, who had served as secretary
of state during his second administration.

The candidates in the 1844 presidential race searched haplessly for issues with which to tar their opponents. Burleson could find few topics
to stir enmity toward the Houstonites. As president, Houston had avoided
war with Mexico; in fact, he pointed out in his address to Congress on
December 4, 1844, that there had been no incursion since 1842, and all
the Texan prisoners but one had come home. The Houston administration, by stringent efforts at retrenchment, had also brought a measure
of economic prosperity to the Republic, and some were predicting that
a small surplus might be achieved that year in the treasury. The mistakes of his administration — most notably the failure to secure annexation by the United States and the fateful decision to move the capital
from Austin — provided little substantial grist for the mill of his opponents.
Both Burleson and Jones promised that they would move the seat of
government back to Austin if Congress requested it, and adopted a wait-
and-see attitude in regard to annexation. The campaign quickly degener-
ated into name-calling, based most often on the actions of the Houston
and Lamar administrations, with which Jones and Burleson respectively
were closely identified.

Jones won with the support of the thickly settled East Texas region,
while Burleson swept West Texas. Jones and Kenneth L. Anderson, the
new vice-president, were inaugurated in a simple ceremony in Washington on December 9, 1844, during which President Jones and outgoing
incumbent Houston confined their remarks on the subject of annexation to simple platitudes, confounding editorial friends and foes alike
who were eager for more definite indications of future policies. The general mood regarding Houston, however, was one of congratulations for
a job well done. Senator Kaufman introduced a warm resolution of gratitude for Houston on inauguration day, which the Senate approved
unanimously.

Anson Jones, last president of the Republic, 1844–46.
Courtesy Texas State Archives.

Jones did indicate that he would remain a loyal supporter of Houston and would continue his efforts in retrenchment and defense while remaining aloof on the question of annexation. Houston, in his opening address to Congress, had not endorsed annexation and indeed spoke as if the independence of the Republic remained his primary objective. Jones's inaugural address presented a series of concrete objectives for the Congress that ignored annexation in favor of providing for a strong and independent Republic. He asked for the cessation of all issues of paper currency, which would be replaced by hard money. He pledged to further reduce the costs of government while establishing a tariff sufficient to support a bare minimum of activity and provide protection in case of emergencies. Among the necessary expenditures of government would be education, and Jones called for the "establishment of a system of common schools and institutions, for the moral and religious culture of the rising generations." Retrenchment would not preclude internal improvements, nor the just settlement of all outstanding claims to headrights and bounties. The incoming president promised a lasting peace with Mexico and vowed to support cooperative efforts to regenerate that country, along with "friendly and just relations with our red brethren, a course not only according with the dictates of humanity, but the principles of acknowledged sound policy, as affording the least expensive protection and greatest safety to our extended frontier." In sum, Jones proposed to continue the policies of the Houston administration and to resolve numerous problems that had plagued the Senate in the past.

Jones clarified his demands in a written message to both houses on December 18. He again requested the cessation of all issues of paper money and the establishment of a hard currency. He would be amenable to a system of treasury drafts drawn against specie in actual deposit, as a commercial convenience. Again he urged economy in government and a lessening of the burden of direct taxes by the raising of tariffs. Turmoil in Mexico once more threatened to spill north across the Rio Grande, so Jones asked for additional companies of Texas Rangers to patrol the southwestern frontier. The controversy over the location of the capital still plagued the government of the Republic, and Jones endorsed the idea of submitting the question to the people of Texas. Without directly mentioning annexation he added a gentle reminder of the necessity of settling land claims and of providing for internal improvements; his public attitude remained that of a president who intended to rule an independent Republic.

The Senate rejected Jones's initiative on the tariff issue. Roman introduced a resolution on December 11 to instruct the Committee on Finance, which consisted of Pilsbury, Grimes, and Pattillo, to investigate the propriety of abolishing the tariff and establishing in lieu thereof direct taxation as the sole means of supporting the government. The measure was adopted, and Pilsbury presented the committee's official report on January 7. It declared that "a considerable reduction may now, safely, be made in the tariff, without, in any degree, impairing the ability to meet, promptly, the just demands against the Government, for all that is necessary for its economical maintenance."

Retrenchment would further reduce the need for a tariff, until the costs of government could be met by direct taxes alone. Among the measures proposed for bureaucratic consolidation were merging the Department of War and Marine with the Department of State, abolishing the Office of Treasurer in favor of the Department of the Treasury, and dismissing the superintendent of Indian affairs, whose duties could be performed by a clerk. Because the United States had recently recovered from a "commercial embarrassment unparalleled in her commercial history," Pilsbury reasoned that "bordering on her territory, and connected with her by commercial as well as social ties . . . we may well expect to share in her prosperity" as an independent and equal Republic. Although it would be, in his opinion, inexpedient to repeal the tariff, a reduction would be in order. Greer, who had been added to the committee, and Pattillo dissented from Pilsbury's report, and Grimes disputed portions of it, but it was adopted by the Senate.

The principal target of the champions of retrenchment within the Ninth Senate became the foreign service. Pilsbury declared in his defiant report: "The *onerous disproportion* [which] the amount appropriated, or to be appropriated, for the maintenance of foreign ministers, bears to the whole support of the Government, (nearly one-third of the estimated amount,) [exposes] this branch of expenditure [as] sufficiently odious and oppressive, without comment from your committee." Pilsbury had proposed a resolution on December 12 to poll every member of the Ninth Congress about the propriety of recalling all ministers to foreign courts. His measure had been referred to the Committee on Foreign Relations, which Pilsbury chaired. He referred a substitute measure, which retained the intent of his first resolution, back to the Senate, and it was adopted on December 31. Three days later, the senators also endorsed a bill introduced by Greer to abolish the office of the secretary of legation. Neither proposal became law.

Jones refused to sign a series of measures intended to reduce tariff rates, except for a bill that exempted ice from import duties. He did approve a bill that levied an impost of one dollar on all neat cattle, horses, and mules brought into Texas, except those owned by immigrants. Because

Congress did not provide for higher tariffs, Jones was forced to endorse direct tax measures, including an additional poll tax of fifty cents on every white male from the ages of twenty-one to fifty, a twenty-five-dollar license fee for every retail merchant, and a livestock tax of one cent per head on all neat cattle and one dollar on all other cattle, horses, and mules. To facilitate the development of a system of transportation, Jones also authorized a law for the collection of road taxes.

The Senate did follow the executive lead on the matter of paper money. A bill to repeal acts that authorized the issuance of exchequer notes was received from the House on January 23. As the proposal echoed sentiments expressed in Pilsbury's report, he reported in its favor after a week of deliberation. The Senate passed the bill unanimously on February 1, and it was signed two days later. The intent of the new law was clear:

> From and after passage of this act, it shall not be lawful for the Secretary of the Treasury, or any other officer of the Government, to issue or cause to be issued, any bonds, bills, notes, or any description of paper representing money, intended either for circulation, or to be received in payment for any class of revenue: the intention of this section being not merely to prohibit the issue of paper, but also the reissue of any such paper which has, or may be returned to the Treasury Department.

The debts of the Republic would be paid only with specie, and as paper money was received as revenue it would be destroyed. During the called session, a joint resolution originated in the House for the issuance of exchequer notes, but passed the Senate only after the adoption of Caldwell's amendment to delete the section that would repeal all laws prohibiting the issue of such bills. The appropriation was limited to ten thousand dollars and was signed by Jones on June 28.

Continued unrest in Mexico mandated additional appropriations for defense. On December 6 Kinney introduced a joint resolution for his own relief in raising a company of soldiers to defend Corpus Christi. On a motion by Isaac Parker, the measure was sent to the Committee on Military Affairs, which consisted of Kinney, Wright, and Roman. As the troops had been mustered by order of President Houston, the Senate quickly approved Kinney's favorable report, and the bill was signed by Jones on December 14, 1844. Another bill for the relief of Kinney was signed on February 3; it provided for expenses not included in the first measure.

The Committee on Military Affairs also approved the muster of a company of Texas Rangers on the southwestern border, which President

Houston had been compelled to activate, as well as the activation of a company of militia to suppress the Regulator-Moderator feud in Shelby County. Captain Hays's Ranger command stationed along the border with Mexico disbanded, but a new larger unit under his command was authorized to patrol the southwestern frontier. In the same bill, signed on February 1, Kinney received approval to raise an additional company of forty men for the protection of Corpus Christi. Two days later, Jones signed a final act for the payment of Hays's expenses.

Appropriations for Indian affairs also remained immune from the efforts of those determined to cut government expenses to the bare minimum. The Senate rejected Pilsbury's proposal to abolish the office of superintendent of Indian affairs, and then approved $4,049 in additional funds for the expenditures during fiscal year 1844 that had exceeded the original budget. In the projected operating expenses for 1845, the grant of $10,000 for "Indian purposes" was one of the largest provisions. The Senate was encouraged by the signing of a treaty with the Comanche, Keechi, Waco, Caddo, Anadarko, Ioni, Delaware, Shawnee, Cherokee, Lipan, and Tawakoni tribes at Tehuacana Creek on October 9, 1844, and quickly gave its approval.

Preparations for defense did not necessarily include provisions for Texan prisoners held by Mexico. A bill for the relief of the Mier expedition prisoners and other prisoners almost failed to pass the Senate. It was rejected twice on the advice of Pilsbury, the chairman of the Committee on Finance. Recalled once more through a motion by Pattillo on February 1, the bill was amended by Wright to include the men imprisoned by the United States following the Jacob Snively expedition, despite the protests of Roman. On the last day of the regular session, February 3, the Senate passed the measure for the relief of prisoners, but Jones let it expire without his signature.

The issue of the location of the seat of government, although it did not overshadow more important subjects such as finance and defense, remained a thorny topic. Greer on December 17 introduced a bill to provide for the selection of a site for the capital of the Republic by a vote of the people of Texas. Caldwell proposed a measure later that afternoon that would require the president and the heads of the executive departments to return to Austin. Both bills went to the Committee on the State of the Republic, now a standing committee due to a motion by Kaufman, with Greer, Wright, and Roman as members. Greer, as chairman, reported in favor of his own bill, but the adoption of his recommendation was blocked by Caldwell, who successfully moved that both the report and the bill be laid on the table. Roman and Wright, a majority of the committee, recommended passage of Caldwell's bill, which required a return to Austin after the adjournment of the present session, thus making clear the turmoil that threatened to split the pivotal Committee on the State of the Republic.

The imbroglio was quickly solved through a series of legislative maneuvers. Pattillo, on December 23, following the majority report, moved that Caldwell's bill be resubmitted to the Committee on the State of the Republic. The Senate reached a tie vote, with Greer voting in favor of the motion and Smith and Roman opposed, before the new vice-president, Anderson, voted in the affirmative. Greer, as chairman, reported against Caldwell's bill five days later, insisting that the threat of invasion by Mexico still existed, especially as Mariano Paredes had instigated a revolt against Santa Anna and had pledged to invade the Republic. Furthermore, the renovation of the "ruined and dilapidated public buildings at Austin" would require an expenditure of twenty thousand dollars or more. Roman and Smith again reported as a majority in favor of passing the bill, but Greer had had his say.

On December 30, on a motion by McCrearey, the Senate considered Greer's bill. It adopted a series of amendments, most notably a change in the date of election from 1845 to 1847, on the second Monday in March. Greer's bill as amended passed the Senate on January 3, followed immediately by Caldwell's measure. President Jones approved the act for an election to be held two years hence, but vetoed the bill for immediate removal to Austin. In his veto message, which he sent to the House, where Caldwell's proposal had originated, Jones admitted that the seat of government properly lay at Austin, but in language reminiscent of Greer's condemnation said that continued unrest in Mexico presented an immediate danger to the Republic. Consequently, Washington was to be the last capital of the Republic of Texas.

A related subject was the permanent establishment of a supreme court. On December 11 Kaufman introduced a joint resolution for the organization of a supreme court by constitutional amendment. On a motion by Wright the proposal was sent to the Committee on the Judiciary: Kaufman, Lawrence, and Caldwell. Kaufman, as the chairman, reported in favor of the resolution on December 17, and the next day the measure passed the Senate, with Munson casting the only opposing vote. Another bill that stipulated the place and time for the sessions of the Supreme Court was approved by the Senate on January 20, with only Munson and Grimes dissenting. The House returned the joint resolution embodying the amendments to the constitution for the Supreme Court with an additional amendment to give Congress the power to pass naturalization laws, and then also slightly amended the bill, setting the location and time for the semiannual meetings of the court. The Senate concurred in the changes, and both measures became law at the end of the regular session.

The Senate did act on President Jones's directive to settle the land claims against the Republic. Kaufman introduced a bill to grant preemption privileges to settlers on vacant public land as a partial solution to the flood of petitions for patents that were inundating Congress. The bill was initially referred to the Committee on Public Lands, and then, after being reported out with a few amendments, was sent to the Committee on the Judiciary, chaired by Kaufman, for approval. Kaufman, in recommending his bill to the Senate, stated: "This bill, it is hoped and seriously believed, will constitute a valuable substitute for the unfortunate and lavish donation system which has heretofore prevailed." His intent was to give lands to those homesteaders who were already in possession of it, rather than to speculators or land-prospecting companies. Kaufman concluded by saying, "This bill only proposes to give a preference to the occupant and settler, and secures his improvement and labor from a rapacity which, unfortunately for human nature, too often requires the restraining hand of legislation." The Senate adopted amendments that provided for careful record keeping by the county surveyor and the General Land Office; they also ensured that the widows and heirs of claimants would receive the same opportunity to file claims for a half-section of public land. The bill passed the Senate unanimously on December 26 and was signed by Jones on January 22, 1845.

The Senate remained hesitant to endorse colonization companies. Kinney introduced a bill on December 11 for the incorporation of the Texas Land Company. The bill was sent to the Committee on the Judiciary, and on December 21, as one of the committee, Caldwell recommended that the bill be referred to a committee of the whole Senate for consideration. The Senate adopted the report and, in the committee of the whole, approved amendments to frame the bill in the fashion of other incorporations, reserving to the Republic the right to use improvements such as dams and roads free of charge and retaining an option to purchase after thirty years. On a motion by Caldwell, the bill was recommitted to a special committee of Caldwell, Kinney, and Roman on December 31. Caldwell, as chairman, reported in favor of a substitute on January 16, with Roman dissenting, but the Senate, unable to reach a firm decision, allowed the session to expire without further action. The Senate did endorse the establishment of a colony by General Charles Fenton Mercer, without granting any special privileges for the construction of internal improvements.

The incorporation of Mercer Colony was just one act in a flood of new legislation for the development of the Republic. The settlements of Paris, Henderson, Marshall, Boston, and Huntsville received charters, and Goliad County was established. The growth of Galveston was reflected in the signing of bills to incorporate the Galveston Chamber of Commerce, the Galveston Lyceum, and the Galveston Guards, one of several paramilitary infantry units in Texas. Acts for internal improvement provided for lighthouses at both Galveston and Paso Cavallo on Matagorda Bay. A proposal from the House to establish a hospital at Galveston passed the Senate on February 3 and was signed that day. It taxed every commander of a vessel arriving at that port fifty cents for every foreign-born white male cabin passenger over the age of sixteen, and twenty-five cents for each foreign-born white male steerage passenger of the same age. The Senate also endorsed a House bill to incorporate the Texas Cotton and Woollen Manufacturing Company; the bill was signed by Jones on February 3, 1845. The plant was intended to produce "shirtings, sheetings, osnaburgs, jeans, cassinetts, linseys, sattinetts, yarns, negro cloths, bagging, bale ropes, &c., &c.," from Texas wool and cotton, providing a model for further development.

The Ninth Senate, led by Masons Greer, Kaufman, Kinney, Lawrence, Parker, Pattillo, Pilsbury, and Wright, chartered more academies and universities than any of its predecessors. Efforts to provide for education were also enhanced by the passage of legislation to facilitate independent action by the Masonic lodges and other organized groups. The Senate approved a House bill to incorporate the Grand Lodge of the Republic of Texas and subordinate lodges in lieu of its own measure to incorporate the Orphans' Friend Lodge Number 17. Signed by Jones on January 30, 1845, the act incorporated the Grand Lodge along with Holland Lodge Number 1 at Houston, Harmony Lodge Number 6 at Galveston, Orphans' Friend Lodge Number 17 at Fantharps in Montgomery County, and such other lodges as had been or would be established under the Grand Lodge. A general incorporation bill also became law, stipulating that "it shall be lawful for any denomination of Christians, or the citizens of any neighborhood in this Republic, to appoint a board or boards of Trustees, for meeting houses, camp grounds, parsonages, and school houses." Such groups could hold land in trust tax free, but not more than ten acres.

The first bill considered by the Ninth Senate for the incorporation of an institution of higher education was introduced by Pattillo on behalf of R. E. B. Baylor and others who requested a charter for a college or university "for the purpose of a more general diffusion of useful knowledge" on December 28. The measure, which referred to the proposed institution as San Jacinto University, was sent to the Committee on the State of the Republic, whence Greer recommended it for passage on January 3. Following a motion by Pattillo, Milam was substituted for San Jacinto wherever it occurred in the bill on January 7, until Pattillo introduced the final amendment that deleted Milam in favor of Baylor University. Jones signed the act into law on February 1, 1845. Former senators Albert C. Horton and James S. Lester and former chaplain of the Senate William M. Tryon were among the first trustees. It is interesting to note that, as with almost all of these early institutions, provisions were made for the education of females.

On the same day on which Baylor University was incorporated, Jones signed the charter for Rusk County Academy, which apparently was the only institution of higher education chartered by the Ninth Congress that failed to open. The latter bill had originated in the House along with additional measures for the incorporation of Nacogdoches University, Trinity University, Matagorda University, Houston College, Victoria College, and the College of Eastern Texas. Amendments were also made to the original charters of Marshall University, DeKalb College, and Wesleyan College in San Augustine. Each was referred in turn to the Committee on the State of the Republic.

The Ninth Senate struggled heroically to consider every request related to education. Greer attempted to amend the bill to provide a land endowment for Wesleyan College to also include Washington University, but both his amendment and the measure itself were rejected by the Senate. It was reluctant to continue the earlier policy of parceling out the public domain for the support of private education. An interesting amendment to the Matagorda University bill was offered by Caldwell and accepted: "Be it further enacted, That the same amount of land shall be allowed to all the other counties in this Republic which have not heretofore received the same for the endowment of an academy therein." Just moments after the Senate adopted the amendment, however, Pilsbury moved a reconsideration of the vote, and Caldwell withdrew his proposal! On January 31, the Matagorda University bill passed the Senate unamended, as did the bills for Nacogdoches University and DeKalb College. As signed, the acts for Rusk County Academy and Matagorda University provided no landed endowment, despite the fact that former senators Horton and Rugeley were among the petitioners for a charter. The Senate did endorse a grant of two leagues of land for Marshall University and authorized the transfer of lands to DeKalb College and Nacogdoches University; the latter included James H. Starr, James M. Rector, and Thomas J. Rusk on its board of trustees. The bills for Trinity University, Houston College, Victoria College, and the College of Eastern Texas, as well as a measure to supplement the previous land grants to public schools, failed to become law.

The Committee on the State of the Republic recommended a host of other bills for adoption. These included provisions for a system of uniform weights and measures and the repeal of an act creating the Board of Medical Censors. Greer reported in favor of the latter action because the statute to which it referred was obviously "inoperative and of no effect." Parker's proposal for the taking of a census of the Republic, a perennial issue in the newspapers since the early days of independence, was also approved by the committee. Although the Senate endorsed each measure, all of them failed to become law. The provision for a census, particularly, fell prey to sectionalism within the House of Representatives, as the western delegates refused to endorse an action that might reduce their number.

All of the Senate committees during the Ninth Congress received a seemingly endless flow of petitions, but only one rebelled against the demands of the public. Despite having legislated for divorce through the courts, petitions for divorce continued to fill the legislative calendar. Kaufman, as one of the Committee on the Judiciary, to which yet another petition had been referred, exploded eloquently on the subject in a report of December 24, 1844, declaring:

> The expediency of granting divorces by Congress, is as palpable as its unconstitutionality. Our laws are extremely liberal on this subject; more so, perhaps, than the laws of any State of the American Union. If we take jurisdiction of *one* case, our tables will groan with petitions, praying for emancipation from the matrimonial bonds—mole hills will be mag-

nified into mountains—slight misunderstandings incidental to human intercourse will be represented as intolerable grievances, and the poor offender will have neither notice nor opportunity to make a defence [sic]—each petitioner will endeavour to show that his or hers is a very *hard* case, and in discussions of the questions of the relative merits of the different petitioners, the time of Congress will be diverted from *general* legislation, and the treasures of the country squandered.

Kaufman concluded by repeating that the petition of Congress to grant divorces, done in the interests of expediency, was neither expedient for Congress nor even constitutional.

The regular session closed with little mention of the question of annexation on the floor of the Senate. The effective impetus for annexation came not from the Republic of Texas but from the United States. President John Tyler correctly interpreted the victory of James K. Polk as a mandate for annexing Texas. Also, Tyler wished to counteract British influence in the region. In his address to the U.S. Congress on December 4, 1844, Tyler requested a joint resolution of annexation. The measure passed the House on January 25, 1845, but did not receive Senate approval until a rider was attached that allowed the president to negotiate new terms with the Republic of Texas if it became necessary for ratification. Tyler signed the resolution on March 1, 1845, and dispatched it to Texas just hours before the end of his administration two days later.

The terms of the joint resolution for annexation reflected the push and pull of sectional politics. All boundary questions were to be settled by the United States. With the consent of Texas, new states, not to exceed the number of four, might be organized from the territory. Slavery would be prohibited in those that fell north of the extended Missouri Compromise line of 1820, but those lying south of that boundary could accept or reject slavery by a popular vote. The State of Texas would retain its public lands and the debts of the Republic of Texas, which would be amortized through sale of the public domain because the control of customs revenues would pass to the U.S. government. The latter would also assume responsibility for all public edifices and military installations. These terms, of course, could be altered through negotiation if both sides agreed to do so.

The government of the Republic of Texas was under great pressure from abroad, especially from France and Britain, not to accept annexation. President Jones truthfully dragged his heels, as did many of his advisers. Public opinion in Texas, however, was strongly in favor of becoming a state. Jones did attempt to negotiate recognition of the Republic from Mexico through the British minister, Charles Elliot, and the French minister, Alphonse de Saligny, but to no avail. Mexico accepted the terms offered in a desperate attempt to thwart annexation, but the last Senate rejected their overtures during the called session and adjourned without making a counterproposal.

Jones tried to avoid assembling a special convention to consider annexation, calling instead a special session of Congress for June. The people refused to accept this measure. Bowing to public demand, Jones in May called for a convention on July 4, 1845, to consider the question of annexation. Houston announced in favor of annexation, but expressed the opinion that union on the basis of a treaty that would require Senate approval would give the Republic a better chance to bargain for terms. The called session convened on June 16, 1845, and received clear instructions from President Jones. The convention had already been called, and participants in the convention had the responsibility of deciding on annexation and writing a state constitution. But, according to the resolution approved by the U.S. Congress, the "consent of the existing government" had to be given, and that was the reason for the legislators' return to Washington-on-the-Brazos.

Jones turned over to the Senate all correspondence relating to both the peace proposal by Mexico and the annexation resolution of the United States, requesting an impartial review so that

> the alternative of Annexation or Independence, will thus be placed before the people of Texas, and their free, sovereign, and unbiased voice, will determine the all-important issue, and so far as it shall depend upon the Executive to act, he will give immediate and full effect to the expression of their will.

The Senate had received many petitions in favor of annexation by the United States during the regular session and on January 20, 1845, had requested all information available on the subject from Jones. Two days later the Committee on Foreign Relations reported through chairman Kaufman on the memorials submitted in favor of annexation. Although it heartily approved of a union with the United States, the Senate preferred to wait until that country initiated efforts. The opportunity was now before it. On June 18, Kaufman reported in favor of a joint resolution endorsing the annexation of Texas by the United States; it was unanimously adopted by all thirteen senators present on June 19. The House had passed its own resolution, but a compromise was quickly reached and won Jones's immediate approval. The president also signed an appropriation to defray the expenses of the Annexation Convention, which was to be held in July, 1845.

The Senate brushed aside a new flood of petitions in order to provide for a smooth transition of power. On June 21 the members adopted Pattillo's resolution, which stated that only measures pertinent to the consummation of annexation would be considered for the balance of the called session. The Senate did unanimously adopt a memorial of thanks, introduced by Greer, the longtime ally of Houston, to Andrew Jackson, who had died on June 8, 1845, for his "many valuable and important services . . . to the cause of civil and religious liberty." A similar resolution of thanks was introduced by Wright on June 21 for Tyler; it was quickly adopted. Kaufman introduced a bill to set aside a specific portion of the public domain between the Arkansas River and the Red River for the retirement of the national debt of the Republic; the bill was passed after a favorable report from Greer of the Committee on the State of the Republic. An amended version was signed into law at the same time that Jones signed a joint resolution suspending the exchange of outstanding notes and bonds for land scrip.

The reaction of Mexico was of immediate concern; Greer on June 19 proposed a resolution requesting the immediate introduction of U.S. troops into Texas. His fear was that Mexico would strike before protection could be extended to Texas as a state in the union. The Senate approved his measure the next day, but the House added amendments in which the Senate refused to concur. As a compromise, Kaufman offered an amendment that stipulated that troops would be sent only "if the preservation of the integrity of the country demands it," a statement designed to mollify those in the House who regarded with suspicion the entry of U.S. troops into Texas. The Senate vote on the compromise proposal ended in a tie; then Anderson voted against both it and the House amendment. The House requested the formation of a conference committee, on which Kaufman, Caldwell, and Pilsbury served, and on June 25, the House informed the Senate that it had adopted the report of the committee of conference, allowing for passage of the resolution.

Many citizens of the former republic were relieved to learn that there would be no delay in the dispatch of U.S. troops to the border with Mexico. Once the resolution for annexation had passed the U.S. Congress, Juan N. Almonte, minister of Mexico, demanded his passports, foreshadowing the conflict to come. McCrearey introduced a resolution in the Senate during the called session to censure Jones for attempting to negotiate a treaty with Mexico upon the condition that Texas would never be annexed by the United States, indicating the strong feeling in Texas against rejoining Mexico. On the final day of the session, June 28, McCrearey, in the last official act of the Senate of the Republic of Texas, withdrew his resolution after his comrades refused to lay it on the table.

Jones delayed in convening the Annexation Convention, but the unanimous approval by the Senate of the United States' proposal removed any final doubts. Ten former senators of the Republic attended the Annexation Convention: John Caldwell, Albert C. Horton, William L. Hunter, Oliver Jones, Henry L. Kinney, James B. Miller, Francis Moore, Jr., Isaac Parker, Emory Rains, and George W. Wright. The convention accepted the original terms of the resolution offered by the United States for annexation and penned a state constitution before adjourning. President Polk signed the measure on December 29, 1845, precipitating the climactic confrontation with Mexico which heralded the arrival of a new imperial power, the United States, in whose constellation the Lone Star was irrevocably fixed.

PART II

Senates of the State of Texas:
Early Statehood to Secession

CHAPTER 10

Early Statehood:
The Senate of the First Legislature, 1846

W̶hen eighteen state senators met in the diminutive frame capitol at Austin on the morning of February 16, 1846, the flag flying outside was still that of the Republic of Texas, whose president had not yet spoken his last word. Becalmed in a nameless time between sovereignty and statehood, these senators of the First Legislature, in the absence of their constitutionally designated leader, the lieutenant governor, perforce organized themselves and waited.

The first order of business for the Senate was to elect a presiding officer. Isaac Parker, a fifty-three-year-old plantation owner from Georgia who had emigrated to Texas in 1833 and served as a representative and a senator in the Congress of the Republic and as delegate to the annexation and constitutional convention of 1845, moved that Jesse Grimes be called to the chair. This may have been in deference to Grimes's age, for, born in North Carolina in 1788, he was the senator who was oldest both in years and in his political experience; his political career had begun soon after his arrival in Texas in 1827, after which he had held local offices as *síndico procurador* and *regidor,* followed by vigorous and conspicuous activity in the revolutionary movement. Grimes had signed both the Declaration of Independence and the Constitution of the Republic of Texas, and had served as a representative, senator, and president pro tempore of the Senate in the Congress.

However, Grimes would not be elected to the latter position in the First Legislature. After electing Stephen Z. Hoyle as secretary pro tempore, the assembly chose instead a broadly popular figure, Edward Burleson, for president pro tempore, which may have been either a consolatory motion to him after his defeat in the race for the presidency

Jesse Grimes, senator who served in First through Eighth legislatures.
Courtesy Texas State Archives.

in 1844, or a defiant gesture to Houston, who had largely brought about that result. Burleson had met Houston, as well as his senatorial colleague George Tyler Wood, while serving under Andrew Jackson in the Creek Indian War in Georgia, and thus could claim an acquaintance with him well before Texas became home to either of them; and, although they had served together in the Texas Revolution and Burleson had been vice-president in Houston's second administration, Houston had supported Dr. Anson Jones for the presidency. It is thought that Houston did not support Burleson because he still resented what he saw as Burleson's bid for military glory during the Mexican invasion of 1842.

Burleson presided over an assembly of some heterogeneity in origins, though the majority were southerners, born and bred. One exception was the obscure John F. Miller, a planter settled on land granted for services during the revolution; he was said to be from Scotland. Another was Henry J. Jewett, born in Maine and at thirty the youngest in a distinctly middle-aged body. Jewett had come to Texas as a land attorney in 1839, but during that same year was appointed chief clerk of the treasury department; he became secretary to President Lamar in 1840, district attorney from the Third Judicial District in 1841–42, secretary of the Senate in the Ninth Congress, and a delegate to the 1845 convention. He was also an occasional translator of French for the government. All of this suggests that he could scarcely have given full time to a law practice. Alexander H. Phillips was from Montgomery County, New York, and had first moved to Refugio County, which he represented in the Eighth Congress. Neither he nor Jewett—and this was unusual among the lawyers of this time and place—seems to have made any effort to enter the planter class, unlike their southern contemporaries.

The remaining northerner, Henry Lawrence Kinney, was born in Sheshequin, Pennsylvania, in 1814 and reached Texas in 1838 after adventures in Illinois. He came with promises of northern financial backing and an idea that while East Texas was rapidly filling up with surplus gentry from the Old South, the coastal area below the Balcones Escarpment, if not as rich as the river bottoms and the piney woods, had possibilities and was almost unexploited. By the time of his election, Kinney was the founder of Corpus Christi, which was little more than a tent city, had a modest private army, and was a prolific promoter of land schemes. He had been a member of the Ninth Congress and would be elected to the Senate of the Second Legislature, but before taking his seat resigned in order to see what might be gleaned from the Mexican War, then in progress.

Kinney would return to the Senate for the Fourth Legislature, but in 1854 went haring off to Nicaragua. The federal government, alerted by the Nicaraguan minister, had him and his partners arrested and indicted in New York, from which they and thirty-five colonists planned to sail. A naval blockade was placed around his steamship, the *United States*, but they escaped on another ship that ran aground on an island in the West Indies, and finally arrived at San Juan del Norte, Nicaragua, in a British vessel. Soon after, Kinney wrote to a friend in Corpus Christi: "I believe that I have previously written you that I have concluded the purchase of the Mosquito grant as it is called extending 350 miles on the coast and contains [*sic*] about 30 million acres of the most productive and beautiful country in the world. I expect to make a million of dollars out of this place if I live." He had just been elected "civil and military governor" by the colonists, not by the Indian natives, who are today called the Miskito, and said, "I do not intend to stop until I am President."

Unfortunately, William Walker at this moment made his famous incursion and captured the capital, Granada. Kinney's attempts to make deals with both Walker and President Rivas resulted in a sojourn in Honduras and then Panama, whence he tried to sell his grant to the Utah Mormons, who were interested but in the end did not buy. Heartened by the appointment of his old friend Mirabeau B. Lamar as U.S. minister to Costa Rica and Nicaragua, Kinney and a dozen desperados tried an armed assault on San Juan del Norte and barely escaped lynching by the infuriated citizens. By the end of June, 1858, Kinney was back in Corpus Christi and running for office again, this time as a representative in the Eighth Legislature, only to be purged from that body when he refused to subscribe to the Confederate oath. He died soon after, shot in a murky Mexican border skirmish. His most notable legislative achievement was creating a county named for himself, a common practice of the time.

Of the senators of southern origin, only one was not in some sense a planter. Thomas F. McKinney was born in Kentucky in 1801 and had traversed Texas on the Chihuahua trade route before joining the Old Three Hundred Colonists and settling on a league of land in present Brazos County in 1824. McKinney did not plant but, early realizing that trading in and transporting cotton could be at least as profitable as growing it, took a partner and founded McKinney, Williams and Company, a commission-merchant cotton firm with subsidiary interests in lumbering, milling, keelboating, and the like. This enterprise was quite successful and lent large sums to the revolutionary cause and the early Republic. It is possible that McKinney became senator in order to be on the spot when the new state found some money to pay old debts.

Landowners dominated the Senate. Nine or ten members could be called simply plantation owners, although some had subsidiary interests as merchants, dealers in land, or lawyers. George Tyler Wood from Georgia, who had met Houston and Burleson there during the Creek Indian War, was clearly a member of the planter class well before coming to Texas in 1839, as most of the others were not, for he had been a member of the Georgia legislative assembly and had set out for his new country in great style on a chartered ship bearing his family and thirty slaves. He soon established a plantation in Liberty County and took up his political career, serving as a representative in the Sixth Congress and a delegate to the 1845 convention.

Joseph Lewis Hogg is now chiefly remembered as the father of James Stephen Hogg, the first native-born governor. The elder Hogg was a Georgian by birth; he came to Texas by way of Alabama in 1839 and like Wood brought his slaves with him. A sometime lawyer, he quickly acquired more land and slaves. His entry into politics and his friendship with Houston were supposedly facilitated by his striking physical resemblance to Andrew Jackson. Strangely, the *Texas Democrat*, an Austin newspaper that closely followed the new legislature, called him a Whig, a party that was almost defined by its opposition to the personality and policies of Jackson. Since true Whiggishness would require Senator Hogg to favor banking, which was strictly forbidden by the Constitution of 1845, which he had just signed, and to favor protective tariffs, which were abhorred by southern planters, who had to import almost all manufactured goods, his supposed Whiggery may have been a flippant response to a reporter's comment on his looks, which by that time must have been more burden than advantage. Whigs also vehemently opposed the Mexican War, but Hogg was so eager to join the fray that he left on May 4, 1846, to recruit troops for Governor James P. Henderson, who also could not wait for the end of his term.

Planting and the law were sometimes supplemented by a variety of other sources of income; Benjamin Rush Wallace, for example, was a merchant and land speculator. He owed his prominence to his close friendships with the major figures in events from the revolution on, and these friendships, perhaps, to his lifelong devotion to Freemasonry, a factor of evident but imprecise importance in the political life of the time. William M. Williams was even more versatile: besides being a landowner and a lawyer, he was at various times quartermaster and commissary of the Texas Army, a mail carrier, and a surveyor, which kept him supple enough to return in one house or the other of the legislature for six sessions.

William Thomas Scott had been a merchant in his native Mississippi, but in Texas in the 1830s began acquiring land and slaves until he was the largest slaveowner in Harrison County. He married the daughter of William Pinckney Rose of Shelby County, organizer and head of the Regulators in the Regulator-Moderator War. A late episode in that deplorable period was part of the legend attached to one of Scott's fellow senators, Robert McAlpin Williamson, who had not yet taken his seat on that February morning.

In many ways the most remarkable presence that day was that of a man who was neither a planter nor a southerner; he was the only Hispanic and the only Texas-born member of the government, José Antonio Navarro. Navarro's district, although called Bexar, was nothing like the present county, but covered the whole northern and western wasteland beyond the Balcones Escarpment to the vague borders that would cause so much trouble in the future. It remains a mystery why this son of a Corsican father connected by marriage to the most distinguished Mexican families of Texas should have taken as a personal cause the interests of the Anglo-American Texans, but his commitment began at least as early as 1821 with his close friendship with Stephen F. Austin. He had nothing to gain from it himself and everything to lose, as had been alarmingly shown very recently. In 1841, after Navarro's term as representative in the Third Congress, President Lamar appointed him a commissioner in the ill-conceived Santa Fe expedition, apparently because Lamar believed he could coax the people of Santa Fe, still a part of Mexico, into becoming part of the Republic of Texas. Indeed, Navarro was an impressive orator in the Hispanic tradition. But what this honor meant, in fact, was that when the disheveled Texan expedition fell into Mexican hands, the other members were sent off to captivity in Mexico City, where society ladies took pity on them and gave them food and clothing, while José Antonio was placed on trial for his life and condemned to be shot. His sentence was commuted by Santa Anna, who was serving one of his eleven terms as president of Mexico. Navarro spent some time in

José Antonio Navarro.
Courtesy Texas State Archives.

the nasty prison of San Juan de Ulloa in the harbor of Veracruz, was allowed to escape, and made his way through Havana and New Orleans, reaching his home in San Antonio on February 18, 1845, a year and two days before the first session of the legislature and in plenty of time to be elected a delegate to the Convention of 1845. The convention began on a symbolic July 4 and ran to August 27; the delegates ratified annexation and wrote the state constitution, to which Navarro made notable contributions, having had experience in drafting that of the Republic ten years before. In 1846 he was fifty years old, a lawyer, merchant, and the owner of large ranch properties. In the early days of the session he would request and be granted an interpreter shortly before he delivered an admirable speech on escheat in Anglo-American law.

The remaining senators present on the morning of February 16 reflected the variety of interests and backgrounds that was typical of antebellum Texas. John Greenville McNeel was the earliest immigrant among the senators, having come from Kentucky as a member of a large family joining Stephen F. Austin's Old Three Hundred Colonists. His plantation, Ellersly, was a well-known showplace. Virginia-born planter-cum-lawyer Ballard Bagby, according to the *Texas Democrat*, was an adherent of an obscure faction, the Locofocos, named for an early safety match and originally a New York radical wing of the Democrats. By 1846, however, they had succumbed to the embraces of John C. Calhoun's philosophy of states' rights.

One senator was a former slave dealer, and others may have done a certain amount of semiprofessional trading. James Bourland, the so-called floatorial senator from a district comprised of Bowie, Red River, Fannin, and Lamar counties, was originally from North Carolina, but had resided in both Kentucky and Tennessee before arriving in Texas in 1840 to trade—in horses, this time, not slaves—with the Indians. At the time of his election he was a collector of customs for the Red River District, an important post, for these duties were almost the sole source of income of the Republic and for some time of the state. His brother, William, represented Lamar County in the House.

Together with two more planters, Jesse Robinson and Philip Cuney, these were the senators who presented their credentials at the first meeting of the Senate under statehood.

After an adjournment for lunch, Burleson took the chair at three o'clock on February 16, and welcomed a latecomer. His name, Robert M. Williamson, did not necessarily win him instant recognition, but the men-

Robert M. "Three-legged Willie" Williamson.
Courtesy Barker Texas History Center, University of Texas at Austin.

tion of "Three-Legged Willie" then and now in East Texas could be counted on to set the flow of anecdote running, for he was one of the great originals of the Texas adventure, a master of frontier rant, of verbal assault and battery, of orotund periods, and of the law as he saw it. He could say of himself, in the genre of the Texas brag:

> I killed a man in North Carolina, and then I crossed over into Tennessee. I killed a man there. Then I went to Alabama and there I laid low my third man. This occasioned my visiting Mississippi, where I killed the fourth. Only after this fourth, gentlemen, did I consider myself practiced to claim myself the honor of becoming a citizen of Texas.

Williamson's verifiable biography begins with his birth in Georgia in 1804. At the age of fifteen he had an attack of what was then called "white swelling," evidently a form of polio, which left his right leg bent back at the knee and useless. He strapped a wooden leg to the kneecap and became "Three-Legged Willie," an arrangement that can be seen in the portrait of him presented to the Senate in 1891, now hanging in the Legislative Reference Library. In practice as a lawyer by the age of nineteen, he reached Texas in 1827 without, so far as is known, any qualifying murders and at once put his rhetorical brilliance at the service of the revolutionary cause, initially as a newspaper editor. Despite his handicap, he fought in the Battle of San Jacinto and immediately on the establishment of the Republic was elected judge of the Third Judicial District, which under the Constitution of 1836 made him a justice of the Supreme Court.

It was probably at this time that he had the legendary encounter with the rival gangs of Moderators and Regulators in Shelby County; it is a tale with as many variants as there are tellers of it. In essence the story is that he rode into Shelbyville on circuit for the first time and announced that court would be held. A leading Moderator or Regulator, it does not matter which, strode up to the table at which he was seated and slapped down a bowie knife, saying, "This is the law in Shelby County." Willie immediately produced a loaded pistol, slapped it down beside the knife and replied, "And this is the Constitution which is the supreme law of the land and I am here to enforce it. The honorable court is in session, everybody rise." In addition to his strenuous circuit riding, he was a representative in the Fifth, Sixth, Seventh, and Ninth congresses, a senator in the Eighth Congress, and a delegate to the 1845 convention.

He was so ardently for annexation that he named a son born at the time William Annexus.

When Williamson took his seat in 1846, he was somewhat beyond his best days, in poor health, and feeling left out of the heady process of determining the future of Texas. The enervated atmosphere of the first legislatures, which were without real power and confined to petty duties, did not offer the dramatic vehicle of earlier years. But he was never insignificant, and a contemporary summed up his lawmaking career in these terms:

> While it is not claimed for him that he originated many great measures, yet as a conservative his influence was widely felt and acknowledged. He stood ever as a faithful and incorruptible sentinel over the rights and interests of the state. . . . He was inaccessible to the threats or flatteries of the cormorants whose object it was to prey upon the public treasury or the public domain. Individuals who had bills of doubtful merit before congress or the legislature feared the sleepless eye and invective of Williamson more than all others.

It must also be said that in a society conspicuous for using position and ability of any kind to acquire wealth, particularly in land, there was never a suspicion of his actions or motives, and he lived and died poor among rich men.

After the swearing in of this formidable addition to the roster, the first meeting was adjourned. The following day, the Senate convened to canvass the votes for governor and lieutenant governor, and declared that J. Pinckney Henderson and Nicholas H. Darnell, respectively, had been elected—not, as it turned out, accurately. The last senator, Isaac Wright Brashear, was received. He had come to Texas from Tennessee in the 1830s and flourished as a merchant, land speculator, and planter.

On Friday, February 19, the two houses of the First Legislature, together with the elected officials of government past and government future, met at eleven o'clock in the morning in front of the Capitol. Anson Jones, last president of the Republic of Texas, bade a melancholy farewell to what he regarded as his true country, and offered no welcome to the statehood that he had opposed, saying merely in the end: "The Republic of Texas is no more." Governor Henderson took the oath of office and spoke briefly in a hopeful vein; however, the lieutenant governor–elect did not appear.

The senators could now begin their work. There were certain imme-

Anson Jones bids farewell to the Republic, in "The Annexation of Texas to the Union,"
painting by Donald M. Yena. Courtesy Texas State Archives.

diate chores to get through, the first of them being the election of a permanent secretary. Those familiar with the long-established way of installing the functionaries of both houses – by a slate agreed on and passed at the beginning of the session as the merest of formalities – would be startled by the hard-fought contests that were common in the first session and many sessions thereafter. Hoyle, the secretary pro tempore, lost to Hamilton P. Bee of Charleston, South Carolina, on the second ballot to break a tie vote. Having barely won the job, Bee resigned shortly to see what the Mexican War could do for his fortunes, leaving the records of the Senate, according to his successor, N. C. Raymond, in such disorder that a day of the Senate journal had to be reprinted from the *Texas Democrat's* account of it. Bee, however, was not utterly lost to Senate history, for after the war he settled in Laredo and was a member of the

J. Pinckney Henderson, first governor of Texas. Reproduced from holdings of Texas State Archives.

House of Representatives from 1849 to 1859, becoming Speaker of the House in the Sixth Legislature. He was one of those so active in the Confederate cause that he found it prudent to live in Mexico for a time. His son Carlos was born there; he would be a senator of considerable distinction from 1915 to 1919, the only one to be born in that country after the Texas Revolution.

N. C. Raymond, the eventual successor of Bee, was elected engrossing and enrolling clerk, also on a second ballot, the two offices combined on a floor motion. Thereafter until the late 1920s there was a clerk for each function. The twenty-five-year-old Raymond was fortunate in his family connections, for his brother, James Hervey, was the first Speaker of the House of Representatives until he resigned to become state treasurer; but whatever influence this implied it did not protect him from the peculiar intensity of these internal races. When he ran for secretary in the Second Legislature, it required six ballots to win over William Cake by one vote.

The senators considered the appointment of a chaplain, but on the motion of Senator Williamson, the question was "indefinitely" postponed. It was a long postponement, and there was in fact to be no regular chaplain of either house until the Fifth Legislature in 1853, following a chaplain crisis in the Senate of the Fourth Legislature.

With these and the other positions filled (sergeant at arms, J. H. Neeley; doorkeeper, Frances Hughes; and assistant secretary, A. W. Luckett), the Senate could proceed in joint session to the election of the first U.S. senators from Texas, who were not elected by popular vote until a federal constitutional change in 1913. Houston and Thomas Jefferson Rusk were the leading candidates, and indeed won, but there were dissenters led by the still-miffed presiding officer, Burleson, who voted for a very minor place-seeker. In the end, Houston had one vote less than Rusk.

Members were quickly assigned to committees, of which there were ten, a large number for a house of only twenty-one senators. The titles suggest the concerns of the times: Judiciary, Military Affairs, Indian Affairs, Internal Improvements, County Boundaries, Privileges and Elections, Claims and Accounts, Printing and Contingent Expenses, and Engrossed and Enrolled Bills.

Later, on a motion of Senator Williams, an eleventh committee was added to the list: the Committee on Education. This was the first manifestation of one of the great themes of special Senate concern, then and to the present day.

N. C. Raymond, engrossing and enrolling clerk in First Legislature, secretary of the Senate in Second Legislature. Courtesy Texas State Archives.

The constitution also required that the senators classify themselves, that is, arrange for staggered terms so that the entire body did not stand for election every two years. To that end, on March 3, eleven slips of paper marked "first class" and ten slips marked "second class" had been placed in a hat and drawn by the senators in alphabetical order. The first-class two-year terms were drawn by Bagby, Brashear, Bourland, Cuney, Grimes, Hogg, McNeel, Miller, Navarro, Robinson, and Williams. The second-class four-year terms went to Burleson, Jewett, Kinney, Mc-Kinney, Parker, Phillips, Scott, Wallace, Williamson, and Wood. The efficacy of this arrangement was perhaps less than intended, for of the short-term senators, one resigned and six were reelected, and of the full-term senators, seven returned, three having resigned for one reason or another.

The Committee on Privileges and Elections soon had work to do, for on February 21 the seat of Brashear was contested by Dr. Cornelius McAnelly on the grounds of irregularities in the conduct of the election. The evidence indicated that McAnelly had the slightly better claim to the seat, but also that the irregularities were pervasive and the actions of the officials so negligent as to place the outcome beyond equity. The committee therefore reported on February 25 a resolution to the effect that the seat be "declared vacant." Senator Navarro, a member of the committee, filed a minority report proposing a new election. Meanwhile, Brashear had been functioning as a particularly energetic senator, and was making friends. On March 3, when the committee resolution came up on the Orders of the Day, Three-Legged Willie rose to move that "declared vacant" be struck and "confirmed" be inserted; the motion carried fourteen to six, and ended the first Senate election contest, firmly if not quite fairly. McAnelly would have to wait until 1853 to join that honorable body.

The Committee on Privileges and Elections also played a pivotal role in a potentially more divisive decision. On February 23, at the beginning of the session, Burleson, president pro tempore, had announced the presence of the Honorable Nicholas H. Darnell, lieutenant governor and president of the senate, who advanced to the podium and made a short speech saying that he was not in fact either of those things. When the votes had been counted, the returns from Fannin County had not been included, and the county being larger then than it is now and relatively populous, there was justifiable concern over the announced results. Mr. Darnell went on to assure the senators that he would not attempt to assume office or challenge the result, and called for a committee to resolve the difficulty.

Senator Navarro then rose to offer a resolution "that the Senate consider this generous and republican act of patriotism as worthy of the highest regard." It was unanimously adopted.

The committee must have had more trouble with this apparently simple affair than the records reflect, for Burleson continued to preside until May 1 when the real lieutenant governor, Albert C. Horton, was at last inaugurated twelve days before the end of the session, with the knowledge that he would immediately have to act as governor, for Henderson was off to invade Mexico. Horton was fortunately a man of tolerable experience; he was a very wealthy cane and cotton planter who had been a senator in his native Alabama and in the first two congresses of the Republic. As a founding member of the Philosophical Society of Texas he presumably had the consolations of that discipline available to steady him through these unsettled times.

A very peculiar bill concerning elections was unfortunately passed by both houses, to an almost immediate outcry by the press. Protests that it would lead to government by inebriates secured its repeal by the Second Legislature. The bill allowed *viva voce* voting in general elections and may have been intended to legitimize a common practice, although not a desirable one. Candidates of the time were expected to provide food and whiskey to enliven the election day, and the confinement of the franchise to those who could still manage to mark a ballot was a real if slight contribution to government by an informed or informable electorate.

Within the legislative arena, the Senate did not hesitate to carry out its unique duty of advice and consent to appointments, making clear that it took this responsibility seriously. Governor Henderson had submitted the name of Volney E. Howard for attorney general, a post he wanted filled at once. Howard, then a member of the House of Representatives, had resigned his seat in expectation of assuming the new position. Howard, who had a history of brash confrontations, having fought duels with two successive governors of Mississippi, may have been personally unpopular, but in any event, a bare majority, eleven to ten, thought his action unconstitutional. Governor Henderson, suitably chastened, dropped the matter for a while and then submitted the name of the jurist who would be a leading influence on the codification of the penal laws in the mid-1850s; John W. Harris was unanimously approved on May 8, so that the first officer to be confirmed was not Howard, as planned, but David G. Burnet, as secretary of state on March 23.

The two houses were then occupied with electing in joint session a long list of officials, including all judges and district attorneys, a stupefying chore that filled many legislative days until an amendment of the constitution in 1850 provided for putting them on the ballot.

Both houses separately had to deal, as well, with a number of matters now long since relegated to the courts: the legitimation of children and the validation of marriages; changes of name; the removal of the disabilities of minority; and the like.

Under the strongly Jacksonian constitution, the legislature also had to charter corporations by a two-thirds vote of both houses, and was severely enjoined from passing bills establishing banking in any form, a requirement that it followed to almost comic excess when it chartered railroad corporations over the next decade and a half. Among the corporations chartered in the cumbersome way laid down by the constitution were two that hoped to build railroads showing that some Texans were aware of the great technological innovation then rapidly changing the northeastern United States. Their efforts came to nothing but were harbingers of a concern that would for good and ill increasingly preoccupy the Senate in the decades to come. As a kind of corollary to the antibanking provisions, the constitution further instructed the Senate to pass — and it did — a bill forbidding private individuals to issue paper money.

But these necessary and time-consuming tasks barely ever rise above the level of housekeeping. Where were the great issues addressed, the major debates, and the bold strokes that would impel the neonatal state's advance among the perils that threatened it then and those quite visible just ahead? There were none. Three factors inhibited decisive action. First, the Mexican War brought into frantic activity all of the high destinarians and opportunists and swept through the state like an epidemic; citizens and elected officials, including the governor, neglected responsibilities and fell to freebooting adventure. Second, controversy stemmed from the conditions that obtained from the manner and matter of annexation itself, whereby a relatively small populated area ruled over a vast if ill-defined area of what were called public lands, the retention of which was a subject of great pride but which were not available for any purpose so long as they were home to an estimated two hundred thousand Indians that the ten-year-old Republic had done nothing to tame. Third and last but far from least, the crushing burden of old debts and negligible income under which all squirmed in a state of helplessness continued to fuel partisan political squabbles.

It was fairly certain that the cash flow problem would grow worse with time. Almost the only source of state funds was the trickle of customs duties; these were a perquisite of the federal government and clearly doomed as soon as Washington gave attention to the fact that Texas was no longer a country. The logical place to look for new money was in the pockets of the landowners, and that was perhaps why there were so many of them in the Senate: to ensure that there would be no bothersome tax on productive land. This meant that, in education for example, the constitutionally mandated permanent school fund was so small as to be useless, a fact painfully brought home, to those who did not know, in an embarrassing speech of the governor to the first special session of a Texas legislature four years later. Senator Williams's Committee on Education could do nothing more than urge the passage of two bills permitting the cities of New Braunfels (then a very new city indeed) and Galveston to levy local taxes for support of free public schools. In every way, Texas was an infant polity reduced to waiting on a distracted federal government.

Not that the senators were idle. They were for the most part models of diligence in attendance; their duties, however small in significance, were often onerous; and the calendar, then called Orders of the Day, was often long. Much time was usefully given to reorganizing the administration of justice, which had lagged behind demographic changes. This was also related to the constant shifts in boundaries occasioned by a fondness for creating or reshaping counties, which would be for many years a favorite recreation of senators. Ten counties were created or reformed in the first session, and one might have been forgiven for supposing that, in those days, senatorial courtesy meant the naming of new counties for each other. The constitution required the legislators to provide for a census to be completed in 1850, and there was quite a debate over the information to be gathered. The much-amended bill passed, as did one exempting from taxation household furniture and goods up to $210 in value, one of the several inheritances from Spanish law still kept in the codes of the state. A bill on escheat was debated at length, occasioning the already mentioned speech by Senator Navarro, whose supposed need for an interpreter was quite possibly a defensive device.

Amid the stresses of a declared war in the neighborhood and rampaging Indians in the front yard, with nothing in the larder and little coming in, the first Senate of the State of Texas adjourned *sine die* on May 13, 1846.

CHAPTER 11

The Senate of the Second Legislature, 1847–48

Although there were nine new sena-
tors and a new lieutenant governor when the Second Legislature convened on December 13, 1847, there was little change in the internal con-
sistency of the Senate and, deplorably, none in the external circumstances
under which it operated. Many of those who did not return probably
chose not to run from motives unrelated to politics. All were, without
known exception, southern states' rights proponents committed to the
preservation and extension of slavery. Nueces County had been created
and was added to the Nineteenth District, in which the tireless oppor-
tunist Kinney had been reelected but immediately resigned to follow the
flag in Mexico. He was replaced by Edward Fitzgerald, an early settler
of Refugio County, who had represented that district in the Fourth Congress, been tax assessor, and practiced law there. Planters like McNeel
doubtless found their one term a costly distraction from the affairs of
their plantations, and went back to them; it was an eye infection, however, that caused William Scott to give up the second half of his four-
year term, only to return later. Scott's Harrison County seat passed to
Edward Clark, of note in 1861 as the pro-Confederate lieutenant governor who took Houston's place and who fled to Mexico with Governor
Pendleton Murrah in 1865. McNeel was replaced by another planter,
Stephen W. Perkins, who came to Texas from Kentucky and had previously served in the House of Representatives during the Ninth Congress and the First Legislature.

Wood and Henderson returned from the Mexican War with conflicting stories about their exploits in the always controversial battles of that
dubious campaign, and took their quarrel into the gubernatorial race.

George T. Wood, governor of Texas, 1847–49. From *The Texas Capitol*, p. 57, courtesy Texas State Archives.

Not himself a candidate, former major general Henderson let it be known that he considered former colonel Wood "a great *dog*." At the commencement of the Second Legislature on December 13 there may have been election returns yet uncounted, but, on December 17, the joint committee appointed to collect the returns made a report to the Senate through its chairman, Senator Perkins, stating that the committee found no additional returns; the report recommended the adoption of a resolution calling for the Speaker of the House to preside over the opening and declaring of the votes cast and to announce the names of the persons who had been elected governor and lieutenant governor to the two houses. The resolution was adopted by the Senate that day, and by the House the next. Wood won the governor's office this time, although it is thought that the same issue, that of his credibility, caused his defeat in two later attempts at the office, the voters having changed their minds about him. Wood's position in the Senate was filled by W. C. Abbott. The lieutenant governor, John A. Greer, president pro tempore of the last four congresses of the Republic, was duly elected and installed without incident.

McKinney, the businessman, did not run for his senatorial position, but did run for a seat in the House; however, the voters allowed him instead to become a gentleman horsebreeder in Manor, near Austin. His Galveston senatorial seat was hotly contested. Among the candidates was Richard Bache, who in earlier life had benefited from the hereditary sinecure of postmaster of Philadelphia established by his grandfather, Benjamin Franklin. But fifty thousand dollars of the funds of that office could not be accounted for, and he abandoned Philadelphia, his wife, and his nine children, surfacing in due time as a Louisiana Volunteer at the Battle of San Jacinto, where he was one of Santa Anna's guards on the night of his capture. Settling in Galveston, he held a succession of government posts of trust and responsibility, including the very important one of collector of customs, and was a justice of the peace when he was elected a delegate to the 1845 Annexation Convention. There he cast the lone vote against annexation, allegedly because he did not wish to enlarge the domain of his brother-in-law, George Dallas, vice-president of the United States. Nevertheless, he is also said to have contributed worthily to drafting the Constitution of 1845.

Bache seems to have been reconciled with at least one of his family, his son, Dr. Alexander Bache, the brilliant cartographer who made the first scientific maps of the Texas coast and who came to live in Galveston during the time when his father was running for the Senate. Once during this campaign, Richard Bache faced a well-informed opponent who neither hesitated to bring up the ugly suspicions of the past nor refrained from mentioning Bache's notorious tippling. Bache was so shocked by the latter insult that he stumbled and fell off the platform, but in the alcoholic climate of Texas in those days, it did him no political harm, and he was elected handily.

Another conspicuous newcomer took the seat of Miller, the obscure Scot. Jon (as he liked to spell it) Winfield Scott Dancy, a South Carolinian of Huguenot ancestry and a leading planter of Fayette County, had been a representative in the Sixth Congress who gloried in his reputation for a bludgeoning verbosity. He loved to tell the story of a boat trip to New Orleans on which he found an unusually receptive listener who never interrupted, did not try to escape, and, although he closed his eyes in thought or possibly rapture, did not snore. The next morning the man was found to be dead. Dancy insisted that he had been alive at the beginning of his harangue and that he, Dancy *qui parle,* had talked him to death. As congressman, he had once assaulted the ears of his fellow members for nine hours on behalf of a scheme of his to annex California, then a part of Mexico, and connect the two discontinuous chunks of empire by a railroad that would have been, in 1841, the first west of the Mississippi and the longest in the world. He said, truly enough, "But I tell you, gentlemen, railroads are the only Key that Texas has to unlock her casket of costly gems." Nine hours of discourse had overstated the case and alienated his audience. Nothing daunted, he tried to win adoption of the metric system, which had been used in France since 1799, and, swollen with pride of ancestry, he slathered his hearers with a mixture of technical terms and supportive quotations in French. At last he yielded the floor, and Gustavus Parker, an Indian trader from Fort Bend County, arose and solemnly addressed the numbed representatives in Choctaw, bringing down the House. In light of these previous performances, one can imagine that when Dancy sought recognition in the Senate, he must have been viewed by his colleagues with alarmed attention.

Hogg was replaced by David Gage, a native Kentuckian who came to Texas at the age of forty-three and settled in Rusk County, where he was a farmer. Before his election to the Senate, Gage had served in the House of Representatives in the Ninth Congress and as a delegate to the Annexation Convention of 1845. The farmer and lawyer Bagby was replaced by the little-known J. B. Wootten, and John McRae took the seat of Robinson, thus completing the makeup of the Senate of the Second Legislature.

The slate of officers for the Second Legislature was completely new, except for Raymond, who returned as secretary of the Senate, a position he had acquired during the previous session with the resignation of Bee. The positions of engrossing clerk and enrolling clerk, which had been combined in the First Legislature, were once again separate offices, with James P. Wallace serving as engrossing clerk and Thomas H. Jones as enrolling clerk. Newcomers to the Senate clerkships were: Thomas Ward, sergeant at arms; R. D. McAnelly, doorkeeper; and James F. Johnson, assistant secretary of the Senate.

One of the first orders of business for the Second Legislature was to elect a senator to represent Texas in the U.S. Congress. On December 15, 1847, the House of Representatives announced that it was organized and ready to proceed, and invited the Senate to meet in Representative Hall that afternoon for that purpose. The Senate accepted. After an address by the outgoing governor, J. Pinckney Henderson, the two houses proceeded to the election. Williamson, on the part of the Senate, nominated Sam Houston. There being no other nomination, and only two votes cast that were not for Houston (Burleson's for Antonio Navarro and Dancy's for James Webb), the Speaker of the House declared Houston duly and constitutionally elected.

The ongoing issues of crime and punishment, adjusting to a new federal system of government, and retiring the debt of the Republic consumed much of the senators' time. Laws were made to raise revenues through *ad valorem* and poll taxes; to create more counties; to organize justice courts and define their jurisdiction; to regulate estrays; and to prohibit tree poaching. The law vesting all escheated property in the state claimed for the sovereign all property of those dying without heirs and of those intestate or absent for seven years and not known to exist.

Problems with race relations continued to fuel debate and provoke questionable legislation. Not passed were bills to prevent the sale of liquor to a slave without the written consent of his master or overseer; to compensate owners for slaves executed as capital offenders (this one was tabled on motion of Dancy); and to confine the invocation of the death penalty against a free white defendant to one crime, that of treason against the state or the United States. Legislation passing the Senate included a resolution by Phillips calling for an inquiry into the propriety of requiring all free Negroes to be removed from the state and an act prohibiting the sale of gunpowder, lead, and alcohol to nontaxpaying Indians. One act concerning slaves amended a law that made a master or overseer "liable to be sued" for abusing a slave and subjected him to a fine of not less than $250 or more than $2,000. The Second Legislature's version, approved on February 14, made the abuser "liable to indictment or presentment, as for a misdemeanor," and imposed a fine, upon conviction, of $20 to $500.

Although Senator Dancy's faith in railroads would have to endure unsatisfied for some years, his desire for the outlying parts of Mexico would receive gratification of a sort almost at once. After General Winfield Scott, to whom the senator owed his middle names, entered Mexico City in triumph on September 14, 1847, the Mexican War was over and, with the American peace negotiator, Nicholas Trist, already on the scene as he had been since March of 1847, treaty arrangements were well under way.

Before final ratification of the Treaty of Guadalupe Hidalgo, however, on January 4, 1848, the Senate considered the report of the Committee on Claims and Accounts regarding the delicate question of relief for citizens whose property was destroyed during the revolution. The committee, through its chairman, Isaac Parker, asserted that if Texas were still sovereign she would surely insist that Mexico provide indemnity for the losses, but, since it was the same war in which the United States was engaged with Mexico and since Texas could no longer negotiate treaties, the United States should so guarantee. Dancy dissented from that part of the committee report, claiming that the first conflict evolved into the latter because Texas waged her war of independence against Mexico, but that Mexico had instigated the present hostilities against the United States.

The debate ended with a joint resolution requesting U.S. congressmen from Texas to protest the relinquishment of captured Mexican land under a peace treaty that did not require Mexico to reimburse the United States for her expenses of war and fully indemnify the nation for the "injuries and aggressions which provoked the war." The resolution also insisted that any territory kept by the United States belonged equally to all of the states, and that any attempt to prevent slaveholding immigrants from bringing their property with them was unconstitutional, "an insult to the southern people, and an outrage upon the sacred rights and privileges, which it is the object of all good governments to protect." The resolution was approved on February 2, the same date on which the peace treaty was signed. Accompanying the resolution to Washington, D.C., was an equally vestigial document, a memorial to His Excellency the President of the United States, which reiterated the position of the committee:

> [Texas, unannexed, would] have been in a position to force from Mexico the acknowledgement of her independence, and to cause to be inserted, a stipulation in the treaty of peace providing for the full indemnity of her injured citizens. She divested herself of all these advantages and rights, when she surrendered her separate existence and became a member of the American Union. And since, so far as Texas is concerned, this may be regarded as the same unfinished war; since during its pendency, her sovereignty . . . has merged in that of the United States. Since the latter has assumed the position of the former in relation to it [the war], surely she should feel the same moral obligation resting upon her, to provide for the remuneration of those injured citizens. . . .

The document, approved on March 20, concluded with a prayer that the president take the memorial into consideration and "cause its object to be carried out by proper provisions in the contemplated treaty with Mexico."

In a bill that originated in the House but was enthusiastically passed by the Senate, the Second Legislature coolly created the County of Santa Fe, authorizing the election of county officers on the first Monday of August and incorporating into the state the enormous territory that stretched almost to Canada. The border followed the boundary defined in the U.S. treaty with Spain and adopted by the First Congress of the Republic on December 19, 1836. The legislators followed through with their efforts to acquire a larger domain by a joint resolution of March 18 declaring Santa Fe an integral territory of the state and instructing the congressional representatives to request that Texas' jurisdiction be extended eastward halfway across the Sabine River, Sabine Pass, and Sabine Lake to thirty-two degrees north latitude and to admonish the U.S. Congress not to lessen the boundaries of the state. On March 20, 1848, a commissioner named Robert S. Neighbors was appointed to assume the governance of the county and to organize it. Because it had also been made the Eleventh Judicial District of Texas, a judge, Spruce Baird, was sent with Neighbors. The session thus closed on a very high note indeed, for the Senate adjourned *sine die* on March 20, the excitement no doubt increased by the dullness of its continuing quotidian duties and the continuing hopelessness of the problems of debt, Indians, and an empty treasury.

Senator Bache, who had turned out to be a diligent but unexceptional legislator, missed these heady events, for he had been felled by a stroke on Congress Avenue in Austin before the County of Santa Fe bill was considered, lingered in a paralytic state for some days, and expired on March 17. He was the first Texas state senator to die in office.

The matter of Santa Fe, meanwhile, aroused the state, or at least its populated portion, which was still not quite half of its full modern extent, from postannexation melancholy, giving the newspapers an opportunity to fill their columns with bellicose writing and providing orators with great and small public meetings to address.

On January 10, 1848, at the first Democratic party state convention, presided over by Governor Wood, Senator Williamson put the issue squarely:

> RESOLVED: That we will as Texans support for the Presidency and Vice-Presidency of the United States such individuals of the Democratic Party as will maintain the Federal Compromise on the subject of slavery, and maintain the establishment of our boundary lines as defined by the laws of the late Republic of Texas.

The juxtaposition of the Missouri Compromise and the Santa Fe question bared an essential consequence of the Texas claim, for as a part of Texas, the new county would be a slave county and represent a victory for the southerners, who looked to overwhelm their opponents by sheer acreage. The Whigs in fact won the presidential election with little help from Texas voters.

Taking into consideration the previous relations of Texas, republic or state, and New Mexico, the convention that met in Santa Fe under the benevolent eyes of the military occupation forces on October 10 with Fr. Antonio José Martinez of Taos as president produced a remarkably mild-mannered, though in no way servile, memorial to Congress anent the ruffles and flourishes in their midst and those growing rapidly louder across the border.

> We, the people of New Mexico, respectfully petition Congress for the speedy organization of a territorial civil government.
>
> We respectfully petition Congress to establish a government purely civil in its character. . . .
>
> We respectfully but firmly protest against the dismemberment of our territory in favor of Texas or from any cause.
>
> We do not desire to have domestic slavery within our borders; and, until

the time shall arrive for admission into the union of states, we desire to be
protected by Congress against the introduction of slaves into the territory.

The adamant decency of expression in this document, which was signed
on October 14, 1848, may have cast its small weight in the balance over
the Texas rant and bluster to determine the final outcome, and so the
Santa Fe lands remained free.

CHAPTER 12

The Senate of the Third Legislature, 1849–50

When Governor George Wood delivered his message to a convening Third Legislature, he handed out an agenda so full that it would keep the senators occupied for a regular session and two called sessions. First, he said that Texas had some housekeeping to do: the state penitentiary had a newly chosen site in Huntsville and was waiting to be constructed; applications by colonists who had once been promised Texas land had to be reviewed; the public school system needed support and maintenance; and Texas needed to come up with a way to protect its citizens from hostile Indians, as the U.S. forces had proved "wholly inadequate."

His speech also foreshadowed the state's resolution of the major issue of the period—what to do about Santa Fe. "The subject of our public debt is one of great importance," he said, insisting that the only way to bail out was if the United States decided to purchase a portion of Texas territory. Although he was referring to a region farther northwest, in the end Santa Fe would be the price Texas would pay for solvency. In his speech Wood noted the state's failure to organize the County of Santa Fe, since the general government there had refused to acknowledge Texas' right to the territory. Regarding the legislature's part in the matter, Wood asked that it confer to him the power "to raise the proper issue and contest it . . . with the whole power and resources of the State." He ended by reminding the legislature of the abolitionists' efforts in Washington, efforts, he said, that had the tendency to "foment and encourage servile insurrection—the conflagration of our homes—the murder of our wives and children."

The Senate began by tending to housekeeping chores of its own. Raymond was reelected secretary of the Senate, and Johnson retained his position as assistant secretary of the Senate. The remaining offices were filled by newcomers: engrossing clerk, John B. Hickey; enrolling clerk, James W. Johnson; sergeant at arms, Gibson Maddox; and doorkeeper, M. B. Irwin. At the end of the balloting, Parker moved that the newly elected officers take the constitutional oath of office, and all but Hickey complied. On the following day Hickey informed the Senate that he could not take the oath of office, and requested that they elect another. William T. Cake, who had lost to Raymond in the hotly contested secretary's race, won on the revote and took the oath as engrossing clerk, completing the slate of officers for the session.

Some new voices would answer roll call in this Third Legislature, reflecting Texas' evolution since the days of the Republic. Two old-timers who would be absent included Three-Legged Willie, who had left the legislature with a final story. It is said that he had fallen into a decline, accelerated by drinking, and was seized by a catalepsy so violent that he could neither talk nor move. Appearing dead, he was declared to be so by a physician summoned to his boardinghouse room. A nurse and carpenter were called in to prepare the body and make a coffin. After the "corpse" had been washed and shrouded, the pair tried to fit Willie into his last resting place. Their struggles with his deformed leg acted as a kind of massage and suddenly broke the rigor. Ripping away the cerecloth, he bellowed in his courtroom roar, "What the hell and damnation are you doing?" He recovered sufficiently to run for the U.S. Congress in 1849 but his name—well known in East Texas—meant little to the now Germanic central counties and nothing to those lining the Rio Grande. After a feeble race for lieutenant governor he retired. He died on December 22, 1859, three days after Lamar, leaving only Houston to represent the mythopoeic period of the Texas frontier.

Navarro also retired. By the convening of the Third Legislature he was devoting his time and energies to matters closer to home—running his law practice, tending his store, and maintaining his extensive ranches. His name came up once in the Third Legislature with Cooke's resolution inviting Navarro to provide the Senate with information on the Santa Fe region. Later he was a delegate to the Secession Convention of 1861, from which he slipped away without voting. But when the Senate met in 1849 it was without a Hispanic member, and it would not have another until the election of Henry B. Gonzalez, also of Bexar County, in 1957. Navarro was succeeded by David C. Vanderlip, a lawyer from

New York who belonged to the incoming generation of Anglos that, together with a torrent of mostly German-born immigrants, was swiftly assuming economic and political leadership in the once solidly Hispanic community.

Among the newcomers to the Senate was Albert H. Latimer, a Tennessee lawyer who arrived in Texas in 1833 and who was to play an important part in the revolution. Latimer attended the Convention of 1836 and there signed the Texas Declaration of Independence. Although he only served one term in the Senate, his influence was a continuing force in the state. He served as state comptroller and associate chief justice of the Supreme Court, and was a delegate to the Constitutional Convention of 1866. Another lawyer joining the Senate was David Y. Portis, who also served just one term but later represented Austin County in the Secession Convention of 1861. Wilds K. Cooke, a doctor and farmer, and John H. Moffitt, a schoolteacher, had both been representatives in the Ninth Congress and would serve in the Senate only for the Third Legislature. Other newcomers to the Senate for the Third Legislature were H. Clay Davis; Hardin Hart; J. F. Taylor; A. M. Truitt, whose father, James Truitt, had been prominent in the days of the Republic and who would serve in the Senate during the Fourth, Sixth, Seventh, and Eleventh state legislatures; and Albert G. Walker, who would not complete his term and would be replaced by Samuel R. Campbell.

A reapportionment bill passed at the last minute of the previous session had laid out twenty-two senatorial districts that had diminished the power of the old eastern and coastal settlements and increased that of the west and north. Even though the bill had originated in the House, the form signed by the governor was almost wholly written in the Senate without House concurrence. A representative of Brazoria County, Elisha M. Pease, published an attack on the constitutionality of the redistricting act. Pease was a Connecticut man whose Texas history began with the first shooting scrape of the revolution; by 1849 he was a partner in a successful law firm. Despite his feelings about the bill, he decided to run in the 1849 race for the Senate seat of the restructured Eleventh District — once Galveston County alone but now incorporating his home county. In response, Democrats in Galveston County nominated another lawyer, John B. Jones, and the ensuing campaign was fought on local rivalries, Galveston against Brazoria.

Predictably, Pease won in Brazoria and Jones in Galveston, but in the total canvass Pease led by seventeen votes. The chief justice of Galveston

County, who tabulated the final ballot count in this Eleventh District battle, rejected the returns from Brazoria on the basis of "informality"— two Brazoria County commissioners, rather than Brazoria's chief justice, had counted and recorded the ballot returns, the chief justice having been out of town at the time. He therefore dismissed the Brazoria election returns altogether and granted the certificate of election to Jones, who took the oath of office with his Senate colleagues on November 5. Pease contested the election by delivering to the president a packet of documents and having Robertson submit a petition on his behalf. The contest was referred to the Committee on Privileges and Elections, which was composed of Senators Gage, Walker, Wallace, Robertson, and Vanderlip. On November 8, a majority of the committee (Gage, Walker, and Wallace) said that they had no hesitation "in declaring that the will of the electors of the 11th district, is plainly and undoubtedly expressed in favor of E. M. Pease." The "informalities" were more "mere omissions of unimportant directory provisions of the election law," according to the committee. Moreover, the committee refused Jones the right to take the seat from a district composed of Galveston County alone, "as the same was not referred to them by the Senate, it was not regarded as before them for consideration."

A minority of the committee presented a counterreport, however, addressing Jones's right to a seat representing Galveston County. The report, written in a somewhat convoluted fashion by the same Robertson who had presented Pease's petition for the Eleventh District seat, declared the Senate's right to recognize Jones as a qualified senator. In order to get Jones his seat, Robertson argued that the Senate could neither judge the election nor qualify its members since the election had occurred prior to the time when the senators had organized. "Most clearly, then," he said, "there had been no rejection of J. B. Jones' credentials by the Senate, nor had their validity ever been questioned even by any Senator in his place up to the time of the reference of the matter to the committee." Portis then presented the petition of Jones accompanied by a certificate of his election as senator from Galveston County that was referred to the Committee on Privileges and Elections.

The majority responded this time with a definitive statement: "The whole number of Senators was fixed by the Legislature and apportioned among the several districts then established by law, according to the number of qualified electors. . . . It has *united* the counties of *Galveston* and *Brazoria*, and of them formed the Senatorial district now represented in the Senate by the Hon. E. M. Pease, under a recent and unequivocal decision of the Senate." The claim of Jones was "indefinitely postponed," they said. The report was voted on by the Senate and passed, settling the matter of the constitutionality of the apportionment bill as well as denying Jones's right to a seat in the Senate that term. Pease stuck to his original stand against the bill, and along with Brashear, Portis, Robertson, and Vanderlip, voted *against* the majority report on November 10. He had, after all, taken his oath of office on November 9.

Pease's committee assignments in the Senate were those already given to Jones: internal improvements, education, and judiciary committees. He sought the chair of the Committee on Internal Improvement because Galveston was interested in incorporating companies planning port and transportation projects. As the representative from Brazoria County, Pease had chaired the Committee on the Judiciary, which drafted the 1848 probate code, a compilation much noted for its retention of Spanish law. Already broken in as a member of that committee, he overwhelmed its titular chairman, the veteran Phillips, by reporting sheaves of bills signed "E. M. PEASE, *One of the Committee.*" Since the public debt kept rearing its ugly head during this Third Legislature, the Committee on Education could do little more than establish manual labor schools. Pease did make a motion in January, 1850, to make provisions for surveying a certain quantity of university land. Later, as governor, he would be remembered for securing a financial base for Texas public schools.

In spite of his active participation in the regular session of the Third Legislature, Pease would miss the extraordinary session called by Governor Bell in August, 1850, and leave for Connecticut to marry his cousin. His colleague from the Eleventh District, Representative Bryan, pleaded with him not to leave. It was, after all, a session called to resolve Texas' shaky relations with the United States over the Santa Fe issue. He said that Pease's political future and the welfare of the state required his "moderate and firm counsel" at a time when "we are I fear on the eve of a civil war." Undeterred, Pease resigned his seat and left to marry his Lucadia.

In February, 1850, the Senate passed a bill directly affecting Pease's Galveston County—an act incorporating the Buffalo Bayou, Brazos and Colorado Railroad Company. The third railroad company to be chartered in the state, its incorporating act contained a clause in dread memory of the Texas Rail Road, Navigation and Banking Company, firmly forbidding it to engage in anything faintly resembling banking. Bills amending the act were passed during successive legislative sessions, with work beginning by the company in late 1852. But the locomotives themselves caused some difficulty. The first to arrive at Galveston "was injured so as to require extensive repairs during the late storm." A second locomotive, "the Texan," was not designed to go around curves and had to be scrapped. Finally, in August, 1853, approximately twenty miles of track between Harrisburg, a town near Houston, and Stafford's Point, the site of a cane mill and cotton gin, were ready to be traveled. By September regular service began, running old Boston horsecars of passengers on Wednesdays and Saturdays. This initial success did not, however, lead to further development of railways in Texas, since the railways could depend only on private money and, with the interminable stretches between settlements, needed government funding.

Several family law bills caught the attention of senators during the Third Legislature. On January 16, 1850, the first piece of legislation in the United States to regulate adoption was passed in Texas. It provided a process for adoption—simply filing an application with the clerk of the county court—and limited the inheritance of the adopted child, where there were legitimate children alive on the death of the adopting parent, to no more than one-fourth of the estate. Because adoption was unknown in English common law, it is probable that the Texas act was based on Spanish law—specifically, the thirteenth-century royal code of Alfonso X the Wise, which restricted the amount of inheritance to one-fifth of the estate.

Vanderlip introduced a bill to prohibit the execution of a mortgage or lien on the homestead by a husband without the consent of his wife. The bill was engrossed on November 29, 1849. Phillips, who chaired the Committee on the Judiciary, put through a bill authorizing clerks of county courts to take the acknowledgment of married women to deeds of property, thus fulfilling the legal requirement that married women be examined apart from their husbands with regard to property actions in which they had an interest. Chairman Phillips also presented to the same committee the petition of executors for a will that emancipated the testator's slaves. The committee pondered over the issue and found that the slaves could be freed, but "because of policy alone" they refused to legislate on the subject. "The only safe plan," they said, is "removing them to free soil territory." The majority rationalized that "the slaves, by their intercourse with those of their own color who are free, are rendered unhappy, discontented and vicious." Latimer and Vanderlip, other members of the committee, produced a counterreport, declaring that it was the testator's wish—upon the feeling of gratitude for past service—that the slaves be freed within the state. They further advised that "such emancipation, by turning them unprotected upon the world, might convert their liberty into a curse instead of a blessing."

When Governor Wood gave his valedictory address in December, 1849, he cited two things that he would be remembered for: his efforts to secure the Santa Fe area of Texas territory and his raising of troops to protect citizens against hostile Indians. The latter he considered to be his greatest accomplishment as, he said, "I should have acted as I did had it exhausted the last dollar [of the state treasury]."

The situation with the Indians had grown worse since Texas had become a state. By 1849 the areas near Corpus Christi and along the Rio Grande were under constant attack. When the U.S. military proved "wholly inadequate," Governor Wood took it upon himself to raise two companies of mounted volunteers. He then asked the legislature for an appropriation and said that it was the duty of the United States to refund the state. A bit riled by the governor's independent action, the Senate replied with a resolution requesting that he identify under what law or authority he had ordered the troops. "This was indicated to me with force and clearness by the common instincts of nature and humanity," he said—not by written code. But now pressed, he continued, citing the sixth article of the constitution, which gave the governor the power to call forth a militia "to repress insurrection and repel invasion."

Wood claimed that the U.S. government had been "addressed directly upon this subject as well as its military officers in immediate command here," but that they had been slow to recognize the necessity of action. The fact that the U.S. infantry and artillery troops were "utterly inadequate or unfit for purposes of protection" was not, however, the fault of the officers or men. Wood further claimed that the troops were an arm of national defense unfit for fighting Indians, as they confronted the enemy while "moving uniformly on horseback and with great clarity"; he suggested that Texas appeal to the patriotism of her own citizens.

The Senate responded this time with the Committee on Indian Affairs urging Congress to remove the Indians from Texas and the Committee on Military Affairs, chaired by General Burleson, presenting an account of $6,114.76 for one hundred mounted volunteers. This money they expected to be refunded by the federal government. Said Burleson:

It is the duty of the General Government to afford protection and security to the inhabitants of all the States, but when, from any cause, it has not been done, the States themselves have, as far as in their power, afforded that protection and the General Government has always admitted the right of the State to demand remuneration, and has invariably liquidated their claims. The evidence is incontestible that the robberies and massacres by hostile bands of Indians have descended upon our South Western frontier.

Burleson—who would be standing in for Lieutenant Governor Greer as presiding officer during the extraordinary session—also had thoughts about the way Texas should protect her citizens. In a report for the Committee on Military Affairs in December, 1849, he said that he was against creating a militia of Texas because "these people would rather volunteer, act on patriotism," than contemplate "the mean paraphernalia and gew gaw show of military exercise."

In his first address to the legislature on December 26, 1849, Governor Bell reiterated the concern of his predecessor: "The frontier of our State must be defended, and I invoke the Legislature to the adoption of such measures as will authorize and require, and enable the Executive, in the event that ample protection is not afforded by the General Government to meet all pressing emergencies (should any unfortunately arise) on the frontiers of the State." He viewed the federal government as the guardian of the Indians as well as the protector of Texas. He continued: "From that day [when Texas became a state], the general management of the numerous Indian tribes, within the limits of the State, was transferred to, and vested in the General Government, and the power to regulate intercourse with them, it was her constitutional right and duty to assume."

In early 1850 the Senate passed a resolution authorizing and instructing its Committee on Indian Affairs to provide statistics on the matter. Kinney, chairman of the committee, reported to the Senate that 204 persons had been "killed, wounded or carried into captivity" within the last year, "besides a great many more which cannot at this time be ascertained by your committee." The committee reported that approximately $103,277 worth of property had been stolen or destroyed by the Indians. These too were safe estimates, and the committee was "fully convinced and satisfied that the losses on our frontier far exceed that herein enumerated."

The committee concluded that the federal government had not "entertained due regard for the lives and property of our citizens," reasoning that the inertia was due to lack of information on the subject. With the documentation prepared by the committee, the Senate announced that it "expected that the general government will no longer delay to place an adequate and efficient force upon our frontier." The Committee on the Judiciary followed with a report on the joint resolution for the removal of Indians beyond the Texas borders. Portis, who made the report as "one of the committee," was blunt: "The Indians must be either removed by the Government of the United States, according to her settled policy, or they must be extinguished by us."

The issue that would take precedence over that of hostile Indians was how to maintain control of the Texas territory that included Santa Fe. As governor, Wood had written messages to President Polk in 1848 and President Taylor in 1849, urging a resolution of the matter. He also sent Judge Baird out to the far western portion of Texas to establish the Eleventh Judicial District, to be composed of the counties of El Paso and Santa Fe. The Senate began the Third Legislature by creating the Special Joint Committee to protest the military government of Santa Fe territory, which had refused to recognize an association with Texas. The Senate requested that Wood transmit to it all previous correspondence between him and the U.S. government and between him and Judge Baird concerning Santa Fe. Senators also passed bills to provide for a "civil organization of counties" in Presidio, El Paso, and Worth, and created a commission on county boundaries to define the boundaries of the "County of Santa Fe."

Then Governor Bell entered the scene. Bell, still fairly fresh from military deeds in the Battle at Buena Vista, came loaded with words and ready for action in settling the Santa Fe dispute:

> [I]f the employment of the necessary force to enable her [Texas] to exercise the right over a refractory population [Santa Fe], should produce a collision with the federal authorities, the fault will not be hers. She will stand exonerated to the judgement of just men, from all the fearful consequences which may result from such a conflict.

He suggested that the legislature send military forces to Santa Fe to enforce Texas' rights over the territory. If the legislature decided against this, "in view of the expenditure," he suggested that the Eleventh Judicial District be altered so that with the addition of other counties the judge could reside in another location "and his services be rendered of some avail to the State."

The legislature responded with a joint resolution demanding that the U.S. government immediately abolish all of its military government within the "Territory of Texas." It also authorized the governor "to employ the whole forces and resources of the state to sustain sovereignty and jurisdiction." The troops would have been volunteers—easy enough to find in this spirited new state—but even they needed guns, ammunition, and food. And the louder the gusts of patriotic rodomontade in the hall of the House and the chamber of the Senate, the more hollow the echoes from the empty coffers in the treasury. Lacking funds, the legislature adjourned *sine die* on February 11, 1850, having done little more than authorize that a commissioner be sent out to Santa Fe to set up the county.

Recognizing the "intrinsic weight of the great question," Governor Bell called an extraordinary session on August 12, 1850. Parker presented a resolution confining Senate business to issues concerning Santa Fe, with a footnote to fireproof the land office to protect the archives of the Republic. Once again, Bell set the tone of the session with a fiery speech supplemented with reports from Major Neighbors, the commissioner the legislature had sent to Santa Fe, and correspondence with various worthies in Washington. As he saw it, "a serious wound was about to be inflicted upon the honor of our State." He began by reviewing the reports from Major Neighbors.

Neighbors had succeeded in El Paso; the people there had welcomed the Texas government and law with open arms. Santa Fe was something else. There the U.S. military commander, Colonel Munroe, snubbed him in public and even called for a convention to form a state government in New Mexico. A federal judge threatened to put him in jail. Governor Bell sent this report to the Texas senators and representatives in the U.S. Congress. He also addressed a letter to President Fillmore with a copy of Munroe's proclamation to form a state government, and asked the president whether he sanctioned Munroe's actions.

Based on this information, Governor Bell saw only one course of action "consistent with honor": "the immediate adoption by your honorable body with perfect unanimity, of such measures as are necessary for the occupation of Santa Fe, with a force ample to quell the arrogant and rebellious spirit now prevailing there, and to enable us to extend and firmly establish the jurisdiction and laws of the State over it. . . ." He requested authorization from the legislature to raise at least two regiments of mounted volunteers for the contemplated move to and occupation of Santa Fe.

In making the recommendation, Bell said that he was "not unmindful of the heavy expenses" that it would involve and the difficulty in raising the funds at a time when Texas was in debt. But the governor had a proposal:

> It may not be improper, in connection with this subject, to remind your honorable body that there is now lying idle and unprofitably in the Treasury the sum of $34,443.00 which has been set apart, in accordance with a provision of the Constitution, as a school fund. It is true that this fund cannot be appropriated to any other object than that for which it was originally designed. But may not its present shape be changed by converting it into one of different and more profitable character for the ultimate attainment of the ends contemplated, without violating any constitutional provision?

Under his plan the school fund would be converted by loan or otherwise into profitable stock-bearing interest. He had suggested this solution during the previous December, but was convinced then that such a conversion was not authorized by the constitution. By now he had arrived at a new interpretation of the constitutional provision and distinguished the value of the school fund—"the essential value of the fund" that could never be applied to another purpose—from the evidences of that value, which he said could be changed or converted into other evidences. "The money now lying idle and profitless in the Treasury, might thus be made auxiliary to the other resources of the State in preparing and fitting out a military expedition, and at the same time the fund would be increased by its employment in this most worthy manner," he concluded.

Next Bell mentioned the Compromise Bill then under consideration in the U.S. Senate. The bill proposed to establish a government for New Mexico, with a boundary extending south to the thirty-second parallel of north latitude and east to the one-hundredth parallel of west longitude, "striking off thereby, unceremoniously, nearly one third of the [Texas] territory." Bell continued:

> This plan is accompanied with a proposition to Texas to give her [blank] dollars for a relinquishment of her claim, or in plainer language, to give her [blank] dollars, provided she will quietly stand aloof, and permit a

In the Compromise of 1850 Texas received $10 million for relinquishing claims to lands to the west and north. Courtesy *Texas Highways* magazine.

party in Congress known to be adverse to certain institutions of the south, and seeking every opportunity to assail them, to partition her territory in a manner consonant with their views to afford them another means of carrying out their favorite policy on that subject.

That "certain institution" Bell feared would be abolished if Texas gave in and helped to create another nonslaveholding state. He pleaded with Senate members not to abandon sister states in the South for monetary gain, and suggested that they consider a proposition to sell only that portion of territory lying north of the thirty-fourth degree of north latitude, with a "sufficient guarantee that the provisions of the Joint Resolutions for annexation in respect to slavery should be observed."

Without undue haste, the Senate prepared and passed what came to be called the "War Bill"—a bill to "organize a militia of the state and to suppress the insurrection existing in the counties of Worth and Santa Fe"—and sent it to the House. The Senate version authorized the governor to call into service three thousand mounted volunteers, "or any less number he deems requisite." (An additional section authorized the governor to call into service additional men.) The volunteers would be furnished with horses, mules, necessary arms and equipments, and a pack mule for every four men, and would be committed to a tour of duty for a length of time that the governor would direct, which was not to exceed twelve months. The regiments of ten companies each, one hundred men in each company, would be regulated by the rules of the late Republic of Texas. The volunteers would get the same pay as mounted volunteers in the U.S. Army, and would not be taxed by the state or county while serving in Santa Fe and Worth. The governor would deliver a proclamation to elect military officers and appoint a quartermaster and commissary of subsistence, each of whom "shall give bond and security for faithful performance of duties of office and shall order necessary subsistence and supplies."

While the House put the War Bill through its wringer, the Senate proceeded to pass a considerable amount of legislation to support the bill. Vanderlip presented a resolution for the Committee on Finance to inquire into selling state property in Austin—approximately five hundred acres of land—to raise funds for the militia. These proceeds, together with receipts from direct taxation, were to be applied to military funding. Another bill, defining treason, was passed. Slipped in was Robertson's proposition that the United States—"in order to settle the public debt and to promote peace and harmony of the union"—offer to sell a portion of Texas territory for $10 million.

Eventually the War Bill came back from the House, much amended. Senator Wallace, once a virulent advocate of the Texas claims, moved to postpone consideration of it for another day. The motion failed to carry, and the bill came up for final passage. There were nine yeas and nine nays when the alphabet led inevitably to Wallace and Ward. Ward, senator from the First District, was a sure yea. There was a moment of apprehensive expectation, and then Wallace announced his nay vote. This meant a ten-to-ten tie, unbreakable because the lieutenant governor was absent and President Pro Tempore Burleson, who had voted yea, was in the chair.

This first special session thus did not permit the governor to lead a Texas militia to fight to get Santa Fe. The legislature adjourned until November, when they could review the articles of the Boundary Act, which the U.S. Congress had passed on September 9. Before the session had ended, however, on September 4 Bell had sent back to the Senate *unsigned* a bill commanding him to submit the U.S. proposition to the voters of Texas. During the second special session, however, he would say that acceptance of the proposition by the State could be manifested only by an act of its legislature, but that he wanted a vote by Texas citizens. A popular referendum was indeed held, although apparently in a somewhat informal manner. The vote found in favor of the federal proposition that the United States pay Texas $10 million in stock bearing 5 percent interest redeemable in fourteen years in consideration of her relinquishment of territory. A later tally showed that three-fourths of the people had approved.

Lieutenant Governor Greer was back for the Senate's second special session, which began on November 18, 1850. A resolution to limit Senate business to issues in connection with the U.S. proposition was laid on the table. Other petitions continued to be introduced: those involving private land claims, bills of relief, and a bill to make plans to hire an architect for fireproofing the land office. By November 20 a bill to accept the U.S. proposition was read for the first time. On November 21 the Senate suspended the rule requiring bills to be read on three several days, and then passed the following:

A bill accepting the proposition made by the United States to the State of Texas, in an act of Congress of the United States, approved on the

9th day of September, A.D. 1850, and entitled "An act proposing to the State of Texas the establishment of her North and West boundaries the relinquishment by the said State of all territory claimed by her exterior to said boundaries, and of all her claims upon the United States, and to establish a Territorial Government for New Mexico."

So there was never a senator from Santa Fe and Worth counties, although a modern handbook lists one, and Judge Baird never held court in the Eleventh Judicial District of Texas. He instead became the first attorney general for the State of New Mexico. The northwestern boundaries of Texas appeared to be fixed, although conflicting surveys clouded title to at least five hundred thousand acres still claimed by New Mexico in its first state constitution. (The land was later awarded to Texas by President Taft for reasons of expediency.) By the end of the Third Legislature there was $10 million, with interest, to the credit of the state in the federal treasury, the first real money it had ever earned.

CHAPTER 13

The Senate of the Fourth Legislature, 1851–53

Adding new counties and shifting the boundaries of old ones yielded twenty-six senatorial districts in 1851, but they were poorly balanced. The census figures available for that year clearly necessitated a complete redistricting of the state as now defined by the Compromise of 1850, for they showed a sharp rise in population, nearly double that of 1845, which was almost entirely from immigration, much of that from Central Europe. Bexar, once a monster in size and shape, had shrunk to a relatively populous county of approximately its modern dimensions, the middle but no longer necessarily the dominant county of three making up the Twenty-Second District, along with Comal, the heart of the vigorous and expanding German community, and Medina, the older Castro Colony of Alemanic-speaking Alsatians, to the southwest.

The Twenty-Sixth District, a by-product of the County of Santa Fe episode, encompassed El Paso County and, officially, Presidio County. The latter, however, had not proved as amenable to organization as the former, and it is unlikely that senatorial elections were held there for some time to come. The senator for the district, Rufus Doane, is the only one in the annals of the Senate whose occupation was given as "mechanic," whatever that may have meant in 1851; in the census of 1860 he was called a farmer. From Massachusetts, he had lived in Chihuahua and was sufficiently acculturated to have a daughter named Estefanía born in Mexico in 1844. By 1850 he was the sheriff of El Paso County. The voters there must have had a predilection for men who could combine public office with the trappings of humble employment, for his successor in 1857, Archibald Hyde, who was county judge in 1850, was an assistant mule driver.

The mechanical Senator Doane probably raised some eyebrows among the planter gentry when the Fourth Legislature convened on November 3, 1851. However, lifetime farmer Joseph H. Burks surely felt at home in this his first session and indeed would return to the Senate for the Fifth Legislature. Experienced lawmaker and negotiator James Truitt joined the Senate after having served in the House in the Eighth and Ninth congresses and the First and Second legislatures. He continued to serve the people of East Texas as senator during the Fifth, Sixth, and Eleventh legislatures. William M. Williams and the ebullient Jon Dancy were back after an absence of one session, and William Scott returned after being absent for two. Burleson, Grimes, and Parker continued their uninterrupted tenure, and Kinney was there, as well as an engineer, William S. Day, who, harbinger of the economic future, was about to go into the cattle business, but would eventually die as the result of a stampede. Two new senators, Stephen Reaves and Peter W. Gray, were prominent lawyers who commanded great respect. Reaves was born in Georgia and came to Tyler in 1846, quickly establishing himself and winning the confidence of area residents. During his one term in the Senate, he was offered a position on the Supreme Court by Governor Bell, but refused in order to remain in the Senate and complete his term of office. Gray, born in Virginia in 1819, followed his father to Texas, arriving at his father's Houston law office in 1838. A man of diverse abilities and interests, Gray was at times an Indian fighter, military officer, judge, politician, district attorney, and successful lawyer. He was deeply concerned with education and was one of the founders of the Texas Literary Institute, which was dedicated to the promotion of education in Texas. Although he too served in the Senate only one term, Adolphus Sterne brought with him a long history of service to Texas. A delegate to the 1833 convention and an agent in the provisional government during the revolution, he was postmaster at Nacogdoches during the Republic, fought in the Cherokee War and the Battle of the Neches, and was a member of the House in the Second and Third legislatures. Other newcomers to the Senate included James Armstrong, Israel B. Bigelow, Z. Williams Eddy, and Frank H. Merriman. There was a large number of doctors in the legislature—twenty-two, according to Travis County annalist Brown, with at least two of these in the Senate, to be joined by a third toward the close of the session. One, Senator George W. Hill, had been secretary of war and the navy during the presidencies of Houston and Jones. The second deserves notice for his extraordinarily long devotion to the legislative idea. Senator Marion Dekalb Taylor had already served in the Alabama legislature when he came to Texas in 1847 and settled in Cass County. (Named for a U.S. senator from Michigan, this county had been carved from Bowie County in 1846. Cass County would be Davis County from 1861 to 1871, in honor of Jefferson Davis, but would then revert to Cass and remain that to the present, or rather in that part of Cass County that was not designated Marion County in 1860.) Taylor was a representative from his county in the Third Legislature, and for the next twenty-four years was in one house or the other, being twice Speaker of the House of Representatives.

A colleague of Taylor's in the third House and the fourth Senate was James C. Wilson, a lawyer and itinerant Methodist preacher, amateur it is to be supposed for otherwise he would fall under the constitutional ban on elected men of the gospel. Wilson brought with him to the dog-trot frame Capitol fading memories of a city whispering from her towers the last enchantments of the Middle Ages, for sometime after his birth in Yorkshire and before his emigration in 1837, he attended Oxford, the first senator to have done so.

All titles were diminished, however, by the arrival of a genuine German baron. Otfried Hans, Freiherr von Meusebach — in 1851 Senator John O. Meusebach of New Braunfels — was altogether different in history and interests from the earlier German immigrants, and so were the people he represented. Of a family rich both in ancestry and attainments, his very broad education and considerable governmental experience were severely tested when he accepted the position of commissioner-general of the Adelsverein, Prince Karl von Solms-Braunfels's society of noble immigrants and their often highly educated and idealist colonists. He plunged at once into relief measures for the nearly eight thousand *Auswanderer* who had been left in the lurch by the prince. He brought many from the miseries of an impoverished camp at Indianola to their promised land north of San Antonio, supervised the development of New Braunfels, and founded Fredericksburg and a host of other communities in what rapidly developed into a German corridor in Central Texas. Despite the hardships of the fresh start, the colonists had scarcely picked their first crop of black-eyed peas when they petitioned the legislature for permission to tax themselves to support free public schools. During that same year, in 1847, they had already drawn the favorable attention of Governor Wood, who recommended that the laws be printed in German as well as English and Spanish.

In an episode unthinkable for his Senate contemporaries, Senator Meusebach joined forty utopian socialists, including Gustavus Schleicher, senator in the Eighth Legislature, to found Bettina, an agrarian collective. The collective soon failed, and Meusebach returned to cope with a swelling inundation of refugees from the European eruptions of 1848. The refugees were aristocrats, intellectuals (radical and otherwise), well-educated bourgeois, and dirt farmers. Some were absorbed into the barely established agricultural life; others contributed to and quickly dominated the second phase of the Germanic extrusion into the commercial, professional, and cultural life of, first, San Antonio, and a little later Austin and Houston.

Senator Meusebach, however, served quietly in a Senate not notable for brilliant accomplishments and still marked by the declining power of the planters, led by men like Burleson, Grimes, and Parker. Concerned chiefly with attempts to secure the effective financing of public education, better Indian relations, and the mare's nest of German land claims, his mere presence indicated a new force to be reckoned with, and so in another way did that of Senator Doane, the mechanic of the far, far west.

In March of 1850, as the constitution directed, an election was held to fix the seat of government for the next twenty years, or, as it turned out, twenty-two years. Austin sent an old settler of just-organized El Paso County to the area to plead its case, and the El Paso vote proved decisive. With money in the treasury for the first time as a result of the Santa Fe Compromise, one of the legislators' first thoughts was to make the capital more worthy of the honor and dignity of the State of Texas. Plans were drawn, contractors seemed to spring from the earth, and a modest beginning was made with a stone General Land Office building on a site now covered by the present Capitol. With the prospect in immediate view of meeting in its cramped frame predecessor, Texas' legislators dreamt that they dwelt in marble halls, and set out to reify those visions with such success that they reached the stage of electing the supervisory personnel in joint session three days before the adjournment of the Fourth Legislature, on February 13, 1852. On March 8 the first spades cut the earth, and the cornerstone was dedicated with Masonic ceremonies on July 4.

The Senate started its work on November 3, 1851, with President

Sen. John O. Meusebach negotiating treaty with twenty Comanche chiefs, March 2, 1847. From painting by Mrs. Ernest Marschall, reproduced from holdings of Texas State Archives.

James W. (Smoky) Henderson in the chair, and soon got to the election of its officials. The race for secretary of the Senate would appear to have been a polite war between Burleson and Grimes, for although others made nominations, Raymond, who held the office in the Third Legislature and was Burleson's man, and W. D. Miller, Grimes's man, led through three ballots, the issue being decided in a fourth ballot, which was won by Miller by one vote. Johnson, who had been temporarily replaced in a special session of the Third Legislature by Bird Holland, was returned without opposition to his position as assistant secretary of the Senate. It took eight ballots to elect Nathan Mitchell engrossing clerk, two for Lewis G. Clapton to become enrolling clerk, and two for Lewis Wells to become sergeant at arms; a large field was outdistanced by Miller, Grimes's man, Burleson having temporarily retired from the fray. After four ballots Joseph Mangum was elected doorkeeper.

Senator Grimes then moved that Secretary Miller be "instructed to cause a copy of Hartley's Digest, and the Journals of the Senate, to be furnished to each Senator." Visitors to Austin during this period frequently remarked on the paucity of the resources of the law library. Even the library of the Supreme Court was meager, and *A Digest of the Laws of Texas*, compiled in 1849 and published (in Philadelphia) by Oliver Cromwell Hartley, a Galveston lawyer, must have been very welcome; it offered for the first time not only the statutes of the state, annotated, but much else besides in one volume. It is easy to forget that lawmakers then worked without offices, secretaries, unless they had private ones, or any of the research facilities that are now routinely provided.

At the same meeting, Senator Burleson offered a resolution, which was accepted, "that the Senate will go into an election for Chaplain on Wednesday, the 5th inst." On that day, a "resolution relative to the election of Chaplain [was] read and adopted" by a vote of fourteen to ten, suggestion enough of trouble to come, with Burleson on the affirmative side and Grimes on the negative. Unfortunately, resolutions of this kind, affecting only one house, are not preserved in the records, but from the further proceedings in the *Senate Journal*, certain inferences can be drawn.

The next day, after the uncontested election of the Senate reporter, on motion of Mr. Burleson, the previous day's vote adopting the resolution to elect a chaplain was reconsidered. However, Senator Dancy offered a substitute: "*Resolved*, that the ministers of the different religious denominations, be requested to make arrangements to give us morning prayers in the Senate, and that the pay for Chaplain be equally divided amongst those ministers who may perform the service." This was rejected by a vote of fourteen to ten, with Grimes voting for and Burleson against it.

Burleson then nominated the Reverend William A. Smith; Sterne, the Reverend A. J. McGowan; Dancy, the Reverend J. H. Ainsworth; Day, the Reverend Thomas Wooldridge; Merriman, the Reverend Edward Fontaine; and Davis, the Reverend G. G. Baggerley.

On Sunday, November 2, Senator Sterne had recorded in his diary, "rd an other letter from A.J.M.g. who wants to be chaplain of the Senate — no go." Archie P. McDonald, editor of *Hurrah for Texas! The Diary of Adolphus Sterne, 1838–1851* (Waco: Texian Press, 1969), expands the *g* to *Gowan*, and assuming that the Senate journal is correct, this is the McGowan that Sterne loyally, although not hopefully, nominated. That it was at least a second letter and that Sterne already knew there was "no go" suggest that a campaign, with lobbying, had been going on for some time. The senator, who does not seem to have had a doctrinal commitment and on occasion attended Catholic mass, twice in the same period of his Austin residence mentions Fontaine: he "went to church (the Episcopal) heard a very exelent Sermon by the revd Mr. Fontain [*sic*]," and "went to church, and heard a splendid discourse on Education by the revd Mr. Fountain [*sic*]." But there would be no go for Fontaine, either.

The Reverend Mr. Smith led the first ballot, but without a majority, and Senator Day withdrew his candidate. A second ballot gained the leader, Smith, one vote, which may have been that of Day, but still no victory, and the Senate adjourned until three o'clock.

At the appointed hour, Senator Sterne successfully moved that "the vote which carried the motion to go into the election of Chaplain" be reconsidered, and Senator Bogart moved "to reconsider the vote which adopted the resolution that the Senate should elect a Chaplain." The motion carried by seventeen to seven, with Grimes on the winning and Burleson on the losing side.

Doggedly, Senator Dancy then offered a more precisely worded version of his substitute: "*Resolved,* That the Pastors of the different Religious denominations residing in the City of Austin be requested to make arrangements to give the Senate morning prayers, during the present session, and that the pay for Chaplain be equally divided amongst those Ministers who perform the services." This time the resolution was adopted. The old Oxonian, Senator Wilson, then moved "to lay the resolution on the table until the 4th July next," a standard ploy to indicate displeasure with the whole subject; the motion failed, as such motions usually did, but not by much, thirteen to ten, Grimes voting yea and Burleson nay.

A further diversionary motion to lay the resolution on the table without date also lost, and a vote was taken on the resolution as substituted, which was adopted by thirteen to eleven, with Burleson for and Grimes against, a reversal of their positions on the first version of Dancy's substitute. This might be thought to be a modest triumph for ecumenism and the end of the matter, but the ministers hadn't been heard from.

When the Senate assembled on the following Tuesday, November 11, with no morning prayer, communications from three of the candidates for chaplain were read, refusing the position. References in one letter to "a large part of the Senate . . . opposed to having any Chaplain" might be explained by a sensitivity of the eleven senators voting against the chaplaincy to the constitutional mandates that no "minister of the Gospel, or priest of any denomination whatever" shall be eligible for the legislature and that "no preference shall ever be given by law to any religious societies or mode of worship." Yet there is certainly the possibility that Senator Sterne's "no go" had to do with the chances of any chaplain being elected, rather than the candidacy of the Reverend Mr. McGowan. In any case, Senator Wilson was there to move that the communications be laid on the table.

On November 12, another letter was received:

To the Honorable the Senate of Texas:

In compliance with the request annexed to the resolution passed by your Honorable Body, on the 6th inst., a copy of which was placed in my hands by your Secretary, I have notified the several ministers included in that resolution. We have not been able, however, to hold a general meeting, and I can only reply for myself.

Believing that the office of Chaplain ought to be filled, and that the resolution of the Senate, to divide the duties between the several Pastors, to be right, and feeling the weight of the command, "first of all things, to offer up prayers for those who are in authority, and for rulers," I have the honor to accept your kind invitation, and hope others may also accept. I am therefore prepared to enter upon the duties of the office, or to co-operate with any one, or all of the ministers included.

I have the honor to be yours, with profound respect,

G. G. BAGGERLY [sic].

Baggerley, who was called "reverend" by his sponsor, Senator James Davis, in the abortive balloting on the "6th inst.," does not sign himself so and is at some pains to at once suggest that he must be, without quite saying that he is. In the only available history of Texas Baptists that discusses him, he is carefully called an "elder," which would mean that he was an active layman rather than an ordained minister; the same history indicates that he was at the time of the letter conducting a "female school" in Austin with some interest in a similar school in Tyler, in his sponsor's district. He is described as aggressive and severe, and was so much so in a controversy over the governance of the Tyler school that he brought about a complete change in the statewide organization of Baptists, apparently in an effort to put a spoke in his wheel. In 1853, he became "pastor" of the First Baptist Church of Tyler for three years, which would not necessarily mean that he had been ordained, for that church was founded and probably run by elders in its early years. At any rate he did not, like the other three letter writers, claim a cure of souls in Austin.

His offer was taken up at once, and the next day the session opened with a prayer by the "Rev. Mr. Baggerley," as did those working days that followed, including November 17, when yet another communication was read into the record:

> To the Senate of the State of Texas, now in session:
>
> GENTLEMEN: At the suggestion of the Rev. Mr. Baggerly [*sic*], who has accepted of the appointment to serve you as chaplain, and at the request of some of my friends in your body, I have reconsidered my decision, and have concluded to take a part in the performance of the duties of chaplain to your branch of the State Legislature.
>
> Respectfully,
W. A. Smith.
of Meth. Church.
Austin City, Texas, Nov. 15, 1851.

The letter is dated the day after Baggerley's debut in the Senate chamber. Thereafter, to the end of the session, the two alternated irregularly in the role of chaplain, except on a few days when no prayer was given, the other ministers still refusing, it would seem, to compromise. The Reverend Mr. Smith would have to wait until the Ninth Legislature (Confederate) to become the only chaplain of the Senate, winning a race with, among others, the Reverend Mr. Baker, one of the recusants of 1851. The idea of having prayers led by different ministers each day would not be put into real effect until the Sixty-Third through Sixty-Fifth legislatures.

The problem of their spiritual needs having found an ad hoc solution, the Fourth Senate took up again the already noticed theme of improved housing for government. Together with plans for a grand new Capitol, it passed a bill that pointed out that "many of the counties of the State are in debt and in want of Courthouses, Jails, Jury Fund, et cetera," and provided for their relief by appropriating nine-tenths of the state tax to them for two years (a relatively small sum, although enough to build mortgages on). State taxes were Texas' only source of self-produced revenue now that the federal government, under the Compromise of 1850, had taken over the collection of the customs duties, in partial payment of certain state debts, that were formerly its principal income. The Senate could not appropriate the remaining one-tenth because the constitution required that it be dedicated to education.

Before any building could take place, however, the money had to be secured. To that end, a Senate bill was passed on December 17 authorizing the comptroller of public accounts, encouraged by the receipt of $1,000 for expenses, to proceed to Washington and there take delivery of $5 million, with interest, in bonds from the U.S. Treasury. This was done, and the Senate passed and the House approved a bill setting $1 million of the bonds for sale. The other $5 million due under the agreement was to be held in the treasury until the creditors of Republic and state were satisfied and gave a release, an arrangement that, although properly ratified before, was already giving rise to ominous murmurings about impugning the honor of Texas.

Establishing the amount of public debt and the validity of claims were subjects of bills in this and subsequent legislatures, while friction continued over the money in escrow. What particularly irritated the Texans was the thought that the federal government would eventually decide who got what; they were also embarrassed by having the payments made by officials of the U.S. Treasury, who were beyond their control, rather than those of the state.

While considering these sticky problems, the Fourth Legislature passed an extravagant number of special bills dealing with individuals, corporations, and the like, and not with the whole state. Among these were ten acts incorporating new railroad companies and five amendments or supplements to previous acts. One of the companies was to bring the iron horse to the Rio Grande Valley; and three others had ambitions to reach El Paso and beyond. The tireless voice of Dancy crying in the wilderness of 1841 had at last been joined by a swelling chorus of hope and praise for the railroad, a chorus that achieved a resonant *mezzo forte* and was still led by Dancy, who was now chairman of the Committee on Internal Improvements. Dancy had learned to concentrate his fire, and spoke much more briefly but as strongly for a state-built and state-owned system, but there ran headlong into the old Jacksonian bias against government enterprise and of course into the teeth and claws of rising, largely northern, investment capitalism.

Some remained unconvinced, namely those who had great hopes of at least putting off the triumph of the railroad by improving the navigability of rivers and building canals; this was highly desirable in any event, and legislation to this effect was indeed passed. These proponents of river travel were mostly from East Texas, for obvious topographical reasons, and were perhaps to some degree motivated by a wish to avoid the certain battles over state-versus-private ownership and the tremendous alienation of public lands that either type of ownership would involve. Despite the fact that not a foot of track had been laid by the day of adjournment *sine die*, it is arguably true to say that in this session and in the Senate particularly, the railroad passion took firm hold of both the legislative and the executive mind, and would only increase from this point, however meager the actual result. The Senate had already reached the point where it was as important to curb the excesses of its enthusiasm as to rouse it from apathy, and one member of Dancy's committee proposed, unsuccessfully, the immediate sale of the coastal islands, the proceeds to be used for financing railroads.

The pressure of all of those special bills and a continuing debate over the debts of the Republic kept the Senate at work on Christmas Eve. Senator Dancy proposed adjournment until the following Monday, but his motion was ruled out of order. Senator Dancy appealed the ruling; the members sustained the chair, and then adjourned until ten o'clock on December 26.

At the appointed hour, after a prayer by the Reverend Mr. Smith, who was on duty during this period, Senator Grimes arose to announce that President Pro Tempore Burleson had died at "20 minutes past seven o'clock." Burleson does not seem to have been in conspicuously poor health before, and all indications are that the news was a shock, but two senators were able to produce instantly speeches of some finish. The fact that the first was Senator Wilson, the itinerant Methodist preacher, who clearly drew on his stock of funerary sermons, and the other was Senator Dancy, diminished the remarkableness of the performance somewhat.

After saying, mysteriously, that the request that he speak came from a "quarter which leaves me no option in the matter," Wilson went on to a review of Burleson's career, saying that "from the date of his arrival in Texas to this the hour of his death, the history of Edward Burleson is the history of Texas"; he later lapsed into the stagy tropes then popular:

> The eye which never quailed before a foe in his ire, nor looked coldly upon a friend in his distress, is set and glassy in death! The honest, manly heart that never throbbed with an ignoble emotion, is now but a clod of the field! The icy finger of the king of terrors has touched the source of life, and the warrior's pulses have ceased to play! He is gone from among us! The old Texian—the patriot—the hero—is no more! No more shall his voice be heard in this chamber, nor his quiet, kindly smile greet our eyes when we turn towards his vacant chair!

Senator Dancy began by saying, delightfully:

> It is unnecessary for me to add anything to what has been so truly and eloquently said of the deceased by the member from Matagorda. Repre-

Sen. Edward Burleson. Courtesy Texas State Archives.

senting, as I do, a district in which General Burleson spent most of the last twenty years of his life, a district in which more of his relatives now reside than in any other in the State, I feel that I would be doing injustice to myself and those whom I represent, if I were to remain silent on the present occasion.

The remainder of his "unnecessary" speech is a decorous and warm expression of appropriate sentiments. On a motion of Senator Scott, one thousand copies of these remarks were printed.

Ten senators, led by Wilson, were appointed to a committee to make arrangements for the funeral and interment, which Senator Grimes had spoken of as planned for the "city burying-ground"; Senator Thomas H. Duggan, however, had the felicitous idea of moving that the committee be "instructed to select a suitable place for a State Burying-ground." On December 27, a cooperating committee of the House, with the agreement of the senators, chose for that purpose Lot 5, Division B, a property belonging to Andrew J. Hamilton, the representative from Travis County and chairman of the House committee. Burleson lies there today surrounded by many of the illustrious dead of Texas. In February of 1854, the Fifth Legislature by joint resolution appropriated one thousand dollars to build Burleson a tomb and authorized the comptroller of public accounts to reimburse Hamilton by making over to him equivalent state land in Austin.

The funeral was quite elaborate and was attended by members of the legislature, the judiciary, the executive, the military, city officials, soldiers of the Republic, and the mourning citizenry. The solemn procession started from the house of Raymond, former secretary of the Senate and recent unsuccessful candidate for the same position, for that was where Burleson had died. The chaplain was probably Smith, who merely gave an opening prayer, but the principal clergyman seems to have been Fontaine, grand chaplain of the Grand Lodge of Texas; he is the one who had been admired by Senator Sterne, who delivered a graveside address as part of the Masonic rite. The orator was Guy M. Bryan, then in his third term as representative from Brazoria County. Bryan was soon to be senator from the Twenty-Fourth District; the peroration of his "Eulogium" bore a noticeable resemblance to the extempore efforts of Senator Wilson.

On December 30, the temporary presiding officer of the First Senate, Senator Grimes, was unanimously elected to succeed Burleson as president pro tempore, and on January 12, 1852, it was announced that Dr. John S. Ford had been duly elected to fill Grimes's seat for the remainder of the term. In the brief time remaining in the session, Ford could not be expected to be conspicuous, but he was well known before and after this as the editor of the *Texas Democrat* and other newspapers and as a military man in all the available wars, ending with the notorious Battle of Palmito Ranch near Brownsville, where he commanded the Cavalry of the West, which he had founded. The cavalry was not a part of the Confederate Army, but it fought the last engagement on behalf of the Confederacy under Colonel Rip (for Rest in Peace) Ford more than a month after General Lee's surrender. He would be a senator again in the Fifteenth and Sixteenth legislatures.

In February, a portrait of Burleson was hung over the chair in which he had presided so long. The Senate had commissioned it from T. Flintoff, an artist working in Texas; Flintoff would receive the first prize for fine arts at Senator Kinney's lavish Lone Star State Fair in Corpus Christi later that year. As it was ordered after Burleson's death, the Flintoff picture may have been painted from a photograph, as was the one by Freeman Thorp of Chicago. The Thorp portrait now hangs in the hall of the House to the right of the podium, the Flintoff painting having perished in the Capitol fire of 1881.

With the last farewells said to Burleson, the torrent of special bills flowed faster as time narrowed before adjournment. One bill that did not make it all the way would have given one-third of a league of land each to former senator Robert Wilson and Senator Sterne for services rendered during the revolution. Sterne had indeed almost gotten himself shot by the Mexican authorities for sundry acts of gunrunning and the like until he was rescued by his Masonic fraternity brethren, but the bill may have been thought unsuitable, and, although engrossed by the Senate, did not return from the House.

Senate Bill 120, which had the same fortune, touched a still lively nerve, for it would have required tax assessors and collectors to conduct a census of those eligible, by virtue of their age and other factors, for military duty. This bill was probably not a prelude to a draft, which was not in use in this country until the federal Militia Act of 1862; rather, the census would have served as a survey of available manpower for volunteers to fight Indians.

After annexation, Indian control was the responsibility of the federal government under the secretary of war and a matter of some moment

Sen. John S. Ford, elected to fill Senator Grimes's unexpired term in 1852. Courtesy Texas State Archives.

to the federal treasury as well, for Texans could lay claim to compensation for losses sustained through Indian depredations, claims difficult to investigate or adjudge; such claims were in fact made with increasing frequency. During the Mexican War, few troops were available for this purpose, and the Indians took full advantage of the hiatus in law enforcement, but once the war was over, with considerable dispatch a line of forts was built and staffed. The U.S. Department of War felt that the protection they afforded was adequate, but many Texans did not agree, and the aggressive Governor Bell, who clearly loved a slanging match with those people in Washington, D.C., would be their spokesman in the coming extraordinary (now referred to as special) session.

A Senate bill that passed and was signed by the governor on the last day of the regular session is of interest. It was the first attempt under statehood to deal with a subject that had once set off a skirmish known as the Archive War, in which a sometime Austin innkeeper, Angelina Belle Eberly, had won a certain celebrity by firing a cannon at the Texas Rangers who had been sent by President Houston to remove the government documents to Washington-on-the-Brazos when the capital was temporarily moved there during a Mexican invasion in 1842. The intensity of the former furor was chiefly caused by the existence of a large body of records relating to landownership, which was of passionate interest to Texans. While the laws passed by the legislatures indeed dealt with land more often than not, the election of 1850 had firmly established the capital at Austin for at least the next twenty years.

Houston had long been at Washington-on-the-Potomac, and Mrs. Eberly had moved to Indianola in 1849, so "An Act concerning the Archives of the Legislature" raised no hackles. It required

that it shall be the duty of the present Secretary of the Senate, and Chief Clerk of the House of Representatives to carefully arrange, and file the entire archives of the Congress of the late Republic of Texas and of the State Legislature, and place the same under proper labels, in a safe and convenient receptacle to be provided for the purpose; and also, to record in suitable blank books of uniform size and manufacture, to be procured for that purpose by the said Secretary and Chief Clerk, to complete journals of the said Congress and State Legislature, with ample and convenient side notes and indexes, so far as the same have not heretofore been recorded; the whole to be executed with the utmost uniformity, neatness and accuracy; for which they shall be entitled to receive compensation at the rate of fifteen cents per hundred words for the work so executed by them respectively.

Because the General Land Office occupied the only stone structure in what would now be called the government complex and was therefore safer from fire than the others, the act further provided "that the said books when prepared as aforesaid, together with the archives, to be arranged and filed as contemplated by this act, shall be deposited in the General Land Office building, for their better security and preservation, until other provision shall have been made by the Legislature."

A new arrangement was made for printing the *Senate Journal*. The secretary of the Senate and the chief clerk of the House no longer sent copies of the journal to the printer, but first recorded the documents in blank books and then sent the originals to the printer, or so it seems, for the whole description of the procedure is difficult to follow. This might account for the sometimes fragmentary state of the manuscript journals that have survived. Several of the strikingly handsome index volumes from this period are still kept in the present State Archives.

On February 10, a packet of three resolutions from the Senate was passed commending U.S. senator Sam Houston to the delegates to the Democratic party convention and to the voters of the nation as a candidate for the presidency. Attempts to weaken the resolutions by amendment or quash them entirely were led by Senator Dancy, but were quickly defeated. On the last day of the session, February 16, he took time to register a protest, saying in part:

> Although I moved to strike out Sam Houston and insert Douglas [Stephen A., leader of the Young America faction of the Democrats and the man who brought the railroad to Chicago], and then Cass [Lewis, supporter of the annexation of Texas and the Compromise of 1850 as senator from Michigan and the man for whom Cass County was named], because I preferred either of them to Houston, candor requires me to state that I would have voted against the resolutions if either name had been inserted, because I did not believe that the resolutions came within the range of our duties as legislators, and I am not willing to see a Legislature converted into a political meeting, to manufacture capital for politicians. It is certainly humiliating for a Legislature to request the delegates to a party political convention to nominate their favorite.

"The enactment of a law to apportion representation throughout the State is imperatively required at your present session," announced Governor Bell in his opening address to the extraordinary session he had called for January 10, 1853. The current practice of passing important legislation at the end of a session has a long history, as evidenced by Governor Bell's remarks:

> A bill for this purpose was passed at the last regular session of the legislature. The circumstances under which it was presented to me, are well known to you, and I presume to the country generally. It is sufficient to state that, although this bill was reported on the 15th day of January last [in the Senate], it was not presented to me until 10 o'clock of the night of the 16th of February following; one hour before the time fixed by the legislature for its adjournment. During this short interval, other bills were presented for Executive action, so that it was impossible for me to read over and duly examine the provisions of the important and complex act in question, and enable me either to approve the same or return it with my objections.
>   Under these circumstances . . . I did not sign the bill. . . .

Bell reminded the legislators of "the necessity that exists for a classification of the Senate, as required by the constitution," his language suggesting that this had been neglected by the seven senators added in the ramshackle reapportionment made by the House in the Second Legislature.

In the bill passed on February 2, 1853, there are in fact thirty-three senatorial districts and ninety representative districts, the maximum allowed by the Constitution of 1845, altogether including ninety-three counties, an increase of nearly sixty over those in existence in 1846. One county, Madison, was created on January 27 and was included in the new apportionment, but Hill County, lopped from Navarro County on February 7, seems not to have been included in a district until the Ninth Legislature (Confederate), although it is unreasonable to suppose that the former Navarro countians abruptly ceased voting for offices of such importance to them.

The governor, recognizing that the movement toward railroads as the primary solution to the state's transportation had by now reached indefectible momentum and that the largely flat terrain compensated for the scarcity of timber in much of the state, addressed the question of how the railroads were to be built. Senator Dancy and others favored a plan that provided for state-constructed railroads financed by money borrowed on the public credit; but the governor, noting that the constitution could be amended to remove the bar to this procedure, stated:

> I am not prepared to say that a change of the constitution in this respect would be either wise or salutary in the present attitude of our State affairs. The inhibition against loaning the credit of the State, was intended,

and I think wisely so, to avoid the embarrassments into which the Republic of Texas and many of the States of the Union had fallen. Without such inhibition, combinations, or hasty legislation might lead to such improvident uses of State credit as would involve difficulties requiring years for their removal; and although it might seem to afford a temporary impetus to the prosperity of the country, yet would result ultimately in the prostration of its energies and power.

He then advanced an argument heard frequently today at the highest levels of policymaking, although in less eloquent prose:

> I likewise entertain doubts of the propriety of the State engaging in works of internal improvement, to the exclusion of all individual enterprize. Experience has shown that governments pay higher for public works or supplies than individuals engaged in similar undertakings, and there is, generally speaking, much less dispatch in their prosecution. The capital invested by individuals prompts them to energy and economy, while public agents have not the same incentives of personal interest to urge them to either the one or the other.

Governor Bell rejected a plan, already proposed in a House bill during the regular session, for a permanent internal improvement fund combined with donations of public land, which would provide loans to private companies, the interest from which would go to form a general education fund; this plan was also open to constitutional objections. He suggested a permanent education fund as the basis for the loans; this arrangement was not prohibited by the constitution, and was likely to yield more benefit to the state. Since under this plan a degree of state control could be exercised "under certain prescribed guarantees," the plan might appeal as a compromise measure to the proponents of state ownership. This was in essence the plan that was eventually adopted by succeeding legislatures.

However, Bell believed that the most important use of the money now burning a hole in the Texas pocket was to pay the public debt:

> It is my anxious desire, then, that in our zeal, laudable though it may be, to develope the resources and add to the prosperity of our State, we should do nothing that would cast a blemish upon her good faith. Let this be kept free from stain, and I will go "heart in hand" with you, in any measure of internal improvement calculated to advance her interest, and give her a prominent place among the States of our glorious Union.

In point of fact, the public debt was paid in the end almost wholly by the federal government in appropriations supplementary to those in the

Compromise of 1850. Needless to say, there was an extended grumble by the governor about the bonds still held in the federal treasury to satisfy the creditors of the state under that agreement.

By far the largest part of his speech was devoted to his dogged pursuit of financing three volunteer companies to fight the "renegade Mexicans and savage Indians," which, as he said, he had been asking for since December, 1849, although as yet "these references and suggestions [had] failed to elicit any action from the legislature." He described as "deplorable" the situation of the citizens along the Rio Grande and launched into an attack on the secretary of war, Charles Conrad from Louisiana, who had already turned his office over to his successor, Jefferson Davis, by the time Bell vented his anger. Dealing out documentary exhibits with both hands and spewing heavy sarcasm at "the Honorable Secretary," the governor succeeded at least and at last in evoking a response from the legislature, which fairly quickly gave him what he asked for.

One subject that the governor introduced late in his address, with evident reluctance, was of great importance: "It is with much regret, I am again under the necessity of calling your attention to the condition of Peters' Colony." The convoluted and dismal history of the Peters Colony is not easy to summarize, but a lingering glance at it is needed to explain the Senate's peculiar part in its later phases. The name came from William S. Peters, a British citizen long resident in the United States, whose family and associates were in the piano-manufacturing and music-publishing business principally in Louisville, Kentucky. It is not certain how he and his associates became interested in Texas land speculation, but by 1841 they had formed an investment company with nine British and eleven American members, and had applied successfully for an empresario contract, that is, one that rewarded the company with land for bringing colonists to settle on land grants obtained through the company, the land to come from the public domain, which was also to provide the colonists with goods and services incidental to establishing working farms. The first contract negotiated was followed by the acquisition of three larger tracts of land, until the final one of January, 1843, covered all or part of present Archer, Baylor, Callahan, Clay, Collin, Cooke, Dallas, Denton, Eastland, Ellis, Erath, Grayson, Hood, Jack, Johnson, Montague, Parker, Shackelford, Stephens, Tarrant, Throckmorton, Wichita, Wilbarger, Wise, and Young counties.

From the beginning there were conflicts between the Texas Emigration and Land Company, as it was called during most of its life, the colonists, and the state, and the situation was muddled further by the intrusion of squatters, land locators, miscellaneous speculators, and, inevitably, politicians. The most conspicuously troublesome were the land locators, a raptor flock who dealt in certificates entitling the holder to claim land in the public domain, the site unspecified, and who found unclaimed or unpatented land to match the certificates, which circulated virtually like lottery tickets. The land locators then sold both to emigrants at disproportionate profits. The enormous expanse of Peters Colony was legally out of bounds to them. However, while pretending to make common cause with colonists disappointed with the company's performance for one reason or another and using corrupt state and local officials and surveyors, the land locators engaged in all manner of trespass on Peters Colony.

Into this fermenting compost, the company had unwittingly introduced a catalyst of eruption, an energetic, conscientious, efficient, and tactless agent of London origins, Henry Hedgecoxe, whose efforts to bring order for the advantage of both company and colonists were consistently misunderstood by the colonists, who distrusted all foreigners, and by their allies among the confidence men.

Things began to take a nasty turn after July, 1848, when the last contract expired and many of the colonists suspected that they were being cheated of their due share of land and other perquisites through the wily schemes of Hedgecoxe at the instance of the company. The colonists turned to the legislature for relief, aided by a young representative, John H. Reagan. (Reagan later became a lawyer of great stature, austere reputation, and undoubtedly laudable achievements; he was a judicial reformer, postmaster general of the Confederacy, a moderate leader in the Reconstruction period, an influential congressman, and finally an elder statesman of the newly established Railroad Commission of Texas, retiring to a nearly universal chorus of praise in 1903 to write his memoirs.) Senator David Gage had passed a bill in aid of the colonists which had their support and was expected to clear the House of Representatives; it was defeated, however, by a vote of fourteen to twenty-eight because of ill-considered amendments by Reagan, as was angrily charged by Gage, the colonists, and Samuel Bogart, representative from old Fannin County in the heart of the colony. In an 1849 campaign for the senatorial seat of the Third District, within the Peters Colony grant, fought exclusively over colonists' issues, Albert G. Walker, another surveyor who had come to the colony from Kentucky and who was greatly helped by the ardent stumping of Bogart, defeated Reagan because, he claimed, he had refused to make extravagant promises to the electorate.

A joint legislative committee produced a bill, which was finally passed on January 21, 1850, that yielded almost entirely to the colonists' demands, chief among which was the granting of land titles directly by the state rather than through the company, an arrangement that disregarded the company's legitimate interests. A functionary appointed by the governor under this act set out to interview claimants and issue patents from the General Land Office. True to a prediction of Reagan's, the company turned to the courts, securing an immediate injunction stopping the issuance of grants and organizing for a long legal battle. His prescience in this matter, together with extensive speechmaking at the meetings that began to spring up over the disputed territory, improved his standing with the colonists and land locators, who with his guidance resorted to vigorous lobbying. The result was a law of December 2, 1850, allowing colonists and land locators to intervene in suits "connected with said colony contracts, where they have an interest."

In August, 1851, the stockholders of the company sent their own lobbyist from Kentucky, Willis Stewart, to consult with Hedgecoxe and Isaiah A. Paschal, a San Antonio lawyer for the company who would be a senator in the Fifth, Seventh, and Eighth legislatures. Stewart, Hedgecoxe, and Paschal prepared a memorial for use in the coming legislative conflict that seems to have considerably exaggerated the number of colonists and the services performed for them and consequently the amount of land owed to them. Stewart also apparently caught the ear of now Senator Bogart, who immediately after the opening of the Fourth Legislature on November 3, 1851, introduced a bill to amend the procolonist law of February, 1850, and saw it passed to third reading on November 10. The governor, however, bombarded by petitions from the colonists and representations from the company, delivered on the same day a message calling for stronger measures, lest "the immense litigation which will be involved in this controversy, if permitted to continue, will greatly retard the growth of one of the finest districts in the State, as nothing is more detrimental to the permanent improvement and advancement of a country, than uncertainty of tenure in its lands."

Bogart's bill was dropped and cooperating special committees were appointed. The Senate committee was chaired by Hill, who as a representative in the Fifth Congress of the Republic had been a member of the committee that approved the original Peters Colony contract. A bill that urged the acceptance of some loss to the state and profit to the company in public lands in order to avoid both colonists and company languishing "under the baneful and withering influences of delayed litigation" was reported from the Senate committee. A slightly amended form of the bill was passed, giving seventeen hundred instead of two thousand sections to the company, contingent on the performance of certain acts by officers of the company; the bill was quickly secured, and was signed on February 10, 1852, amid a general feeling that all would now be well.

It probably would have been if the colonists had understood that now they were likely to get what they wanted. Many of the colonists, however, persisted in not believing Hedgecoxe when he tried to explain the bill to them; they were egged on by the land locators, who were seeking a legislative fiat that would validate without much scrutiny all land claims except those of the company. These land locators, with Reagan as their loudest and most persistent voice, hammered away at the huge body of land – over one million acres – accruing to the company under the compromise bill. On March 9, Reagan said, "If the Committee and the Legislature had known as well as every colonist knew, how false the statements contained in the Report were, their actions would have been different." This is true enough, but probably in degree rather than in kind, for although the statements in the report were inflated, the legislature was by now determined to throw out both bathwater and baby if need be to have peace, and would merely have reduced further the grant to the company if it had been reliably informed that the memorial figures were not unvarnished verity. Reagan soon said that they had known this from the beginning.

A mass meeting was held in Limestone County on April 28, organized entirely by noncolonists. Resolutions, couched in language of near-criminal violence, were passed urging the colonists to join forces and act in defiance of the compromise law. Meantime, the hapless Hedgecoxe had, in strict obedience to the law, opened an office in the colony and published a handbill, no copy of which and no unprejudiced account of which survives. The handbill detailed the duties required of the colonists and of Hedgecoxe, those of the latter being a somewhat confusing subject, seeing that he was acting as the company agent and a bonded official of the state simultaneously. No one paid any attention to what he said, in any case, for his manner was perceived as so arrogant that he was thereafter called Lord Hedgecoxe and other less seemly epithets.

The meetings organized by noncolonists continued, and the colonists also began holding meetings. The first one was held on May 15, with Reagan as speaker; he described at length and in the most sensational language the reasons for war, and then in brief, feeble terms called for peace. The feeling of the colonists that they had been abandoned by their government was exacerbated when, on June 3, Ebenezer Allen, who was alleged to be a former counsel to the company and now attorney general, published an opinion upholding the despised law. The number and intensity of the meetings grew.

Accounts of the crucial meetings of July held in Dallas County differ, but the sequence of events confirmed by common report would seem to begin with a July 10 meeting at which a committee headed by Walker, former senator and Reagan's former foe, was appointed to request Reagan to speak. Reagan spoke, and a resolution was then passed appointing another committee, of which Reagan was a member, to request Hedgecoxe "to submit to them all the books of the office, together with the papers, field-notes, &c., of the colonists for their investigations and see what arrangements may be made between the agent and the colonists to quiet the excitement now existing."

Exactly what followed is unclear, but some kind of report was prepared by the committee, based on a peaceful visitation, and was presented by Reagan to a meeting, held perhaps on the 13th but probably on the 15th, detailing the wickedness of Hedgecoxe and his masters. According to the *Texas State Gazette*, two thousand copies were ordered printed for distribution, in part to committees of correspondence to be set up elsewhere in the colony. It should be noted that one respectable source, Claude Elliott's life of James W. Throckmorton, *Leathercoat, the Life History of a Texas Patriot* (San Antonio: Standard Printing Co., 1938), states that the report, for reasons unknown, was not read at all. Even if the report was not read, and whatever its content if it was, something moved those assembled beyond the pacific measures often, if briefly, advocated by Reagan, and leadership was assumed by the assistant secretary, John Jay Good, who was referred to as General Good.

The aftermath has abundant testimony. On the night of July 15, led by General Good, an armed force estimated at from forty to over one hundred men marched to Hedgecoxe's office and home in or near Mc-

Kinney. He had been warned by James Throckmorton, representative from Collin and Denton counties who, despite expressed sympathies with the colonists, had voted for the detested compromise bill and was thus regarded as a traitor. Hedgecoxe managed to remove some papers and surveyors' equipment and escape to the shelter of a neighboring cornfield. The raiding party arrived, broke into the office, and stole whatever they thought was of significance. Before departing with their booty into the night, they left messages for Hedgecoxe telling him to quit the colony within twenty-four hours or be lynched, which next day he did after arranging for transportation to safekeeping of the instruments and records he had hidden. This was either the first or the second engagement of what is called the Hedgecoxe War, depending on belief in a previous raid by the investigatory committee.

By the time the loot-laden marauders returned to Dallas and deposited their cache in the courthouse, it was the early morning of July 16. As the twenty-five-year-old Good wrote, they "met with a brilliant reception from the citizens of Dallas County, at whose expense we have been feasting and revelling until this time (3 o'clock) and still the excitement is up. Sam Bogart was promenaded around the square, in effigy, on a rail, then [they] swung him to a black jack [a common oak] and burned him." Bogart is believed to be the first senator so singled out by his constituents.

A meeting at Denton on July 24 heartily commended the deeds of the Dallasites and resolved "that it is the wish of the citizens of Denton County, that our Senator Sam Bogart and our Representative James W. Throckmorton, resign their seats in the State Legislature." The general response, in or out of the colony, was unfavorable, and a kind of convention was called to meet at the scene of the crime, McKinney, on July 29. The participants at the convention blamed Hedgecoxe for the whole thing, appealed to the legislature for a remedy in the coming special session, and appointed various committees. Senator Bogart chaired the committee to hire counsel and chose Reagan at a fee of ten thousand dollars. At the beginning of the July turbulence Reagan had been informally offered one thousand dollars for the same services, but had refused. The offer was renewed by resolution at the July 15 meeting, but Reagan again refused. He did not, however, refuse the ten-thousand-dollar offer, and the convention quickly adjourned, with attention now fixed on the legislative extraordinary session.

The company was ready to do almost anything that would rid it of the colonists and allow it to realize a profit on its land bonanza. It was commonly understood that it would offer no resistance to measures short of confiscation. Consideration of remedies began in January, 1853, and it was for some a necessary but loathsome task. A correspondent in the Clarksville *Standard* noted:

> The Senate has been engaged in the discussion of that endless subject—Peters Colony. I was much amused (although I to some extent coincide in his views), in the remarks of a Senator, who stated that for thirteen years, he had been seeking for light by voting for every measure calculated to terminate the difficulties existing in that colony, and give to the colonists the right to their homesteads, but instead of this accomplishing its object, legislation has but involved us in more impenetrable darkness, and he was now disposed to retrograde, and seek in repeal what they had failed to effect by enactments. I find that many agree with that gentleman, as will be seen by reference to the vote on the demagogues who have been inciting the colonists to pursue a suicidal policy, have induced them to act with great indiscretion and to be lavish in their denunciations, and abundant in the use of Billingsgate abuse of those who acted with an eye solely directed to their benefit and prosperity.

An attempt was made to wipe out the company's seventeen-hundred-section bonanza by repealing the February 1852 law, but it failed. A Senate bill with House amendments was passed on February 5 by a vote of twelve to seven, Bogart voting yea, with the opposing votes all from beyond the colony's borders. The company increment was untouched, but it had to yield to the colonists in choice of location and the survey used. Virtually all claims made before the effective date of the law were confirmed. Those colonists who had not located land or had not filed were given three months in which to do so. The bill was signed on February 7, and this period therefore ended on May 7. The basic conflict was thus at last settled, although it was not precisely at an end, for there were lawsuits and legislative repairs over the next twenty years, but the only remaining warlike acts were verbal. Indeed, the abuse took on a phosphorescence of its own well after the embers of the original fire had grown cold, and Reagan and Bogart carried on a slanging match in the public press whose range of rumor, innuendo, and libel was far removed from the cause of it all.

The urgent business of the extraordinary session—Indians, apportionment, and the Peters Colony—was dealt with efficiently enough by the Senate, the House concurring, and there was time for another clutch of special bills and some significant general legislation. While the Senate deliberated in its drafty old wooden chamber, bereft of its portrait of the lamented Burleson, which had been put for safekeeping in the General Land Office at the end of the regular session, the new limestone Capitol could be seen rising on the little hill at Mesquite (now Eleventh) Street and Congress Avenue. Two construction bills were passed and approved, one adding to the Capitol a chamber for the Supreme Court, for which fifty thousand dollars was appropriated, and the other providing for a detached "fire-proof building, for the Treasury Department and the Comptroller's offices," at an initial cost of twenty-nine thousand dollars, which would require supplementation.

A bill and a joint resolution concerning free Negroes and slaves were introduced. The bill contained what amounted to a penal code and a code of criminal procedure for Negroes, with a definition of Negro. With regard to crimes, punishments, and procedures, there was an appearance of a careful distinction made between slaves and free Negroes in some sections of the act, but this did not save the free Negro from flogging. The county court, with three-man bench, served as "a criminal tribunal for the trial of negroes and slaves charged with felony." One slight advantage reserved to the slave was that in a trial for felony, "the court shall assign counsel to defend, if none be employed, and allow him such fee, not to exceed one hundred dollars, which shall be paid by the owner of the slave." However, in criminal cases before a county court, a prosecutor could be retained either by a private person or by the court.

The free Negro had a very slight advantage in one type of case, for "if a slave plot or conspire to rebel or make insurrection, or commit an offence for the commission of which a free negro is punishable by death, or confinement in the penitentiary for not less than three years, he shall be punished with death." The peculiar sense of uneasiness about free Negroes (of whom there were fewer than four hundred in Texas according to the census of 1850) exuded by this act and other legislation of the period is intelligible in the light of popular southern racial theory, which held that slavery was the natural condition of the Negro and that therefore there was something profoundly unnatural about a Negro who was in any sense free, even within such constraints as the law could set. As early as 1835 there was a law forbidding the importation of free Negroes or mulattos, and in 1858 the legislature made it possible for those free Negroes who had the laudable intention of getting right with the natural order to select masters and become slaves.

The U.S. Congress had recently shown the effectiveness of southern political dominance by passing a series of harsh fugitive slave laws, and a joint resolution approved on February 7 may have received its impetus from this disposition. Mexico had no slavery or racial laws and did not recognize those of the United States, so that the temptation for slaves to flee south of the Rio Grande rather than north of the Mason-Dixon line was strong. It was even widely alleged in Texas that Mexican agents were constantly at work fomenting and aiding escapes, although this seems unlikely, but it was indeed chancy for a slaveowner to take slaves to Mexico and expect to bring them back. The resolution directed the Texas Congressional Delegation "to call the attention of the Government of the United States to the necessity of a further treaty with the Republic of Mexico," which would restore "to the citizens of the United States, all slaves belonging to them and which are now within the said Republic, as well as all which may hereafter escape thereto; and, also, for the prompt restoration of any other property of American citizens which may have been carried or taken against the will of the respective owners thereof into the said Republic." No such treaty was ever negotiated.

Also on the last day of the session, the governor signed a Senate bill to regulate railroad companies; someone had done a very thorough job of research on the bill, for it is unsparing of circumstantial detail. Covered are the organization of the companies and the payment of dividends; the costumes of conductors, baggagemasters, engineers, brakemen, and other employees; the erection of warning signs at crossways; the method of checking baggage; and the rights of passengers. Required were locomotive bells "of at least thirty pounds weight, or a steam whistle" that "shall be rung, or whistle blown, at the distance of at least eighty rods from the place where the railroad shall cross any road or street, and to be kept ringing or blowing until it shall have crossed such road or street, or stopped, under a penalty of fifty dollars for every neglect." Any person who shall, "while in charge of a locomotive engine, running upon the railroad of any such corporation, or while acting as the conductor of a car, or train of cars on any such railroad, be intoxicated, he shall be guilty of a misdemeanor, and be punished by fine or imprisonment, or both." Furthermore, "the width of the track or guage [sic] of all roads in the state shall be six feet"; this reference is to the so-called Erie gauge, the width of which was later amended to five feet, six inches and in 1875 to four feet, eight and one-half inches, the gauge of ancient Roman chariots. The bill also stipulated that "each company shall have a good and sufficient brake upon the hindmost car on all trains transporting passengers and merchandize, and also permanently stationed there a trusty and faithful brakeman, under a penalty of not exceeding one hundred dollars for each offence, to be recovered by suit in the name of the State."

The vexed question of financing was touched on, and there were quite a few words more on various related topics, and a last one on proxies. The act was passed at this time, perhaps from a sense of urgency to regulate the first twenty miles of track laid in the state, the line running from Harrisburg to Stafford's Point; this project was supposed to be finished that same month but, as has been mentioned, it was not completed until August. In any event, when Texas did have a railroad it would be regulated.

During the extraordinary session the unpleasantness over the chaplaincy seems to have been resolved for the moment. Smith and Baggerley lost their tag-team hold on the office, and Baker, one of those who had earlier refused to serve, offered prayers together with the familiar Fontaine and Thomas and Taliaferro.

CHAPTER 14

The Senate of the Fifth Legislature, 1853–54

The Fifth Legislature, the largest parliamentary body in Texas to that date, convened for a single session from November 7, 1853, to February 13, 1854. A full complement of thirty-three senators, seven more than in the previous assembly, was elected, but after a few months it became difficult to assemble a quorum because fully one-third habitually absented themselves for various reasons. The senators who did attend, however, adopted a legislative program that addressed some of the lingering problems of the young state, including education, frontier defense, and internal improvements. The last to meet in the old wooden Capitol, they were also the last to meet in relative harmony before the Civil War, free from the fractiousness that would increasingly characterize politics in Texas as partisan arguments became divisive.

Due to the awkward schedule of the legislative sessions during the antebellum period, lame-duck Governor Peter H. Bell greeted the assembled legislators on November 9, 1853. Less than three weeks later, he resigned to take a seat in the U.S. House of Representatives. Bell left the executive duties in the hands of his lieutenant governor, James W. (Smoky) Henderson, an unsuccessful candidate for governor in 1853. Henderson presided over state government until the inauguration of Elisha M. Pease, the man who had defeated him, on December 21, 1853.

Pease had won a close race in 1853 as a Democrat on a platform that incorporated several planks from Bell's program as governor: free public schools, the expulsion of the Indians from the settled portions of Texas, and internal improvements, especially in transportation. He was opposed by William T. Ochiltree, a Whig with a large personal following, but

P. Hansborough Bell, governor of Texas, 1849–53.
Courtesy Texas State Archives.

Pease gained the nomination of his party and the electoral victory after the two other strong Democrats contending for the office of governor— Middleton T. Johnson and Henderson—withdrew and threw their support to him. In the general election, Pease received only 13,091 votes and Ochiltree 9,178, while 13,893 Texans cast their votes for other candidates.

Most of Pease's support came from the southern and western parts

James W. Henderson, governor of Texas in 1853, filling Bell's unexpired term.
Courtesy Texas State Archives.

of the state, which explains his political orientation toward a more active
government, but he attracted many voters from East Texas by pledging
to support their efforts to have the proposed transcontinental rail line
built through their area. He also enjoyed popular favor as an "Old Texan."
A native of Connecticut, he had come to Texas in 1835, at the age of
twenty-three, and studied law. He occupied several public offices during
the Republic period; was a district attorney after founding a successful
private practice; served in the Texas House during the First and Second

The Fifth Legislature was the first to meet in the new limestone capitol, November 21, 1853, situated on site of present-day granite building. Reproduced from holdings of Texas State Archives.

legislatures; and spent part of a term in the Texas Senate in 1849 and 1850.

Unlike Pease, David C. Dickson handily won the office of lieutenant governor, defeating his nearest opponent by a margin of more than two to one. Born in Mississippi in 1818, Dickson attended medical school in Kentucky before emigrating to Texas in 1841. He served briefly as a surgeon in the army of the Republic of Texas before founding a private medical practice, which he left to serve as a member of the House of Representatives in the First and Third legislatures after annexation and as Speaker of the House in the Fourth Legislature.

In part due to the redistricting and the increase in the number of members, the returning senators found themselves a minority of six: James H. Armstrong, Joseph H. Burks, Rufus Doane, Hardin Hart, William T.

Elisha M. Pease, governor of Texas, 1853–57.
Courtesy Texas State Archives.

Scott, and M. D. K. Taylor. These veterans were joined by a former state senator, David Gage, who had served during the Second and Third legislatures. Gage, a native of Kentucky, had come to Texas in 1839 at the age of forty-three. He commanded a company of minutemen in 1840 and 1841, after which he was elected as a representative to the Eighth and Ninth congresses of the Republic and as a delegate to the Convention of 1845. He died soon after the Senate adjourned in 1854.

Among the newcomers were many who had served previously in the Texas House of Representatives. Foremost among them was Guy M. Bryan, who had been elected to the Second, Third, and Fourth legislatures. He came to Texas from his native Missouri in 1831 at the age of ten and then returned east and graduated in 1842 from Kenyon College in Ohio. Too young to serve in the army during the revolution, he did join a ranger company during the Mexican War. In the legislature he attracted notice as a prudish man who did not drink, gamble, or swear. He left the Texas Senate to take a seat in the Thirty-fifth Congress, where he made his reputation as a rabid secessionist. After leading the walkout of the Texas delegation from the Democratic National Convention of 1860, he became a Confederate staff officer. He returned to the Texas House in 1873, when he served as speaker, and again in 1879 and 1887. His last public position was as president of the Texas Veterans' Association, where he served from 1892 until his death in 1901.

Charles G. Keenan was perhaps better known than Bryan in Texas before the Civil War. He had worked as an army surgeon among the Indians before he came to Texas during the Republic period. For ten years, from 1850 to 1860, he served as treasurer of the Grand Lodge of Texas. After serving in the First and Second Texas Houses and as Speaker of the House during the Third Legislature, Keenan campaigned unsuccessfully for lieutenant governor in 1851. One of his companions in the Senate, Elisha E. Lott, had served with him in the House during the Second and Third legislatures, as well as in the House in the Fourth Legislature and as a representative in the Eighth Congress of the Republic. A native of Mississippi, Lott came to Texas in 1840, at the age of twenty. After establishing a plantation, he worked his way into politics by assisting in the survey of both Smith County and its seat of Tyler. He remained in the Texas Senate for four terms, after which he resigned to enlist in the Confederate Army. He died in service in 1864.

Henry W. Sublett, unlike Lott, lost his race for the Congress of the Republic in 1845. A native of Kentucky, he had come to Texas in 1835 at the age of eighteen. He was appointed attorney for the Sixth Judicial District in 1842 and represented his county in the First Legislature. Elliott M. Millican, who emigrated to Texas from his native South Carolina in 1821 at the age of thirteen, claimed to be a planter but was far more successful in politics, being elected constable of Washington County in 1839, sheriff of Navasota County in 1841, sheriff of Brazos County in 1843, and a representative to the Ninth Congress of the Republic and the First, Second, and Third legislatures. The town of Millican, in Brazos County on the Texas and New Orleans Railroad line, was named in his honor.

Most of Bryan's former companions in the House did not enjoy such glamorous public careers, but they had impressive backgrounds. James K. Holland, born in Tennessee in 1822, came to Texas from Mississippi in 1842. He served in the army during the Mexican War, then in the Texas House during the Third Legislature. Prior to coming to the Senate, he worked as a U.S. marshal for several years. Holland refused to accept a nomination to the secession convention but became a colonel on Governor Pendleton Murrah's staff during the Civil War. William G. W. Jowers, who had served in the House in the Third and Fourth legislatures, was a native of North Carolina. Born in 1812, he had graduated from Transylvania University in Kentucky in 1835 before moving to Texas four years later. He would serve in the Senate in the Tenth and Eleventh legislatures during the Civil War.

The remaining four House veterans came from diverse backgrounds. William C. Edwards, who had been in the House in the First, Second, and Fourth legislatures, was a planter from Louisiana. James W. McDade, from the House in the Fourth Legislature, was a farmer from Alabama, and a town in Bastrop County on the Texas and New Orleans Railroad line was later named in his honor. Mark M. Potter, an attorney born in Connecticut, had served in the House in the Second Legislature and would return there for the Ninth Legislature after four terms in the Senate. Johnson Wren, who had served in the House in the Second, Third, and Fourth legislatures, was a farmer from Kentucky who, like most of the members of the Senate, found that politics suited him better than staying on the land all year.

Among the newcomers to the Senate were several "Old Texans" who had fought for the Republic. Isaac L. Hill, born in 1814 in Georgia, had come to Texas in 1835 and fought at the Battle of San Jacinto. Cornelius McAnelly, a physician who immigrated to Texas during the period of the

Republic, had been active in civic and government affairs and enlisted as colonel and brigade surgeon for the abortive Somervell expedition in 1842. Like Ochiltree, McAnelly was a member of the ailing Whig party; he had won a seat in the Senate only after long and bitter campaigning, an experience that probably contributed to his uniquely obstinate opposition to almost every issue considered by the Senate.

Several of the legislative neophytes enjoyed impressive tenures in the Texas legislature. Robert H. Guinn, a Tennessee attorney, served seven terms in the Senate, through the Civil War, and was elected president pro tempore of the Senate for the Ninth, Tenth, and Eleventh legislatures. Another Tennessee native, the farmer Claiborne Kyle, remained only a short time in the Senate, but served in the House in the Tenth and Eleventh legislatures during the Civil War.

Jefferson Weatherford, who moved to Texas from his native Alabama in 1846, served two terms, then went off briefly to the Confederate Army and returned to the Senate for the Ninth and Tenth legislatures. A fellow Alabamian, William H. Martin, studied law and was admitted to practice before moving to Athens, Texas, in 1850 at the age of twenty-seven. Later he commanded a company in the Fourth Texas Regiment, which served for the duration of the Civil War in the Army of Northern Virginia. In peace, he turned his attention to national politics, filling the seat vacated by John H. Reagan in the Fiftieth Congress and winning reelection to the Fifty-first Congress.

A Southern lawyer of rather different cut was Isaiah A. Paschal, born in Georgia in 1808 and admitted to the bar in 1830. Three years later he moved to Louisiana, where he soon became closely identified with the German settlers then rising in the business, agricultural, and professional life of the area. Like many of them, he was a staunch Unionist throughout the Civil War. He attended and took an aggressively punitive part in the Constitutional Convention of 1866. On February 21, 1868, he died with Texas still under military rule and no legislature in the capitol.

The election of one newcomer, Edwin B. Scarborough, was marred slightly by accusations of impropriety. He was the editor and owner of Brownsville's *American Flag* and often referred to the paper as his "little pet," indicating its role in his public career. His rival, E. B. Barton, contested his seat, alleging that Mexicans who were not American citizens had been allowed to vote for Scarborough. Lott, as chairman of the Committee on Privileges and Elections, reported on November 12, 1853, that the testimony was "so conflicting, irreconcilable and unsatisfactory" that it was "next to an impossibility to form a conclusion free from doubt." He concluded that while it was "not improbable that irregularities happened, and that illegal votes were given on both sides," Scarborough should retain his seat, thereby preserving a degree of decorum in the Senate. Scarborough survived the investigation unscathed and served five consecutive terms in the Senate.

The eight remaining new senators—Malachi W. Allen, James H. Durst, James T. Lytle, Simpson C. Newman, Henry C. Pedigo, Henry W. Sublett, Antoine Superviele, and M. G. Whitaker—represented a diverse spectrum of interests. Durst enjoyed the distinction of being the first Anglo senator born in the state; in fact, he was alleged to be the first white child born in East Texas. He was a farmer, as were four of the others. Lytle, Pedigo, Sublett, and Superviele, a native of France and the only foreign-born member of this Senate, were all attorneys. Unfortunately, the talents of seven of the new Senators lay outside the legislative arena, for they did not remain long in the Texas legislature. The abilities of Lytle remained untried; he requested sick leave in late November, 1853, and, sadly, died on February 5, 1854, at the age of thirty-one.

Of the elected officers of the Senate of the Fourth Legislature, only the doorkeeper, Joseph Mangum, retained his job. Senators of the Fifth Legislature elected almost an entirely new complement, including James F. Johnson as secretary, M. D. Herring as first assistant secretary, Caleb J. Garrison as second assistant secretary, H. W. Raglin as enrolling clerk, R. W. Martin as engrossing clerk, and Ward Taylor as sergeant at arms. Senator Taylor was elected president pro tempore at the outset, but after his appearances became infrequent and finally ceased altogether, Senator Bryan was chosen to be his successor.

The first priority in Pease's program was education. He signed an act on January 31, 1854, that set aside $2 million of the 5 percent bonds given to the state by the United States as part of the Compromise of 1850 for the endowment of public schools. This fund was to be used only to pay the salaries of teachers, not to build or equip schools. The chief justice and commissioners of each county were responsible for organizing their counties into school districts and conducting elections to choose three trustees. The public school money was to be distributed according to the number of free whites between the ages of six and sixteen in each district and was to be administered solely by the trustees. The trustees had exclusive power to hire and fire teachers, who had to be of "suitable moral character and qualifications." If the appropriation did not cover the teacher's entire salary, the balance was to be paid by the patrons. The latter soon found that the endowment, which yielded only sixty-two cents per capita annually, left them with a substantial obligation, but it was a start.

The Senate of the Fifth Legislature chartered a number of private schools, as well as providing for public education. Senator Taylor was among the trustees of the Sharon Union School in Cass County, incorporated on November 30, 1853. The other educational institutions included the Linden Male and Female Hall and Masonic Academy, also in Cass County, the Indian Creek Academy in Jasper County, the Mound Prairie Institute in Anderson County, the New Danville Masonic Female Academy, the Alam Institute in Lavaca County, the Newburn Male and Female Academy in Shelby County, the McKenzie Institute in Red River County, the Milam Masonic Institute in Sabine County, the Gilmer Male Academy in Upshur County, and the Church Hill Male and Female Academy in Rusk County.

Many of these schools, such as the Indian Creek Academy, never opened their doors, but some earned a measure of distinction for their practical, if not classical, curricula. Among the latter was the McKenzie Institute, which proved to be both popular and effective for several years. Most of the schools, like McKenzie, were coeducational, and many of their charters banned all alcoholic beverages in the immediate neighborhood, in deference to the public campaign for temperance. They were strictly segregated by race, with one notable exception: Aranama College, chartered on January 25, 1854, at Goliad, taught Mexican children under the aegis of the Presbyterian church.

Both Bell and Pease strongly recommended that immediate action be taken to establish the two state universities provided for by an earlier act, but a bill to that effect failed to pass. Some semblance of higher education was provided by Tyler University, which had opened in East Texas in 1853 under the control of the Cherokee Baptist Association. Governor Pease signed its charter on February 11, 1854. Like almost all of the private schools, it admitted both males and females, but struggled to remain open during the antebellum period due to chronically low enrollments.

Indian attacks remained a daily problem for settlers along the Texas frontier. Governor Bell endorsed the proposal of Indian agent Robert S. Neighbors and the federal government for a reservation in Texas, saying:

Humanity loudly demands that something of this kind should be done as a provision for the poor Indian, who now has no other alternative left than to perish by famine or the sword; who, goaded to desperation at the loss of hunting grounds that furnished his forefathers with subsistence, and year after year driven further and further, by remorseless fate, from fertility to barrenness, feels that the existence of the white race sounds the knell of extinction to his own.

Pease endorsed Bell's request for a reservation, albeit in a more practical plea that stressed the benefits to accrue to the white race rather than the red.

Two days after he endorsed an appropriation of five thousand dollars for the ransom of captives held by Indians, Pease signed an act setting aside twelve leagues of land for a permanent reservation. It was to be located no more than twenty miles south or east of the most northern of the military posts established by the United States along a line from the Red River to the Pecos River, so that the soldiers could guard against an uprising. Jurisdiction over the reservation was surrendered to the federal government, but Texas reserved the right to arrest "any person other than an Indian for any offense committed upon the person or property of any one within the limits of this State."

It proved to be the white settlers in the area, not the Indians, who were the more troublesome. Two reservations were established in 1855. About a thousand surviving members of the Caddo, Ioni, Anadarko, Waco, Tonkawa, Tawakoni, and other small tribes were located on a reservation of about eight square leagues at the junction of the Brazos River and its Clear Fork, near present-day Graham. The Penateka Comanche settled on a preserve of about four square leagues on the Clear Fork in modern Throckmorton County. Unfortunately, many hostile nomads remained at large, and their activity led to clashes between the white settlers and the reservation Indians and their guardians. Finally, all of the Indians were removed to reservations north of the Red River in 1859, and the lands set aside in 1854 reverted to the state. A final sad note was sounded when Neighbors returned to the state to conclude his business affairs. While on the streets of Fort Belknap, the town outside the now-abandoned post near the former reservations, he was assassinated by an Indian-hating townsman.

The state reservation created for the Alabama Indians through an act signed on February 3, 1854, proved to be more successful, in part because settlers in East Texas, where it was located, had not experienced

Indian attacks in several decades. Two sections of vacant public land, comprising 1,280 acres, were reserved in Polk County, although if no suitable free public land had been available, the commissioners chosen to locate the reservation were empowered to buy property at no more than two dollars an acre. According to the organic act, no part of the reservation was located within four miles of the home of a white person. The Alabama Indians, forbidden to "alien, lease, rent, let, give, or otherwise dispose of [their] land or any part thereof to any person whatsoever," have remained on the tract for more than a century.

One of the cornerstones of Pease's plan for internal improvements was that the cost to the state government would be very little. Texas, after paying the revenue debt from the Republic period with the 5 percent bonds given by the U.S. government as part of the Compromise of 1850, still had enough on hand to allow state government to operate with a very low tax rate. Continuing a practice initiated during the Fourth Legislature, nine-tenths of the state tax on real and personal property for 1854 and 1855 was relinquished to the county governments for their use, leaving the one-tenth already earmarked by the state constitution of 1845 for the common school fund. Pease vetoed this bill, but after it was repassed endorsed several bills to continue the trend toward placing much of the responsibility for internal improvements on county governments, thereby achieving his goal through a popular legislative sleight of hand that reinforced the Democratic call for greater local autonomy. The Senate endorsed only one bill for a major public building project, setting aside seventeen thousand dollars to build and furnish a new governor's mansion.

As the legislature intended and Pease reluctantly accepted, the money channeled back to the counties was used by them for public buildings and other purposes. This was reinforced with gentle prodding from the legislators. An act approved on February 4, 1854, required county courts to supervise the construction of public roads. The commissioners were to appoint road overseers for all precincts; those who refused to serve could be fined from ten to forty dollars. A petition from eight householders in a precinct was required to open or close a road, and decisions on construction were made by a "jury" of five householders. A similar committee of five decided all cases of eminent domain. All free white males between the ages of eighteen and forty-five and all slaves and free blacks between the ages of sixteen and fifty were required to work on the roads for ten days each year. Ministers, students, public millers and

The Texas Governor's Mansion, circa 1864. The Fifth Legislature authorized expenditure of $17,000 to build and furnish an executive mansion, to be completed by December 21, 1855. Courtesy Texas State Archives.

ferrymen, teachers, and county commissioners and judges were exempt; all others had to pay a fine of one dollar per day for failing to work. To reduce collusion, any overseer who failed to prosecute such a case had to pay a fine of five dollars.

The major internal improvement projects, principally railroads, were left to private investors. Several of the senators, notably Hill, Potter, and Paschal, were active promoters of the virtues of private capital for the construction of railroads. They had their hearts set on securing a transcontinental line through Texas, which would bring settlers and commerce into the state and greatly enhance its economy. Unfortunately, when the U.S. Congress in 1853 appropriated funds for the survey of three possible routes, none of them crossed Texas. Bell in his opening address proposed that a "liberal donation" of the public domain, of which 102.7 million acres were as yet unclaimed, to encourage a "responsible company" to invest might demonstrate Texas' support for the project and might persuade Congress to endorse a more southern route. Pease generally agreed with Potter that "all capitalists are generally sensible and cautious," and endorsed Bell's idea to undermine the proponents of a northern railroad to the Pacific.

Senator Gage introduced the organic bill for the construction of the Mississippi and Pacific Railroad, the linchpin of Texas' plans for a transcontinental route, and the governor signed it on December 21, 1853. The measure called for a line to be built from some point on the eastern boundary of the state, "not north of the town of Fulton in the State of Arkansas," westward to a "suitable point on the Rio Grande, at or near the town of El Paso." Twenty sections of public land would be given to the contracting company for every mile of track completed. The first fifty miles had to be laid within eighteen months, and one hundred miles each year thereafter, or the charter was void. The officers were permitted to sell $20 million in stock.

The Mississippi and Pacific Railroad bubble burst quickly. A performance bond of $300,000 in gold or silver had to be posted in order to secure the construction contract from the state government. The bidding opened in August, 1854, when the Texas Western Company, a railroad firm whose finances were questionable, submitted its proposal. Pease stood firm and did not accept its stock in lieu of specie, and finally the bid was withdrawn when the company admitted that it could not post the required bond in gold or silver. Alarmed perhaps by Pease's conservative stance, other companies refused to bid, and the Mississippi and Pacific Railroad reserves were declared open to settlers by the Sixth Legislature.

The collapse of the Mississippi and Pacific Railroad scheme left the Jefferson Railroad Company, incorporated on February 2, 1854, to connect that town with the proposed line to the West Coast, high and dry, and the investors did not bother to organize. The directors of the Gilmer and Sulphur Springs Railroad Company, chartered on February 8, 1854, to build a line from a point on the Texas Western Railroad between Marshall and the Sabine River south to the town of Gilmer, found themselves in a similar quandary. Due to legal troubles and a chronic lack of capital, the Texas Western Railroad completed only about twenty miles of track east of Marshall before the beginning of the Civil War. Although construction began again after the war, and the line eventually became part of the Texas and Pacific Line in 1872, the dreams of the Gilmer and Sulphur Springs Railroad promoters had long since dissipated.

One Texas promoter in 1854 offered an alternative to the plans for a transcontinental line entirely through the United States. The Sabine and Rio Grande Railroad Company was chartered on February 6, 1854, to construct a line from a point on the Sabine River near thirty-one degrees north latitude, thence running through Burkeville in Newton County to Austin, and then south through San Antonio to the Rio Grande near Presidio de Rio Grande, between Las Moras and Palafox. There it could link up with a Mexican route to the West Coast. The legislature promised eight sections of public land for every mile completed, but the company never even did any surveying.

An act signed by Pease on January 30, 1854, provided public land subsidies for the construction of railroads to link the interior of Texas with the ports along the coast. Any company that built a line twenty-five miles in length or more would receive sixteen sections of land for each mile completed. The first twenty-five miles had to be completed within two years of the enactment date, with an additional twenty-five miles laid annually thereafter to completion, or the land would not be granted. The sections, once transferred, had to be completely alienated within twelve years, a common requirement for charters granted in Texas before the Civil War. Only one company, the Gulf Coast and Austin City Railroad Company, took advantage of the offer during the Fifth Legislature, but this was a ploy by investors in the ports to forestall efforts by Virginia City capitalists to monopolize trade with the capital, and proved to be short-lived and unproductive.

A number of local projects were similarly unsuccessful, largely because they were created to generate capital, not to build railroads. The Tyler and Dallas Railroad Company was chartered to connect the Texas and New Orleans Railroad in East Texas with Dallas by way of Tyler. The legislature imposed no limit on its capitalization and pledged eight sections of the public domain for every mile completed. Not a single track was ever laid. A more substantial project was the Columbia, Wharton, and Austin Railroad Company, incorporated to build a line from Columbia to Austin, providing transport for planters along the coast. In spite of its intentions, the company failed to sell enough stock to organize and folded quickly.

Some companies proved to be remarkably persistent in failure. Investors for the Brazos Branch Railroad Company, chartered to connect the town of Washington with one of three proposed trunk lines, failed twice, both before and after the Civil War. A firm under the direction of Thomas J. Chambers received its first charter on February 11, 1854. It proposed to construct a line from the point where the Mississippi and Pacific crossed the Brazos River to the town of "Chambersia" at the mouth of the Trinity River and then to build east of the Trinity "by the best route" north to the Red River. This association underwent several rather interesting transformations through the next few years but ultimately failed to produce anything.

Even more numerous than railroad companies were organizations and individuals proposing to build and operate toll roads and bridges in antebellum Texas. Senator Taylor was a director for the Black Cypress Bridge, Ferry and Turnpike Company, organized to provide a toll road with a ferry or bridge across Black Cypress Creek in Cass County. The Austin and Houston Turnpike Company proposed to link those two growing towns. Along the Neches River, Stinson's Ferry Turnpike Company received a charter for a causeway, bridge, and ferry project, and Jesse Gibson was authorized to build a toll bridge on the road from Rusk to Palestine. Both Ridley B. Thomas and the Dallas Bridge and Causeway Company proposed to bridge the upper Trinity River at two widely separated points. The Mann's Bluff Turnpike Company pledged to build a toll road from Panola County across the Sabine River to Shreveport, Louisiana. That same stream was the focus of efforts by the Sabine and Lake Fork Bridge Company, while the McWilliams Turnpike Company proposed to bypass it while linking Shreveport with Shelbyville, Texas. Other projects included John Mooney's plans to bridge the San Marcos River near Gonzales, Zill McCaleb's proposal to bridge the San Jacinto River in Montgomery County, and the Rock Creek Bridge and Turnpike Company's scheme to span that waterway with a toll bridge in Hopkins County.

Water travel along the coast remained one of the principal modes of transporting freight. Senators of the Fifth Legislature endorsed land bonuses for persons and associations who built seagoing ships in Texas, either steam or sail, of at least fifty tons displacement, or steam-powered boats for inland waterways. The Galveston Wharf and Cotton Press Company, chartered on February 4, 1854, did not receive any land grants, but it did materially improve the cargo-handling facilities of that port by uniting control of the waterfront in one association. The Trinity River and

Galveston Bay Dredging Company pledged to dig a channel through the sandbar at the mouth of the Trinity River to facilitate navigation by steamboats. Its costs were to be repaid through the imposition of tolls on water traffic, but the Senate endorsed the transfer of ninety-four sections of land to the Galveston and Brazos Navigation Company, contingent upon its completion of a canal from West Galveston Bay to the Brazos River, as provided in an 1850 act of the Texas legislature. When the Nueces and San Patricio Causeway Company received a charter for a viaduct from Nueces County to San Patricio County, it included provisions for a drawbridge to facilitate navigation.

The Senate of the Fifth Legislature approved charters for a variety of other projects. The Texas and Red River Telegraph Company, chartered on January 5, 1854, proposed to string a line from Galveston to the Red River. A little over a month after being incorporated, the firm opened its first office in Marshall; its competitor, Western Union, opened its office on the same day. On a similarly progressive note, John Grumbles was permitted to construct and operate a steam-powered "Grist, Flour, Saw, and Planing Mill" on public property between Lavaca and Colorado streets on the Colorado River in Austin. A charter was forwarded as well to Clarksville, where the new Red River and Texas Insurance Company promised to insure produce and merchandise shipped on the Red River and the Mississippi River and their tributaries; they also promised to insure the structures connected with the shipping industry, "dwelling-houses, mill-houses, and all other buildings, the lives of persons, and all other matters and things that said company, acting through the President and Directors thereof may deem it expedient to insure."

Remarkably, although the cultivation of cotton was becoming an important enterprise in Texas, the Fifth Legislature did not issue a charter for a single textile mill in the state. The only proposal for such a facility came from the superintendent of the state penitentiary, who after a tour of the plants run by prisoners in Louisiana and Mississippi submitted a request for a plant to employ fifty convicts. The Senate approved his scheme and endorsed an appropriation of thirty-five thousand dollars to fund the project. The coarse cotton and woolen goods were used primarily at the penitentiary, but some were sold outside, and the textile operation contributed to the self-sufficiency of that institution.

These internal improvements and new corporations served a rapidly increasing populace in Texas. Despite both the continuing controversy over the rights of settlers, which were mired in the intricate legal tangles of the organized empresario colonies, and the reduction of the homestead donation to 160 acres by the Fifth Legislature, people continued to pour into Texas. The Senate of the Fifth Legislature endorsed charters for the towns of Columbus, Corsicana, La Grange, and McKinney, and approved the creation of four new counties: Bosque, Coryell, Johnson, and Kendall.

In keeping with the human instinct, the people of Texas quickly came together in organizations, either to fraternize or to work together to improve their surroundings. Senators endorsed charters for lodges of the International Order of Odd Fellows at Centerville and San Antonio and for a chapter of the Sons of Temperance in Seguin. The Medical Association of Texas, which actually organized at Austin in January, 1853, was incorporated through a bill introduced by Senator Paschal and signed by Pease on November 28, 1853. Among its members were the former surgeon general of the Republic, Ashbel Smith, Lieutenant Governor Dickson, and Senator Jowers. The new association met for the first time on November 14 in Austin, but despite a generally favorable reception did not convene again until 1869. The Howard Association of Galveston took a different approach to a common medical dilemma of the period, pledging in its charter, issued on January 18, 1854, to provide relief to the indigent sick during epidemics, especially yellow fever epidemics.

The Fifth Legislature set aside funds for the publication of a new criminal code and adopted several amendments to be included in the forthcoming edition. Among the more interesting changes were those involving race. One law mandated a prison term of up to ten years for selling a free person into slavery or holding a free person as a slave, knowing that he was lawfully free. The punishment for murder or manslaughter of a slave was the same as that for the same crime against a white person. At the same time, any white who married a black or a descendant of a black or who continued to cohabit with such a person after coming to Texas was to be imprisoned at hard labor in the state penitentiary for up to five years. If any person conspired with a slave to induce a rebellion, he or she was to be executed whether the rebellion or insurrection took place or not. Attempts to steal or entice a slave to run away could earn one up to ten years; if successful, the culprit could be jailed for up to fifteen years. Simply advising a slave to run away could land a person in jail for three to five years.

The new criminal statutes evidenced a strong moralistic streak among the legislators. In fact, the Fifth Legislature became the first in Texas to adopt a statewide law for the regulation of alcoholic beverages. Henceforth, the retail sale of liquor in quantities of less than a quart was prohibited unless the voters of a county decided otherwise. A general referendum was to be held on August 1, 1854, to decide which counties would be dry and which would not. If a county cast its vote in favor of selling liquor in quantities smaller than a quart, then a second election could be called a year later, but the measure did not provide for a subsequent election in counties that went dry.

The Senate mustered only twenty members on February 13, 1854, and on a motion by Lott adjourned *sine die*. The senators had worked harmoniously on most issues, with only an occasional jibe or accusation of improper personal interest in a bill. Within a few months, however, Texas politics would begin to polarize along new lines, and much that had been done by the members of the Fifth Legislature would be undone. The Indian reservations would be abandoned, the school fund would be drained for frontier defense and preparations for civil war, and Texas would not be crossed by a transcontinental line for several more decades. Of course, this was something that the legislators could not know as they returned home to accolades for their labors; within the scope of their cognizance, they had done a good job.

CHAPTER 15

The Senate of the Sixth Legislature, 1855–56

The Senate of the Sixth Legislature met in an atmosphere of heightened sectional tension, brought on by the appearance of a secretive political party in Texas. Resentment of the powerful political influence wielded by foreigners, especially the Irish, in northern cities along the Atlantic seaboard had resulted in a strong nativist movement, which incorporated a definite tinge of anti-Catholicism as well. Originally a loose collection of local secret societies, the American party grew rapidly and earned the popular sobriquet of "Know-Nothings" from its members' customary response to inquiries from the uninitiated. Its strong pro-Union stance attracted Whig refugees, whose own party had disintegrated under the stress of sectional politics, as well as Democrats who were unhappy with the growing identification of their party with the support of slavery.

Nativism, Unionism, and abolitionism made strange bedfellows of a polyglot of political activists under the rubric of the Know-Nothings. The new party first appeared in Texas in 1854, when it elected a complete slate of city officials in San Antonio. By the next spring several newspapers, most of them former Whig publications, had aligned with the party, and they elected a mayor and several councilmen in Galveston. Texas Democrats initially paid little attention to the usurpers; the Democratic convention in 1855 attracted delegates from only twelve counties, and they routinely gave their nomination to the incumbent governor, Elisha M. Pease, and Lieutenant Governor David C. Dickson.

Soon after the Democrats adjourned, however, the Know-Nothings assembled for a caucus in Washington-on-the-Brazos on June 11, 1855. They nominated Dickson for governor and State Senator W. G. W. Jowers for lieutenant governor, and laid plans to organize "committees of vigilance" in every county. Their crowning achievement came when they received the endorsement of U.S. senator Sam Houston, who had been read out of the Texas Democratic party for opposing the Kansas-Nebraska Act, which would have allowed slavery in any territory if the residents voted to accept it. The Democrats hurriedly assembled for another, better-attended caucus, known as the "Bomb Shell Convention." They withdrew their nomination of Dickson and threw the nomination to Hardin R. Runnels, a native of Mississippi and an ardent supporter of slavery.

Other Democrats were persuaded to withdraw to close ranks against the usurpers. Dickson fought hard, assailing Pease for espousing the "state plan," which focused on Galveston as a hub, to build railroads; for opposing the Pacific railroad; and for failing to protect the frontier. Pease defeated Dickson by a margin of less than eight thousand votes to remain in office, although Runnels did make a better showing. Dickson quickly rebounded, winning election to the House to fill a vacated seat during the Sixth Legislature and then serving in the House in the Eighth Legislature and in the Senate in the Ninth and Tenth legislatures.

By 1856, the Know-Nothing party in Texas was virtually moribund as many former supporters scrambled to disassociate themselves from it. The repercussions of the campaign for the members of the Senate, which met for a regular session from November 5, 1855, to February 4, 1856, and then again from July 7 to September 1, 1856, proved to be less fleeting. The Know-Nothings claimed to have won eleven of thirty-three seats in the Senate in 1855. Although only five—John Caldwell, William H. Martin, William M. Taylor, James W. Flanagan, and Elisha E. Lott—can be positively identified, making the boasts of the Know-Nothings somewhat specious, the influence of the uprising on the legislation endorsed by the Senate was obvious. Despite opposition from Pease, whose outrage against the Know-Nothings bordered on hysteria, the legislators adopted a program that combined internal improvements, a sop to former Whigs, with fiscal conservatism, a Democratic tenet.

Nineteen members of the Senate retained their seats from the Fifth Legislature: Malachi W. Allen, James H. Armstrong, Guy M. Bryan, Rufus Doane, Robert H. Guinn, Isaac L. Hill, Elisha E. Lott, William H. Martin, James W. McDade, Elliott M. Millican, Henry C. Pedigo, Mark M. Potter, Edwin B. Scarborough, William T. Scott, Antoine Superviele, M. D. K. Taylor, Jefferson Weatherford, Madison G. Whitaker, and Johnson Wren. A veteran of the first four state senates, Jesse Grimes, returned to the chamber after only a brief interlude in private life. James Truitt, a veteran of the House in the First and Second legislatures and of the Senate in the Fourth Legislature, also regained his seat.

A newcomer to the Texas State Senate, but not to the activities of a senator, caused some stir when he took his seat. John Caldwell was alleged to be the president of the Know-Nothing party in Texas. He had come to Texas in 1831, at age twenty-nine, from Alabama (he was originally from Kentucky), and served in the House during the Third, Fifth, Sixth, Seventh, and Eighth congresses of the Republic and in the Senate in the Ninth Congress. He signed the resolution calling for the Annexation Convention, which he attended as a delegate. His support of the Know-Nothings probably stemmed from his devotion to the Union and his dismay at the increasingly sectional nature of the Democratic party. After leaving the Senate, he staunchly opposed disunion as a delegate to the Secession Convention in 1861, one of very few to do so.

Other Senate newcomers had also served in the Congress of the Republic. Preeminent among this group was Samuel A. Maverick, a South Carolina native who boasted a degree from Yale University. He had served in the South Carolina legislature until he was forced to flee the state following a duel over his opposition to John C. Calhoun's nullification doctrine. He moved to Texas from Alabama in 1835 and joined the Texas Army. Arrested after the capture of Goliad in October, 1835, he escaped from his prison in San Antonio in December and served as a guide for the siege of that city. He was elected to the 1836 convention and signed the Texas Declaration of Independence, and then went back to Alabama for two years. After returning to San Antonio in 1838, he was elected mayor the next year. Captured by Mexican general Adrian Woll during his raid in 1842, Maverick was released after six months, in time to serve as a representative in the Eighth Congress of the Republic. After Texas joined the Union, he served in the House in the Fourth and Fifth legislatures. He served two terms in the Senate and was elected president pro tempore *ad interim* of the Senate in the Seventh Legislature before returning to the House for the Eighth and Ninth legislatures.

Several other veterans of the Republic had scarcely less distinguished careers. Sam Addison White had served as a representative in the First Congress of the Republic. Born in Tennessee, he had come to Texas in 1830 from his native state and worked as an overseer while studying law. He fought at Velasco in 1832, served in the Texas Army in 1835 and 1836, and took part in the Indian fight at Plum Creek in 1840. After a single

Samuel A. Maverick served in the Senate from District 31 during the Sixth and Seventh legislatures. Courtesy Texas State Archives.

term, he worked as owner and editor of the *Victoria Advocate* from 1857 until his death in 1869. He was returned to the Senate for the Tenth Legislature, elected mayor of Victoria during the last years of the Civil War, and appointed district judge in 1865. James M. Burroughs, an Alabama native, had emigrated to Texas in 1844 at the age of twenty and served the following year as a delegate to the Annexation Convention. He sat in the House in the First and Second legislatures as well and in 1861 attended the Secession Convention. He was elected to the U.S. House of Representatives in 1866, but was denied a seat because of his service in the Confederate Army.

Most of the Senate rookies had some prior legislative experience. Edward R. Hord, Edward A. Palmer, and Robert H. Taylor had served together in the House in the Fourth and Fifth legislatures. Hord, who would return to the Senate in the Tenth Legislature, and Palmer did not enjoy long political careers, but Taylor remained in public life for well over two decades. Taylor was an attorney who had emigrated to Texas from his native South Carolina in 1844 at the age of nineteen and fought in the Mexican War. He returned to the House for the Eighth Legislature after two terms in the Senate. Although he opposed secession, after Texas left the Union he participated in the organization of three regiments for the Confederacy. He allegedly spent the last six months of the war in the brush, hiding from Confederate officials who wanted to try him for treason. After the war he served as a delegate to the Constitutional Convention of 1866, as state comptroller, and as judge of the Eighth District. He failed in his bid to be elected lieutenant governor in 1873, but in 1878 he was returned to the House, serving in the Sixteenth Legislature.

Jonathan Russell and James W. Flanagan served together in the House in the Fourth Legislature. The former won little distinction as a state senator, but the latter earned notoriety in a tempestuous career that spanned two score years. Born in Virginia in 1805, Flanagan had come to Texas in 1843 after presiding for ten years in the circuit court of Breckenridge County, Kentucky. He had been a successful planter, attorney, and land speculator in Kentucky and continued to amass wealth in Texas. Like many wealthy men, his conservatism made him a Whig and later a Know-Nothing in opposition to the growing Democratic radicalism in Texas. He gave some lip service to the nativist platform of the American party, but more importantly he endorsed Houston's moderate position on the issues that were dividing the country; he opposed secession. After the Civil War, he attended the 1866 and 1868 constitutional conventions, and in 1869 was elected lieutenant governor on the radical Republican ticket. Before he could be inaugurated, however, he was appointed to the U.S. Senate, where he served from 1870 to 1875.

The three remaining newcomers to the Senate reflected the broad diversity of Texas' antebellum legislators. Henry E. McCulloch, who had served in the House in the Fifth Legislature, was a native of Tennessee who had settled in Texas in 1838 at the age of twenty-two. He had won a reputation for exceptional bravery as an Indian fighter and would serve with distinction as a Confederate officer, although he lived constantly in the shadow of Ben McCulloch, his more talented and popular brother, who died a hero's death at the Battle of Elkhorn Tavern in 1862. Solomon Pirkey was a less spectacular character; he served in the Senate in the Sixth and Seventh legislatures and then served in the House for the Eighth Legislature, where he ended his public career by resigning at the outset of the Civil War. The aspirations of William M. Taylor had apparently collapsed with those of his party; he was a Know-Nothing, and he was never reelected to the Texas legislature after his brief tenure in the Senate.

Only two elected officers of the Senate retained their seats from the Fifth Legislature: Secretary James F. Johnson and Sergeant at Arms Ward Taylor. The roster of newly elected officers included First Assistant Secretary Richard T. Brownrigg, Second Assistant Secretary Adolphe Menard, Engrossing Clerk Caleb J. Garrison, Enrolling Clerk Frank Gildart, Doorkeeper S. W. Pipkin, Assistant Doorkeeper A. M. Clare, and Chaplain J. M. Wesson. John F. Morgan succeeded Garrison as engrossing clerk for the special session.

The senators had scarcely settled in their seats before endorsing a joint resolution, introduced by Senator Potter, excoriating the Know-Nothings and Sam Houston. Adopted on November 20, 1855, the missive declared that the Texas legislature considered that the Compromise of 1850 "fully settled" the "great questions which have unhappily divided the Northern and Southern States of the Union." The Fugitive Slave Act, which had been one of the keys to the compromise, was praised as a "measure of constitutional right and justice to the slave-holding States, essential to their peace and the preservation of their rights." Texas would consider any repeal or modification of the act to be an "invasion of her constitutional rights, and a just cause of alarm to herself and her sister States of the South." Furthermore, the legislators applauded the Kansas-Nebraska Act as a "measure founded in the true spirit of the Federal Constitution of justice to all parts of the Union." They applauded U.S. Senator Thomas J. Rusk's support for the bill and condemned Houston for opposing it.

In his inaugural address to the legislators on December 21, 1855, Pease scorned the Know-Nothing party as being led by "fanatics" who would endanger the government of the United States for the "fancied advantages of freedom to a race who are incapable of appreciating or enjoying it." Moving on to more substantive matters, he recommended the undertaking of an extensive program of internal improvements for transportation, including railroads, roadways, and canals. These would be funded by the state through sales of the public domain, moderate internal improvement taxes, and the investment of the surplus funds set aside by the federal government to redeem the nonrevenue debt of the Republic.

Pease and the Democrats in the legislature combated Dickson's allegations of neglecting the frontier by enacting no fewer than three bills to pay the expenses of ranger companies mustered for various campaigns. The largest appropriation, of $51,000, covered the costs of six companies of volunteers mustered on November 1, 1854, upon the request of U.S. brevet major general Persifor F. Smith, in command of the federal troops in Texas. The national government paid a majority of the expense, but the state had to pay for the time when the troopers had been in the field but had not actually been in federal service. This imposition on the state's financial resources added to the total debt that Texans believed the national government owed to them, a lingering controversy that was not settled until long after the Civil War.

The Senate of the Sixth Legislature also attempted to cope with the Indian problem by setting aside more land for reservations. A bill endorsed by Pease on August 30, 1856, during the called session, provided for the allotment of 640 acres in Liberty, Polk, or Tyler County for the benefit of the Coushatta Indians. This tract, which was to have been located in the public domain or purchased for no more than two dollars an acre, was unfortunately never acquired. The Coushatta eventually joined the Alabama Indians on their Polk County reservation, which had been provided for by the Fifth Legislature, and were assimilated into that tribe. Similarly, an act signed on February 4, 1856, which set aside five leagues of public land for the establishment of an Indian reservation west of the Pecos River, failed to bring about the creation of a new preserve.

The Indian problem, or rather the state's expenses in coping with it, was an influential factor in the settlement of the revenue debt of the Republic, which consisted of bonds that had been sold to fund the operations of that defunct government. In the Compromise of 1850, the United States Congress had pledged to set aside $5 million for the retirement of those securities. This amount was combined with the existing debt of the national government to the state for Indian depredations, plus interest, in a bill passed by Congress on February 28, 1855, that set aside a total of $7.75 million to settle all accounts.

In accordance with the wishes of the state government of Texas, and despite the protests of those holding the bonds, the amount set aside by Congress was to be distributed to creditors *pro rata*, giving each about seventy-seven cents on the dollar. This was far more than most of the creditors had paid because the Republic had originally sold the securities at less than par, and many of the holders were speculators who had bought bonds at even greater discounts. The voters of Texas had rejected the offer of $7.75 million from the national government in a referendum in the fall of 1855, but Pease in his opening address had declared the vote not binding because little more than half of the active electorate had given an opinion, and those who did returned only a narrow majority against acceptance.

A majority of the Senate Committee on the Public Debt, chaired by M. D. K. Taylor, rebelled against the directive of Governor Pease to ignore the plebiscite against accepting the settlement. They insisted that a popular mandate could not be ignored and added that the amount offered for Indian depredations was not nearly enough. Most of the other members of the Senate, however, did endorse the bill after several concessions were offered. The measure as adopted included the stipulation that although the state agreed to abandon all claims against the United States for Indian depredations, this did not include those of individuals for their losses. A supplemental act signed by Pease on February 2, 1856, directed the state comptroller to issue current state bonds for the difference between the (*pro rata*) amount that seventeen petitioners were to receive from the federal government and the face value of the Republic securities that they held. The latter ranged from $200, held by Lucian Navarro, to $88,900, held by the partnership of McKinney and Williams, for a total of $126,777, a pittance well spent for compromise.

The senators, like many other people in Texas, were concerned with the potential for fraud in the final settlement of the Republic's debt. An act approved by Governor Pease on February 2, 1856, directed the comptroller to travel to Washington to review the certificates being submitted for claims in order to reject all fraudulent and counterfeit documents.

He was to keep a register of all approved certificates as well as of those he rejected. A separate act signed that same day strengthened the statutes against counterfeiting public documents for the acquisition of land or money from the state or local governments. The measure provided a penalty of up to twenty years for a conviction and set aside ten thousand dollars for the arrest and prosecution of offenders.

The Senate also endorsed a measure intended to settle another long-standing dispute. During the special session, an act was adopted establishing the office of commissioner of claims to review all land disputes arising from the operations of the Peters, Mercer, Castro, and Fisher and Miller colonies; the German Immigration Company; all grants for internal improvements; and all preemptions. The commissioner was to be appointed by the legislature and hold office until the first day of January, 1858, although the petitioners could present claims for two years beginning on September 1, 1856. Claims could be approved via either the surviving documentation of the General Land Office attesting to their validity or the testimony of "two credible witnesses" in deference to the records destroyed by a disastrous fire that year. Anyone entitled to a land certificate who had not received one could apply to the commissioner, giving evidence as required under whatever law applied, as well as producing two witnesses to confirm residence or service. To house the new records, the Sixth Legislature set aside forty thousand dollars to build a new "fireproof" General Land Office building in Austin.

In response to the rapid westward shift of population, the Senate endorsed the creation of a number of counties. The first act signed by Governor Pease during the Sixth Legislature on December 12, 1855, was one creating Parker County. Its county seat was later named in honor of Senator Weatherford. Other counties were created in rapid succession: Wise, Atascosa, Erath, Comanche, Kerr, Bandera, Lampasas, Llano, San Saba, Kinney, Live Oak, Uvalde, Young, Maverick (named for the popular senator from San Antonio), Jack, Brown, McCulloch (named for Ben McCulloch, brother of Senator Henry McCulloch), and Palo Pinto counties. The Senate also approved new charters for the municipalities of Austin, Anderson, Bellville, Boston, Cameron, Chappell Hill, Dallas, Fairfield, Helena, Indianola, Lavaca, Lexington, Linden, Marshall, Moscow, Mount Pleasant, New Salem, Paris, Rusk, San Antonio, Texana, Tyler, Wheelock, and Woodville.

Pease recommended that the surplus 5 percent bonds set aside by the federal government to redeem the nonrevenue debt of the Republic be

The old Land Office Building, completed in 1857, is one of the oldest in the capitol complex.
Courtesy Texas State Archives.

used to endow public institutions. Foremost in his proposal was the ap-propriation of three hundred thousand dollars in these bonds as a per-manent endowment for a university. The bond money was to be sup-plemented by the proceeds from land sales. The legislators refused to endorse his proposal for a bonded endowment, but did pass a bill on August 30, 1856, directing that the public lands set aside for two state universities—a total of fifty leagues—be surveyed into 160-acre tracts, and alternate plots offered for sale at three dollars an acre through twenty-year notes bearing 8 percent interest. The profits were to be reserved for the support of either one or two universities, a question that still had not been resolved, while the remaining sections were to be held in reserve awaiting disposition by the legislature.

Education in antebellum Texas remained largely a private affair. Many schools chartered by the Sixth Legislature were sponsored by church organizations. The Eastern Texas Annual Conference of the Methodist Episcopal Church, South, opened Starrville Female High School in Smith County and Gilmer Female College, which actually was coeducational for most of its six-year operation, in Upshur County. The Texas Conference of the Methodist Episcopal Church, South, established the Paine Female Institute in Goliad County, which remained open for twenty years and boasted a four-year collegiate department, and Soule University, which offered higher education in Washington County periodically for over thirty years. Texas Baptists founded Luther Rice Baptist Female Institute in Harrison County, while Larissa College in Cherokee County operated under the aegis of the Brazos Synod of the Cumberland Presbyterian Church. Not to be outdone, the Christian Church received a charter for the establishment of Texas Christian College, to be located in the Christian Church district having the greatest number of subscribers. In connection with their college, the trustees were permitted to establish primary schools throughout the state as auxiliaries. The scheme was never implemented.

Private, nonsecular educational institutions were also chartered by the Sixth Legislature. Henderson Female College received a charter, as did Franklin College, which professed to be "purely literary and scientific," in Anderson County. Others included the Milam Male and Female Institute in Bowie County; the Mechanic's Institute, Waco Female Seminary, and Waco Female Academy in McLennan County; and Woodville College in Tyler County, which specified that no denomination would have a majority of the faculty or officers. The charter granted to Galveston Island University on July 18, 1856, empowered it to "possess all the privileges granted to institutions of learning of the highest grade." Nearby, the University of St. Mary was incorporated on August 23, 1856, to instruct males "in all those branches of Literature, science and the arts which are now, or may hereafter be taught in the higher classes of Seminaries in the United States of America"; no religion was specified.

Many of the private, nonsecular educational institutions were supported by fraternal organizations such as the Masons or the International Order of Odd Fellows. The latter were particularly vigorous in 1856, receiving charters from the Sixth Legislature for lodges in Anderson, Austin, Cartmell, Gonzales, Henderson, Huntsville, Ida, La Grange, Lockhart, Marshall, Palestine, Paris, and Waco. Others sponsored educational efforts aimed at an adult audience. Publisher Ferdinand Flake headed a list of members who received a charter as the "Galveston Reading Club," a private circulating library, on September 1, 1856, five days after a new "Lyceum" was incorporated in Houston.

The Senate also endorsed a desperate attempt by a failing private educational institution to save itself. Rutersville College was combined with the Texas Monumental Committee and the Texas Military Institute in a measure signed on August 6, 1856. The resulting institution, to be known as the Texas Monumental and Military Institute, pledged to build a mausoleum to serve as a monument to those who had died or would die in the service of Texas and to establish an institution of higher education for Texas youth "as a most suitable monument in honor of the dead." The superintendent was to be commissioned a colonel in the state militia by the governor and was to direct the "Military and Academic operations" of the organization "according to Military principles." The former site of Rutersville College would now house the Rutersville Female College, to be administered by the same board of trustees. The main campus was to confer the degrees of bachelor and master of arts and bachelor and master of civil engineering, and general degrees were to be conferred by the Female College. The gambit did not work; in 1859, after twenty years of service, the school closed its doors.

Pease recommended that U.S. 5 percent bonds in the amount of $250,000 each be reserved for buildings and for the operation of a lunatic asylum and schools for the deaf, dumb, and blind. Senator Flanagan introduced a successful bill establishing the state Lunatic Asylum; it was signed reluctantly by Pease on August 28, 1856. The measure set aside only $50,000 in bonds for construction, but two days later Pease endorsed another bill appropriating one hundred thousand acres of the public domain for the support of the institution. Identical parcels of land were set aside for the Institute for the Education of the Deaf and Dumb, founded at Austin under an act approved on August 26, 1856, and the Institute for the Education of the Blind, established in Austin under a bill signed by Pease on August 16, 1856. The latter two institutions received no bonds to support construction; they had to settle for ten thousand dollars each in state funds.

The specie held in trust for the schools of Texas was exchanged for federal 5 percent bonds through a measure introduced by Senator Potter and passed on August 29, 1856. The act combined the General School Fund with the Special School Fund created by the Fifth Legislature and then replaced all currency held in the joint account with bonds. The interest from the combined fund was to be used for the support of all public schools in the state. The only restriction was that no school could receive support unless it provided instruction in the English language.

Many states allowed their school funds to be loaned to railroad companies during the antebellum period. Senator Palmer, as well as many railroad promoters in Texas, thought that this was a fine idea, and introduced a bill to that effect. As chairman of the Senate Committee on Public Education, he reported his bill favorably, asserting that the proposal would make "Education and Internal Improvements . . . handmaids in advancing the prosperity and greatness of the State."

Pease agreed, and signed Palmer's bill into law on August 13, 1856. The exchange of school funds for railroad bonds was to be regulated by the governor, comptroller, and attorney general sitting as an ex officio board of school commissioners. The fund would be given to the companies at no less than par for ten years at 6 percent interest, plus 2 percent interest paid each year into a sinking fund. By the terms of the act, half of the fund was reserved for companies building east of the Trinity River, and the balance for companies building west of that waterway. Only six thousand dollars per mile could be disbursed, and to qualify for funding a minimum of twenty-five miles had to be completed, and another twenty-five had to be graded, ready for rails. The loans were to be secured by a lien on all of a railroad company's property and income. Companies that received more than sixteen sections of public land per mile under the terms of their charter could not receive a loan from the school fund, nor could any firm building a line between Houston and Galveston or any line less than fifty miles in length. Few companies took advantage of the offer, and those that did proved to be a mixed blessing for the state, draining specie in return for unsecured bonds that proved worthless when the company folded.

Judicious use of the federal 5 percent bonds along with fiscal conservatism permitted the Sixth Legislature once more to turn over nine-tenths of the state tax revenue to the counties, despite an attempted veto by Pease. Also, several counties were authorized to levy special taxes for various projects. The school trustees of Comal County collected a school tax equivalent to the state tax on real and personal property to augment the proceeds from the state school fund. A similar levy was permitted in Dallas and Travis counties to build courthouses, while in McLennan County the commissioners were allowed to collect a property tax twice that of the state for their courthouse.

A unique act approved on January 28, 1856, extended the authority of the Brazoria County commissioners over private as well as public roads in their county. Requests for all new roads had to be accompanied by a petition from twelve householders. While the closing of a road required a petition from twelve householders and a public hearing, a remarkable provision allowed farmers who wanted to cultivate land where a road lay to petition for removal of the road to another site. Such a request could be granted upon the review and approval of inspectors appointed by the court, without a public hearing. The commissioners of Brazoria County were empowered to collect a tax of six cents on every hundred dollars in real and personal property and a poll tax of fifty cents to supplement their road fund. These taxes could be paid by working on the road for one dollar a day or furnishing slaves to do so at the same rate of compensation.

Brazoria County was the exception to the rule of private road and bridge construction in antebellum Texas. Senators in the Sixth Legislature endorsed many charters for toll bridges. The Austin City Bridge Company was incorporated on August 11, 1856, to bridge the Colorado River. Nearby, E. P. Sawyer bridged Walnut Creek, while farther south John Torrey and associates were allowed to build and operate a toll bridge across the Guadalupe River at New Braunfels. William M. Lee and his partners were authorized to build a span across the East Fork of the Trinity River in Collin County. In East Texas, Mathew Worell built a toll bridge across the Navasota River on the old colonial road from Bexar to Nacogdoches, and Caroline Stafford built and operated a toll bridge across Mud Creek in Cherokee County. Near Beaumont another woman, Nancy Hutchinson, went into partnership with A. J. Livis to build a causeway across the Neches River. Yegua Creek was the focus of two enterprises: the Yegua Turnpike and Bridge Company near Independence and Albert G. Hunt's proposed span in Washington County near Blake's Crossing.

Pease, keeping in mind the charges made by Dickson, accepted a bill from the Sixth Legislature to revive a failing Pacific railroad line. After three years of inactivity, on February 4, 1856, the Memphis, El Paso and Pacific Railroad Company received a new charter from the Sixth Legislature. Its pledge to build a line from a point on the eastern boundary line of the state between the Red River and Sulphur River to a junction with the Rio Grande near El Paso was renewed, but its land grants were increased from eight sections per mile to sixteen, to be surveyed in a strip of alternating sections eight miles wide on either side of the line. Again, it could combine with another westward-building company to provide one trunk line through the state. A supplemental bill signed on March 20, 1856, allowed the company to claim land for each mile it graded rather than completed. Although it laid a total of only six miles of rails, which were abandoned in 1872, before the Civil War the company received 230,000 acres for grading fifty-seven miles of roadbed.

The Sixth Legislature proved to be more successful in bailing out another ailing railroad company by rechartering it. The Galveston and Red River Railroad became the Houston and Texas Central Railroad, which survived the Civil War and prospered. The new charter deleted the right of the company to build branch lines, so when the citizens of Washington County wanted to connect their county seat to the main line, they had to build their own; the Washington County Railroad Company was chartered on February 2, 1856. The line, built at low cost by slave labor, started at Hempstead and reached Brenham in 1861. It was reputed to have cost less per mile than any other railroad in the United States. To cover expenses, the state donated a total of 236,610 acres of land and loaned the company sixty-six thousand dollars, while the county provided a loan from its school fund for the rolling stock. Other companies were not so fortunate: the Henderson and Logansport Railroad Company, incorporated on September 1, 1856, to build a line from Henderson to the latter town on the Sabine River, lost its charter through inactivity, stymied by poor management and lack of funds.

The Houston and Texas Central Railroad owed much of its success to local government support. The Sixth Legislature allowed Houston officials to levy a tax of one percent on all taxable property in the city to support the construction of a railroad. They were also permitted to collect a license tax equal to that levied by the state for the same purpose on taverns, groceries, bars, "tippling-houses," bowling alleys, and billiard halls. A similar bill permitted the commissioners of Brazoria County to impose a special levy of one-fourth of one percent on taxable property, plus twice the state license tax on taverns, groceries, bars, "tippling houses," bowling alleys, and billiard halls. Like the Houston tax, it had to be approved in a popular referendum before imposition, but the Brazoria County revenues could be spent on either a railroad or a canal.

Water transportation was a special concern of the planters living along the Texas coast. Senator Potter introduced an act, signed on January 8, 1856, that authorized the federal government, with the approval of the governor, to build breakwaters, jetties, dams, and other improvements for navigation along the coast. During the special session, Pease dodged another override vote by declining to veto an act setting aside $300,000 for the improvement of the navigable waterways of Texas. This amount was used as a matching fund in a ratio of four to one; for every $1,000 raised by private subscription, the state donated $4,000 to a limit of $50,000 for each project. Only 5 percent of any subscription had to be paid in cash up front, but another 20 percent had to be paid in every sixty days. A new officer, the state engineer and superintendent, was to inspect each proposal before disbursement and supervise the work of all contractors.

The state waterway improvement fund was severely limited in its utility by restrictions imposed by the Sixth Legislature. If Louisiana provided funds for the improvement of the Sabine River, or Arkansas for the Red River, or Mexico for the Rio Grande, a matching amount from the Texas fund could be drawn for that purpose, but no more than $15,000 could be drawn for each project. A supplemental bill limited the disbursement of state matching funds to $50,000 for all the bays on the coast, and directed that not more than $10,000 was to be spent on any one bay. No more than $20,000 was to be spent on any stream other than the Brazos, Colorado, Sabine, and Trinity rivers, and no Texas waterway that was not naturally navigable for at least ten miles was to be proposed for improvement.

One transportation proposal endorsed by the Senate purported to combine the best features of roads, rails, and canals. Thomas J. Chambers, who had received a charter from the Fifth Legislature for a transport company, was granted a new charter on February 6, 1856, for the "Terraqueous Transportation Company." He told the legislators that he had invented a vehicle for the transport of freight and passengers that was "capable of traversing equally the land and the sea," and claimed it was "equal, if not superior in safety, speed, accommodation and capacity" to any "first class vessels by water, and railroad conveyances by land." Flanagan chaired the joint select committee that recommended the adoption of Chambers's proposal. The committee referred to the machine as "novel," and admitted that they were not entirely convinced of its utility, but were willing to give Chambers a chance to prove himself. The Sixth Legislature gave him a charter for an unprecedented one hundred years to "locate, survey, construct, equip, alter, maintain, own, and operate" four thousand miles of roads in the state. A right-of-way three hundred feet in width was granted through all public lands, and the power of eminent domain was bestowed to acquire similar easements through private property.

The remainder of the charters granted by the Sixth Legislature were for more ordinary and more successful projects. The Powder Horn Bayou and Matagorda Bay Dredging Company was authorized to dredge that waterway in Calhoun County. Farther up the coast, the Texas Marine Railway and Building Association was incorporated on August 13, 1856, to build a drydock facility in Harris County to repair steam and sailing vessels. Senator Potter introduced a bill to allow the Texas and New Orleans Telegraph Company to string a line from Galveston to the Louisiana state line on the east and the cities of Austin and San Antonio on the west. The company had some trouble laying line under Galveston Bay, but it was in place by 1860 and continued to be used well into the middle of the twentieth century. The Galveston Gas Company received a charter on August 23, 1856, to provide natural gas service to the port city for the first time. Finally, the Brazoria County Insurance Company received a charter, through a bill introduced by Senator Bryan, to sell marine and fire insurance in Brazoria, Fort Bend, Wharton, and Matagorda counties, and to sell it for all of the vessels navigating on the Brazos River.

Most of the industries chartered in Texas before the Civil War were simple affairs designed to process agricultural products into useful commodities. George W. Baird was given a charter for a water-powered "saw, grist, and flouring mill" on the Elm Fork of the Trinity River in Dallas County, while James H. and Simpson C. Dyer were empowered to build a grist and flour mill on the Brazos River near Fort Graham in Hill County. A few enterprises were more ambitious. The Texas Cotton Seed, Oil, and Paper Manufacturing Company was incorporated on August 7, 1856, to make oil and paper from cottonseed in Harris County. To the south, the Galveston Rope Cordage and Cotton Manufacturing Company was chartered on September 1, 1856, to produce cotton and woolen goods, while farther north, the Harrison Manufacturing Company received a charter on August 15, 1856, to produce textiles in that county.

The increasing importance of cotton to the Texas economy was attested to by the passage on September 1, 1856, of a bill creating the office of weigher of cotton at the ports of Indianola, Lavaca, Houston, and Galveston. An unusual bill designed to protect the interests of planters was signed by Pease two days earlier, making it unlawful for anyone who found a cotton bale floating in a Texas waterway or along the coast to keep his windfall. The finder had to place the bale or bales in a secure place and advertise the find until the owner replied. Upon delivery, the finder was to be compensated for costs and be rewarded with five dollars. If the owner did not respond in three months, the cotton was to be sold at auction by a "wreck-master," who received a commission of 5 percent of the sale price for his trouble, paid the finder his costs plus five dollars, and held the remainder in trust for the owner. If the owner never appeared, then the money was given to the county treasurer, who gave it to the state treasurer, who then returned it to the finder if he could prove his claim satisfactorily. If a person decided to ignore the new law and use the found cotton as his own, the penalty for such violation was a fine of up to five hundred dollars and a prison sentence of one year.

At the suggestion of Governor Pease, the Sixth Legislature adopted, during the special session, both a new criminal code, introduced in the House, and a new code of criminal procedure, introduced in the Senate. These proved to be quite durable; the latter was not fundamentally revised until 1965, and the former not until 1973. They did, however, contain some provisions that were peculiar to their time. For instance, the law of April 9, 1840, restricting the immigration of free blacks to Texas was included and was amended to impose a fine of up to two thousand dollars on any person who brought or helped to bring a free black into Texas. Another section forbade any black to carry a gun or other deadly weapon without the permission of his or her owner or another responsible white person. Any white person was empowered to take a gun from any black who did not have permission to carry one or was not escorted.

The Senate of the Sixth Legislature adjourned in a flurry of angry accusations of impropriety and incompetence, the fallout from the tensions accompanying the Know-Nothing "bombshell" that exploded before the session began. Pease, furious that his directives on key issues such as the federal bonds had been questioned, denounced the legislators as "foolish, improvident, and corrupt." Like many other Texas Democrats, he viewed dissension within party ranks in such a time of partisan crisis to be tantamount to treason. The Know-Nothings faded quickly into obscurity, but a new enemy, the "Black Republicans," had already appeared to take their place. The result for Texas politics was a further closing of the ranks by the Democrats, who developed an intransigence that precluded compromise with anyone who questioned their policies, especially their support of slavery, and forced the state to secession.

CHAPTER 16

The Senate of the Seventh Legislature, 1857–58

The Seventh Legislature met from November 2, 1857, to February 16, 1858, under Governor Elisha M. Pease and Governor Hardin R. Runnels, who had served as lieutenant governor with Pease and was succeeded by Francis R. Lubbock. The inauguration of Runnels and Lubbock on December 21, 1857, was a triumph for the radical faction of the Democratic party in Texas, a faction composed of partisans who fervently espoused the primacy of states' rights over the authority of the federal government and were committed to the expansion of slavery, even at the expense of the national union. Runnels had defeated Sam Houston, the hero of the Republic and a U.S. senator, who had lost favor in Texas after voting against the Kansas-Nebraska Act of 1854, a measure that repudiated the Missouri Compromise of 1820 and allowed the voters in each organized territory of the United States to decide whether the "peculiar institution" would expand into their community.

Houston knew that his dissenting vote would jeopardize his Senate seat; Texas had become a Democratic stronghold after the collapse of the Know-Nothings, a pro-Union party with whom he had dallied briefly. He stumped for the governorship in 1857, as an outgoing U.S. senator without a party, and lost for the first and only time in a bitter struggle. Almost all of his speeches were accompanied by a rebuttal from Louis T. Wigfall or J. Pinckney Henderson, both known as "fire-eaters" in the developing sectional parlance of the period. The voters took their cue from the strongest organization in the field, one that increasingly presented itself as the only choice for salvation from a federal government that had fallen under the control of fanatical abolitionists, and the Democrats pushed Houston offstage to await a return to reason.

Runnels and Lubbock, unlike Houston, had proved to be good party men in their support for the increasingly radical Democrats in Texas. Runnels was a native of Mississippi who had served as a representative in the Second, Third, and Fourth Texas legislatures, and then was elected Speaker of the House for the Fifth Legislature. Lubbock was a native of South Carolina who had been appointed comptroller of the Republic by President Houston in 1837, when Lubbock was only twenty-two. An active states' rights partisan, Lubbock had been a leader in the crucial reorganization of the Texas Democratic party in the wake of the Know-Nothing challenge, and the revitalized convention system had rewarded him, together with Runnels, with a historic victory over Houston.

Although Lubbock and Runnels lost their bid for reelection to Houston and Edward Clark in 1859, when the voters of Texas temporarily balked at the perilous choices offered by the radicals, Lubbock nevertheless forged ahead, serving as a radical Texas delegate to the national Democratic convention in 1860, where he took part in the walkout by several southern delegations. In 1861, after Houston had been removed from office for refusing to take an oath of loyalty to the nascent Confederate States of America, Lubbock was elected governor. He did not stand for reelection in 1863 but instead accepted a military commission. As an aide-de-camp to Jefferson Davis, Lubbock was captured with the Confederate president in Georgia and jailed at the end of the Civil War, but rebounded once more to become a successful businessman and state treasurer of Texas for six terms beginning in 1878. The tenacity of radical Democrats such as Lubbock ensured that the issues leading to the secession crisis would not be ignored during the Seventh Legislature, even as the members concentrated on other matters.

Of the thirty-three senators who actually attended the Seventh Legislature, a total that does not include Hiram G. Runnels or Elliott M. Millican, neither of whom appeared, eighteen had served in the Senate in the Sixth Legislature: James M. Burroughs, John Caldwell, Jesse Grimes, Robert H. Guinn, Elisha E. Lott, William H. Martin, Samuel A. Maverick, Henry E. McCulloch, Henry C. Pedigo, Solomon H. Pirkey, Mark M. Potter, Jonathan Russell, Edwin B. Scarborough, M. D. K. Taylor, Robert H. Taylor, William M. Taylor, James Truitt, and Johnson Wren. This large cadre of returning senators lent a strong element of political stability to the deliberations within the Senate, especially through the leadership of such moderate veterans as Jesse Grimes, who had run as Houston's candidate for lieutenant governor in 1857. Their position was reinforced with the support of legislative neophytes such as John N. Fall, Archibald C. Hyde, George Quinan, Chauncy B. Shepard, and David M. Whaley, who took Millican's place after his resignation. Forbes Britton, a West Point graduate with a long and distinguished career, provided conservative professional leadership on issues involving frontier defense, a topic that would become the source of much resentment against the federal government.

Among the newcomers were others who had some previous legislative experience. Isaiah A. Paschal returned from the Senate of the Fifth Legislature, and Albert G. Walker had served in the Senate in the Third Legislature until his resignation. George B. Erath had sat in the House during the First Texas Legislature, along with Ben F. Tankersly, who also served in the House in the Second and Fourth legislatures. Erath had fought at San Jacinto, campaigned with the fateful Somervell expedition, and served as a representative in the Eighth and Ninth congresses of the Republic. He remained a fighter for Texas all of his life. At the outbreak of the Civil War he mustered a company for Confederate service but was active also in civilian affairs, surveying many tracts such as the present sites of Waco and Caldwell. Erath would return for a second time to the Texas Senate in 1874 at the age of sixty-one to aid in the Democratic reclamation of the state from Republican rule. Little is known of Tankersly; he was elected to take the place of Hiram G. Runnels, who failed to appear for the session. Runnels, who was not related to the governor-elect, had his seat contested on November 9, 1857, when Grimes presented a petition to the Senate Committee on Privileges and Elections. Runnels had been elected once before, in 1855, to the Texas Senate, to fill Pease's seat when he was elected to the governorship, but had failed to qualify then, too. Runnels was apparently chronically ill; on December 21, 1857, Senator Potter offered a resolution of condolence following his death. To fill the vacancy left by Runnels, the election was called that brought Tankersly to the Senate in the Seventh Legislature.

The careers of two legislative veterans who were newcomers to the Texas Senate during the Seventh Legislature illustrate the critical division on the states' rights issue that was already threatening the Union and plaguing Texas politics. James W. Throckmorton had resigned from the House in the Fourth Legislature and then succeeded himself after a special election and served in the House in the Fifth Legislature. A native

Archibald C. Hyde represented District 33 in the Senate during the Seventh and Eighth legislatures. Courtesy Texas State Archives.

of Tennessee and a confirmed Whig who had served as an army surgeon during the war with Mexico, Throckmorton won distinction for his vocal opposition to those who advocated sectionalism, including Governor Runnels. He remained a stalwart supporter of Houston, and Throckmorton would be one of only eight delegates elected to the Secession Convention who voted against dissolving the Union. Throckmorton would not fight against his state, however, and he became a brigadier general in the Texas militia during the Civil War. Later he served as president of the Constitutional Convention of 1866, and then as governor of Texas until he was removed by General Philip H. Sheridan as an "impediment to reconstruction," an epithet that must have galled such a staunch Unionist. Once the Democrats had wrested control of the Texas government from the Republicans, however, Throckmorton served a number of terms in the U.S. Congress.

Throckmorton's constant opponent was Louis T. Wigfall, who had won his first Texas election to fill a partial term in the House in the Third Legislature. Wigfall was a formidable states' rights partisan with a well-deserved reputation for a venomous tongue. A native of South Carolina, he had served as a sergeant during the Seminole War and had fought at least two duels, killing his challenger in the first. As a member of the House in the Third Legislature he had led the opposition to the Compromise of 1850, protesting that it would permit New Mexico to become a "free soil" territory. He later became a champion of the movement to reopen the slave trade with Africa. Naturally, his politics made him an enemy of Houston, who was unable to prevent Wigfall's election to the U.S. Senate in 1859.

In Washington, Wigfall condemned Democrats who supported Stephen A. Douglas and sectional compromise, and worked unceasingly for secession. He taunted the Lincoln administration from the floor of the Senate during the crisis at Fort Sumter and then resigned to accept an appointment as aide-de-camp to General Pierre G. T. Beauregard at Charleston, where Wigfall negotiated the surrender of Fort Sumter. He was commissioned a brigadier general in the Confederate Army, but resigned following his election as one of two senators for Texas in the Confederate Congress. There, he became a thorn in Jefferson Davis's side by loudly demanding ruthless prosecution of the war; Wigfall's opposition to centralizing the Confederate war effort, however, hindered the prosecution he demanded. After the war, Wigfall fled to England from

Galveston and did not return to Texas until January, 1874, dying a month later in the "Island City."

Wigfall's states' rights stance was shared by many other members of the Senate, including Malcolm D. Graham, who served as the attorney general of Texas from 1858 to 1860 before he was elected to the Confederate Congress as a representative along with Claiborne C. Herbert. In May, 1864, Davis appointed Graham as presiding judge advocate of the Trans-Mississippi Department. Graham was captured by Union forces and imprisoned until he was exchanged in March, 1865, after which he returned to private practice in Texas. Herbert joined Wigfall in his opposition to the centralization of the southern war effort, threatening that Texas would secede from the Confederacy if the issue was forced; he retained his seat for the duration of the war. He was elected to the U.S. Congress in 1865 and 1867 but was refused a place because of his Confederate war record. Fletcher S. Stockdale was a delegate to the Democratic National Convention in 1860 and followed Lubbock's lead in withdrawing. Stockdale became a leading member of the Secession Convention in Texas, an aide to Lubbock, and finally lieutenant governor in 1863, a position that left him with the unhappy task of restoring order after Governor Pendleton Murrah fled to Mexico in 1865. After the war, Stockdale remained active in business and politics, returning to the Texas Senate for a term in 1868 and serving in the Constitutional Convention of 1875.

The election of officers for the Senate proceeded peacefully until the selection of a chaplain. The balance of the roster was quickly filled: James F. Johnson, secretary; Richard T. Brownrigg, first assistant secretary; Thomas P. Samford, second assistant secretary; Stephen Cummings, engrossing clerk; J. Pat Henry, enrolling clerk; William A. Pitts, sergeant at arms; L. M. Truitt, doorkeeper; A. M. Clare, assistant doorkeeper; and Episcopalian Reverend Edward C. Fontaine as chaplain. Senator Graham, on November 10, 1857, presented a petition signed by 198 people requesting that the selection of chaplains for the Texas legislature, the U.S. Congress, and the military forces of the United States be discontinued. The signers of the petition contended that the appointment of these religious officials clearly violated the first amendment of the U.S. Constitution and the corresponding sections of the state charter that prohibited the establishment of a national religion. Senator Wigfall, chairman of the Committee on State Affairs, delivered a typically angry re-

Claiborne C. Herbert from District 32 served in the Senate during the Seventh and Eighth legislatures. Courtesy Texas State Archives.

Malcolm D. Graham served in the Seventh Legislature as senator from District 9. Courtesy Texas State Archives.

pudiation of the petitioners' assertion, and the matter was dropped without further consideration.

Most of the Senate's calendar was occupied with more substantial matters. Governor Pease's annual message was read to the Texas Senate on November 4, 1857. In it, he addressed several pressing issues. Crops in some areas of the state had failed for the previous two years because of a drought "unexampled in the annals of the country." Also, a financial panic afflicted the United States as a whole, decreasing "the value of every description of property" and suspending, "for a season, the operation of almost every branch of industry." Governor Pease, like most Democrats, laid the blame for the panic on the "rapid increase of banks," whose "improvident issues of paper currency" had encouraged "reckless speculation and an extension of credit beyond the reasonable demands of business." Texas, however, was "but slightly affected" by the Panic of 1857 because "no paper currency has ever been able to obtain a general circulation," and the governor asked that the policies against the establishment of banks and an expenditure of state funds for general relief be continued. His advice was heeded by the Seventh Legislature; a joint committee did recommend the adoption of several individual relief bills but failed to muster support for a general fund of one hundred thousand dollars.

The overall prosperity of the state, due to its increasing export of cotton despite a decline in prevailing prices, sustained an atmosphere of financial optimism. Although other state officers questioned his figures, Governor Pease predicted a large surplus in the state coffers, including the school fund, and recommended a reduction in *ad valorem* and poll taxes. At the same time, a recognition that in the future the expenses of state government would increase—as more judicial districts were established for the new frontier counties, for example—prompted the governor to ask that the general policy of releasing taxes back to the counties be discontinued in favor of a more parsimonious method of authorizing local taxes for internal improvements. He urged the payment of outstanding bonds to preserve the credit of the state, including those for the debts of the Republic, a bill that the House had refused to pass during the Sixth Legislature.

Fiscal optimism also led Governor Pease to stress the immediate importance of establishing a state university while the state treasury was full. Pease declared: "no country was ever better situated to commence such an undertaking." In addition to the "ample means" in the treasury, 220,400 acres had already been reserved for an endowment, and the remainder of the fifty leagues provided by the Constitution of 1845 were being surveyed, albeit haphazardly, in accordance with an act of the Sixth Legislature. Pease insisted that the proceeds from the sale of these lands, "if properly managed," would be a "liberal endowment," enabling the state to employ "the ablest professors in every department of learning." He concluded: "The necessity for such an institution is felt and acknowledged by everyone; and I trust that you will not let this session pass, without adopting measures for its establishment at an early day." Pease also asked that permanent quarters for the Institute for the Education of the Deaf and Dumb and the Institute for the Education of the Blind be purchased in Austin and reported that the Lunatic Asylum, after some difficulty, was finally in the planning stages of construction.

The first order of business was maintenance of internal order in Texas and defense of the frontier against Indian attacks. The Senate appropriated sixteen thousand dollars to pay the mounted volunteer company commanded by Captain G. H. Nelson that had been dispatched during October, 1857, to provide an escort for Mexican carters along the long road from Port Lavaca to San Antonio. These troopers had been enlisted in order to provide protection from Anglo settlers in the region who resented Mexican competition and demonstrated their antipathy by ambushing the Mexicans. The attackers rarely killed their victims, but they had wounded several and destroyed their carts.

The Anglo settlers were quite bold, occasionally attacking even U.S. Army sutlers and their escorts. Governor Pease was extremely concerned; the appropriation on December 14, 1857, was in response to his request for a continuance of Nelson's unit. A joint committee of investigation that included all of the members of the Senate Committee on State Affairs—Graham, Paschal, Potter, Shepard, Stockdale, Robert H. Taylor, and Wigfall—was formed. The joint committee introduced a bill to expedite trials in such cases, which proved to be of such narrow interest that the bill did not pass; the appropriation measure was adopted only as amended by a conference committee cochaired by McCulloch for the Senate.

Frontier defense proved to be a much more divisive issue. In an act introduced by Senator McCulloch, four thousand dollars was appropriated to reimburse three units of minutemen, commanded by John W. Sansom, John H. Davenport, and Reading W. Black, for their service

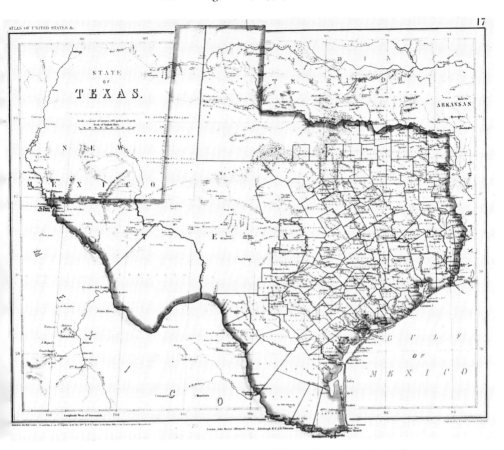

This 1857 map of Texas shows the westward advance of the settlers and the land still occupied by Indians. Reproduced from holdings of Texas State Archives.

along the border during 1856. Brevet Major General David E. Twiggs, in charge of the U.S. troops on the western frontier, sent a tactful request for more aid and a suggestion that it might be obtained by pressuring Congress. Two joint resolutions passed on November 17, 1857. The first, introduced by Senator Britton as chairman of the Committee on the Militia, asked Texas congressmen to secure federal funds for a unit of mounted volunteers for the western frontier. The other, introduced by Senator Scarborough of the joint committee established to investigate reports of Indian depredations in San Saba County, authorized Governor Pease to enlist a company of one hundred mounted volunteers for three months and provided twenty thousand dollars for that purpose. Eight days later, on November 25, the legislature adopted an angrier resolution initiated by Senator McCulloch that directed the federal government to repay Texas for its expenses in defending the frontier.

The administration of the federal Indian reserves also occasioned some friction. The Senate followed the recommendation of Senator Caldwell, chairman of the Committee on Indian Affairs, and tabled Senator Hyde's bill to enlarge the Texas Indian reserve from five to nine leagues. Senators Erath, McCulloch, Throckmorton, Britton, and Scarborough were appointed to a special committee as a result of a motion by Erath to create a commission to look into the Indian policy and its administration and recommend alternatives to federal control of the Indians. The commission continued beyond the end of the Seventh Legislature; on the eve of the Civil War, Erath resigned his seat in the Texas Senate to continue his investigation into Indian affairs. He faced an almost hopeless task: in August, 1859, the Texas Indian reservation was removed to the Indian Territory under the supervision of Major Robert Neighbors. When Neighbors returned, he was ambushed and killed by a man who disagreed with the policy of protecting Indians on reservations.

Erath's special committee did produce some results during the Seventh Legislature. A joint resolution on January 16, 1858, asked for a prompt settlement of private claims resulting from raids in Texas conducted by Indians living on federal reservations in adjacent territories. Another joint resolution on January 29 requested the establishment of a federal military post near the junction of the Washita River and the Red River in order to prevent Indians from crossing into Texas at that point from the Indian Territory. Additionally, the resolution demanded stricter regulation of the Texas Indian reserve by the agents present there and requested that the agents be assigned a sufficient military force to carry out the Texas legislature's instructions. Yet another resolution adopted on the same day, January 29, added to the responsibilities of the agents by directing that all of the Indians in the Trans-Pecos region be rounded up and placed on the reserve by a federal agent. Finally, the Senate requested that the Alabama-Coushatta Indians be removed from Polk and Tyler counties by the state government; first, however, the permission of the chiefs had to be obtained. When the Civil War began, the Alabama-Coushatta were still in East Texas, so apparently their leaders had refused to comply with the Senate's relocation plan. A bill by Senator Scarborough to authorize the governor to appoint an agent for the Alabama-Coushatta failed to become law in 1858, indicating the Seventh Legislature's disinterest in forcibly disturbing "friendly" Indians.

The concern of Texans to counteract "unfriendly" Indians was another matter. On January 27, 1858, a bill introduced by Senator Britton was signed, providing for the muster of a company of one hundred mounted volunteers for six months. These troopers would be funded by an appropriation of seventy thousand dollars, which would be replenished if the federal government did not act for frontier defense and it became necessary to continue or expand the force in the field against the Indians. This unit, which was basically an extension of that provided for in November, 1857, was mustered into service in San Antonio under the command of John S. Ford. It left in April, 1858, for the Panhandle region, where its most noted accomplishment was its defeat of the noted Comanche chief "Iron-Jacket" in a running battle. Such victories by state troops reinforced the arguments of those who insisted that Texas could make its own way outside the Union and might do even better within a new confederation.

The Senate of the Seventh Legislature endorsed one final measure for state defense. On February 15, 1858, the uniformed militia companies in Texas—the Galveston Artillery Company and the Lone Star Military Company of Galveston; the Washington Light Guards, Milam Rifles, and Turner Rifles of Houston; the Refugio Riflemen; and the Alamo Rifles of San Antonio—were incorporated as self-governing organizations and exempted from militia duty. As military units they would be equipped by the state in times of emergency and be subject to the command of the governor. Arming these companies and the militia taxed the resources of the state. Governor Runnels on January 19, 1858, was authorized to petition the U.S. government for a periodic requisition of arms and accoutrements to be issued to the militia, to every uniformed volunteer company, and to the military colleges and schools in Texas that applied for equipment. Many people in Texas recognized that these preparations went beyond those necessary for frontier defense; along with Runnels's increasingly belligerent stance, these activities indicated that a much bigger conflict was afoot.

The imposition of internal order included a sweeping revision of the penal code adopted by the Sixth Legislature, especially those provisions governing slaves. An act introduced by Senator Herbert and signed on January 27, 1858, allowed "free persons of African descent" over the age of fourteen to choose a master and become a slave through a petition to the district court. A black female could request that her children be enslaved along with herself if they were under fourteen years of age. If she were deceased, then a guardian could request enslavement of the orphans, with no provision for emancipation upon reaching their majority. These revisions seem to have been adopted in response to several court cases, notably in Galveston, where the right of a white to enslave a free black had been called into question. Wigfall did introduce a bill to prevent the emancipation of slaves by will, a measure designed, together with the act permitting voluntary enslavement, to reduce the number of free blacks in Texas, but the bill failed to pass.

The revised law did provide some remedy for those free blacks who correctly believed that the new provisions had opened a Pandora's box regarding their civil liberties. Any person convicted of falsely enslaving a free man or woman could be fined up to two thousand dollars. If by abduction a woman was forced into marriage, then the miscreant could be jailed for up to five years. If she was forced into prostitution, then the sentence could be increased to ten years. A seduction by a promise of marriage to a female under the age of twenty-five that resulted in "carnal knowledge" could bring both a fine of five thousand dollars and a prison term of five years. This obsession with female virtue was probably intended only to apply to white women. The obsession is reflected in the reduction of a murder charge to manslaughter, which was not a capital offense, if it avenged an insult to a woman, although one had to "prove the general character of the female insulted, in order to ascertain the extent of the provocation."

Whipping was the milder of two alternatives for punishing slaves. The new penal code required that a slave be whipped for trespassing, "improper language," or "indecent or turbulent conduct" in the presence of whites. Death was mandatory for slaves guilty of murder, rape upon a free white woman, insurrection, arson, robbery of a free white person, or an assault with intent to murder, rape, or rob a free white person. The same capital offenses applied to "free persons of color," who could also be executed for aiding in an insurrection or kidnapping a free white woman. Forced labor was an option to whipping or fining free persons of color. Slaves who killed their masters in the course of being punished were guilty of murder.

Under the existing law, the state was obligated to pay a master one-half of the value of a slave executed for a capital offense. The Senate was confronted with an interesting case in December, 1857, when three men petitioned separately for compensation for their slaves, who had been lynched. Each of the three slaves had been taken into custody for a capital offense but had been "rescued" by a mob in each instance and hanged without trial. A majority of the Committee on State Affairs refused to pay the owners any indemnity, opining that to do so would provide no obstacle to a repetition of such ugly incidents in the future. The slaves should have been tried, and to award money for a lynching would only encourage masters or their neighbors to continue to take justice into their own hands. Paschal and Graham dissented from the majority report, insisting that the state officers who had taken the slaves into custody had assumed responsibility for their safety, and therefore the state was liable for the loss of that investment, regardless of the humane element in the grisly affair.

The Senate adjourned without compensating the irate owners, and even endorsed one revision to the penal code that made masters legally liable for damages or fines levied on their slaves. The legislators did provide another sop for masters by endorsing an act, signed on February 13, 1858, that provided that anyone who captured a runaway Texas slave outside of the slave territory of the United States and delivered him to the Travis County sheriff would be rewarded with up to one-third of the value of the slave. By doing so, the Senate encouraged the kidnapping of free blacks even outside the South, a practice that was not uncommon by 1858.

Internal racial order also required measures for preserving purity of blood. The revised penal code, as it was finally approved on February 12, 1858, included a prohibition on interracial marriage, defined as the marriage of a white with anyone with as little as one-eighth Negro blood. Continued cohabitation could bring a jail sentence of up to five years, and the law applied to any couple residing in Texas whether they married within the state or not. This law was accompanied by other statutes providing that adulterers could be fined up to one thousand dollars, but keepers of a "disorderly house," one kept not only for purposes of prostitution but also as a "common resort" for vagabonds, slaves, or free blacks, would be fined up to five hundred dollars. Abortions were illegal, and even an unsuccessful attempt could bring up to one thousand dollars in fines. Apparently, however, none of these last-mentioned offenses even approached the heinousness of interracial marriage, the penalties for which eclipsed those for a white man found guilty of kidnapping a woman to force her into an unwanted marriage or kidnapping a free black to sell him or her into bondage.

The maintenance of internal order also required strong permanent institutions for enforcement. Through a bill that originated in the House, the itinerant Texas Supreme Court was required to meet in Austin in October for twelve weeks, in Galveston in January for ten weeks, and in Tyler in April for ten weeks. The Senate adhered to Governor Pease's mandate for renewed parsimony in disbursing state funds, but provided for local law officers in other ways. Palo Pinto County was given 320 acres to be surveyed and sold to raise funds for a courthouse, a jail, and other public buildings. Gonzales and Bell counties were authorized to levy special taxes to build courthouses. Only Hidalgo, Starr, and Cameron counties were given state revenues to build jails: nine-tenths of the taxes collected within their boundaries in 1858 and 1859. A joint resolution passed on January 27, 1858, requested funds from the federal government to build U.S. district courthouses and post offices in Tyler, Austin, and Brownsville.

The legislators also followed Governor Pease's lead in reducing taxes. On February 16, 1858, Governor Runnels signed a bill to reduce state levies from 15 cents to 12.5 cents per $100 of real and personal property. The poll tax, however, remained 50 cents on every mentally competent free male from twenty-one to fifty years of age. Every company having money loaned out for interest was to pay 20 cents per $100 on that working capital, and a similar tax was levied on the stock of merchants and liquor retailers. Direct taxes also continued to be levied on entertainers; street vendors; the owners of saloons, billiard parlors, race tracks, tenpin alleys, hotels, and restaurants; and professional men such as realtors, brokers, auctioneers, attorneys, and doctors. County courts assessed and collected taxes, although they now had little opportunity to retain them for their own use.

A dependable supply of capital for the state was necessary during this period of rapid expansion. A remarkable thirty-seven counties were created by the Seventh Legislature: Archer, Baylor, Bee, Blanco, Buchanan (later renamed Stephens), Callahan, Chambers, Clay, Coleman, Concho, Dawson (later abolished), Dimmit, Duval, Eastland, Edwards, Encinal (later abolished), Frio, Hardeman, Hamilton, Hardin, Haskell, Jones, Kimble, Knox, La Salle, Mason, McMullen, Menard, Montague, Runnels, Shackelford, Taylor, Throckmorton, Wichita, Wilbarger, Zavala, and Zapata. Legislation also passed for the organization of Presidio County. A measure signed on January 26, 1858, provided for the election of county surveyors in all counties that did not have a district surveyor.

The next day a general act was signed for the incorporation of municipalities. Several towns changed their names: Madison, in Orange County, became Orange; Madisonville, in Madison County, became Madison; Hamilton, in Burnet County, became Burnet; Mesquiteville, in Jack County, became Jacksboro; Taylorsville, in Wise County, became Decatur; and the county seat of Palo Pinto County became Palo Pinto. Newly incorporated towns included Bonham, Clinton, Gilmer, Indianola, and Weatherford.

The tide of new immigration and the financial crisis had raised serious questions about the human and natural resources of Texas. Following Governor Pease's recommendation, a thorough census was authorized to be taken in 1858, at the same time as the scholastic census, by the tax assessor and collector in each county. These officers were to be paid at the rate of five cents apiece for the first thousand people counted; four cents apiece for the next thousand; and three cents apiece for all those over two thousand. Previously, many of the school fund apportionments had to be made on the basis of estimates because the assessors failed to make a return; therefore, a schedule of penalties was attached for noncompliance. A geological and agricultural survey was authorized on February 10, 1858, when Governor Runnels signed a bill introduced by Senator Wigfall as chairman of the Committee on State Affairs. This last effort unfortunately would not proceed far before the advent of the Civil War, when it had to be suspended.

The increasing influx of settlers and the organization of local government made the settlement of claims, especially those that involved land, even more imperative. The state office of the commissioner of claims, created through a measure signed during the Sixth Legislature, was extended through the first day of 1859, and James C. Wilson, who had resigned, was replaced by James O. Illingsworth, the choice of the Senate. Illingsworth's thankless task was to confirm title to land, a job made even more difficult by the number of special acts passed by the Seventh Legislature in response to private petitions for grants. A special act created a separate board of three commissioners appointed by the governor to inspect the records of the controversial Peters Colony and to hold hearings to resolve the conflict. The General Land Office, through an act signed on February 11, 1858, began selling the remaining public domain to settlers at one dollar per acre in 160-acre sections, with a limit of 1,280 acres, except for those claimed as part of railroad, school, or other reserves, in which case they would be sold for slightly more.

A more lucrative group of claims, those that involved the debt of the Republic of Texas, had been settled through the Compromise of 1850 and the Public Debt Act of the U.S. Congress in 1856, which provided for a payment of 76.4 cents on the dollar. Senator Throckmorton reported for the select committee formed by the Senate to consider the claims of those who requested that the state make up the difference between the settlement and the face value of the bonds. This group included such luminaries as Samuel Swartout. Throckmorton insisted that nonpayment of "so just and sacred a debt" would "cause the brow of every honest Texan to mantle with shame, and the heart of every patriot to throb with mournful sorrow at such wretched meanness and degradation." In spite of such inspired rhetoric, the Democrats in the Senate and their compatriots in the House were unmoved by the straits of those who had speculated in Texas bonds, and refused to authorize additional compensation.

A final group of claims that involved the rights of homesteaders who had intruded into the lands reserved for the Mississippi and Pacific Railroad brought the sectional conflict to the forefront once more. Governor Pease in his address recommended against the petition of the squatters, who had requested a donation of the land that they had preempted. These tracts had been appropriated by the legislature in 1853 for the financial support of the company, which proposed to build a transcontinental railroad line through Texas from the eastern border to El Paso. Pease did recommend an extension of time for the settlers to pay for their sections, as that portion of the state had been impoverished by the drought of the previous two years.

The ensuing debate in the Senate became nasty; some portrayed the settlers as abolitionists and "Black Republicans," who were derided by the Democratic press in Texas as the "Coon Party." Senator Lott led the arguments in favor of donating the contested sections to the squatters, but was successfully opposed by Senator Wigfall. However, in a measure introduced by Senator Walker and signed by Governor Pease on November 28, 1857, a compromise was reached. The deadline for the settlers to pay for their claims, which were limited to no more than 160 acres each, was extended from January 1, 1858, to October 1, 1859. In order to placate the company, the northern boundary of its reserve was redefined in an act signed on December 21, 1857, to extend from the point where the states of Arkansas, Louisiana, and Texas met to the southwest corner of Young County, and thence due west to the New Mexico border, which it followed to its junction with the Rio Grande.

The Senate endorsed other legislation that imposed stricter controls on all railroad companies that enjoyed the state's favor. An act supplementing the previous measures for the regulation of railroad companies became law on December 19, 1857. It required that all records of stock transactions be available for public inspection, that a majority of the directors and officers of the company reside in Texas, and that in the case of a forced sale the roadbed, track, franchise, and all chartered powers and privileges be considered an "entire thing."

The desire for greater control by the state did not indicate an end to public support for railroad construction. Wharton County was authorized to levy a tax of one-fourth of one percent on all real and personal property in the county and a tax of twice the state rate on "all taverns, groceries, barrooms, tippling houses, nine- and ten-pin-alleys and billiard tables in said county." This tax, which had to be approved in a countywide referendum, was intended to raise fifty thousand dollars to buy stock in the Houston Tap and Brazoria Railway Company. Several other new railroad corporations received broad charters endorsed by the Senate, including the Indianola Railroad Company, to connect that municipality with the San Antonio and Mexican Gulf Railroad; the Eastern Texas Railroad Company, to connect Galveston Bay with the Galveston, Houston and Henderson Railroad; the Opelousas and Texas Western Railroad Company, to link the Sabine River settlements with the Southern Pacific or the Memphis and El Paso Railroad; and the Columbus, San Antonio, and Rio Grande Railroad Company to link East Texas with the Mexican trade through Eagle Pass.

Railroads were not the only internal improvements approved by the Seventh Legislature. The establishment of several new mail lines was requested from the federal government in joint resolutions, and the first transcontinental mail route from Texas to the Pacific coast was inaugurated on July 9, 1858, when the mail left San Antonio for San Diego along a newly blazed trail. These and other enterprises required better transportation, often through areas that the railroads would not reach for at least another quarter-century, even in the most optimistic estimates. An act approved on February 1, 1858, authorized the governor to contract for the drilling of artesian wells between the Nueces River and the Rio Grande on each of the major routes between the settlements in the region. The drillers were to be paid in land grants. A few private citizens operated public utilities; for example, Senator Maverick served as a director of the newly incorporated San Antonio Water Company, along with John James and Gustavus Schleicher.

The state shared the burden of public road maintenance. County courts were made responsible for local road construction through a bill signed on February 8, 1858. They were to survey the counties into "road precincts," each with an appointed overseer. The roads were to be laid out by a jury of five householders from the county who were appointed by the county court as well. First-class roads were to be thirty feet wide with stumps cut down to within six inches of the surface; second-class roads only had to be twenty feet wide. All free white males eighteen to forty-five years of age and all black males, slave or free, sixteen to fifty years of age were required to work on the roads every year for ten days. Clergy, teachers, students, public millers and ferrymen, chief justices, and county commissioners were exempt. As the roads were completed, mileposts were to be placed to mark distances from courthouses, and "index boards" were to be erected to give directions at forks and intersections.

Texas industry began diversifying, despite the national recession. Several companies received charters to operate water-powered mills: the West Fork Mill Company, to build and operate a grist, saw, and flour mill on the Trinity River in Dallas County; the Lynchburg Steam Saw Mill and Ship Yard Company in Harris County; and the Tellico Manufacturing Company in Ellis County. The latter company had $300,000 in capital to build a textile, saw, flour, and grist mill. A separate bill allowed the Tellico Manufacturing Company to build a toll bridge across the Trinity River, and similar bills were endorsed for other individuals to construct and operate bridges across the Angelina, Navasota, Nueces, and Guadalupe rivers, as well as smaller tributaries in the state. The Nash Iron, Steel, and Copper Manufacturing Company proposed to open in Cass County, and the San Antonio Cotton and Woolen Manufacturing Company laid plans for producing textiles and cordage. The Houston Insurance Company was chartered with a stock issue of $100,000 and a board of directors that included such luminaries as Thomas W. House, William M. Rice, and W. J. Hutchins. At least two other firms tried their hand at selling insurance during this period: the Western Texas Life, Fire, and Marine Insurance Company of San Antonio and Galveston and the Lavaca Insurance Company. In the Island City, too, the expanding Galveston Dry Dock Company gained exclusive rights to Pelican Flats for the construction of facilities.

The Seventh Legislature incorporated many new social institutions as well. A Fire Association and a Casino Association were founded in San Antonio; the latter organization, which had an all-German membership, was the first established in San Antonio for "social purposes" and for the encouragement of "literary pursuits." The German Free School Association was chartered in Austin. The Grand Lodge and subordinate chapters of the Royal Arch Masons of Texas received a charter for "educational and charitable purposes," as did the grand and subordinate lodges of the Free and Accepted Masons. The Richmond Masonic Hall Association was established in Fort Bend County; its affiliation is not clear. In Dallas, Lodge Number 44 of the Independent Order of Odd Fellows was incorporated. The Preachers Aid Society of the East Texas Annual Conference of the Methodist Episcopal Church, South, was founded to further the missionary aims of that sect, while the Texas Baptist Publication Society, located in Anderson, was incorporated to print the *Texas Baptist*, a weekly newsletter, as well as the minutes and proceedings of the various Baptist associations and conventions in Texas.

Private organizations and individual citizens were also active in the field of education. The Seventh Legislature incorporated Colorado College, the first Lutheran college in Texas, in Colorado County. The Methodists received a charter for the Union Female Institute in Waco. Other institutions included Bosque College and Seminary, Corpus Christi Academy, the Freestone School Association, Union Hill High School, Melville Male and Female Academy, New Braunfels Academy, and the Tennessee Colony Masonic Institute, whose act of incorporation called for a county election on the prohibition of the drinking of alcoholic beverages for one mile around the school.

The Senate opposed the adoption of general prohibition bills. Senator Potter, for the Committee on the Judiciary, in response to a petition from Knoxville, in Cherokee County, reported against the passage of such a sweeping measure, declaring:

> The many crying evils growing out of the use of intoxicating liquors are well known to all, and are greatly to be lamented, but in the opinion of a majority of the committee, the propriety of prohibiting [*sic*] liquor laws, as a remedy for these evils, is more than questionable; public opinion is more certain and efficient in furnishing a remedy against the use of the intoxicating cup than any prohibitory legislation can be.

The public opinion that would be strong enough to win and enforce a prohibition law should be "sufficiently strong to frown down the use of the accursed poison," or the "exhortation and example of the good and virtuous" should be enough to "lure the wanderer back to the paths of temperance." The exception to the rule was an act that prohibited the sale of any liquor to Indians in the Chickasaw or Choctaw territories, which bordered Texas along the Red River.

The state did not leave education entirely in the hands of private interests. A state university for Texas was established in a bill introduced by Senator Wigfall, as chairman of the Committee on State Affairs, and approved by Governor Runnels on February 11, 1858. Through this act, one hundred thousand dollars in U.S. bonds was set aside for an additional endowment, and the earlier constitutional grant of fifty leagues of land for two institutions was confirmed for the use of the one university, despite long and heated debate to the contrary by those who saw the opportunity for building an institution of higher education in their home district slipping away. This largesse was supplemented by the reservation of every tenth section of land granted to railroads, with the governor selecting the sections to be reserved for university support. Ten state "administrators," including the governor, the chief justice of the Supreme Court of Texas, and eight others appointed by the governor with the approval of the Senate, would serve four-year terms to supervise construction of the university. Because of its endowment, the university would not charge tuition. Unfortunately, the Civil War interrupted plans for higher education in Texas, and the bonds of the endowment were spent on frontier defense.

The state also took its first hesitant steps in the care of the infirm and the disabled. On February 5, 1858, Governor Runnels signed an act, introduced by Senator Quinan, that authorized the appointment of five "managers" to found the State Lunatic Asylum in Austin. The managers were to meet quarterly to supervise the affairs of the asylum and employ a superintendent, who had to be a "married man and a skillful physician, experienced in the treatment of the Insane," for its daily maintenance. Commitment was to be by jury trial, presided over by the chief justice of the county or with the written request of a relative or guardian accompanied by the endorsement of both a physician and a chief justice. The asylum was not a charitable institution and was not to accept any person who could "be safely kept in the county to which he belongs, nor any person laboring under a contagious or infectious disease. . . ."

Indigent patients and those committed by the county were to pay two dollars per week board, and all others no less than five dollars per week. Two additional acts signed on February 5 and 11, 1858, provided money for the purchase of permanent sites for the Institution for the Education of the Deaf and Dumb and the Institution for the Education of the Blind in Austin, both of which had been created by the Sixth Legislature and had occupied leased quarters during 1857, the first year of their operation.

Despite the assurance of Governor Pease in his annual address on November 4, 1857, that the election of James Buchanan as the president of the United States would ensure that the rights of the southern states were respected by the federal government, the sectional conflict continued to fester. Governor Runnels devoted his inaugural address on December 21 to the "impending danger" northern abolitionists posed to southern interests. He said that the South would grow steadily weaker as the North gained in strength, declaring that the "equilibrium has been destroyed which afforded the only sure and permanent guarantee of protection against abolitionist intervention." Runnels called on the Seventh Legislature to help him make preparations for the crisis to come, including provisions for military defense, education, internal improvements, and agriculture. Thus, although Runnels supported almost all of Pease's initiatives, his motives were quite different.

An issue of particular interest to proslavery Democrats in Texas was the filibustering expedition to Nicaragua led by William Walker. M. D. K. Taylor introduced an unsuccessful resolution to censure U.S. Commodore Hiram Paulding for his "arrest" of General William Walker. Actually, Paulding's intervention came as a blessing to the beleaguered Walker, who was besieged by angry Nicaraguans, but many Texans did not see it that way. A special committee of M. D. K. Taylor, Graham, Caldwell, Walker, Wigfall, and McCulloch was formed to consider the joint resolution. Taylor reported for the majority in favor of his measure, but he was opposed by Wigfall, who denounced Walker, and all filibusterers in general. Maverick joined Wigfall in his condemnation, pointing out to those who equated Walker's efforts with the aid given by the United States to Texas during its revolution that the Texans had asked for help, which the hapless Nicaraguans had not. Taylor was joined by Stockdale, Pedigo, Graham, Herbert, Shepard, and Britton, but they did not prevail. Britton, however, did cause an uproar when he compared Walker to Moses leading the Israelites out of bondage and warned the United States to remember God's destruction of the Pharaoh's armies in the Red Sea.

H. R. Runnels, governor of Texas, 1857–59.
Courtesy Texas State Archives.

Louisiana, Alabama, and Virginia condemned Paulding, as did Buchanan, but the Seventh Texas Legislature did not.

The states' rights issue in 1858 centered on the submission of the pro-slavery Lecompton constitution for Kansas. Radical Democrats adver-tised it as the test for the federal government's protection of their in-terests, especially slavery, and President Buchanan endorsed the charter. Governor Runnels in a special message on January 20, 1858, requested that a convention of delegates from southern states be organized if Con-gress rejected the Lecompton bill. A joint resolution passed by the Sev-enth Legislature on the last day of the session condemned the free-state partisans in Kansas for their "violent determination" to "exclude, by force, the citizens of the slave holding States from a just, equal, and peaceful participation in the use and enjoyment of the common property and territory of the members of the confederacy." Fearing that the influence of the "political feeling in the Northern States" upon the federal govern-ment might make that exclusion permanent, the Seventh Legislature authorized an election of seven delegates to meet in convention with representatives from other southern states to discuss the situation. If the State of Texas were forced to act alone, the governor was requested to call a special session of the legislature to arrange for a state convention. Although Congress did not endorse the Lecompton constitution, and other southern states such as Virginia and Alabama also passed bills call-ing for a regional caucus, the anticipated rebellion simmered for a few more years.

The ubiquitous nature of the sectional crisis was most clearly dem-onstrated by the election of two secessionists to the U.S. Senate by the Seventh Legislature. The two chambers convened in a joint session on November 9, 1857, to elect two senators for Texas, because Thomas J. Rusk, who had often been opposed to the states' rights Democrats' posi-tion, had committed suicide, and Houston was *persona non grata*. Both of the Senate's nominees, former governor of Texas J. Pinckney Hender-son and Chief Justice of the Texas Supreme Court John Hemphill, were elected unanimously. Henderson's selection can be attributed as much to his stance in favor of the radical Democrats as to his record of service to Texas. The election of Hemphill, a native of South Carolina and a stalwart states' rights partisan, required twenty-three ballots, but his even-tual victory was a strong indictment of Houston's opposition to the Demo-cratic party stance on the Kansas-Nebraska Act. Tempers had not yet heated to the boiling point; Houston's term expired quietly in March,

1858, after a resolution introduced by M. D. K. Taylor, requesting that Houston resign, failed to pass. Houston would win another election to become governor of Texas in 1859, but it was symptomatic of the disintegration of Texas politics that he was unable to prevent the selection of Wigfall, a "fire-eater," to fill the seat of Henderson, who died on June 4, 1858. The ensuing turmoil would destroy much that the antebellum legislatures of Texas had accomplished.

CHAPTER 17

Secession:
The Senate of the Eighth Legislature, 1859–61

The Senate of the Eighth Legislature of Texas met in a political atmosphere charged with tension over the slavery issue and the concurrent sectional issues that accompanied the conflict between two divergent American life-styles. The Senate met three times, first in a regular session from November 7, 1859, to February 13, 1860, which was primarily dominated by mundane affairs of state, then in an extra session from January 21 to February 9, 1861, and in an adjourned session from March 18 to April 9, 1861, in which they endorsed the secession of Texas from the United States and provided for an alliance with the nascent Confederate States of America. Throughout the whirlwind of events that climaxed with Texas' involvement in the Lost Cause, members of the Senate remained divided on the issue of dissolving the Union, but they did act in response to what they perceived to be the opinion of a majority of the people of the state.

The population of Texas had increased rapidly between 1850 and 1860, from 212,592 to 604,215. Ninety percent of the newcomers were from slaveholding states, with pronounced sentiments in favor of the continuance of slavery and the defense of states' rights. As national issues heated up, the regular Democrats in Texas became more aggressive and gravitated toward the extreme proslavery and secessionist position of the political factions east of the Mississippi River. Houston, who defended the constitution and the Union, won the gubernatorial race in 1859 through the force of his personality, but it was clear that the states' rights leaders had won the upper hand on almost every other political front. John Brown's insurrectionary raid and a wave of mysterious fires in North Texas, said to be the work of abolitionist incendiaries, strengthened the secessionists' grip on the emotions of the people. The Senate through 1860 made little effort to meet the issue head on, apparently considering it to be of no immediate concern. Lincoln's election put the issue into sharper focus, and when the Senate convened again in the winter of 1861, secession was almost a foregone conclusion.

Thirty-four senators sat during the regular session, and four more were elected to replace those who resigned on the eve of the special session. There were fifteen newcomers to the Senate in the regular session: John G. Chambers, John R. Dickinson, Thomas H. Duggan, Abram M. Gentry, Lewis G. Harmon, Martin D. Hart, Francis M. Martin, Jesse H. Parsons, Enoch S. Pitts, Alexis T. Rainey, Emory Rains, Gustavus Schleicher, James W. Sims, Eggleston D. Townes, and Henry C. Wallace; and E. A. Blanche replaced Louis T. Wigfall after his election to Congress. Replacements for the special sessions included Ben F. Neal for Britton, H. P. C. Dulany for Dickinson, Steward A. Miller for Rainey, and Franklin B. Sexton for Wallace. Of the original complement, seven were not natives of slaveholding states. Three senators were foreign born: George B. Erath had been born in Austria; George Quinan, in Ireland; and Gustavus Schleicher, in Germany. The interests of all were diverse, as reflected in their occupations. Twelve listed "lawyer" as their primary occupation, including James W. Throckmorton, who also held the credentials of a physician. Eleven were farmers or planters. Of the balance, four worked as surveyors, three as merchants, and one each as a printer, doctor, soldier, and civil engineer.

Perhaps the easiest vote cast by the Senate was that given in the election of officers. James F. Johnson served as secretary; N. C. Raymond and John R. Woolridge as first and second assistant secretaries, respectively; Thomas J. Johnson as engrossing clerk; J. Pat Henry as enrolling clerk; D. C. Burleson as sergeant at arms; and Joel Williams as doorkeeper. Albert Weir was elected messenger, a new office created after the adoption of a timely resolution introduced by Martin D. Hart. The Reverend William H. Seat served as chaplain, another position formalized through the passage of a resolution introduced by Senator Guinn. William H. Wheelock replaced Williams as doorkeeper during the special session, and the Reverend W. Thomas took Seat's place.

The most immediate concern when the Senate convened in November, 1859, was the defense of the Rio Grande frontier, especially the Brownsville area, from the depredations of Juan N. Cortina and his guerrillas. They had attacked at several points along the river, killing many

A. M. Gentry, senator from District 18, served in the Eighth Legislature. Courtesy Texas State Archives.

Albert Weir served as messenger for the Senate in the Eighth Legislature. Courtesy Texas State Archives.

people and causing uncounted losses in crops, livestock, and other valuable property. Forbes Britton, the U.S. Military Academy graduate who listed his occupation as "soldier," although he had resigned his commission in 1850 and moved to Corpus Christi, introduced a series of bills that earned him distinction as the "Father of the Texas Militia."

On November 10, Britton introduced a bill to authorize Governor Hardin R. Runnels to raise without delay a mounted military corps of one thousand men to be designated as the Texas Rangers. Four days later, he introduced a joint resolution to authorize the governor to enlist a force of one thousand mounted men immediately to "suppress rebellion and resist invasion of the State" along both the southern and western frontiers. On the day on which the joint resolution was taken up and read for the first time, Senator James W. Sims offered a substitute that the Senate did not adopt, but which indicates the urgency of the situation:

> Be it Resolved by the Legislature of the State of Texas, That the Legislature adjourn on the 17th inst. [the next day], and that each member of the same, as well as the officers thereof be requested to furnish himself with a good horse, arms, and ammunition, and repair to the City of Brownsville as soon as possible, and show his patriotism and valor by defending the soil of our State from invasion. . . .

Britton's joint resolution was also lost, but the Committee on Indian Affairs reported in favor of his first bill, with the sole amendment being to increase the term of enlistment from one year to two. A second joint resolution that authorized the governor to accept volunteers to quell the "insurrection or invasion of Cortina and followers on the Rio Grande" was approved on November 18, 1859.

The growing hostility of some of the senators toward the federal government, which they held responsible for not providing better defense along the frontier, colored the debate on Britton's bill. The Senate adopted a bellicose preamble for a measure proposed by Senator Stockdale that stated that the reason for the organization of the militia was that the "Federal Government, whose duty it is primarily, to protect the State from such hostilities, has not efficiently afforded such protection." The bill, signed by Houston on January 2, 1860, provided for the enlistment of a regiment of ten companies of eighty-three mounted men each, to serve for a term of one year. Half of them would be stationed immediately along a line from the Rio Grande to the Red River "to act as spies and minute men," and all of them would remain under the control of the governor.

The acceptance of the "minute men" by Houston marked an important step in Britton's campaign. An act for the permanent organization of the militia was signed on February 14, 1860. All free males from eighteen to forty-five years of age were liable for duty, except teachers, postal employees, public ferrymen and millers, judges and clerks of state but not county courts, justices of the peace, and the secretary of state, the auditor, the treasurer, and the comptroller. In cases of "immediate danger, insurrection, or invasion," the exceptions did not apply. The employment of a substitute was permitted. Texas was organized into sixteen divisions of two brigades each. Every senatorial district was to provide two regiments, except for the more sparsely populated Twenty-ninth and Thirty-third districts, which were to muster one each. All ranks were to be decided by election; those of brigadier and major general by a poll of the commissioned officers, and lesser positions by the rank and file. Like all other state units, the militia was to operate under control of the governor as commander in chief.

The organization of a more permanent militia was not the first such provision for frontier defense. The Senate also endorsed appropriations totaling $74,000 to pay the expenses of units commanded by John S. Ford, James Bourland, John H. Brown, and William G. Tobin for their operations during the previous year, along with $7,500 paid for the supplies for John Williams's company of Texas Rangers. Ford, together with U.S. regulars, had engaged and routed Cortina on December 27, 1859. Before adjournment, the Senate approved an additional $300,000 to pay for the future defensive measures for which they had provided. Houston, in the wake of Cortina's defeat, took the opportunity to point out that the victory was almost entirely due to the actions of the federal troops, but the Senate paid little heed. The one important exception was Britton, who was appointed to go to Washington to petition for increased support along the frontier.

The Senate, as a consequence of Cortina's attacks, was deluged with petitions for relief. One of the petitions provides an insight into the unique code of honor that characterized antebellum public service in Texas. A. Baccus Bacon had been elected district attorney of the Twelfth District shortly before the outbreak of the conflict. Bacon, after the dust had settled, estimated that there were at least five hundred people, if not more, within his purview who were guilty of felonies ranging from larceny to murder who would not flee to Mexico or be killed by soldiers. He therefore asked for additional compensation to undertake the monumental task of capturing and trying these felons. Hart, as chairman of the Committee on the Judiciary, reported against Bacon's request, declaring that the state constitution did not allow additional compensation. Hart did offer some advice:

> As the committee are of the opinion that the present salary is entirely too small to justify any *constitutional lawyer* which we are satisfied the *memorialist soon will be,* and more particularly as he has five hundred culprits in his District who ought to be convicted, we therefore recommend to him to resign his office and return to "sublimer themes of sweet repose."

The Senate adopted Hart's report and later amended the criminal code to provide that any county or state official "who wilfully refuses or fails from neglect, to execute any lawful process in his hands requiring the arrest of a person accused of a felony . . . shall be fined not exceeding two thousand dollars." In a separate petition involving the settlement of a land dispute, Bacon received a section of land, which may have been the source of some consolation.

Public lands remained a topic for heated debate. Albert G. Walker, chairman of the Committee on Public Lands, to which was referred a measure to provide for the recording of a certain collection of field notes, reported that the committee's members were of the opinion that the measure should not pass. They declared it to be not only a "little stealing arrangement," but stated also that it was filled "from beginning to end with snakes, putrifying sores, &c., &c." The Senate refused to be a party to land fraud. At the same time, senators acted to provide for the relief of settlers and encourage new immigration. Houston recommended the sale of all public lands surrendered to the state for nonpayment of taxes, but instead the legislature extended the deadline for the redemption of that land by debtors. The Senate also endorsed a measure to enlarge the number of homesteads that would be exempt from all forced sales: "the lot or lots occupied or destined as a family residence, not to exceed in value two thousand dollars." In a curious reversal of this trend toward leniency, the Senate, before adjourning, passed an act abolishing the system of bankruptcy created during the time of the Republic, leaving debtors with little clear recourse for settlement with private creditors.

An act to reorganize the court of claims and to extend the time for presentation of claims for land against the Republic or the state passed over Houston's veto on February 7, 1860. A new commissioner of claims was to be elected by the legislature. The statute provided that any person, or that person's legal heirs or assigns, who was entitled to a headright under the Mexican colonization laws or under any law enacted by the Congress of the Republic and who had not received a valid grant, certificate, or patent could apply by June 1, 1861, and, if entitled, receive a land certificate. Requirements included continuous residence in Texas from the time of the person's birth or immigration to the time of the submission of the application, which could be filed in the county or district court within the county in which the person resided. Any person entitled to bounty lands for military services, or that person's heirs, could also apply to the commissioner of claims. An additional act of February 14, 1860, provided that those disabled in the service of the Republic were to be granted one league of land by the court of claims "as a testimony of the gratitude of this state." The office of commissioner of claims expired in January, 1862, but while it existed served to lessen the burden of petitions to the legislature during its tenure.

Land became the pivotal issue in the provisions made for higher education in Texas by the Senate during the Eighth Legislature. Runnels in his annual address asked for provisions to carry out the act of the Seventh Legislature that had chartered a university in Texas. Sales of university lands were proceeding slowly; indeed, the revenue did not cover the costs of surveying and administration. The Senate ignored the governor's request. On November 9, Hart introduced a motion to repeal the act providing for a university. Although it did not pass, this bill indicated the preoccupation of the Senate with more pressing matters, especially frontier defense. An act signed by Houston on January 31, 1860, authorized the use of one hundred thousand dollars in U.S. bonds, which had been set aside for the endowment of the university, to provide for frontier defense. Provisions were included for speedy repayment if the funds were so used, but the endowment, which was spent during the Civil War, was never replenished. Another act, signed on February 1, 1860, allowed the sale of the lands reserved for the university along with all other reserved portions of the public domain for the benefit of the general revenue. Houston on February 14 endorsed the suspension of the sale of university lands, but returned the one hundred thousand dollars to the general fund, saying, "The establishment of a University, is, in my opinion, a matter alone for the future."

The Senate, despite its stinginess with the state revenue and lands, did foster the development of educational institutions through grants of incorporation. Britton on December 1, 1859, introduced a bill to set aside twenty-five leagues of land for an agricultural college, but it did not pass. Claiborne C. Herbert introduced a measure for the endowment of professorships in the colleges, academies, and seminaries of Texas, which was sent back to the floor with a negative report authored by Hart, of the Committee on the Judiciary. The bill proposed to give five leagues of land to all institutions with over five thousand dollars invested, and Hart declared it to be too generous in its intent. Despite a second report favoring the bill from Quinan, who chaired the Committee on Education, the measure failed to become law. Among the schools that received the Senate's endorsement for a charter, however, were Salado College, Franklin College, the Guadalupe Male and Female College, Starrville Mission Academy, the Masonic Female Institute at Prairie Lea, the McKenzie Male and Female College, the Texas Masonic Institute, Alamo College, Bastrop Academy, Clifton Academy, San Antonio Female College, Waco Female College, and the Texas Medical College. These measures were introduced by a number of senators, were faithfully shepherded through the Senate by Quinan, and were all signed into law, providing a statutory basis for a private school system to supplement the faltering public institutions.

Quinan made an unusual report on January 17, 1860, on a petition submitted by the citizens of Chappell Hill on behalf of Soule University, which had been chartered during the Republic period. The citizens requested the prohibition of the sale of liquor in the neighborhood of the school, as it clearly had "an evil effect upon the discipline and influence of the institution." They proposed to prohibit sales within three miles of the university. On Quinan's advice, a bill passed the Senate immediately, as did a later measure of similar import for Starrville Mission Academy.

In the aftershock of John Brown's raid on Harpers Ferry, the Senate acted to tighten legal controls over the slave community and those who would try to destroy the institution of slavery. The key amendments to a proposed alteration of the criminal code were introduced by Stockdale. As signed by Houston on February 11, 1860, the act included among those committing "crimes against nature" any free white person playing cards or any other game of chance with either a slave or a free person of color. If convicted, the person could be fined as much as one hundred dollars or imprisoned for up to three months. New articles strictly defined an insurrectionist as "any person who shall in the presence or hearing of any slave, utter words calculated and with the intent to render such slave discontented with his state of slavery, or who shall by words or writing addressed to a slave, endeavour to render such slave discontented with his state of slavery." The offense was a grave one; those convicted would serve two to five years in the state penitentiary. The same penalty awaited any free person who "privately or otherwise than publicly" declared that masters did not have a right of property in slaves "with purpose to bring the institution of slavery (African) into dispute in the mind of any free inhabitant of this State, or of any resident for the time being therein."

Written opposition to the institution of slavery was perhaps even more greatly feared than the spoken word. Those who publicly aided abolition by writing, printing, or distributing abolitionist literature would be jailed for two to five years. Postal employees were enlisted to police the mails for such publications and to give notice if they found anything suspicious. The prescribed fine for failure to comply was two hundred dollars. This was in fact a weaker version of an earlier resolution that would have required postmasters to destroy all abolitionary or incendiary documents received at their offices. Any person who subscribed to such literature would be fined not more than five hundred dollars and could be imprisoned for as long as six months. Importing slaves who were fugitives from justice in other states was punishable by a fine of from one hundred to one thousand dollars.

It is interesting to note that the senators did not permit their fear of uncontrolled blacks to override completely their sense of legal propriety. They received a petition from W. E. Price, who stated that in 1835 in Alabama he was the owner of a slave who ran away. In 1856, Price found the slave in Texas, living as a free man, and immediately captured him. The black filed suit for his freedom in the district court of Polk County, where he lived. The petitioner, Price, did not explain what the result of the suit was, but insisted that there were other blacks in Polk County living under similar circumstances and asked the legislature to pass a law requiring them to be returned to their former owners as slaves. Mark M. Potter, chairman of the Committee on the Judiciary, advised the senators to ignore the petition, as the "courts of the county are the proper tribunals for the settlement of the legal rights of parties situated as the petitioner says he is, and . . . Legislation on the subject is unnecessary." The Senate refused to act on the matter, allowing the decision of the court to stand. A later bill that would have prevented the manumission of a slave under any circumstances also failed to receive Senate endorsement, although after the secession of Texas a bill provided that captured runaways who were still unclaimed after a period of one year would spend the rest of their lives in the state penitentiary. Such a measure, however, may simply indicate a recognition of the crucial need for manpower, rather than a desire for control.

The Eighth Legislature finally resolved a long-standing issue that had become the focus of vituperative debate. The Senate, in the wake of a slanderous campaign against John Marshall and William S. Oldham, acted to formalize the process for selecting a public printer. Beginning on June 1, 1861, the contract for the production of all official publications was to be let biannually to the lowest bidder following the submission of sealed bids to the secretary of state. The contractor would receive copies of all laws and resolutions from the legislature, as well as the Senate and House journals, and be responsible for publishing in a newspaper those laws of a general nature that were intended to be printed.

Debate on internal improvements occupied much of the legislative calendar during the regular session. The most pressing issue was that of railroads; in addition to several bills for the relief of companies already in operation, the Senate endorsed the issue of charters for seven more corporations: the Houston, Trinity, and Tyler Railroad Company; the Columbus Tap Railway Company; the Texas and Mexican Railway Company; the Palestine Tap Railway Company; the Trinity Valley Railroad Company; the Matagorda Railroad Company; and the Metropolitan Railroad Company. Perhaps the most ambitious proposal was originated by Britton, who introduced a bill for the construction of a canal from the Rio Grande to Corpus Christi. It was reported favorably by chairman Isaiah A. Paschal, of the Committee on Internal Improvements, and adopted by the Senate, but Houston refused to sign it. The governor also turned down a second bill by Britton that contained a slightly less ambitious proposal: the digging of a canal from Corpus Christi to Brazos Santiago.

An act of February 8, 1860, authorized the formation of county and town agricultural societies. During the Eighth Legislature and its predecessors, there had been an increasing flood of petitions for charters for such local organizations, which would provide for development in Texas. Henceforth, county societies could hold $25,000 in real estate, and town societies $10,000. Personal property valued at $10,000 could be managed by county societies, but only $5,000 by town societies. Dues-paying members would become stockholders in the associations, with their elected officers serving as directors. The declared purpose of these organizations was to stage fairs and exhibitions and "to manage the property and concerns of said Society as will best promote the interests of agriculture, horticulture and the mechanic arts." Individual charters were issued to the Navarro County Agricultural and Mechanical Association and the Gulf Coast Fair Association in Victoria.

Even this simple act may have been motivated by sectionalism. Alexis T. Rainey, chairman of the Committee on Agriculture, reported in favor of a bill to incorporate the Washington County Cotton and Woolen Manufacturing Company on January 23, 1860, saying that "present indications unfortunately direct our minds to the painful conclusion, that the time may soon arrive when self dependence will be forced upon the State sovereignties of the union." In preparing for that day, he said: "It would be well to foster and protect those domestic manufactories which in time of need will supply the country with articles of both public and private necessity, thereby securing a consummation, which every one must desire, that of making Texas self-poised and self-reliant in the hour of danger."

The possibility of secession influenced almost every action of the senators, even as early as 1859. On November 10, they met in a joint session with the House to hear the message of Governor Runnels. On the matter of the sectional controversy, he declared: "If there can be no longer unity and harmony of sentiment, if the Southern people are no longer to look to [the Constitution] as the chief reliance for the maintenance of their equal rights, their internal peace and security, the sooner it is known the better. They should neither cheat nor should they submit to be cheated." Runnels compared the situation of the southern states to that of the American colonies in 1776. He concluded with a resounding challenge: "Equality and security in the Union or independence outside of it, should be the motto of every Southern State."

The first test of sectionalism in the Eighth Legislature came when the Senate again met with the House in a joint session on December 5, 1859, to elect a U.S. senator to fill the unexpired term of the late J. Pinckney Henderson. On the initial ballot, Wigfall, a state senator, received sixteen votes from his compatriots and forty-three from the House, but failed to win a majority of the votes cast. A second ballot yielded the same results. Several members of the House began to agitate for adjournment, insisting that a quorum was no longer present. There was much opposition to Wigfall on several counts: he favored reopening the slave trade, was an ardent champion of states' rights, and, because he had not yet resigned his seat in the Texas Senate, it could be argued that his candidacy violated certain provisions of the Texas constitution. The senators watched without interrupting as different factions within the House struggled to gain control of the vote. Many legislators had indeed left the floor, but no one was exactly sure why. Some said that it was to delay a vote because it was clear that Wigfall could not win that day; others insisted that it was an arrangement whereby he could be elected immediately. The representatives repeatedly voted against adjournment until some action was taken.

Representative J. M. H. Martin, with the permission of M. D. K. Taylor, Speaker of the House, turned his invective against Britton, chairman of the caucus that sought Wigfall's election. Britton had declared that he had heard "upon the streets" that if his opponents could not succeed in defeating Wigfall by a fair vote, they would defeat him by preventing an election that day. Martin denied the allegation, then charged that the "trick" being played was by Britton. Martin insisted that a deal had been made for two ballots to be taken, with those who could not vote for Wigfall voting in opposition, then leaving the chamber and allowing Wigfall to be elected by the remaining members. Representative F. F. Foscue, a member of Wigfall's caucus, rose to challenge Martin's accusations, but the latter replied that Wigfall himself had substantiated the rumors. When confronted by Martin, Wigfall had "sneeringly charged us with letting our consciences control our action." Martin ended with a flourish: "I will submit to the unfairness attempted to be practiced, only when I am overpowered and forced to submit."

Representative G. W. Whitmore chastised the Senate for condemning the House for factiousness when it was just as guilty. It was obvious to Whitmore that both caucus leaders had issued instructions to their more squeamish members to leave the chambers before the final vote was taken, in order not to be labeled. Whitmore declared, "I am ready to cast my vote at any time, if gentlemen will take their seats in this House. If a person were to come in here now, he would imagine that it was Christmas Day, and all the members have gone home to see their wives and families." After a few more remarks aimed at specific miscreants, Whitmore said, "Let them come up to the scratch; let every man answer to his name; and let them elect a Senator, a States' Rights man or a Union Saver, as the case may be."

Representative David B. Culberson delivered the most eloquent challenge to the supporters of Wigfall. He explained that

> the course of the Opposition to-day cannot be misunderstood. The democratic party have been defeated, routed horse, foot, and dragoon? Are you not satisfied with your victory? You have impaled upon a halberd of slander the best Governor this State ever had; you have seen the flag under which some of you have rallied, when the sun shone brighter, go down in treachery? Not satisfied with this, here you come to sack the camp and scalp the dead. One crumb is left in the provision wagon of the democratic party, and every effort is now to be made to deprive us of this comfort in our adversity. If gentlemen think that Wigfall cannot be elected—why seek to postpone the ballot. In sunshine and in storm, he has stood by the standard of his party, and to-day he is ready to be martyred for its principles.

To Culberson, it was clear that the secessionists were wrong but would win the day; he would resign his seat after his district voted in favor of secession, but on this day he was indomitable: "I for one, am willing to say to you that the flag of the vanquished has gone up again; the victors cannot garrison the conquered." Wigfall ultimately won the final ballot, taken late at night. The tally indicated that only five legislators had left the hall in the course of the debate.

Senator Walker on December 8 introduced a joint resolution to endorse the actions of President Buchanan and Governor Wise of Virginia in "suppressing the recent outrage at Harpers Ferry, for capturing and bringing to justice and deserved punishment, John Brown and other insurgents." Furthermore, the resolution pledged "that the State of Texas, will stand by her sister States of the South, in the maintenance of their institutions, against all Abolitionists, Insurrectionists and Traitors, and in the preservation of the rights and powers reserved to the States." The resolution was sent to the Committee on State Affairs. Paschal, a Unionist, on December 12 introduced a more moderate resolution that praised Buchanan, Wise, and Governor Packer of Pennsylvania for their "prompt and energetic action" which evidenced a "degree of manliness and patriotism, honorable alike to them, and worthy of our warm admiration." Without any direct mention of states' rights, Paschal's measure called simply for "the utmost vigilance in guarding against the recurrence of similar conspiracies in our own borders, or elsewhere at the South." Shepard, then chairman of the Committee on State Affairs, cautiously reported in favor of the passage of both resolutions. The final version as passed contained elements of each one, indicating the lack of commitment at that time.

On December 21, Runnels delivered his farewell address to the Eighth Legislature. The majority of his speech was devoted to the sectional issue, and his tone was unmistakable: "It is now clearly demonstrated by the history of the past five years that a deep unchangeable determination exists in the Northern States to assail our dearest political rights, and if possible, destroy our domestic institution." He added, "The time has surely arrived when the South should look to her defences [*sic*]." Houston refused to deliver his inaugural address to the legislature, declaring that the legislature did not truly represent the sentiment of the people. The legislators had alienated him by their drift toward an extreme states' rights position and angered him by their election of Wigfall to the Senate. Instead, Houston delivered his inaugural address at the top of the stairs of the Capitol. Most of his address was devoted to mundane affairs; he included only a single concluding passage on sectional tensions. He reminded his listeners that when Texas became a state, "she entered, not into the North, nor into the South, but into the Union." He continued: "When our rights are aggressed upon, let us be behind none in repelling the attack; but let us be careful to distinguish between the acts of individuals and those of a people—between the wild ravings of fanatics and that public sentiment which truly represents the masses of a State." In a message to the legislature on January 14, Houston congratulated the conservatives for holding the line against the radical secessionists.

On January 24, 1860, Houston presented to the Senate resolutions adopted by South Carolina that affirmed the right of a state to secede and called for a convention of the slaveholding states, together with a message from her governor, William H. Gist. With these missives, Houston included a statement of his own. He wrote that the reasons set forth for the consideration of secession did not justify such drastic action and that secession itself had no constitutional sanction. He declared the legacy of the founding fathers of the United States to be union and strength—would Texans turn their backs on that dream? More practically, leaving the Union would leave Texas virtually defenseless, with long and violent borders, and with no recourse for the recovery of runaway slaves. He concluded, "I deem it due to myself, as well as to your honorable body, to enter my unqualified protest against, and dissent from the principles enunciated in the resolutions."

Britton introduced a resolution to endorse Houston's stand on the

BRAVING THE STORM!!!

"I REGARD THE CONSTITUTION OF MY COUNTRY, AND I AM DETERMINED TO STAND BY IT."—*Extract from Gen. Houston's Letter of No*

Sam Houston's unpopular opposition to secession was based on his deep concern for the protection of his beloved Texas and his belief in America's founding principles. Cartoon from *Vanity Fair*, reproduced from holdings of Texas State Archives.

South Carolina resolutions, but instead the message was submitted to the Committee on State Affairs. A majority of that committee reported, through Stockdale, that they agreed on the "determination of this State to preserve, adhere to and defend the Union with the Constitution," but they differed as to the means by which this was to be done. Their proposed resolution began with a pledge to defend the constitutions of both the United States and the State of Texas and to adhere to the Union. At the same time, they condemned the nullification of the fugitive slave laws by several northern states, the intention of the "Black Republican" party to use the national government to abolish slavery, thereby violating the constitutional guarantee to property, and the aims of the abolitionists to foster insurrection in the South. They appealed to the people of other states to demonstrate their devotion to the cause of peaceful union at the ballot boxes and commended the subject to a popular vote in Texas. They did not, as Houston had asked, deny the right of secession. Their report was adopted immediately, but no further action was taken, which indicates that the issue had not yet become urgent.

A minority of the Committee on State Affairs, Paschal, Townes, and Gentry, reported strongly against adhering to the resolutions sent by South Carolina. The resolution they proposed as a response emphatically denied the right of a state to secede peacefully. They defined secession as a "revolutionary act" justifiable only by "dangerous and oppressive infractions of the Constitution by the General Government." This the federal government had not done, and so, they continued, the resolutions of South Carolina were "premature and unnecessary." The proposal did contain a "solemn warning" to the "Northern brethren" against the "mad fanaticism of the Abolitionists and Black Republicans, who are waging war against the institutions of the South." If the time should come when the national government no longer protected the South from this "band of fanatics," then "the sons of Texas will again raise the revolutionary standard," but, for the time being, Texans repledged their faith in the U.S. Constitution and the Union. The minority proposal was tabled and not taken up again.

After the Eighth Legislature adjourned, public support for a convention to be held to write an ordinance of secession grew. Houston bowed to public demand only after impromptu elections were held without his permission for delegates to the proposed convention. He convened the legislature in special session on January 21, 1861, hoping to subvert the popular movement and substitute one that was more under the control of the existing administration. He had made clear his sentiments in favor of maintaining the Union through reasonable compromise in a letter he wrote to J. M. Calhoun, the envoy from Alabama; he stated, however, that "if the Union be dissolved and the gloomy forebodings of patriots be realized in the ruin and civil war to follow, Texas can 'tread the wine press alone.'" He would rather see Texas unfurl the Lone Star flag again than accompany a southern alliance to defeat and ruin.

The senators, like their counterparts in the House, viewed much more favorably the idea of joining the states of the Gulf South, who had already seceded, in a new confederation. On January 26, the Senate adopted a joint resolution that declared "that should . . . the Federal Government attempt to coerce any of our sister States of the South by force of arms

Houston's antisecessionist stance received approbation in Northern periodicals. Cartoon from *Vanity Fair*, reproduced from holdings of Texas State Archives.

into subjection to Federal rule; we assure such State of the sympathies of our people, and . . . shall make common cause with them in resisting by all means and to the last extremity, such unconstitutional violence and tyrannical usurpation of power." Herbert introduced a bill to validate all acts of the convention and to pay the expenses of the delegates. It passed the Senate with only five voting in opposition: Hart, Paschal, Rains, Townes, and Throckmorton, who had introduced an unsuccessful resolution to declare the election of delegates invalid. The convention met for the first time two days later, on January 28, in Austin. Houston reluctantly signed the measure on February 4 "with a protest against the assumption of any powers on the part of said convention, beyond the reference of the question of a longer connection of Texas with the Union to the people."

Several senators and former senators attended the convention. Stockdale and Throckmorton became prominent in the leadership of the opposing factions: Stockdale had seceded from the Democratic convention in Charleston with the rest of the Texas delegation, then served as a member of the committee in Austin who composed the ordinance of secession; Throckmorton was the leader of the tiny Unionist minority. The ordinance was approved by the delegates on February 1. Only seven voted against it, including Throckmorton. When he cast his vote, hisses and applause burst from the galleries, prompting his famous retort: "Mr. President, when the rabble hiss, well may patriots tremble."

A copy of the ordinance was sent to the Senate six days later. The grievances set forth as reasons for secession included the threat from the abolitionists as well as from Mexicans and Indians, from which the federal government had given little protection. Texas therefore would annul the ordinance by which it became a "party to the compact styled 'The Constitution of the United States of America,'" revoke and resume all powers delegated through that compact by Texas to the federal government, and absolve itself and its people from all debts and obligations incurred by that compact and allegiance to the United States. On February 23, 1861, the people of Texas approved the fateful ordinance of secession by a vote of 46,129 to 14,697.

The Senate adjourned on February 9 when it failed to muster a quorum, but convened again on March 18. In the interregnum, the convention had provided for the adherence of Texas to the new Confederate States of America, the removal of U.S. troops, and the transfer of military installations and stores. It had also adopted a loyalty oath and

After Houston lost his struggle to keep Texas in the Union, he was deposed by the Secession Convention and retired quietly to his farm in Huntsville.
Courtesy Texas State Archives.

removed Houston from office when he refused to take it, replacing him with Lieutenant Governor Edward Clark. Senator Blanch came forward on March 19 with an amended oath of loyalty, and the senators all took it, despite the initial opposition of some such as Paschal and Throckmorton.

Edward Clark, who replaced Sam Houston as governor of Texas in 1861.
Courtesy Texas State Archives.

The most pressing issue was that eternal fear, frontier defense. Houston on February 6, 1861, had informed the Senate that Texas was over $817,000 in arrears, including unpaid claims of $300,000 from the Texas Rangers. Something had to be done, and he implored them not to wait "until the call for men and money comes laden with the dying shrieks of women and children." Britton, chairman of the Committee on the

Militia, endorsed Houston's successful request for three thousand men, divided into three regiments, one of infantry and two of cavalry, for patrolling the frontier from Brownsville to El Paso and thence north to the Red River. Another bill that was signed into law provided for a company of forty "minute men" to be raised in each of thirty-seven frontier counties, along with the regular militia and Confederate troops. To pay for these and other measures, the legislature endorsed the issue of $1 million in 8 percent bonds, redeemable in sixteen years.

Senators of the Eighth Legislature had finally confronted the issue of secession and come down firmly, if not unanimously, on the side of the South. Many of them would continue to serve in the Confederate legislatures of Texas, and not a few of them would distinguish themselves as soldiers, including Throckmorton, who became a brigadier general. Although Texas would emerge from the Civil War relatively untouched by the scourges of an invader, it would still lose a horrendous proportion of its young men on the battlefields that scarred other states. To recall that they had remained voices of reason arguing against the clamor for disunion would bring little, if any, satisfaction to Throckmorton, Paschal, and the other senators who had stood against the radicals in 1861. The rest reaped the whirlwind they had so angrily sown.

Appendix A

MEMBERS OF THE FIRST CONGRESS

COLUMBIA
October 3–December 22, 1836
HOUSTON
May 1–June 13, 1837

PRESIDENT David G. Burnet[1]
PRESIDENT Sam Houston[1]
VICE-PRESIDENT Lorenzo de Zavala[2]
VICE-PRESIDENT Mirabeau B. Lamar[2]

SENATE

Member	District
Augustine, Henry W.[3]	San Augustine
Collinsworth, James[4, 5]	Brazoria
Corzine, Shelby[3]	San Augustine
Ellis, Richard	Red River
Everitt, Stephen Hendrickson	Jasper, Jefferson
Grimes, Jesse	Washington
Hill, William G.[5, 6]	Brazoria
Horton, Albert Clinton[7]	Matagorda, Jackson, Victoria
Irion, Robert Anderson[8]	Nacogdoches
Landrum, Willis H.[9, 10]	Shelby, Sabine
Lester, James Seaton	Mina, Gonzales
Morehouse, Edwin[11, 12]	San Patricio, Refugio, Goliad
Robertson, Sterling Clack	Milam
Ruiz, Francisco[13]	Bexar
Somervell, Alexander	Austin, Colorado
Wharton, William Harris[4, 14]	Brazoria
Wilson, Robert	Harrisburg, Liberty

1. Burnet served as president from March 16 to October 22, 1836, when Houston became president.

2. De Zavala served as vice-president from March 16 to October 22, 1836, when Lamar became vice-president.

3. Shelby Corzine resigned on December 16, 1836, after Congress elected him judge of the First Judicial District (*Senate Journal*, First Congress, First Session, p. 96). An election was held on February 25, 1837, to determine his successor, but it was returned to the people (Resolution, Papers of the First Congress, File 595), as apparently it was not conducted pursuant to presidential proclamation (*A Journal of the Coincidences and Acts of Thomas S. McFarland* [Newton County Historical Commission; Burnet: Norten Press, 1981], p. 23). On March 11, 1837, President Houston called an election for April 17, 1837 (*Record Book of Documents under the Great Seal*, no. 37, pp. 7–8). Henry W. Augustine was elected to succeed Corzine for the term expiring September 2, 1839, being seated on May 3, 1837 (*Senate Journal*, First Congress, Second Session, p. 2).

4. William Harris Wharton resigned on November 16, 1836, after Senate confirmation of his appointment by President Houston as minister plenipotentiary to the United States (*Secret Journals of the Senate*, pp. 23–24 [Winkler ed., 1911]). On November 17, 1836, President Houston called an election for November 23, 1836 (*Record Book of Documents under the Great Seal*, no. 37, pp. 1–2; *Senate Journal*, First Congress, First Session, p. 56). James Collinsworth was elected to succeed Wharton for the term expiring September 3, 1838, being seated on November 30, 1836 (*Senate Journal*, First Congress, First Session, p. 66).

5. James Collinsworth resigned on December 16, 1836, upon his election by Congress as Chief Justice (*Senate Journal*, First Congress, First Session, p. 97; Collinsworth to the President and Members of the Senate, December 16, 1836, Miscellaneous Election Returns). On January 31, 1837, President Houston called an election for February 6, 1837 (Certificate, George B. McKinstry, Chief Justice of Brazoria County, February 10, 1837, Election Returns). William G. Hill was elected to succeed Collinsworth for the term expiring September 3, 1838, being seated on May 3, 1837 (*Senate Journal*, First Congress, Second Session, p. 2).

6. William G. Hill resigned on August 22, 1837, citing "circumstances over which I have no control" and "obligations which I have to perform . . ." (Hill to President Houston, August 22, 1837, Election Returns). On September 8, 1837, President Houston called an election for September 20, 1837, at which time Hill's successor was elected to the Second Congress for the term expiring September 3, 1838 (*Department of State Letter Book*, no. 1, p. 12).

7. Albert Clinton Horton's election was unsuccessfully challenged by George Sutherland. The Committee on Privileges and Elections reported unanimously in favor of Horton on October 6, 1836. After Senator Wilson's motion to lay the report on the table was defeated, the Senate adopted the report without a division on the same day (*Senate Journal*, First Congress, First Session, p. 11).

8 Robert Anderson Irion's election was unsuccessfully challenged by Isaac Watts Burton. Irion defeated Burton by a vote of 270 to 252, but Burton asserted that Irion owed his majority to the votes of Mexican citizens from Nacogdoches "opposed to the Government and consequently not entitled to citizenship." The Committee on Privileges and Elections reported unanimously in favor of Irion on October 14, 1836, stating that the challenged voters, being citizens under the constitution, could not be disenfranchised except "by due course of the law." Since the Senate had on the preceding day de-

clared the constitution effective as of March 17, 1836, the Mexican votes were legal. The Senate, by a vote of eight to two, adopted the report on October 14, 1836, and Irion was seated (*Senate Journal*, First Congress, First Session, p. 20; Papers of the Third Congress, File 1098 [incorrrectly filed]).

9. After Willis H. Landrum was seated, his election was unsuccessfully challenged by (Robert O.[?]) Lusk. The Committee on Privileges and Elections reported unanimously in favor of Landrum on October 11, 1836 (Papers of the Fourth Congress, File 1195 [incorrectly filed]), and the Senate adopted the report without a division on the same day (*Senate Journal*, First Congress, First Session, p. 14).

10. Willis H. Landrum resigned on April 24, 1837, because he had "been confined for some time with an old contracted disease" (Landrum to President Houston, April 24, 1837, Election Returns). No successor was chosen for the remainder of his term, which expired on September 4, 1837.

11. Both Edwin Morehouse and James Power claimed victory in the election for senator from the district of San Patricio, Goliad, and Refugio. Although Morehouse won the election by a vote of 231 to 1 (Certificate, John D. McLeod, October 3, 1836 [returns from one precinct missing], Election Returns), Power claimed victory on the basis that Morehouse was not a citizen. Morehouse introduced testimony before the Committee on Privileges and Elections that he had obtained a certificate of citizenship from the agent of Milam Colony in 1832, that he lived in Refugio and owned property there in 1834, and that he intended to return to Refugio after leaving for the United States to purchase goods in late 1834. When he came back to Texas in 1836, he found Refugio evacuated and joined the army. The committee reported unanimously in favor of Morehouse on October 15, 1836 (Papers of the First Congress, File 595). The Senate adopted the report, and Morehouse was seated on the same day (*Senate Journal*, First Congress, First Session, p. 21).

12. Edwin Morehouse resigned on December 22, 1836, upon Senate confirmation of his appointment by President Houston as adjutant general of the army (*Secret Journals of the Senate*, pp. 40–41 [Winkler ed., 1911]; *Senate Journal*, First Congress, First Session, p. 103; Papers of the First Congress, File 595). On March 16, 1837, President Houston called an election for April 17, 1837 (*Record Book of Documents under the Great Seal*, no. 37, p. 32). The election apparently failed, for there was no senator from San Patricio, Refugio, and Goliad in the Second Session of the First Congress. No successor was chosen for the remainder of Morehouse's term, which expired September 4, 1837.

13. Francisco Ruiz resigned on May 22, 1837, due to ill health (Ruiz to Judge Don José Veca [Joseph Baker, Chief Justice of Bexar County], May 22, 1837, Election Returns). His successor was chosen at the next general election for the term expiring September 2, 1839.

14. William Harris Wharton was seated after a second election to determine the Senator from the district of Brazoria. Both Wharton and Walter C. White claimed victory in the initial election on September 5, 1836. Although Wharton won the election, 272 to 230, White challenged the votes of recently arrived volunteer soldiers from the United States, alleging that the constitutional suffrage requirement of six months' residency was in effect on election day. Wharton, on the other hand, argued that the requirement was not in effect on election day because the constitution had not at that time been adopted by the voters. White argued in part: "I consider the Constitution

as binding and of full effect from the time it was adopted in Convention. . . . If it was not binding from that period, the acts of the Government up to this period have been illegal, our Navy have been Pirates, our Army Highland Robbers, our Commissioners to the United States Imposters, and in all our acts we have been faithless and ought no longer to be trusted" (Papers of the Second Congress, File 899 [incorrectly filed]). The Committee on Privileges and Elections agreed, disallowing 119 votes cast by volunteers at Velasco and unanimously recommending on October 7, 1836, that White be seated. On October 10, 1836, Senator Horton's motion to lay the report on the table was adopted, and a resolution was passed that "the contest now pending . . . be referred to the people of the district of Brazoria" (*Senate Journal*, First Congress, First Session, pp. 12–14; Papers of the First Congress, File 499). On October 11, 1836, President Burnet called an election for October 15, 1836 (*Executive Record Book*, no. 35, pp. 91–92). Wharton was elected for the term expiring on September 3, 1838, being seated on October 17, 1836 (*Senate Journal*, First Congress, First Session, p. 21).

Ironically, the Senate voted nine to two on October 13, 1836, to require the president to issue a proclamation declaring that the constitution had been in effect from March 17, 1836 (*Senate Journal*, First Congress, First Session, p. 19). Had this policy been followed in the contest for the district of Brazoria, White would have been seated after the first election.

Note: On November 11, 1836, the senators conducted a lottery to determine length of terms. The following districts drew three-year terms: Bexar; Harrisburg and Liberty; Jasper and Jefferson; and San Augustine. Two-year terms were assigned to these districts: Austin and Colorado; Brazoria; Matagorda, Jackson, and Victoria; Milam; and Mina and Gonzales. One-year terms were assigned to these districts: Nacogdoches; Red River; San Patricio, Refugio, and Goliad; Shelby and Sabine; and Washington (*Senate Journal*, First Congress, First Session, p. 50).

Appendix B

MEMBERS OF THE SECOND CONGRESS

HOUSTON
Called Session, September 25–November 4, 1837
Regular Session, November 6–December 19, 1837
Adjourned Session, April 9–May 24, 1838

PRESIDENT Sam Houston
VICE-PRESIDENT Mirabeau B. Lamar

SENATE

Member	District
Augustine, Henry W.[1]	San Augustine
Barnett, George Washington	Washington
Burton, Isaac Watts	Nacogdoches
Dunn, John	San Patricio, Refugio, Goliad
Ellis, Richard[2]	Red River
Everitt, Stephen Hendrickson	Jasper, Jefferson
Green, Thomas Jefferson[3]	Bexar
Greer, John Alexander[1]	San Augustine
Horton, Albert Clinton	Matagorda, Jackson, Victoria
Lester, James Seaton	Mina, Gonzales
Rains, Emory	Shelby, Sabine
Robertson, Sterling Clack	Milam
Russell, William Jarvis[4]	Brazoria
Seguin, Juan Nepomuceno[3]	Bexar
Somervell, Alexander[5]	Austin, Colorado
Wharton, William Harris[4, 6]	Brazoria
Wilson, Robert	Harrisburg, Liberty

1. Henry W. Augustine resigned on November 23, 1837 (Papers of the Second Congress, File 803), probably to pursue active military duty (*Biographical Directory of the Texan Conventions and Congresses 1832–1845* [Austin: 1941], p. 46). The Senate accepted his resig-

nation the next day (*Senate Journal*, Regular Session, p. 74). On November 25, 1837, President Houston called an election for December 16, 1837. The election apparently failed, because Houston subsequently called another election for February 5, 1838 (*Record Book of Documents under the Great Seal*, no. 37, pp. 12, 13). John Alexander Greer was elected to succeed Augustine for the term expiring September 2, 1839, being seated on April 10, 1838 (*Senate Journal*, Second Congress, Adjourned Session, p. 3).

2. When Richard Ellis appeared to take his seat, his election was challenged. On October 30, 1837, however, the Committee on Privileges and Elections reported that "on a strict examination of the Constitution, Ellis was qualified" (Papers of the Second Congress, Called Session, File 782; *Senate Journal*, Called Session, p. 40). On October 31, 1837, Senator Everitt moved that Ellis's election be investigated by a special committee. The motion was defeated, six to four, and Ellis was thereupon seated by the same vote. The following day, Senators Wharton, Burton, Everitt, and Dunn formally protested Ellis's seating because the United States exercised civil and military jurisdiction over Red River County, the county had never been organized, the election was illegally and improperly conducted, and Ellis's citizenship was doubtful (*Senate Journal*, pp. 40, 42–44). A second resolution to appoint a special investigative committee was also defeated. On November 4, 1837, however, a resolution to appoint a committee to "investigate the political condition of Red River County" was adopted, and Senators Ellis, Horton, and Rains were appointed thereto (*Senate Journal*, pp. 44, 50). No report from this committee has been found.

3. Thomas Jefferson Green was elected on September 4, 1837, for the term expiring September 2, 1839, and was seated on September 25, 1837 (*Senate Journal*, Second Congress, Called Session, p. 4). On September 26, 1837, however, two of Green's defeated opponents, Joseph L. Hood and Horatio A. Alsbury, challenged his election. They alleged that Green had not resided in Bexar County for the requisite one year, that he owed his election to the receipt of many illegal votes, and that "the Election was carried by *violence, threats, fraud,* and *force* and many of the citizens were thereby deterred from tendering their votes and others terrified into voting for General Green and many retired from the polls from a conviction that they would suffer personal violence if they did not vote for General Green and from a knowledge that the whole election was a 'farce and mockery'" (Papers of the Second Congress, Called Session, File 736 [emphasis in original]). Despite the fact that Green won the election with 164 votes out of 189 cast, the Committee on Privileges and Elections withheld a favorable recommendation as to Green's election on November 28, 1837 (*Senate Journal*, Second Congress, Called Session, p. 6). On October 18, 1837, the committee agreed to refer the matter to the entire Senate. On October 20, 1837, the Senate voted nine to one to declare the seat vacant. Senator Isaac Watts Burton, the lone dissenter, argued that Green had represented Bexar in the House of Representatives in the First Congress, had declared an intention to reside in Bexar fifteen months before his election to the Senate, had consummated that declaration by visiting Bexar before the election, and had been disenfranchised in municipal elections outside of Bexar County (*Senate Journal*, pp. 25, 29–30).

On October 20, 1837, President Houston called an election for November 11, 1837 (Certificate, Nicolas Flores, County Judge of Bexar County [Justice of the Peace, First District], November 13, 1837, Election Returns). At that election, Juan Nepomuceno Seguin was elected to succeed Green for the term expiring September 2, 1839. Seguin took his seat on May 15, 1838 (*Senate Journal*, Second Congress, Adjourned Session, p. 73).

4. William Harris Wharton resigned on February 10, 1838 (Robert A. Irion, Secretary of State, to Wharton, March 3, 1838, *Department of State Letter Book*, no. 1, p. 26). On February 26, 1838, President Houston called an election for March 31, 1838 (*Record Book of Documents under the Great Seal*, no. 37, p. 18). At that election, William Jarvis Russell was elected to succeed Wharton for the term expiring September 3, 1838. Russell took his seat on April 9, 1838 (*Senate Journal*, Second Congress, Adjourned Session, p. 3).

5. Alexander Somervell did not take his seat until December 14, 1837 (*Senate Journal*, Second Congress, Regular Session, p. 123). Prior to that date, an attempt was made to declare Somervell's seat vacant and a committee was appointed to investigate the matter (Papers of the Second Congress, Regular Session, File 821; *Senate Journal*, Second Congress, Regular Session, pp. 68, 85–86).

6. William Harris Wharton was elected to succeed William G. Hill on September 20, 1837, for the term expiring September 3, 1838. Wharton took his seat on September 27, 1837 (*Senate Journal*, Second Congress, Called Session, p. 4).

Appendix C

MEMBERS OF THE THIRD CONGRESS

HOUSTON
November 6, 1838–January 24, 1839

PRESIDENT Sam Houston[1]
PRESIDENT Mirabeau B. Lamar[1]
VICE-PRESIDENT Mirabeau B. Lamar[2]
VICE-PRESIDENT David G. Burnet[2]

SENATE

Member	District
Barnett, George Washington	Washington, Montgomery
Burleson, Edward[3]	Bastrop, Gonzales, Fayette
Burton, Isaac Watts	Nacogdoches, Houston
Dunn, John	San Patricio, Refugio, Goliad
Ellis, Richard	Red River, Fannin
Everitt, Stephen Hendrickson	Jasper, Jefferson
Greer, John Alexander	San Augustine
Jones, Oliver	Austin, Colorado, Fort Bend
Kendrick, Harvey W.	Matagorda, Jackson, Victoria
Rains, Emory[4]	Shelby, Sabine
Seguin, Juan Nepomuceno	Bexar
Stroud, Beden	Milam, Robertson
Wharton, William Harris[5]	Brazoria
Wilson, Robert[6]	Harrisburg, Liberty

1. Houston served as president until December 10, 1838, when Lamar became president.

2. Lamar served as vice-president until December 10, 1838, when Burnet became vice-president.

3. Edward Burleson resigned January 21, 1839 (*Senate Journal*, Third Congress, p. 120). His successor was chosen at the next general election for the term expiring September 6, 1841.

4. Emory Rains resigned October 27, 1839, citing "private affairs" (Rains to Acting Secretary of State David G. Burnet, October 27, 1839, Election Returns). On November 18, 1839, President Lamar called an election for December 20, 1839 (*Record Book of Documents under the Great Seal*, no. 37, pp. 47–48), at which time Rains's successor was elected to the Fourth Congress for the term expiring September 7, 1840.

5. William H. Wharton died on March 14, 1839 (*Telegraph and Texas Register*, March 20, 1839). On April 22, 1839, President Lamar called an election for May 12, 1839. The election apparently failed, because on May 16, 1839, Lamar called another election for June 1, 1839 (*Record Book of Documents under the Great Seal*, no. 37, p. 41). Anson Jones was elected to succeed Wharton for the term expiring September 6, 1841, being seated at the commencement of the Fourth Congress (*Senate Journal*, Fourth Congress, pp. 1, 41 [Smither ed.]).

6. On the basis of Wilson's conduct in secret session on December 24, 1838, the Senate voted eight to two to arrest Wilson until the Senate concluded its deliberations (*Secret Journals of the Senate* [Winkler ed.], pp. 119–20). On December 26, 1838, the Senate adopted a special committee report to expel Wilson, ten to one, for using profanity and disclosing secrecy (*Senate Journal*, Third Congress, p. 70). Wilson was reelected to his seat on January 11, 1839, for the term expiring September 2, 1839 (Election Returns). Wilson resumed his seat on January 21, 1839 (*Senate Journal*, Third Congress, p. 121).

Appendix D

MEMBERS OF THE FOURTH CONGRESS

AUSTIN

November 11, 1839–February 5, 1840

PRESIDENT Mirabeau B. Lamar
VICE-PRESIDENT David G. Burnet

SENATE

Member	District
Barnett, George Washington	Washington, Montgomery
Burton, Isaac Watts	Nacogdoches, Houston
Dunn, John	San Patricio, Refugio, Goliad
Ellis, Richard[1]	Red River, Fannin
Everitt, Stephen Hendrickson	Jasper, Jefferson
Gaines, James Taylor[2]	Shelby, Sabine, Harrison
Greer, John Alexander[3]	San Augustine
Jones, Anson	Brazoria
Jones, Oliver	Austin, Colorado, Fort Bend
Kendrick, Harvey W.	Matagorda, Jackson, Victoria
Lester, James Seaton[4]	Bastrop, Gonzales, Fayette
Moore, Francis, Jr.	Harris, Liberty, Galveston
Seguin, Juan Nepomuceno	Bexar
Stroud, Beden	Milam, Robertson

1. Richard Ellis resigned due to ill health on November 28, 1839 (*Senate Journal,* Fourth Congress, pp. 75–76 [Smither ed.]). No election was called to select a successor for the remainder of his term, which expired on September 7, 1840.

2. James Taylor Gaines was elected to succeed Emory Rains on December 20, 1839, for the term expiring September 7, 1840. Gaines took his seat on January 21, 1840 (*Senate Journal,* Fourth Congress, p. 273 [Smither ed.]).

3. John Alexander Greer's reelection was unsuccessfully challenged by Isaac Campbell. Although Greer won the election, 252 to 237, Campbell claimed that the election

was not conducted according to law in certain precincts (*Senate Journal,* Fourth Congress, p. 5, n. 6 [Smither ed.]). On November 14, 1839, the Committee on Privileges and Elections reported that the election be returned to the people (*Senate Journal,* Fourth Congress, p. 34 [Smither ed.]). On November 15, Senator Moore moved in accordance with the report, but the Senate voted to lay the resolution on the table (*Id.,* p. 39). The committee the next day reported in favor of Greer's election. This report was adopted, and Greer thereupon took his seat (*Senate Journal,* pp. 39, 40).

4. James Seaton Lester was elected to succeed Edward Burleson for the term expiring September 6, 1841.

Appendix E

MEMBERS OF THE FIFTH CONGRESS

AUSTIN
November 2, 1840–February 5, 1841

PRESIDENT Mirabeau B. Lamar
VICE-PRESIDENT David G. Burnet

SENATE

Member	District
Barnett, George Washington	Washington, Montgomery
Byrne, James W.	San Patricio, Refugio, Goliad
Daingerfield, William Henry[1]	Bexar
Everitt, Stephen Hendrickson[2]	Jasper, Jefferson
Gaines, James Taylor	Shelby, Sabine, Harrison
Greer, John Alexander	San Augustine
Jones, Anson	Brazoria
Kendrick, Harvey W.	Matagorda, Jackson, Victoria
Lester, James Seaton	Bastrop, Gonzales, Fayette, Travis
Miller, James B.	Austin, Colorado, Fort Bend
Moore, Francis, Jr.	Harris, Liberty, Galveston
Muse, Kindred H.	Nacogdoches, Houston
Potter, Robert	Red River, Fannin
Stroud, Beden	Milam, Robertson

1. Juan Nepomuceno Seguin resigned on October 14, 1840 (Seguin to President Lamar, October 14, 1840, Election Returns), "to lead Texas volunteers into Mexico to aid Antonio Canales," the Federalist commander in Tamaulipas (*Handbook of Texas*, vol. 1, p. 288). On October 22, 1840, President Lamar called an election for October 31, 1840 (*Record Book of Documents under the Great Seal*, no. 37, p. 59). William Henry Daingerfield was elected to succeed Seguin for the term expiring September 5, 1842. Daingerfield took his seat on November 13, 1840 (*Senate Journal*, Fifth Congress, p. 18).

2. Stephen Hendrickson Everitt resigned on December 9, 1840, due to "private affairs"

(Everitt to Vice-President Burnet, December 9, 1840, Election Returns). On December 10, 1840, Burnet, as acting president, called an election for December 26, 1840 (*Record Book of Documents under the Great Seal,* no. 37, p. 62). The election failed because notice of the proclamation was not timely received (M. B. Lewis, Chief Justice of Jasper County, to secretary of state, January 12, 1841, Election Returns). His successor was chosen at the next general election.

Appendix F

MEMBERS OF THE SIXTH CONGRESS

AUSTIN
November 1, 1841–February 5, 1842
HOUSTON
June 27–July 23, 1842

PRESIDENT Mirabeau B. Lamar[1]
PRESIDENT Sam Houston[1]
VICE-PRESIDENT David G. Burnet[2]
VICE-PRESIDENT Edward Burleson[2]

SENATE

Member	District
Barnett, George Washington	Washington, Montgomery
Byrne, James W.	San Patricio, Refugio, Goliad
Colquhoun, Ludovic[3]	Bexar
Daingerfield, William Henry[3]	Bexar
Gaines, James Taylor[4]	Shelby, Sabine, Harrison
Greer, John Alexander	San Augustine
Jack, William Houston[5]	Brazoria
Jones, Oliver[6]	Austin, Colorado, Fort Bend
McFarland, Thomas S.[7]	Jasper, Jefferson
Martin, Wyly[6]	Austin, Colorado, Fort Bend
Moore, Francis, Jr.	Harris, Liberty, Galveston
Muse, Kindred H.	Nacogdoches, Houston
Owen, Clark L.	Matagorda, Jackson, Victoria
Pilsbury, Timothy[5]	Brazoria
Potter, Robert[8]	Red River, Fannin
Randal, Leonard[4]	Shelby, Sabine, Harrison
Shaw, James	Robertson, Milam
Titus, James[8]	Red River, Fannin
Webb, James	Bastrop, Gonzales, Fayette, Travis

1. Lamar served as president until December 13, 1841, when Houston became president.

2. Burnet served as vice-president until December 13, 1841, when Burleson became vice-president.

3. William Henry Daingerfield resigned on February 5, 1842, after Senate confirmation of his appointment by President Houston as secretary of the treasury (*Secret Journals of the Senate* [Winkler ed.], p. 225). On May 24, 1842, President Houston called an election for June 14, 1842 (Proclamations and Colonial Contracts No. 48, 1842–44, pp. 11–12). Ludovic Colquhoun was elected to succeed Daingerfield for the term expiring September 5, 1842, being seated at the commencement of the called session (*Senate Journal*, Sixth Congress, Second Session, pp. 1, 6 [Smither ed.]).

4. James Taylor Gaines, who did not attend the called session, resigned on July 15, 1842, due to advanced age and declining health (*Senate Journal*, Sixth Congress, Second Session, p. 2, n. 5 [Smither ed.]). On September 21, 1842, President Houston called an election for October 29, 1842, to select a successor (Proclamations and Colonial Contracts No. 48, 1842–44, pp. 47–48).

5. Timothy Pilsbury resigned on February 14, 1842 (Pilsbury to Secretary of State Anson Jones, February 14, 1842, Election Returns), having been elected Chief Justice of Brazoria County on January 24, 1842. On May 24, 1842, President Houston called an election for June 14, 1842 (Proclamations and Colonial Contracts No. 48, 1842–44, pp. 11–12). William Houston Jack was elected to succeed Pilsbury for the term expiring September 2, 1844, being seated at the commencement of the called session (*Senate Journal*, Sixth Congress, Second Session, pp. 2, 6 [Smither ed.]).

6. Wyly Martin died on April 26, 1842 (*Biographical Directory of the Texan Conventions and Congresses 1832–1845* [Austin: 1941], p. 134). On May 24, 1842, President Houston called an election for June 14, 1842 (Proclamations and Colonial Contracts No. 48, 1842–44, pp. 11–12). Oliver Jones was elected to succeed Martin for the term expiring September 4, 1843, being seated at the commencement of the called session (*Senate Journal*, Sixth Congress, Second Session, pp. 1, 6 [Smither ed.]).

7. Thomas S. McFarland was elected on September 6, 1841, to succeed Stephen Hendrickson Everitt for the term expiring September 5, 1842. McFarland did not attend the called session of the Sixth Congress (*Senate Journal*, Sixth Congress, Second Session, p. 2, n. 5 [Smither ed.]).

8. Robert Potter was murdered on March 2, 1842 (*Biographical Directory of the Texan Conventions and Congresses 1832–1845* [Austin: 1941], p. 156). On May 24, 1842, President Houston called an election for June 14, 1842 (Proclamations and Colonial Contracts No. 48, 1842–44, pp. 11–12). James Titus was elected to succeed Potter for the term expiring September 4, 1843, being seated on July 11, 1842 (*Senate Journal*, Sixth Congress, Second Session, p. 12 [Smither ed.]).

Appendix G

MEMBERS OF THE SEVENTH CONGRESS

WASHINGTON
Called Session, November 14–December 4, 1842
Regular Session, December 5, 1842–January 16, 1843

PRESIDENT Sam Houston
VICE-PRESIDENT Edward Burleson

SENATE

Member	District
Barnett, George Washington	Washington, Montgomery, Brazos
Byrne, James W.[1]	San Patricio, Refugio, Goliad
Greer, John Alexander	San Augustine
Jack, William Houston	Brazoria
Jones, Oliver[2]	Austin, Colorado, Fort Bend
Lawrence, William	Harris, Liberty, Galveston
Muse, Kindred H.	Nacogdoches, Houston
Owen, Clark L.[3]	Matagorda, Jackson, Victoria
Pattillo, George Alexander	Jasper, Jefferson
Randal, Leonard[4]	Sabine, Shelby, Harrison
Rugeley, John[3]	Matagorda, Jackson, Victoria
Shaw, James	Milam, Robertson
Smith, John William[4]	Bexar
Titus, James	Red River, Fannin, Bowie, Lamar
Webb, James[5]	Bastrop, Gonzales, Fayette, Travis

1. James W. Byrne did not attend either session of the Seventh Congress (Papers of the Seventh Congress, File 2635). No election was called to select a successor for the remainder of his term, which expired on September 4, 1843.

2. Oliver Jones resigned January 17, 1843 (Jones to President Houston, January 17, 1843, Election Returns; Papers of the Seventh Congress, File 2635). His successor was chosen at the next general election for the term expiring September 2, 1844.

3. Clark L. Owen resigned on November 12, 1842 (Papers of the Seventh Congress, File 2635; also, Vice-President Burleson to Secretary of State Jones, November 22, 1842, Election Returns). On November 22, 1842, President Houston called an election December 17, 1842 (Proclamations and Colonial Contracts No. 48, 1842–44, pp. 51–52). John Rugeley was elected to succeed Owen for the term expiring September 2, 1844, taking his seat on January 7, 1843 (*Senate Journal*, Seventh Congress, Regular Session, p. 91). The election was held only in Matagorda County, as the proclamation did not reach the other counties in sufficient time to conduct a vote. (Certificate, J. M. Brown, Chief Justice of Jackson County, December 31, 1842, Election Returns).

4. Leonard Randal was elected on October 29, 1842, for the term expiring September 4, 1843.

5. James Webb resigned on December 5, 1842 (Vice-President Burleson to Secretary of State Jones, November [sic] 5, 1842, Election Returns). The following day, President Houston called an election for December 21, 1842 (Proclamations and Colonial Contracts No. 48, 1842–44, pp. 54–55). Webb was unopposed for reelection to the term expiring September 2, 1844 (Certificate, Greenlief Fisk, Chief Justice of Bastrop County, December 24, 1842, Election Returns), taking his seat on December 31, 1842 (*Senate Journal*, Seventh Congress, Called Session, p. 60).

Appendix H

MEMBERS OF THE EIGHTH CONGRESS

WASHINGTON
December 4, 1843–February 5, 1844

PRESIDENT Sam Houston
VICE-PRESIDENT Edward Burleson

Senate

Member	District
Greer, John Alexander	San Augustine
Grimes, Jesse[1]	Washington, Montgomery, Brazos
Hunter, William Lockhart[2]	San Patricio, Refugio, Goliad
Jack, William Houston	Brazoria
Kaufman, David Spangler	Sabine, Shelby, Harrison
Lawrence, William	Harris, Liberty, Galveston
Parker, Gustavus A.	Austin, Colorado, Fort Bend
Parker, Isaac	Nacogdoches, Houston, Rusk
Pattillo, George Alexander[3]	Jasper, Jefferson
Rugeley, John	Matagorda, Jackson, Victoria
Shaw, James	Milam, Robertson
Smith, John William	Bexar
Webb, James	Bastrop, Gonzales, Fayette, Travis
Williamson, Robert McAlpin[1]	Washington, Montgomery, Brazos
Wright, George Washington[4]	Red River, Fannin, Bowie, Lamar

1. Robert McAlpin Williamson was certified as elected to the Senate of the Eighth Congress (Certificate, William H. Ewing, Chief Justice of Washington County, October 12, 1843, Contested Election Returns) and took his seat on December 12, 1843 (*Senate Journal*, Eighth Congress, p. 6). Jesse Grimes contested the election, however, and on December 29, 1843, the Committee on Privileges and Elections reported that while Williamson had received the largest number of the votes legally returned, such returns "do not present anything like a true statement of the vote which was given . . . in this district." The returns from Brazos County, although legally cast, were not counted because

they were never forwarded to the returning officer, Chief Justice Ewing of Washington County. The returns from Montgomery County, although also legally cast, were not counted because they were improperly forwarded to Ewing. All but two precincts in Washington County were rejected by Ewing for technical reasons. Finally, 83 votes cast in Milam County were rejected by Ewing as lying outside the senatorial district. Thus, the legal returns gave Williamson the victory, with 76 votes to 27 for Grimes and 20 for George Washington Barnett, the incumbent. Counting all votes returned to the various chief justices gave the same result, with Williamson receiving 513 votes, Grimes 506, and Barnett 461. Omitting Milam County, however, would have given Grimes the victory with 496 votes to 459 for Barnett and only 442 for Williamson. Furthermore, Grimes alleged that had the votes in two other precincts in Montgomery County been forwarded to the Chief Justice of Montgomery County, he would have won regardless of the Milam County vote. The majority of the committee recommended that the seat be declared vacant (*Senate Journal,* Eighth Congress, pp. 39–41, 43).

On December 29, 1843, and January 1, 1844, the Senate voted to lay the report of the committee on the table. The Senate took the matter up again on January 4, 1844, when Senator Parker moved to declare Grimes elected. Senator Shaw offered a substitute to allow Williamson to hold his seat until the adjournment of the current session, at which time the seat would be declared vacant. Although Shaw's resolution was defeated four to eight, he did succeed in striking from Senator Parker's resolution that language declaring Grimes elected, eight to four. The Senate then voted nine to three to adopt the original report declaring the seat vacant. The Senate then resolved, seven to five, that the votes cast in Milam County were illegal (*Senate Journal,* Eighth Congress, pp. 43, 52–53, 66–68).

On January 5, 1844, President Houston called a new election for January 14, 1844 (*Record Book of Documents under the Great Seal,* no. 37, p. 187). Jesse Grimes was elected to succeed Williamson for the term expiring September 7, 1846. Grimes took his seat on January 22, 1844 (*Senate Journal,* Eighth Congress, p. 148).

2. William Lockhart Hunter was seated on December 6, 1843 (*Senate Journal,* Eighth Congress, p. 3). On December 28, 1843, however, James Power filed a challenge to Hunter's election (Papers of Eighth Congress, File 2892), which was referred the following day to the Committee on Privileges and Elections. Although Hunter won the election, 52 to 38, Power challenged 40 of Hunter's votes, 2 as being cast by underage voters, 10 as being cast by nonresidents of the districts, and 28 as being cast in an irregular election (*Senate Journal,* p. 39).

On January 9, 1844, the committee made its initial report. After various resolutions were offered, the Senate voted six to five to allow the parties three weeks to take testimony (*Senate Journal,* Eighth Congress, pp. 90–91, 93, 95–96). Various controversies arose over the manner and procedure of gathering this testimony, but a considerable mass of evidence was forwarded to the Senate (Papers of Eighth Congress, File 2892).

On February 3, 1844, the committee reported that Power's challenges were largely without foundation, with only two or three of Hunter's votes having probably been illegal. On the other hand, the committee found substantial evidence that fourteen of Power's votes were illegal (Papers of Eighth Congress, File 2892); (*Senate Journal,* Eighth Congress, pp. 228–31). On February 5, 1844, Senator Parker offered a resolution declaring Power the winner. Senator Smith offered a substitute resolution to declare the seat vacant, which was adopted eight to three (*Senate Journal,* pp. 242–43). No successor was chosen until the next general election for the term expiring September 7, 1846.

3. George Alexander Pattillo was elected for the term expiring September 2, 1844.

4. George Washington Wright never took his seat in the Eighth Congress, but he was active in the Ninth Congress.

Appendix I

MEMBERS OF THE NINTH CONGRESS

President Sam Houston[1]
President Anson Jones[1]
Vice-President Edward Burleson[2]
Vice-President Kenneth Lewis Anderson[2]

Senate

Member	District
Caldwell, John	Bastrop, Fayette, Gonzales, Travis
Greer, John Alexander	San Augustine
Grimes, Jesse	Washington, Montgomery, Brazos
Kaufman, David Spangler[3]	Sabine, Shelby, Harrison
Kinney, Henry L.	San Patricio, Goliad, Refugio
Lawrence, William	Harris, Galveston, Liberty
Luckie, Samuel H.[4]	Bexar
McCrearey, James K.	Austin, Colorado, Fort Bend
Munson, Henry J.	Robertson, Milam
Parker, Isaac	Nacogdoches, Rusk, Houston
Pattillo, George Alexander	Jasper, Jefferson
Pilsbury, Timothy	Brazoria
Roman, Richard	Matagorda, Jackson, Victoria
Smith, John William[2]	Bexar
Wright, George Washington	Red River, Fannin, Bowie, Lamar

1. Houston served as president until December 9, 1844, when Jones became president.
2. Burleson served as vice-president until December 9, 1844, when Anderson became vice-president.
3. David Spangler Kaufman resigned on June 28, 1845 (Kaufman to Ebenezer Allen,

Secretary of State ad interim, June 28, 1845, Election Returns). His successor was chosen at the next general election for the term expiring September 7, 1846.

4. John William Smith died on January 12, 1845 (*Handbook of Texas*, vol. 2, p. 625), or January 13, 1845 (*Biographical Directory of the Texan Conventions and Congresses 1832–1845* [Austin: 1941], p. 173). On January 13, 1845, President Jones called an election for January 24, 1845 (Proclamations and Colonial Contracts No. 48, 1842–44, p. 105). Samuel H. Luckie was elected to succeed Smith for the term expiring September 1, 1845, taking his seat on February 1, 1845 (*Senate Journal*, Ninth Congress, Regular Session, pp. 273–74).

Appendix J

MEMBERS OF THE TENTH CONGRESS

Elected September 1, 1845
Never Seated – Never Convened[1]

Member	*District*
Caldwell, John	Bastrop, Fayette, Gonzales, Travis
Darnell, Nicholas Henry	San Augustine
Franklin, Benjamin Cromwell	Harris, Galveston, Liberty
Grimes, Jesse	Washington, Montgomery, Brazos
Kinney, Henry Lockhart	San Patricio, Goliad, Refugio
McCrearey, James K.	Austin, Colorado, Fort Bend
Munson, Henry J.	Robertson, Milam
Navarro, José Antonio	Bexar
Parker, Isaac	Nacogdoches, Rusk, Houston
Pilsbury, Timothy	Brazoria
Roman, Richard	Matagorda, Jackson, Victoria
Wright, George Washington	Red River, Fannin, Bowie, Lamar
[Middleton T. Johnson or Isaac Van Zandt][2]	Shelby, Sabine, Harrison
_____[3]	Jasper, Jefferson

1. On December 29, 1845, the United States Congress accepted the state constitution, and Texas became a part of the United States.

2. Conflicting reports exist as to the winner of this election. Compare *Telegraph and Texas Register*, October 1, 1845, p. 2, col. 4 ("Johnson reportedly elected by a small majority"); *Red-Lander*, September 11, 1845, p. 3, col. 3 (Johnson elected) with *Texas National Register*, September 18, 1845, p. 327[7], col. 1 (Van Zandt elected). The winner was elected to the term expiring September 7, 1846.

3. The candidates and outcome of the election in the district of Jasper and Jefferson are unknown.

Appendix K

MEMBERS OF THE FIRST LEGISLATURE

Regular Session, February 16–May 13, 1846

GOVERNOR J. Pinckney Henderson
LIEUTENANT GOVERNOR Albert C. Horton

SENATE

Member	District Number	Counties Composing District
Bagby, Ballard C.	2	Fannin, Lamar, Bowie
Bourland, James[1]	(F)	Fannin, Lamar, Bowie, Red River
Brashear, Isaac W.	10	Harris
Burleson, Edward	15	Bastrop, Travis
Cuney, Philip M.	13	Austin, Fort Bend
Grimes, Jesse	9	Montgomery
Hogg, Joseph L.[2]	4	Rusk, Houston, Nacogdoches
Jewett, Henry J.	8	Brazos, Robertson
Kinney, Henry L.	19	Refugio, Goliad, San Patricio
McKinney, Thomas F.	11	Galveston
McNeill, John G.	12	Brazoria, Matagorda
Miller, John F.	14	Colorado, Fayette
Navarro, José A.	18	Bexar
Parker, Isaac[2]	4	Houston, Rusk, Nacogdoches
Phillips, Alexander H.	17	Gonzales, Jackson, Victoria
Robinson, Jesse J.	6	Jasper, Sabine
Scott, William T.[3]	3	Harrison
Wallace, Benjamin R.	5	San Augustine, Shelby
Williams, William M.	1	Fannin, Lamar
Williamson, Robert M.	16	Milam, Washington
Wood, George T.[4]	7	Jefferson, Liberty

1. Bourland was a floatorial senator conjointly elected from Bowie, Red River, Fannin, and Lamar counties.

2. Parker succeeded Joseph L. Hogg, who resigned to become a volunteer in the war with Mexico.

3. William T. Scott resigned in a letter to Governor Henderson dated June 5, 1847, explaining that his resignation was because of "private affairs" and his unwillingness to be separated from his family.

4. George T. Wood resigned to become a volunteer in the war with Mexico.

Appendix L

MEMBERS OF THE SECOND LEGISLATURE

Regular Session, December 13, 1847–March 20, 1848

GOVERNOR George T. Wood

LIEUTENANT GOVERNOR John A. Greer

SENATE

Member	District Number	Counties Composing District
Abbott, William C.	7	Jefferson, Liberty
Bache, Richard[1]	11	Galveston
Bourland, James[2]	(F)	Bowie, Fannin, Lamar, Red River
Brashear, Isaac W.	10	Harris
Burleson, Edward	15	Bastrop, Travis
Clark, Edward	3	Harrison
Cuney, Philip M.	13	Austin, Ford Bend
Dancy, Jon W. S.	14	Colorado, Fayette
Fitzgerald, Edward[3]	19	Nueces, Refugio, San Patricio, Goliad
Gage, David	4	Houston, Rusk, Nacogdoches
Grimes, Jesse	9	Montgomery
Jewett, Henry J.	8	Brazos, Robertson
Kinney, Henry L.[3]	19	Goliad, Refugio, Nueces, San Patricio
McRae, John H.	6	Jasper, Sabine
Navarro, José A.	18	Bexar
Parker, Isaac	4	Houston, Rusk, Nacogdoches
Perkins, Stephen W.	12	Brazoria, Matagorda
Phillips, Alexander H.	17	Jackson, Gonzales, Victoria
Wallace, Benjamin R.	5	San Augustine, Shelby
Williams, William M.	1	Fannin, Lamar
Williamson, Robert M.	16	Milam, Washington
Wootten, James B.	2	Bowie, Red River

1. Richard Bache died on March 17, 1848.
2. Bourland was a floatorial senator conjointly elected from Bowie, Red River, Fannin, and Lamar counties.
3. Henry L. Kinney resigned and was succeeded by Edward Fitzgerald, who took his seat on February 5, 1848, but resigned on March 20, 1848.

Appendix M

MEMBERS OF THE THIRD LEGISLATURE

Regular Session, November 5, 1849–February 11, 1850
First Called Session, August 12–September 6, 1850
Second Called Session, November 18–December 3, 1850

GOVERNOR Peter H. Bell
LIEUTENANT GOVERNOR John A. Greer

SENATE

Member	District Number	Counties Composing District
Brashear, Isaac W.	12	Harris
Burleson, Edward	16	Bastrop, Caldwell, Fayette, Hays, Travis
Campbell, Samuel R.[1]	4	Collin, Dallas, Denton, Grayson, Henderson
Cooke, Wilds K.	15	Brazos, Leon, Limestone, Navarro, Robertson
Davis, H. Clay	21	Cameron, Starr, Webb
Gage, David	5	Panola, Rusk
Grimes, Jesse	13	Grimes, Montgomery, Walker
Hart, Hardin	3	Hopkins, Hunt, Fannin
Jones, John B.[2]	11	Brazoria, Galveston
Kinney, Henry L.	19	Cameron, Goliad, Nueces, Refugio, San Patricio
Latimer, Albert H.	2	Lamar, Red River
McRae, John H.	8	Jasper, Newton, Sabine, San Augustine, Angelina
Moffitt, John H.	9	Jefferson, Liberty, Polk, Tyler
Parker, Isaac	10	Anderson, Houston, Cherokee
Pease, Elisha M.[2]	11	Brazoria, Galveston
Phillips, Alexander H.	18	Calhoun, DeWitt, Gonzales, Jackson, Matagorda, Victoria
Portis, David Y.	17	Austin, Colorado, Fort Bend, Lavaca, Wharton
Robertson, Jerome B.	14	Burleson, Milam, Williamson, Washington

350

Member (cont.)		*Counties Composing District (cont.)*
Taylor, James F.[3]	6	Harrison, Smith, Upshur
Truitt (Truit), Alfred M.	7	Nacogdoches, Shelby
Vanderlip, David C.	20	Comal, Bexar, Guadalupe
Walker, Albert G.[1]	4	Collin, Dallas, Denton, Grayson, Henderson
Wallace, Benjamin R.	22	All counties east of Trinity River
Ward, Matthias	1	Bowie, Cass, Titus

1. Albert G. Walker resigned and was succeeded by Samuel R. Campbell, who took the oath of office on August 12, 1850.

2. John B. Jones took the oath of office on November 5, 1849, but his petition for seat for Galveston County was denied on November 10, 1849. Elisha M. Pease was declared the winner in the contested election and took the oath of office on November 9, 1849.

3. Taylor resigned on September 30, 1850, but was reelected before the Second Called Session.

Appendix N

MEMBERS OF THE FOURTH LEGISLATURE

Regular Session, November 3, 1851–February 16, 1852
First Called Session, January 10–February 7, 1853

GOVERNOR Peter H. Bell
LIEUTENANT GOVERNOR James W. Henderson[1]

SENATE

Member	District Number	Counties Composing District
Armstrong, James H.	14	Brazos, Burleson, Leon, Milam, Robertson, Williamson
Bigelow, Israel B.	24	Cameron, Starr
Bogart, Sam	3	Cooke, Dallas, Denton, Collin, Grayson
Burks, Joseph H.	1	Bowie, Red River
Burleson, Edward[2]	21	Gillespie, Hays, Travis
Dancy, Jon W. S.	20	Caldwell, Bastrop, Fayette
Davis, James	13	Jefferson, Liberty, Polk, Tyler
Day, William S.	16	Austin, Fort Bend, Washington
Doane, Rufus	26	El Paso, Presidio (Santa Fe, Worth)
Duggan, Thomas H.	23	DeWitt, Goliad, Gonzales, Guadalupe, Lavaca
Eddy, Z. Williams	10	Jasper, Newton, Sabine, San Augustine
Ford, John S.[2]	21	Gillespie, Hays, Travis
Gray, Peter W.	17	Harris
Grimes, Jesse	15	Grimes, Montgomery, Walker
Hart, Hardin	4	Hopkins, Hunt, Kaufman, Van Zandt
Hill, George W.	6	Henderson, Limestone, Navarro
Kinney, Henry L.	25	Kinney, Nueces, Refugio, San Patricio, Webb
Merriman, Franklin H.[3]	18	Brazoria, Galveston
Meusebach, John O.	22	Bexar, Comal, Medina
Miller, Steward A.[4]	11	Angelina, Houston, Nacogdoches

Member (cont.)		Counties Composing District (cont.)
Parker, Isaac	7	Anderson, Cherokee
Potter, Mark M.[3]	18	Brazoria, Galveston
Reaves, Stephen	8	Rusk, Smith
Scott, William T.	9	Harrison, Upshur
Sterne, Adolphus[4]	11	Angelina, Houston, Nacogdoches
Taylor, Marion D. K.	5	Cass, Titus
Truit, James H.	12	Panola, Shelby
Williams, William M.	2	Fannin, Lamar
Wilson, James C.	19	Calhoun, Colorado, Jackson, Matagorda, Victoria, Wharton

1. Henderson served as governor November 23, 1851–December 21, 1853.

2. Edward Burleson died on December 26, 1851, and was succeeded by John S. Ford, who took the oath of office on January 19, 1852.

3. Mark M. Potter succeeded Franklin H. Merriman in special session.

4. Adolphus Sterne died on March 27, 1852. Steward A. Miller was elected for the unexpired term and took his seat in the special session.

Appendix O

MEMBERS OF THE FIFTH LEGISLATURE

Regular Session, November 7, 1853–February 13, 1854

GOVERNOR Elisha M. Pease

LIEUTENANT GOVERNOR David C. Dickson

SENATE

Member	District Number	Address	Counties Composing District
Allen, Malachi W.	4	McKinney	Collin, Cooke, Kaufman, Denton, Grayson
Armstrong, James H.	23	Georgetown	Bell, Falls, Milam, Williamson, McLennan
Bryan, Guy M.	24	Gulf Prairie	Brazoria, Fort Bend, Matagorda, Wharton
Burks, Joseph H.	1	DeKalb	Bowie, Red River
Doane, Rufus	33	San Elizario	El Paso, Presidio
Durst, James H.	29	Rio Grande City	Nueces, San Patricio, Starr, Webb, Refugio, Kinney
Edwards, William C.	15	San Augustine	Jasper, Newton, Sabine, San Augustine
Gage, David	9	Mount Enterprise	Rusk
Guinn, Robert H.	11	Rusk	Cherokee
Hart, Hardin	3	Greenville	Fannin, Hunt
Hill, Isaac L.	32	Round Top	Austin, Colorado, Fayette
Holland, James K.	14	Carthage	Panola, Shelby
Jowers, William G. W.	12	Palestine	Anderson, Houston
Keenan, Charles G.	19	Huntsville	Grimes, Madison, Montgomery, Walker
Kyle, Claiborne	27	San Marcos	Caldwell, Hays, Comal, Gonzales, Guadalupe

354

Member (cont.)			Counties Composing District (cont.)
Lott, Elisha E.	10	Tyler	Smith, Van Zandt
Lytle, James T.[1]	26	Lavaca	Calhoun, DeWitt, Goliad, Jackson, Lavaca, Victoria
Martin, William H.	22	Athens	Freestone, Limestone, Henderson, Navarro
McAnelly, Cornelius	18	Houston	Harris
McDade, James W.	20	Chappell Hill	Washington
Millican, Elliott M.	21	Millican	Brazos, Burleson, Leon, Robertson
Newman, Simpson C.	6	Coffeeville	Upshur, Wood
Paschal, Isaiah A.	31	San Antonio	Bexar, Gillespie, Medina, Uvalde
Pedigo, Henry C.	16	Woodville	Jefferson, Liberty, Orange, Polk, Tyler, Trinity
Potter, Mark M.	17	Galveston	Galveston
Scarborough, Edwin B.	28	Brownsville	Cameron, Hidalgo
Scott, William T.	8	Marshall	Harrison
Sublett, Henry W.	25	Austin	Bastrop, Burnet, Travis
Superviele, Antoine	30	San Antonio	Bexar
Taylor, Marion D. K.	7	Smithland	Cass, Titus
Weatherford, Jefferson	5	Pleasant Run	Dallas, Ellis, Tarrant
Whitaker, Madison G.	13	Nacogdoches	Nacogdoches, Angelina
Wren, Johnson	2	Black Jack Grove	Hopkins, Lamar

1. James T. Lytle died on February 5, 1854. He had tendered his resignation on January 30, 1854, but it was not received by the Senate until February 8.

Appendix P

MEMBERS OF THE SIXTH LEGISLATURE

Regular Session, November 5, 1855–February 4, 1856
Adjourned Session, July 7–September 1, 1856

GOVERNOR Elisha M. Pease
LIEUTENANT GOVERNOR Hardin Richard Runnels

SENATE

Member	District Number	Counties Composing District
Allen, Malachi W.	4	Collin, Cooke, Kaufman, Denton, Grayson
Armstrong, James H.	23	Bell, Falls, Milam, Williamson, McLennan
Bryan, Guy M.	24	Brazoria, Fort Bend, Matagorda, Wharton
Burroughs, James M.	15	Jasper, Newton, Sabine, San Augustine
Caldwell, John	25	Bastrop, Burnet, Travis
Doane, Rufus	33	El Paso, Presidio
Flanagan, James W.	9	Rusk
Grimes, Jesse	19	Grimes, Madison, Montgomery, Walker
Guinn, Robert H.	11	Cherokee
Hill, Isaac L.	32	Austin, Colorado, Fayette
Hord, Edward R.	29	Nueces, San Patricio, Starr, Webb, Refugio
Lott, Elisha E.	10	Smith, Van Zandt
Martin, William H.	22	Freestone, Limestone, Henderson, Navarro
Maverick, Samuel A.	31	Bexar, Gillespie, Medina, Uvalde
McCulloch, Henry E.	27	Caldwell, Hays, Comal, Gonzales, Guadalupe
McDade, James W.	20	Washington
Millican, Elliott M.	21	Brazos, Burleson, Leon, Robertson
Palmer, Edward A.	18	Harris
Pedigo, Henry C.	16	Jefferson, Liberty, Orange, Polk, Tyler, Trinity
Pirkey, Solomon H.	1	Bowie, Red River
Potter, Mark M.	17	Galveston
Russell, Jonathan	6	Upshur, Wood

Member (cont.)		*Counties Composing District (cont.)*
Scarborough, Edwin B.	28	Cameron, Hidalgo
Scott, William T.	8	Harrison
Superviele, Antoine	30	Bexar
Taylor, Marion D. K.	7	Cass, Titus
Taylor, Robert H.	3	Fannin, Hunt
Taylor, William M.	12	Anderson, Houston
Truit, James	14	Panola, Shelby
Weatherford, Jefferson	5	Dallas, Ellis, Tarrant
Whitaker, Madison G.	13	Nacogdoches, Angelina
White, S. Addison	26	Calhoun, DeWitt, Goliad, Jackson, Lavaca, Victoria
Wren, Johnson	2	Hopkins, Lamar

Appendix Q

MEMBERS OF THE SEVENTH LEGISLATURE

Regular Session, November 2, 1857–February 16, 1858

GOVERNOR Hardin Richard Runnels
LIEUTENANT GOVERNOR Francis R. Lubbock

SENATE

Member	District Number	Address	Counties Composing District
Britton, Forbes	29	Corpus Christi	Nueces, San Patricio, Starr, Webb, Refugio, Kinney
Burroughs, James M.	15	Milam	Jasper, Newton, Sabine, San Augustine
Caldwell, John	25	Webberville	Bastrop, Burnet, Travis
Erath, George B.	23	Waco	Bell, Falls, Milam, Williamson, McLennan
Fall, John N.	13	Cherino	Nacogdoches, Angelina
Graham, Malcolm D.	9	Henderson	Rusk
Grimes, Jesse	19	Anderson	Grimes, Madison, Montgomery, Walker
Guinn, Robert H.	11	Rusk	Cherokee
Herbert, Claiborne C.	32	Columbus	Austin, Colorado, Fayette
Hyde, Archibald C.	33	San Elizario	El Paso, Presidio
Lott, Elisha E.	10	Tyler	Smith, Van Zandt
Martin, William H.	22	Athens	Freestone, Limestone, Henderson, Navarro
Maverick, Samuel A.	31	San Antonio	Bexar, Gillespie, Medina, Uvalde
McCulloch, Henry E.	27	Seguin	Caldwell, Hays, Comal, Gonzales, Guadalupe
Millican, Elliott M.[1]	21	Millican	Brazos, Burleson, Leon, Robertson

			Counties Composing
Member (cont.)			*District (cont.)*
Paschal, Isaiah A.	30	San Antonio	Bexar
Pedigo, Henry C.	16	Woodville	Trinity, Jefferson, Liberty, Orange, Polk, Tyler
Pirkey, Solomon H.	1	Boston	Bowie, Red River
Potter, Mark M.	17	Galveston	Galveston
Quinan, George	24	Wharton	Brazoria, Fort Bend, Matagorda, Wharton
Runnels, Hiram G. [2]	18	Houston	Harris
Russell, Jonathan	6	Webster	Upshur, Wood
Scarborough, Edwin B.	28	Brownsville	Cameron, Hidalgo
Shepard, Chauncy B.	20	Long Point	Washington
Stockdale, Fletcher S.	26	Indianola	Calhoun, DeWitt, Goliad, Jackson, Lavaca, Victoria
Tankersly, Benjamin F. [2]	18	Houston	Harris
Taylor, Marion D. K.	7	Jefferson	Cass, Titus
Taylor, Robert H.	3	Bonham	Fannin, Hunt
Taylor, William M.	12	Crockett	Anderson, Houston
Throckmorton, James W.	4	McKinney	Collin, Cooke, Kaufman, Denton, Grayson
Truit, James	14	Truitts Store	Panola, Shelby
Walker, Albert G.	5	Birdville	Dallas, Ellis, Tarrant
Whaley, David M. [1]	21	Centerville	Brazos, Burleson, Leon, Robertson
Wigfall, Louis T.	8	Marshall	Harrison
Wren, Johnson	2	Black Jack Grove	Hopkins, Lamar

1. Elliott M. Millican did not attend and resigned his seat. He was succeeded in special election by David M. Whaley, who took his seat on January 12, 1858.

2. Hiram G. Runnels was elected but did not attend, and died on December 17, 1857. He was succeeded by Benjamin F. Tankersly, who took his seat on January 25, 1858.

Appendix R

MEMBERS OF THE EIGHTH LEGISLATURE

Regular Session, November 7, 1859–February 13, 1860
First Called Session, January 21–February 9, 1861
Adjourned Session, March 18–April 9, 1861

Governor Sam Houston[1]
Lieutenant Governor Edward Clark[1]

Senate

Member	District Number	Address	Counties Composing District
Blanch, E. A.[2]	8	Marshall	Harrison
Britton, Forbes[3]	29	Corpus Christi	Nueces, San Patricio, Starr, Webb, Refugio, Kinney
Chambers, John G.	7	Daingerfield	Cass, Titus
Dickinson, John R.[4]	14	Bethany	Panola, Shelby
Duggan, Thomas H.	27	Seguin	Caldwell, Hays, Comal, Gonzales, Guadalupe, DeWitt
Dulany, H. P. C.[4]	14	Carthage	Panola, Shelby
Erath, George B.	23	Waco	Bell, Falls, Milam, Williamson, McLennan
Fall, John N.	13	Cherino	Nacogdoches, Angelina
Gentry, Abram M.	18	Houston	Harris
Grimes, Jesse	19	Anderson	Grimes, Madison, Montgomery, Walker
Guinn, Robert H.	11	Rusk	Cherokee
Harmon, Lewis G.	2	Tarrant	Hopkins, Lamar
Hart, Martin D.[5]	3	Greenville	Fannin, Hunt
Herbert, Claiborne C.	32	Columbus	Austin, Colorado, Fayette
Hyde, Archibald C.	33	San Elizario	El Paso, Presidio
Lott, Elisha E.	10	Tyler	Smith, Van Zandt

Member (cont.)			*Counties Composing District (cont.)*
Martin, Francis M.	22	Corsicana	Freestone, Limestone, Henderson, Navarro
Miller, Steward A.[6]	12	Palestine	Anderson, Houston
Neal, Benjamin F.[3]	29	Corpus Christi	Nueces, San Patricio, Starr, Webb, Refugio, Kinney
Parsons, Jesse H.	9	Henderson	Rusk
Paschal, Isaiah A.[7]	30	San Antonio	Bexar
Pitts, Enoch S.	16	Woodville	Jefferson, Liberty, Orange, Polk, Tyler, Trinity
Potter, Mark M.	17	Galveston	Galveston
Quinan, George	24	Wharton	Brazoria, Fort Bend, Matagorda, Wharton
Rainey, Alexis T.[6]	12	Palestine	Anderson, Houston
Rains, Emory	6	Springville	Upshur, Wood
Scarborough, Edwin B.	28	Brownsville	Cameron, Hidalgo
Schleicher, Gustavus	31	San Antonio	Bexar, Gillespie, Medina, Uvalde
Sexton, Franklin B.[8]	15	San Augustine	Jasper, Newton, Sabine, San Augustine
Shepard, Chauncy B.	20	Long Point	Washington
Sims, James W.	1	Clarksville	Bowie, Red River
Stockdale, Fletcher S.	26	Indianola	Calhoun, DeWitt, Goliad, Jackson, Lavaca, Victoria
Throckmorton, James W.	4	McKinney	Collin, Cooke, Kaufman, Denton, Grayson
Townes, Eggleston D.[9]	25	Webberville	Bastrop, Burnet, Travis
Walker, Albert G.	5	Birdville	Dallas, Ellis, Tarrant
Wallace, Henry C.[8]	15	San Augustine	Jasper, Newton, Sabine, San Augustine
Whaley, David M.	21	Centerville	Brazos, Burleson, Leon, Robertson
Wigfall, Louis T.[2]	8	Marshall	Harrison

1. Houston, refusing to take the oath of allegiance to the Confederate States Government, was deposed, and Clark assumed the duties of governor on March 16, 1861, and served out the unexpired term.

2. Louis T. Wigfall's resignation was acknowledged in the *Senate Journal* on December 7, 1859. E. A. Blanch was elected for the unexpired term and took the oath of office on January 13, 1860.

3. Forbes Britton resigned prior to the adjourned session, and the Senate adopted

on March 20, 1861, a memorial resolution on his death. He was succeeded by Benjamin F. Neal, who took the oath to the Confederacy on March 19, 1861.

4. John R. Dickinson resigned prior to the First Called Session and was succeeded by H. P. C. Dulaney, who took the oath of office on January 28, 1861.

5. Martin D. Hart resigned, with no successor.

6. Alexis T. Rainey resigned prior to the First Called Session and was succeeded by Steward A. Miller, who took the oath of office on January 21, 1861.

7. Isaiah A. Paschal resigned, with no successor.

8. Henry C. Wallace resigned and was succeeded by Franklin B. Sexton, who was elected on March 4, 1861, but did not appear.

9. Eggleston D. Townes resigned on March 13, 1861. The outcome of the special election is uncertain because of missing election returns. He was probably succeeded by N. G. Shelley, who did not, however, appear until the Ninth Legislature.

The Texas Senate, 1836–61
A Bibliographic Essay

The Eugene C. Barker Texas History Center at the University of Texas at Austin proved to be the richest source of information on the Texas Senate, both published and archival. The staff members were always helpful and remained patiently so even under the most histrionic demands from historians rushing to meet a deadline. The collections of the Texas State Library and Archives Commission in Austin were mined as well for facts to be incorporated into a history of the Senate. Although time did not allow extensive research in the official records archived there, surveys were accomplished with the help of the excellent finding aids compiled by the archivists. This bibliography, then, must serve as little more than a starting point for future research.

As with any historical project, historians of the Texas Senate must begin with general sources. The most authoritative single volume on the history of Texas is Rupert N. Richardson, Ernest Wallace, and Adrian N. Anderson, *Texas: The Lone Star State* (Englewood Cliffs, N.J.: Prentice-Hall, 1981). Now in its fourth edition, this textbook, which first appeared in 1943, provides a synoptic overview of the history of the state that is unmatched by any other effort. Each chapter is accompanied by brief bibliographic essays, which facilitate further research in specific topics. Several other works serve as good supplements to this book. Probably the most important source of Texas history is Walter P. Webb, H. Bailey Carroll, and Eldon S. Branda, *The Handbook of Texas* (Austin, Tex.: Texas State Historical Association, vols. 1 and 2, 1952; vol. 3, 1977). This historical encyclopedia is being revised and vastly expanded, but until the new edition appears the original remains unsurpassed for its broad comprehensive work on Texas. The *Texas Almanac*, first published by the *Galveston News* in January, 1857, and since 1904 by the *Dallas Morning News*, serves as a dependable contemporary reference for many periods. T. R. Fehrenbach's *Lone Star: A History of Texas and the Texans* (New York: American Legacy Press, 1968) is a lively narrative written by one who obviously loves the state.

The period of the Texas Republic has been studied extensively by historians, but few broad overviews of this era have been written. A good brief account is Seymour V. Connor, *Adventure in Glory* (Austin, Tex.: Steck-Vaughn, 1965). Two more narrowly focused works which proved to be indispensible are William R. Hogan, *The Texas Republic: A Social and Economic History* (Norman: University of Oklahoma Press, 1946), and Stanley Siegel, *Political History of the Texas Republic, 1836–1845* (Austin: University of Texas Press, 1956). An overriding concern of the Texas Republic was defense, the subject of two books by J. M. Nance, *After San Jacinto: The Texas-Mexican Frontier, 1836–1841* (Austin: University of Texas Press, 1963), and *Attack and Counterattack: The Texas-Mexican Frontier, 1842* (Austin: University of Texas Press, 1964). Marquis James, *The Raven: A Biography of Sam Houston* (New York: Blue Ribbon Books, 1929), gives an entertaining and informative narrative of the life of the Republic's premier statesman. The career of Houston's chief foe is detailed in Herbert P. Gambrell, *Mirabeau Buonaparte Lamar* (Dallas, Tex.: Southwest Press, 1934). The best recent analysis of the events surrounding the end of the Republic and the annexation of Texas is David M. Pletcher, *The Diplomacy of Annexation: Texas, Oregon, and the Mexican War* (Columbia: University of Missouri Press, 1973). Frederick Merk and Lois Bannister Merk's *Slavery and the Annexation of Texas* (New York: Knopf, 1972) centers on the great controversy.

The early period of statehood for Texas is delimited here as the years from the adoption of the first state constitution in 1845 to secession in 1861. The best general survey of the period is Ernest Wallace, *Texas in Turmoil* (Austin, Tex.: Steck-Vaughn, 1965). Some topics required more extensive explanation. Progress in Texas education is detailed in Frederick Eby, *The Development of Education in Texas* (New York: Macmillan, 1925), with an informative sidelight provided in Horace Bailey Carroll, *Masonic Influence on Education in the Republic of Texas* (Waco: Texas Lodge of Research, A.F. & A.M., 1960). Thomas L. Miller, *The Public Lands of Texas, 1519–1970* (Norman: University of Oklahoma Press, 1972), explains clearly a subject that remains a problem for Texas. Marilyn Mc-

Adams Sibley's *Lone Stars and State Gazettes: Texas Newspapers Before the Civil War* (College Station: Texas A&M University Press, 1983), is a mine of information, not confined to newspapers, of a time when the legislative halls were filled with editors and publishers. A very unorthodox editor and no legislator candidly tells of his impact on the German community and beyond in "Autobiography of Dr. Adolf Douai: Revolutionary of 1848, pioneer, Introducer of the kindergarten, Educator, Author, Editor, 1819–1888; Translated from the German by Richard H. Douai Boerker, his grandson" (Typescript, Barker Texas History Center, University of Texas). The campaign pronouncements of several candidates such as Isaiah Paschal and Antoine Superviele in Douai's *San Antonio Zeitung* are worth reading, although they may have been as much written as translated by Douai. Some figures in the chaplain controversies of the early senates can be identified with the help of such books as James Milton Carroll's *A History of Texas Baptists: Comprising a Detailed Account of Their Activities, Their Progress, and Their Achievements* (Dallas: Baptist Standard, 1929). Pat Ireland Nixon, *The Medical Story of Early Texas: 1528–1853* (Lancaster, Pa.: Mollie Bennett Lupe Memorial Fund, 1946), supplies information on a number of the many doctors in the early legislatures and on the origin of the Texas Medical Association.

The background of the German immigration to Texas that was so important in this period is deeply explored in Terry G. Jordan's *German Seed in Texas Soil: Immigrant Farmers in Nineteenth-Century Texas* (Austin: University of Texas Press, 1966), and a leading senatorial figure in it is given a full-length biography by Irene Marschall King, *John O. Meusebach: German Colonizer in Texas* (Austin: University of Texas Press, 1967). Earl Wesley Fornell's admirable *The Galveston Era: The Texas Crescent on the Eve of Secession* (Austin: University of Texas Press, 1961) deals with an important German enclave, as it became in the 1850s, and with much related to railroads, commerce, and other vital concerns of the day.

Forces at work leading to the sundry attempts on the Santa Fe territory and the Compromise of 1850 are clarified in William C. Binkley's *The Expansionist Movement in Texas: 1836–1850* (Berkeley, Calif.: 1925 [New York: Da Capo, 1970]).

The development of penitentiaries, dealt with by Herman Lee Crow in "A Political History of the Texas Penal System, 1829–1951" (Dissertation, University of Houston, 1964), was of particular interest to the protean Elisha M. Pease, although his name is more widely associated with education; the dissertation of Roger Allen Griffin, "Connecticut Yankee in Texas: A Biography of Elisha Marshall Pease" (Austin: University of Texas, 1973), deals with this and the more resounding concerns of his life, both in general and in fine particular.

Attempted Fourierist colonization by the French can be traced in William J. and Margaret F. Hammond's *La Reunion, a French Settlement in Texas* (Dallas: Royal Publishing Company, 1958); in Dr. Augustine Savandan's *Un naufrage au Texas: Observations et impressions recueillies pendant deux ans et demi au Texas et à travers les États-Unis d'Amérique* (Paris: Garnier frères, 1858); and in Victor Prosper Considerant's *Du Texas: Premier rapport a mes amis* (Paris: Librairie societaire, 1857), as well as in his petition to the legislature and the response in committee reports of the *Senate Journal* of the Sixth Senate. The Peters Colony imbroglio is given extensive treatment in Seymour V. Connor's *The Peters Colony of Texas: A History and Biographical Sketch of the Early Settlers* (Austin: Texas State Historical Association, 1959), and in the relevant portions of Ben H. Proctor's *Not Without Honor: The Life of John H. Reagan* (Austin: University of Texas Press, 1962).

The basic study of the rocket flight of the Know Nothings and the strange role of Sam Houston in their machinations is still Litha Crews's "The Know-Nothing Party in Texas" (master's thesis, University of Texas, 1925), supplemented by Waymon L. McClellan's "1855: The Know-Nothing Challenge in East Texas," *East Texas Historical Journal* 12, and Ralph A. Wooster's "An Analysis of Texas Know Nothings," *Southwestern Historical Quarterly* 70 (January, 1967), as well as Llerena Friend's *Sam Houston: The Great Designer* (Austin: University of Texas Press, 1954), and M. K. Wiseheart's *Sam Houston: American Giant* (Washington, D.C.: R. B. Luce, 1962). There is also a peculiar but not useless sketch by H. Budd, "The Know-Nothing Party in Texas" (typescript, Barker Texas History Center, 1923).

St. Clair Griffin Reed's *A History of the Texas Railroads and of Transportation Conditions Under Spain and Mexico and the Republic and State* (Houston: St. Clair Publishing Co., 1941) is a defense of the railroad industry and all its works, but contains data of value and may be corrected by reference to such articles as A. B. Armstrong's "Origins of the Texas and Pacific Railways," *Southwestern Historical Quarterly* 56 (April, 1953) and Earl F. Woodward's "Texas's Internal Improvements Crisis of 1856: Four Remedial Plans Considered," *East Texas Historical Journal* 13 (January, 1967).

No history of the Texas Senate has been published previously. The individual members of the Congress of the Republic of Texas were the subject of brief biographies in *A Biographical Directory of the Texan Conventions and Congresses,* compiled by E. R. Linley (Austin: Book Exchange, 1941). Those who have served in the legislature since statehood are listed in *Members of the Texas Legislature,* most recently updated and published in 1982. This work, however, provides no biographical detail; for that one must consult *The Handbook of Texas* or the numerous privately printed directories that were published in Texas and other states around the turn of the century. The notes to W. W. Mills, *Forty Years at El Paso: 1858–1898* (El Paso: C. Hertzog, 1962), give biographical data on early senators from this region not easily available elsewhere, and a few senators and other legislators, besides those already mentioned, receive extensive treatment in Joseph Martin Dawson's *José Antonio Navarro: Co-creator of Texas* (Waco: Baylor University Press, 1969), Yancy Parker Yarbrough's "The Life and Career of Edward Burleson (1798–1851)" (Master's thesis, University of Texas, 1936), Duncan W. Robinson's *Judge Robert McAlpin Williamson: Texas' Three-Legged Willie* (Austin: Texas State Historical Association, 1948), Elizabeth Silverthorne's *Ashbel Smith of Texas: Pioneer, Patriot, Statesman, 1805–1886* (College Station: Texas A&M University Press, 1982), and Claude Elliott's fine study of James W. Throckmorton, *Leathercoat, the Life History of a Texas Patriot* (San Antonio: Privately published, 1938).

Typical of the general collections of miscellaneous sketches of public figures that are often the only source of information about individuals of less than stellar rank are Frank Brown's "Annals of Travis County and of the City of Austin: From The Earliest Times to the Close of 1875" (typescript, Texas State Archives), John Henry Brown and William S. Speer's *The Encyclopedia of the New West* (Marshall, Tex.: United States Biographical Publishing Co., 1881), Sidney Smith Johnson's *Some Biographies of Old Settlers: Historical, Personal and Reminiscent* (1900; facsimile edition, Tyler, Tex.: Smith County Historical Association, 1965). Restricted to one region is Frederick Charles Chabot's *With the Makers of San Antonio: Genealogies of the Early Latin, Anglo-American, and German Families with Occasional Biographies, Each Group Being Prefaced with a Brief Historical Sketch and Illustrations* (San Antonio, Tex.: Privately published, 1937). For a more complete understanding of the issues at hand, E. W. Winkler, *Platforms of Political Parties in Texas* (Austin: University of Texas Press, 1916), is essential. The best periodical containing articles on Texas and the legislature is the *Southwestern Historical Quarterly*, published since 1898 by the Texas State Historical Association.

Because of time constraints, few primary research materials could be consulted beyond the *Senate Journals,* files of which can be found in both the Barker Texas History Center and the Texas State Library. Many committee reports were reproduced separately and provide informative insights into the routine of the Texas state politics. Legislation adopted during the Republic and early statehood can be found in H. P. N. Gammel, *The Laws of Texas 1822–1897* (10 vols.; Austin: Gammel Book Company, 1898). Newspapers housed at the Barker Texas History Center provided in-depth information on legislative debate and defined the context of public opinion. For the Republic period, the most useful newspapers were the Houston *Telegraph and Texas Register* and *Morning Star;* the Galveston *Civilian and Galveston Gazette;* the *Matagorda Bulletin;* the Austin *Texas Sentinel, Texian,* and *Daily Bulletin;* and the *Texas National Register* from Washington-on-the-Brazos. After statehood, the *Telegraph and Texas Register* in Houston continued publication, but the *Galveston News* took the place of the *Civilian and Galveston Gazette,* which enjoyed a brief revival from 1857 to 1862.

Finally, the personal papers of some former senators have been perused during the course of this project. Unique in this period are the daily jottings of a busy senator, *Hurrah for Texas! The Diary of Adolphus Sterne, 1838–1851,* edited by Archie P. McDonald (Waco: Texian Press, 1969). The reminiscences of a long and extraordinary career by a journalist of great experience, including widely separated terms in the legislature and vigorous political activity, are to be found in John Salmon Ford's *Rip Ford's Texas,* edited by Stephen B. Oates (Austin: University of Texas Press, 1963). Self-revelation also comes from Guy Morrison Bryan, particularly in his correspondence with Rutherford B. Hayes, "Bryan-Hayes Correspondence II," *Southwestern Historical Quarterly* 25 (July 1921–April 1922), and in his most famous speech, "The Unity of Texas" (typescript, Barker Texas History Center, University of Texas). An old-fashioned view of his career, as the title would indicate, is by Fannie Baker Sholars, "Life and Services of Guy M. Bryan" (master's thesis, University of Texas, 1930). Cofounder of the Texas State Historical Association with Bryan was Senator James K. Holland, whose "Diary of a Texas Volunteer in the Mexican War," *Southwestern Historical Quarterly* 30, and "Reminiscences of Austin and Old Washington," *Quarterly of the Texas State Historical Association* 1, are, like the Bryan-Hayes correspondence, most valuable perhaps for the notes of their editor, Ernest Winkler. Most of the personal papers, however, were left undisturbed, providing ample material for future historians.

Index